UNIVERSITY CASEBOOK SERIES®

2018 CASE SUPPLEMENT AND STATUTORY APPENDIX TO

COPYRIGHT

CASES AND MATERIALS

NINTH EDITION

ROBERT A. GORMAN
Kenneth W. Gemmill Professor of Law Emeritus
University of Pennsylvania

JANE C. GINSBURG
Morton L. Janklow Professor of Literary and Artistic Property Law
Columbia University School of Law

R. ANTHONY REESE
Chancellor's Professor of Law
University of California, Irvine

CASE SUPPLEMENT AND STATUTORY APPENDIX

by

JANE C. GINSBURG
R. ANTHONY REESE

FOUNDATION
PRESS

University Casebook Series is a trademark registered in the U.S. Patent and Trademark Office.

© 2017 LEG, Inc. d/b/a West Academic
© 2018 LEG, Inc. d/b/a West Academic
    444 Cedar Street, Suite 700
    St. Paul, MN 55101
    1-877-888-1330

Printed in the United States of America

ISBN: 978-1-64242-397-6

TABLE OF CONTENTS

TABLE OF CASES

The principal cases are in bold type.

UNIVERSITY CASEBOOK SERIES®

2018 CASE SUPPLEMENT AND STATUTORY APPENDIX TO

COPYRIGHT

CASES AND MATERIALS

NINTH EDITION

CHAPTER 2

COPYRIGHTABLE SUBJECT MATTER

A. IN GENERAL

1. ORIGINAL WORKS OF AUTHORSHIP

a. WHAT IS AUTHORSHIP?

Page 94. Add at the end of the first paragraph:

The Ninth Circuit affirmed the district court's decision. Applying precedent requiring a plain statement in Congressional enactments of any grant of standing to nonhuman animals, the court concluded that the "Copyright Act does not expressly authorize animals to file copyright infringements under the statute." 888 F.3d 418, 425–26 (9th Cir. 2018).

D. DERIVATIVE WORKS

2. ORIGINALITY IN DERIVATIVE WORKS

Page 214. Add a new Question 5:

5. The song "We Shall Overcome" is "strongly associated with the Civil Rights movement in the United States and, according to the Library of Congress, 'the most powerful song of the 20th century.' The song originated as an African-American spiritual." *We Shall Overcome Foundation v. The Richmond Organization, Inc.*, 221 F.Supp.3d 396 (S.D.N.Y. 2016). The earliest known printed reference to the song is in 1909 and refers to the song as "We Will Overcome."

The following version of the lyrics to the song's first verse are in the public domain:

> We will overcome,
>
> We will overcome,
>
> We will overcome some day,
>
> Oh down in my heart, I do believe,
>
> We will overcome some day.

Music Publisher claims copyright in the following version of the lyrics to the song's first verse as a derivative work:

> We shall overcome,
>
> We shall overcome,
>
> We shall overcome some day,

Oh deep in my heart, I do believe,

We shall overcome some day.

Are the lyrics claimed by Music Publisher sufficiently original to be protected by copyright as a derivative work of the public domain lyrics? See *We Shall Overcome Foundation v. The Richmond Organization, Inc.*, 2017 WL 3981311 (S.D.N.Y. 2017) (finding changes in lyrics lacked originality necessary for copyright).

F. PICTORIAL, GRAPHIC AND SCULPTURAL WORKS

2. THE PROBLEM OF APPLIED ART

d. SEPARABILITY

Pages 274–295. Replace *Pivot Point* and *Varsity Brands* with the following new case:

Star Athletica, L.L.C. v. Varsity Brands, Inc.

580 U.S. ____, 137 S.Ct. 1002, 197 L.Ed.2d 354 (2017).

■ JUSTICE THOMAS delivered the opinion of the Court.

Congress has provided copyright protection for original works of art, but not for industrial designs. The line between art and industrial design, however, is often difficult to draw. This is particularly true when an industrial design incorporates artistic elements. Congress has afforded limited protection for these artistic elements by providing that "pictorial, graphic, or sculptural features" of the "design of a useful article" are eligible for copyright protection as artistic works if those features "can be identified separately from, and are capable of existing independently of, the utilitarian aspects of the article." 17 U. S. C. § 101.

We granted certiorari to resolve widespread disagreement over the proper test for implementing § 101's separate identification and independent-existence requirements. We hold that a feature incorporated into the design of a useful article is eligible for copyright protection only if the feature (1) can be perceived as a two- or three-dimensional work of art separate from the useful article and (2) would qualify as a protectable pictorial, graphic, or sculptural work—either on its own or fixed in some other tangible medium of expression—if it were imagined separately from the useful article into which it is incorporated. Because that test is satisfied in this case, we affirm.

I

Respondents Varsity Brands, Inc., Varsity Spirit Corporation, and Varsity Spirit Fashions & Supplies, Inc., design, make, and sell cheerleading uniforms. Respondents have obtained or acquired more than 200 U. S. copyright registrations for two-dimensional designs appearing on the surface of their uniforms and other garments. These designs are primarily "combinations, positionings, and arrangements of elements" that include "chevrons . . ., lines, curves, stripes, angles, diagonals, inverted [chevrons], coloring, and shapes." At issue in this case are Designs 299A, 299B, 074, 078, and 0815. See Appendix, *infra*.

Petitioner Star Athletica, L.L.C., also markets and sells cheerleading uniforms. Respondents sued petitioner for infringing their copyrights in the five designs. The District Court entered summary judgment for petitioner on respondents' copyright claims on the ground that the designs did not qualify as protectable pictorial, graphic, or sculptural works. It reasoned that the designs served the useful, or "utilitarian," function of identifying the garments as "cheerleading uniforms" and therefore could not be "physically or conceptually" separated under § 101 "from the utilitarian function" of the uniform.

The Court of Appeals for the Sixth Circuit reversed. In its view, the "graphic designs" were "separately identifiable" because the designs "and a blank cheerleading uniform can appear 'side by side'—one as a graphic design, and one as a cheerleading uniform." (quoting Compendium of U. S. Copyright Office Practices § 924.2(B) (3d ed. 2014) (Compendium)). And it determined that the designs were "'capable of existing independently'" because they could be incorporated onto the surface of different types of garments, or hung on the wall and framed as art.

Judge McKeague dissented. He would have held that, because "identifying the wearer as a cheerleader" is a utilitarian function of a cheerleading uniform and the surface designs were "integral to" achieving that function, the designs were inseparable from the uniforms.

II

. . .

B

. . .

1

The statute provides that a "pictorial, graphic, or sculptural featur[e]" incorporated into the "design of a useful article" is eligible for copyright protection if it (1) "can be identified separately from," and (2) is "capable of existing independently of, the utilitarian aspects of the article." The first requirement—separate identification—is not onerous. The decisionmaker need only be able to look at the useful article and spot some two- or three-dimensional element that appears to have pictorial, graphic, or sculptural qualities.

The independent-existence requirement is ordinarily more difficult to satisfy. The decisionmaker must determine that the separately identified feature has the capacity to exist apart from the utilitarian aspects of the article. See 2 OED 88 (def. 5) (defining "[c]apable" of as "[h]aving the needful capacity, power, or fitness for"). In other words, the feature must be able to exist as its own pictorial, graphic, or sculptural work as defined in § 101 once it is imagined apart from the useful article. If the feature is not capable of existing as a pictorial, graphic, or sculptural work once separated from the useful article, then it was not a pictorial, graphic, or sculptural feature of that article, but rather one of its utilitarian aspects.

Of course, to qualify as a pictorial, graphic, or sculptural work on its own, the feature cannot itself be a useful article or "[a]n article that is normally a part of a useful article" (which is itself considered a useful article). § 101. Nor could someone claim a copyright in a useful article merely by creating a replica of that article in some other medium—for example, a cardboard model of a car. Although the replica could itself be copyrightable, it would not give rise to any rights in the useful article that inspired it.

2

The statute as a whole confirms our interpretation. The Copyright Act provides "the owner of [a] copyright" with the "exclusive righ[t] . . . to reproduce the copyrighted work in copies." § 106(1). The statute clarifies that this right "includes the right to reproduce the [copyrighted] work in or on any kind of article, whether useful or otherwise." § 113(a). Section 101 is, in essence, the mirror image of § 113(a). Whereas § 113(a) protects a work of authorship first fixed in some tangible medium other than a useful article and subsequently applied to a useful article, § 101 protects art first fixed in the medium of a useful article. The two provisions make clear that copyright protection extends to pictorial, graphic, and sculptural works regardless of whether they were created as freestanding art or as features of useful articles. The ultimate separability question, then, is whether the feature for which copyright protection is claimed would have been eligible for copyright protection as a pictorial, graphic, or sculptural work had it originally been fixed in some tangible medium other than a useful article before being applied to a useful article.

3

This interpretation is also consistent with the history of the Copyright Act. . . . Shortly [after the Court decided *Mazer*], the Copyright Office enacted a regulation implementing the holdings of *Mazer*. . . . Congress essentially lifted the language governing protection for the design of a useful article directly from the post-*Mazer* regulations and placed it into § 101 of the 1976 Act. Consistent with *Mazer*, the approach we outline today interprets §§ 101 and 113 in a way that would afford copyright protection to the statuette in *Mazer* regardless of whether it was first created as a standalone sculptural work or as the base of the lamp.

C

In sum, a feature of the design of a useful article is eligible for copyright if, when identified and imagined apart from the useful article, it would qualify as a pictorial, graphic, or sculptural work either on its own or when fixed in some other tangible medium.

Applying this test to the surface decorations on the cheerleading uniforms is straightforward. First, one can identify the decorations as features having pictorial, graphic, or sculptural qualities. Second, if the arrangement of colors, shapes, stripes, and chevrons on the surface of the cheerleading uniforms were separated from the uniform and applied in another medium—for example, on a painter's canvas—they would qualify as "two-dimensional ... works of ... art," § 101. And imaginatively removing the surface decorations from the uniforms and applying them in another medium would not replicate the uniform itself. Indeed, respondents have applied the designs in this case to other media of expression—different types of clothing—without replicating the uniform. The decorations are therefore separable from the uniforms and eligible for copyright protection.

The dissent argues that the designs are not separable because imaginatively removing them from the uniforms and placing them in some other medium of expression—a canvas, for example—would create "pictures of cheerleader uniforms." Petitioner similarly argues that the decorations cannot be copyrighted because, even when extracted from the useful article, they retain the outline of a cheerleading uniform.

This is not a bar to copyright. Just as two-dimensional fine art corresponds to the shape of the canvas on which it is painted, two-dimensional applied art correlates to the contours of the article on which it is applied. A fresco painted on a wall, ceiling panel, or dome would not lose copyright protection, for example, simply because it was designed to track the dimensions of the surface on which it was painted. Or consider, for example, a design etched or painted on the surface of a guitar. If that entire design is imaginatively removed from the guitar's surface and placed on an album cover, it would still resemble the shape of a guitar. But the image on the cover does not "replicate" the guitar as a useful article. Rather, the design is a two-dimensional work of art that corresponds to the shape of the useful article to which it was applied. The statute protects that work of art whether it is first drawn on the album cover and then applied to the guitar's surface, or vice versa. Failing to protect that art would create an anomaly: It would extend protection to two-dimensional designs that cover a part of a useful article but would not protect the same design if it covered the entire article. The statute does not support that distinction, nor can it be reconciled with the dissent's recognition that "artwork printed on a t-shirt" could be protected.

To be clear, the only feature of the cheerleading uniform eligible for a copyright in this case is the two-dimensional work of art fixed in the tangible medium of the uniform fabric. Even if respondents ultimately succeed in establishing a valid copyright in the surface decorations at issue here, respondents have no right to prohibit any person from manufacturing a cheerleading uniform of identical shape, cut, and dimensions to the ones on which the decorations in this case appear. They may prohibit only the reproduction of the surface designs in any tangible medium of expression—a uniform or otherwise.[2]

D

Petitioner and the Government raise several objections to the approach we announce today. None is meritorious.

1

Petitioner first argues that our reading of the statute is missing an important step. It contends that a feature may exist independently only if it can stand alone as a copyrightable work *and* if the useful article from which it was extracted would remain equally useful. In other words, copyright extends only to "solely artistic" features of useful articles. According to petitioner, if a feature of a useful article "advance[s] the utility of the article," then it is categorically beyond the scope of copyright. The designs here are not protected, it argues, because they are necessary to two of the uniforms' "inherent, essential, or natural functions"—identifying the wearer as a cheerleader and enhancing the wearer's physical appearance. Because the uniforms would not be equally useful without the designs, petitioner contends that the designs are inseparable from the "utilitarian aspects" of the uniform.

The Government raises a similar argument, although it reaches a different result. It suggests that the appropriate test is whether the useful article with the artistic feature removed would "remai[n] *similarly* useful." In the view of the United States, however, a plain white cheerleading uniform is "similarly useful" to uniforms with respondents' designs.

The debate over the relative utility of a plain white cheerleading uniform is unnecessary. The focus of the separability inquiry is on the extracted feature and not on any aspects of the useful article that remain after the imaginary extraction. The statute does not require the decisionmaker to imagine a fully functioning useful article without the artistic feature. Instead, it requires that the separated feature qualify as a nonuseful pictorial, graphic, or sculptural work on its own.

Of course, because the removed feature may not be a useful article— as it would then not qualify as a pictorial, graphic, or sculptural work— there necessarily would be some aspects of the original useful article "left behind" if the feature were conceptually removed. But the statute does

---

[2] The dissent suggests that our test would lead to the copyrighting of shovels. But a shovel, like a cheerleading uniform, even if displayed in an art gallery, is "an article having an intrinsic utilitarian function that is not merely to portray the appearance of the article or to convey information." 17 U.S.C. § 101. It therefore cannot be copyrighted. A drawing of a shovel could, of course, be copyrighted. And, if the shovel included any artistic features that could be perceived as art apart from the shovel, and which would qualify as protectable pictorial, graphic, or sculptural works on their own or in another medium, they too could be copyrighted. But a shovel as a shovel cannot.

not require the imagined remainder to be a fully functioning useful article at all, much less an equally useful one. Indeed, such a requirement would deprive the *Mazer* statuette of protection had it been created first as a lamp base rather than as a statuette. Without the base, the "lamp" would be just a shade, bulb, and wires. The statute does not require that we imagine a nonartistic replacement for the removed feature to determine whether that *feature* is capable of an independent existence.

Petitioner's argument follows from its flawed view that the statute protects only "solely artistic" features that have no effect whatsoever on a useful article's utilitarian function. This view is inconsistent with the statutory text. The statute expressly protects two- and three-dimensional "applied art." § 101. "Applied art" is art "employed in the decoration, design, or execution of useful objects," Webster's Third New International Dictionary 105 (1976) (emphasis added), or "those arts or crafts that have a *primarily utilitarian function*, or . . . the designs and decorations used in these arts," Random House Dictionary 73 (1966) (emphasis added). An artistic feature that would be eligible for copyright protection on its own cannot lose that protection simply because it was first created as a feature of the design of a useful article, even if it makes that article more useful.

Indeed, this has been the rule since *Mazer*. In holding that the statuette was protected, the Court emphasized that the 1909 Act abandoned any "distinctions between purely aesthetic articles and useful works of art." Congress did not enact such a distinction in the 1976 Act. Were we to accept petitioner's argument that the only protectable features are those that play absolutely no role in an article's function, we would effectively abrogate the rule of *Mazer* and read "applied art" out of the statute.

Because we reject the view that a useful article must remain after the artistic feature has been imaginatively separated from the article, we necessarily abandon the distinction between "physical" and "conceptual" separability, which some courts and commentators have adopted based on the Copyright Act's legislative history. See H. R. Rep. No. 94–1476, p. 55 (1976). According to this view, a feature is *physically* separable from the underlying useful article if it can "be physically separated from the article by ordinary means while leaving the utilitarian aspects of the article completely intact." Compendium § 924.2(A). *Conceptual* separability applies if the feature physically could not be removed from the useful article by ordinary means.

The statutory text indicates that separability is a conceptual undertaking. Because separability does not require the underlying useful article to remain, the physical-conceptual distinction is unnecessary.

2

Petitioner next argues that we should incorporate two "objective" components into our test to provide guidance to the lower courts: (1)

"whether the design elements can be identified as reflecting the designer's artistic judgment exercised independently of functional influence," and (2) whether "there is [a] substantial likelihood that the pictorial, graphic, or sculptural feature would still be marketable to some significant segment of the community without its utilitarian function."

We reject this argument because neither consideration is grounded in the text of the statute. The first would require the decisionmaker to consider evidence of the creator's design methods, purposes, and reasons. The statute's text makes clear, however, that our inquiry is limited to how the article and feature are perceived, not how or why they were designed.

The same is true of marketability. Nothing in the statute suggests that copyrightability depends on market surveys. Moreover, asking whether some segment of the market would be interested in a given work threatens to prize popular art over other forms, or to substitute judicial aesthetic preferences for the policy choices embodied in the Copyright Act.

3

Finally, petitioner argues that allowing the surface decorations to qualify as a "work of authorship" is inconsistent with Congress' intent to entirely exclude industrial design from copyright. Petitioner notes that Congress refused to pass a provision that would have provided limited copyright protection for industrial designs, including clothing, when it enacted the 1976 Act, and that it has enacted laws protecting designs for specific useful articles—semiconductor chips and boat hulls, see 17 U.S.C. §§ 901–914, 1301–1332—while declining to enact other industrial design statutes. From this history of failed legislation petitioner reasons that Congress intends to channel intellectual property claims for industrial design into design patents. It therefore urges us to approach this question with a presumption against copyrightability.

We do not share petitioner's concern. As an initial matter, "[c]ongressional inaction lacks persuasive significance" in most circumstances. [cit.] Moreover, we have long held that design patent and copyright are not mutually exclusive. Congress has provided for limited copyright protection for certain features of industrial design, and approaching the statute with presumptive hostility toward protection for industrial design would undermine Congress' choice. In any event, as explained above, our test does not render the shape, cut, and physical dimensions of the cheerleading uniforms eligible for copyright protection.

III

We hold that an artistic feature of the design of a useful article is eligible for copyright protection if the feature (1) can be perceived as a two- or three-dimensional work of art separate from the useful article and (2) would qualify as a protectable pictorial, graphic, or sculptural work either on its own or in some other medium if imagined separately from the useful article. Because the designs on the surface of respondents' cheerleading uniforms in this case satisfy these requirements, the judgment of the Court of Appeals is affirmed.

APPENDIX TO OPINION OF THE COURT

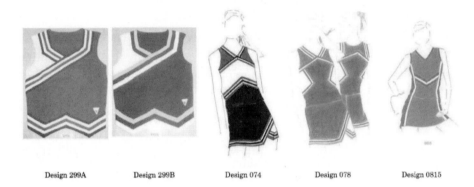

Design 299A   Design 299B   Design 074   Design 078   Design 0815

■ JUSTICE GINSBURG, concurring in the judgment.

I concur in the Court's judgment but not in its opinion. Unlike the majority, I would not take up in this case the separability test appropriate under 17 U. S. C. § 101.[1] Consideration of that test is unwarranted because the designs at issue are not designs *of* useful articles. Instead, the designs are themselves copyrightable pictorial or graphic works *reproduced on* useful articles.

A pictorial, graphic, or sculptural work (PGS work) is copyrightable. § 102(a)(5). PGS works include "two-dimensional and three-dimensional works of fine, graphic, and applied art." § 101. Key to this case, a copyright in a standalone PGS work "includes the right to reproduce the work in or on any kind of article, whether useful or otherwise." § 113(a). Because the owner of a copyright in a pre-existing PGS work may exclude a would-be infringer from reproducing that work on a useful article, there is no need to engage in any separability inquiry to resolve the instant petition.

The designs here in controversy are standalone pictorial and graphic works that respondents Varsity Brands, Inc., et al. (Varsity) reproduce on cheerleading uniforms. Varsity's designs first appeared as pictorial and graphic works that Varsity's design team sketched on paper. Varsity then sought copyright protection for those two-dimensional designs, not for cheerleading costumes; its registration statements claimed "2-

---

[1] Courts "have struggled mightily to formulate a test" for the separability analysis. 799 F. 3d 468, 484 (CA6 2015); see 2 W. Patry, Copyright § 3:136, p. 3–420 (2016) (noting "widespread interpretative disarray" over the separability test); Ginsburg, "Courts Have Twisted Themselves into Knots": U. S. Copyright Protection for Applied Art, 40 Colum. J. L. & Arts 1, 2 (2016) ("The 'separability' test . . . has resisted coherent application . . . ."); 1 M. Nimmer & D. Nimmer, Copyright § 2A.08[B][6], p. 2A–84 (2016) (separability is a "perennially tangled aspect of copyright doctrine").

Dimensional artwork" and "fabric design (artwork)." Varsity next reproduced its two-dimensional graphic designs on cheerleading uniforms, also on other garments, including T-shirts and jackets.[3]

In short, Varsity's designs are not themselves useful articles meet for separability determination under § 101; they are standalone PGS works that may gain copyright protection as such, including the exclusive right to reproduce the designs on useful articles.

■ Justice Breyer, with whom Justice Kennedy joins, dissenting.

I agree with much in the Court's opinion. But I do not agree that the designs that Varsity Brands, Inc., submitted to the Copyright Office are eligible for copyright protection. Even applying the majority's test, the designs *cannot* "be perceived as . . . two- or three-dimensional work[s] of art separate from the useful article." *Ante,* at 1007.

Look at the designs that Varsity submitted to the Copyright Office. See Appendix to opinion of the Court, *ante.* You will see only pictures of cheerleader uniforms. And cheerleader uniforms are useful articles. A picture of the relevant design features, whether separately "perceived" on paper or in the imagination, is a picture of, and thereby "replicate[s]," the underlying useful article of which they are a part. *Ante,* at 1007, 1031. Hence the design features that Varsity seeks to protect are not "capable of existing independently o[f] the utilitarian aspects of the article." 17 U.S.C. § 101.

I

The relevant statutory provision says that the "design of a useful article" is copyrightable "only if, and only to the extent that, such design incorporates pictorial, graphic, or sculptural features that can be identified separately from, and are capable of existing independently of, the utilitarian aspects of the article." *Ibid.* But what, we must ask, do the words "identified separately" mean? Just when is a design separate from the "utilitarian aspect of the [useful] article?" The most direct, helpful aspect of the Court's opinion answers this question by stating:

> "Nor could someone claim a copyright in a useful article merely by creating a replica of that article in some other medium—for example, a cardboard model of a car. Although the replica could itself be copyrightable, it would not give rise to any rights in the useful article that inspired it." *Ante,* at 1010.

Exactly so. These words help explain the Court's statement that a copyrightable work of art must be "perceived as a two- or three-dimensional work of art separate from the useful article." *Ante,* at 1007,

---

[3]   That Varsity's designs can be placed on jackets or T-shirts without replicating a cheerleader's uniform supports their qualification as fabric designs. The dissent acknowledges that fabric designs are copyrightable, but maintains that Varsity's designs do not count because Varsity's submissions depict clothing, not fabric designs. But registrants claiming copyrightable designs may submit drawings or photos of those designs as they appear on useful articles. And, as noted in text, Varsity's registration statements claimed "2-Dimensional artwork" and "fabric design (artwork)." . . .

1015–1016. They help clarify the concept of separateness. They are consistent with Congress' own expressed intent. And they reflect long held views of the Copyright Office.

Consider, for example, the explanation that the House Report for the Copyright Act of 1976 provides. It says:

> "Unless the shape of an automobile, airplane, ladies' dress, food processor, television set, or any other industrial product contains some element that, *physically or conceptually,* can be identified as separable from the utilitarian aspects of that article, the design would not be copyrighted. . . ." H.R. Rep., at 55 (emphasis added).

These words suggest two exercises, one physical, one mental. Can the design features (the picture, the graphic, the sculpture) be physically removed from the article (and considered separately), all the while leaving the fully functioning utilitarian object in place? If not, can one nonetheless conceive of the design features separately without replicating a picture of the utilitarian object? If the answer to either of these questions is "yes," then the design is eligible for copyright protection. Otherwise, it is not. The abstract nature of these questions makes them sound difficult to apply. But with the Court's words in mind, the difficulty tends to disappear.

An example will help. Imagine a lamp with a circular marble base, a vertical 10-inch tall brass rod (containing wires) inserted off center on the base, a light bulb fixture emerging from the top of the brass rod, and a lampshade sitting on top. In front of the brass rod a porcelain Siamese cat sits on the base facing outward. Obviously, the Siamese cat is *physically separate* from the lamp, as it could be easily removed while leaving both cat and lamp intact. And, assuming it otherwise qualifies, the designed cat is eligible for copyright protection.

Now suppose there is no long brass rod; instead the cat sits in the middle of the base and the wires run up through the cat to the bulbs. The cat is not physically separate from the lamp, as the reality of the lamp's construction is such that an effort to physically separate the cat and lamp will destroy both cat and lamp. The two are integrated into a single functional object, like the similar configuration of the ballet dancer statuettes that formed the lamp bases at issue in *Mazer v. Stein,* 347 U.S. 201 (1954). But we can easily imagine the cat on its own, as did Congress when conceptualizing the ballet dancer. See H.R. Rep., at 55 (the statuette in *Mazer* was "incorporated into a product without losing its ability to exist independently as a work of art"). In doing so, we do not create a mental picture of a lamp (or, in the Court's words, a "replica" of the lamp), which is a useful article. We simply perceive the cat separately, as a small cat figurine that could be a copyrightable design work standing alone that does not replicate the lamp. Hence the cat is *conceptually separate* from the utilitarian article that is the lamp. The pair of lamps pictured at Figures 1 and 2 in the Appendix to this opinion illustrate this principle.

Case law, particularly case law that Congress and the Copyright Office have considered, reflects the same approach. . . .

By way of contrast, Van Gogh's painting of a pair of old shoes, though beautifully executed and copyrightable as a painting, would not qualify for a shoe design copyright. See Appendix, fig. 3, *infra*; 17 U.S.C. §§ 113(a)–(b). Courts have similarly denied copyright protection to objects that begin as three-dimensional designs, such as measuring spoons shaped like heart-tipped arrows, *Bonazoli v. R.S.V.P. Int'l, Inc.,* 353 F.Supp.2d 218, 226–227 (D.R.I.2005); candleholders shaped like sailboats, *Design Ideas, Ltd. v. Yankee Candle Co.,* 889 F.Supp.2d 1119, 1128 (C.D.Ill.2012); and wire spokes on a wheel cover, *Norris Industries, Inc. v. International Tel. & Tel. Corp.,* 696 F.2d 918, 922–924 (C.A.11 1983). None of these designs could qualify for copyright protection that would prevent others from selling spoons, candleholders, or wheel covers with the same design. Why not? Because in each case the design is not separable from the utilitarian aspects of the object to which it relates. The designs cannot be physically separated because they themselves make up the shape of the spoon, candleholders, or wheel covers of which they are a part. And spoons, candleholders, and wheel covers are useful objects, as are the old shoes depicted in Van Gogh's painting. More importantly, one cannot easily imagine or otherwise conceptualize the design of the spoons or the candleholders or the shoes *without that picture, or image, or replica being a picture of spoons, or candleholders, or wheel covers, or shoes.* The designs necessarily bring along the underlying utilitarian object. Hence each design is not conceptually separable from the physical useful object.

The upshot is that one could copyright the floral design on a soupspoon but one could not copyright the shape of the spoon itself, no matter how beautiful, artistic, or esthetically pleasing that shape might be: A picture of the shape of the spoon is also a picture of a spoon; the picture of a floral design is not.

To repeat: A separable design feature must be "capable of existing independently" of the useful article as a separate artistic work that is not itself the useful article. If the claimed feature could be extracted without replicating the useful article of which it is a part, and the result would be a copyrightable artistic work standing alone, then there is a separable design. But if extracting the claimed features would necessarily bring along the underlying useful article, the design is not separable from the useful article. In many or most cases, to decide whether a design or artistic feature of a useful article is conceptually separate from the article itself, it is enough to imagine the feature on its own and ask, "Have I created a picture of a (useful part of a) useful article?" If so, the design is not separable from the useful article. If not, it is.

In referring to imagined pictures and the like, I am not speaking technically. I am simply trying to explain an intuitive idea of what separation is about, as well as how I understand the majority's opinion. So understood, the opinion puts design copyrights in their rightful place. The law has long recognized that drawings or photographs of real world objects are copyrightable as drawings or photographs, but the copyright does not give protection against others making the underlying useful objects. That is why a copyright on Van Gogh's painting would prevent others from reproducing that painting, but it would not prevent others from reproducing and selling the comfortable old shoes that the painting depicts. Indeed, the purpose of § 113(b) was to ensure that " 'copyright in a pictorial, graphic, or sculptural work, portraying a useful article as such, does not extend to the manufacture of the useful article itself.' " H.R. Rep., at 105.

II

To ask this kind of simple question—does the design picture the useful article?—will not provide an answer in every case, for there will be cases where it is difficult to say whether a picture of the design is, or is not, also a picture of the useful article. But the question will avoid courts focusing primarily upon what I believe is an unhelpful feature of the inquiry, namely, whether the design can be imagined as a "two- or three-dimensional work of art." *Ante,* at 1007, 1015—1016. That is because virtually any industrial design can be thought of separately as a "work of art": Just imagine a frame surrounding the design, or its being placed in a gallery. Consider Marcel Duchamp's "readymades" series, the functional mass-produced objects he designated as art. See Appendix, fig. 4, *infra.* What is there in the world that, viewed through an esthetic lens, cannot be seen as a good, bad, or indifferent work of art? What design features could not be imaginatively reproduced on a painter's canvas? Indeed, great industrial design may well include design that is inseparable from the useful article—where, as Frank Lloyd Wright put it, "form and function are one." F. Wright, An Autobiography 146 (1943) (reprint 2005). Where they are one, the designer may be able to obtain 15 years of protection through a design patent. 35 U.S.C. §§ 171, 173. But, if they are one, Congress did not intend a century or more of copyright protection.

III

The conceptual approach that I have described reflects Congress' answer to a problem that is primarily practical and economic. . . .

The Constitution grants Congress primary responsibility for assessing comparative costs and benefits and drawing copyright's statutory lines. Courts must respect those lines and not grant copyright protection where Congress has decided not to do so. And it is clear that Congress has not extended broad copyright protection to the fashion design industry. Congress has left "statutory . . . protection . . . largely unavailable for dress designs." 1 Nimmer § 2A.08[H][3][a].

Congress' decision not to grant full copyright protection to the fashion industry has not left the industry without protection. Patent design protection is available. 35 U.S.C. §§ 171, 173. A maker of clothing can obtain trademark protection under the Lanham Act for signature features of the clothing. 15 U.S.C. § 1051 *et seq.* And a designer who creates an original textile design can receive copyright protection for that pattern as placed, for example, on a bolt of cloth, or anything made with that cloth.

The fashion industry has thrived against this backdrop, and designers have contributed immeasurably to artistic and personal self-expression through clothing. But a decision by this Court to grant protection to the design of a garment would grant the designer protection that Congress refused to provide. It would risk increased prices and unforeseeable disruption in the clothing industry, which in the United States alone encompasses nearly $370 billion in annual spending and 1.8 million jobs. That is why I believe it important to emphasize those parts of the Court's opinion that limit the scope of its interpretation. That language, as I have said, makes clear that one may not "claim a copyright in a useful article merely by creating a replica of that article in some other medium," which "would not give rise to any rights in the useful article that inspired it." *Ante,* at 1010.

IV

If we ask the "separateness" question correctly, the answer here is not difficult to find. The majority's opinion, in its appendix, depicts the cheerleader dress designs that Varsity submitted to the Copyright Office. Can the design features in Varsity's pictures exist separately from the utilitarian aspects of a dress? Can we extract those features as copyrightable design works standing alone, without bringing along, via picture or design, the dresses of which they constitute a part?

Consider designs 074, 078, and 0815. They certainly look like cheerleader uniforms. That is to say, they look like pictures of cheerleader uniforms, just like Van Gogh's old shoes look like shoes. I do not see how one could see them otherwise. Designs 299A and [299B] present slightly closer questions. They omit some of the dresslike context that the other designs possess. But the necklines, the sleeves, and the cut of the skirt suggest that they too are pictures of dresses. Looking at all five of Varsity's pictures, I do not see how one could conceptualize the design features in a way that does not picture, not just artistic designs, but dresses as well.

Were I to accept the majority's invitation to "imaginatively remov[e]" the chevrons and stripes *as they are arranged* on the neckline, waistline, sleeves, and skirt of each uniform, and apply them on a "painter's canvas," *ante,* at 1011–1012, that painting would be of a cheerleader's dress. The esthetic elements on which Varsity seeks protection exist only as part of the uniform design—there is nothing to separate out but for dress-shaped lines that replicate the cut and style of the uniforms. Hence, each design is not physically separate, nor is it conceptually separate, from the useful article it depicts, namely, a cheerleader's dress. They cannot be copyrighted.

Varsity, of course, could have sought a design patent for its designs. Or, it could have sought a copyright on a textile design, even one with a similar theme of chevrons and lines.

But that is not the nature of Varsity's copyright claim. It has instead claimed ownership of the particular " 'treatment and arrangement' " of the chevrons and lines of the design as they appear at the neckline, waist, skirt, sleeves, and overall cut of each uniform. The majority imagines that Varsity submitted something different—that is, only the surface decorations of chevrons and stripes, as in a textile design. As the majority sees it, Varsity's copyright claim would be the same had it submitted a plain rectangular space depicting chevrons and stripes, like swaths from a bolt of fabric. But considered on their own, the simple stripes are plainly unoriginal. Varsity, then, seeks to do indirectly what it cannot do directly: bring along the design and cut of the dresses by seeking to protect surface decorations whose "treatment and arrangement" are *coextensive with that design and cut.* As Varsity would have it, it would prevent its competitors from making useful three-dimensional cheerleader uniforms by submitting plainly unoriginal chevrons and stripes as cut and arranged on a useful article. But with that cut and arrangement, the resulting pictures on which Varsity seeks protection do not simply depict designs. They depict clothing. They depict the useful articles of which the designs are inextricable parts. And Varsity cannot obtain copyright protection that would give them the power to prevent others from making those useful uniforms, any more than Van Gogh can copyright comfortable old shoes by painting their likeness.

I fear that, in looking past the three-dimensional design inherent in Varsity's claim by treating it as if it were no more than a design for a bolt of cloth, the majority has lost sight of its own important limiting principle. One may not "claim a copyright in a useful article merely by creating a replica of that article in some other medium," such as in a picture. *Ante,* at 1010. That is to say, one cannot obtain a copyright that would give its holder "any rights in the useful article that inspired it." *Ante,* at 1010.

With respect, I dissent.

APPENDIX TO OPINION OF BREYER, J.

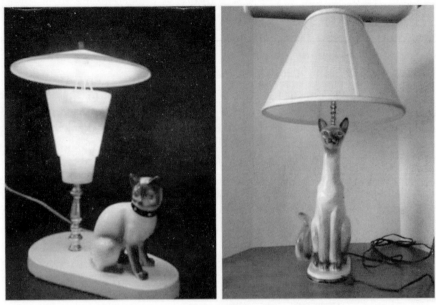

Fig. 1   Fig. 2

APPENDIX TO OPINION OF BREYER, J.

Fig. 3: Vincent Van Gogh, "Shoes"

APPENDIX TO OPINION OF BREYER, J.

Fig. 4: Marcel Duchamp,
"In Advance of the Broken Arm"

[While the Court majority noted that its decision did not address other issues about the copyrightability of the uniforms, including whether the designs satisfied the originality requirement, the case settled on remand with no further decision on those issues. Anandashankar Mazumdar, *Insurance Settlement Ends Cheerleading Uniform Copyright Dispute*, 94 PATENT, TRADEMARK & COPYRIGHT J. 1101 (Aug. 18, 2017).]

Pages 295–299. Replace Question 1 with the following Question 1, and in Questions 4, 5, and 6, evaluate whether the designs have any separable PG&S features under the test announced in *Star Athletica*:

QUESTIONS

1.   *Star Athletica* concerned "surface decorations." The court distinguished decorations that follow the entire contours of a useful article from the "shape, cut, and physical dimensions" of the article. But the court also held "that an artistic feature of the design of a useful article is eligible for copyright protection if the feature (1) can be perceived as a two- or *three*-dimensional work of art separate from the useful article . . ." (emphasis supplied). Can a three-dimensional work of art constitute the entire shape of the article yet still be "separable"?

J. GOVERNMENT WORKS AND OTHER PUBLIC POLICY ISSUES

1. GOVERNMENT WORKS

Page 353. After Question 8, add the following:

———————

In another controversy concerning government incorporation of private code writing organizations' standards, **American Society for Testing & Materials v. Public.Resource.org, Inc.,** 2018 WL 3431738 (D.C. Cir. July 17, 2018), the D.C. Circuit declined to rule whether Constitutional principles barred copyright protection.

> Although PRO [Public Resource.org] raises a serious constitutional concern with permitting private ownership of standards essential to understanding legal obligations, we think it best at this juncture to address only the statutory fair use issue—which may provide a full defense to some, if not all, of the SDO's infringement claims in this case—and leave for another day the question of whether the Constitution permits copyright to persist in works incorporated by reference into law. This approach not only allows us to resolve the appeal within the confines of the Copyright Act but is also more faithful to our responsibility to avoid "pass[ing] on questions of constitutionality . . . unless such adjudication is unavoidable." [Citation] Avoiding the constitutional question is all the more pressing here given that the record reveals so little about the nature of any given incorporation or what a constitutional ruling would mean for any particular standard. After all, it is one thing to declare that "the law" cannot be copyrighted but wholly another to determine whether any one of these incorporated standards—from the legally binding prerequisite to a labeling requirement, see 42 U.S.C. § 17021(b)(1), to the purely discretionary reference procedure, see 40 C.F.R. § 86.113–04(a)(1)—actually constitutes "the law."
>
> Our narrower approach, focusing on fair use, has two additional virtues. First, it limits the economic consequences that might result from the SDOs losing copyright—which they repeatedly emphasize would jeopardize the continued development of high-quality standards, by allowing copying only where it serves a public end rather than permitting competitors to merely sell duplicates at a lower cost. Second, it avoids creating a number of sui generis caveats to copyright law for incorporated standards. For instance, we need not determine what happens when a regulation or statute is revised to incorporate newer versions of a particular standard. Do the older, now unincorporated versions regain the copyright they might have

lost with the initial incorporation? Likewise, we need not resolve what happens when only part of a standard is incorporated by reference into law. Although copyright law speaks of "works," see 17 U.S.C. § 102 ("Copyright protection subsists . . . in original *works. . . .*" (emphasis added)), does a partial incorporation cause the entire work to lose copyright or just the relevant portions?

Can you reconcile the *Veeck* majority's view of "the law" with the D.C. Circuit's?

CHAPTER 4

FORMALITIES

D. DEPOSIT AND REGISTRATION

2. REGISTRATION

c. WHEN IS A WORK "REGISTERED"

Page 491. Add after the first full paragraph:

The Eleventh Circuit has held that the statute requires the "registration" approach, concluding that registration is made when " 'the Register . . . register[s] the claim,' " and that "[f]iling an application does not amount to registration." Fourth Estate Public Benefit Corp. v. Wall-Street.com, LLC, 856 F.3d 1338 (11th Cir. 2017) (quoting 17 U.S.C. § 410(a)). In June 2018, the Supreme Court granted certiorari in this case, promising resolution to the circuit split over the proper approach to determining when registration occurs. 585 U.S. ___.

CHAPTER 5

DURATION AND RENEWAL, AND TERMINATION OF TRANSFERS

C. TERMINATION OF TRANSFERS

1. IN GENERAL

Page 590. Add a new Question 5:

5. In 1980, Songwriter writes, and transfers to Music Publisher the copyright in, a song called "Pop Song #1." The song quickly becomes a hit. On July 31, 2014, in anticipation of terminating the 1980 transfer, Songwriter signs a contract with Rights Enforcement Company (REC). REC agrees to administer the rights Songwriter recovers in "Pop Song #1" in return for retaining ten percent of the revenues from users of the song. On August 1, 2014, Songwriter served on Music Publisher a valid termination notice, with an effective termination date of August 31, 2016. Is Songwriter's contract with REC valid and enforceable? See § 203(b)(5); *Artists Rights Enforcement Corp. v. Estate of Benjamin E. King*, 224 F.Supp.3d 231 (S.D.N.Y. 2016) (applying parallel provision § 304(c)(6)(D)).

2. SCOPE OF THE TERMINATION RIGHT

b. "ANY AGREEMENT TO THE CONTRARY"

Page 602. Insert the following Problem after Question 7:

PROBLEM

Between 1980 and 1983 the members of the British rock group Duran Duran entered into agreements transferring all their rights to a British music publisher. One of the contract's clauses provided:

> The Writer as beneficial owner (and by way of assignment of future copyright and rights where appropriate) hereby assigns to the Publishers all the copyrights and all other rights whatsoever and howsoever now or hereafter known (subject as hereinafter provided) in all musical compositions and/or lyrics and/or original arrangements of musical works (whether or not such musical works so arranged are in the public domain) which may prior to the date hereof have been written composed or created in whole or in part by the Writer and not been assigned by the Writer to any third party and which may during the term hereof be written composed or created in whole or in part by the Writer including the titles words and music thereof (all of such musical compositions, lyrics and arrangements being hereinafter together called 'the said works') throughout the world and the right to renew and extend

such copyrights and other rights and the ownership of such renewed and extended copyrights and other rights as may now or hereafter be conferred by the laws of any territory *so that the entire copyrights and all other rights in the said works shall be vested in the Publishers absolutely free from the adverse claims of any third party . . .*

Emphasis supplied. In 2014, the members of Duran Duran filed with the U.S. Copyright Office (and served on the British publisher) notices of termination of their grant of rights for the United States. The British publisher sues in the United Kingdom, seeking an injunction restraining Duran Duran from effecting termination under the U.S. statute on the ground that termination would breach the group's obligations under the English-law contract. The group responds that the publisher's interpretation of the contract makes the relevant clause an unenforceable "agreement to the contrary." Do the group's U.S. termination rights prevail over the English contract? See *Gloucester Place Music v. Le Bon*, [2016] EWHC 3091 (Ch), *appeal pending.*

Suppose that instead of contending that the authors are contractually barred from taking any action inconsistent with the foreign grant (which would include terminating the grant of rights as to the United States), the publisher asserts that under the law of the country of origin, the relationship between the author and the commissioning party publisher was equivalent to a U.S. work made for hire. How should a U.S. court evaluate the foreign law claim? See *Ennio Morricone Music Inc. v. Bixio Music Group Ltd.* 2017 U.S. Dist. LEXIS 177643 (S.D.N.Y. October 6, 2017), *appeal pending.*

CHAPTER 6

EXCLUSIVE RIGHTS UNDER COPYRIGHT

A. THE RIGHT TO REPRODUCE THE WORK IN COPIES AND PHONORECORDS UNDER § 106(1)

1. THE RIGHT TO MAKE COPIES

a. WHAT IS A "COPY"?

Page 630. Add before Questions:

The Ninth Circuit, like the Second Circuit in *Cartoon Network* and the Fourth Circuit in *CoStar Group* (discussed in *Cartoon Network*, *supra* main casebook at 626) has endorsed the *Netcom* volition approach for liability of Internet service providers. *Perfect 10, Inc. v. Giganews, Inc.*, 847 F.3d 657 (9th Cir. 2017).

b. PROVING INFRINGEMENT

iii. Proving That Copying Infringed

Page 732. Add new Questions 6 and 7.

6. Songwriter *A* writes a musical composition. The first two lines of the lyrics of the chorus are "Playas, they gonna play / And haters, they gonna hate." Songwriter *B* later writes a song featuring a chorus with the first two lines " 'Cause the players gonna play, play, play, play, play / And the haters gonna hate, hate, hate, hate, hate." If *B* copied from *A*'s song, has *B* copied protectable expression? See *Hall v. Swift*, 2018 WL 2317548 (C.D.Cal. 2018).

7. Jacobus Rentmeester, a renowned photographer, took the photo of Michael Jordan below, in 1984, when Jordan was a student at the University of North Carolina. The photo

> depicts Jordan leaping toward a basketball hoop with a basketball raised above his head in his left hand, as though he is attempting to dunk the ball. The setting for the photo is not a basketball court, as one would expect in a shot of this sort. Instead, Rentmeester chose to take the photo on an isolated grassy knoll on the University of North Carolina campus. He brought in a basketball hoop and backboard mounted on a tall pole, which he planted in the ground to position the hoop exactly where he wanted. Whether due to the height of the pole or its placement within the image, the basketball hoop appears to tower above Jordan, beyond his reach.
>
> Rentmeester instructed Jordan on the precise pose he wanted Jordan to assume. It was an unusual pose for a basketball player

to adopt, one inspired by ballet's grand jeté, in which a dancer leaps with legs extended, one foot forward and the other back. Rentmeester positioned the camera below Jordan and snapped the photo at the peak of his jump so that the viewer looks up at Jordan's soaring figure silhouetted against a cloudless blue sky. Rentmeester used powerful strobe lights and a fast shutter speed to capture a sharp image of Jordan contrasted against the sky, even though the sun is shining directly into the camera lens from the lower right-hand corner of the shot.

Rentmeester v. Nike, Inc., 883 F.3d 1111, 1115–16 (9th Cir. 2018).

Soon after Rentmeester's photo appeared in *Life* magazine, Nike hired a photographer to produce the second photograph below. In 1987, "Nike created its iconic 'Jumpman' logo [shown below], a solid black silhouette that tracks the outline of Jordan's figure as it appears in the Nike photo," and has used that logo over three decades in marketing billions of dollars of merchandise. *Id.* at 1116.

Assuming that Rentmeester can demonstrate that Nike had access to his photograph before it created the Nike photograph and the logo, can Rentmeester show improper appropriation in order to prevail on an infringement claim against Nike? See *id.*

Nike's photograph

Rentmeester's photograph

Nike's Jumpman logo

B. THE RIGHT TO PREPARE DERIVATIVE WORKS UNDER § 106(2)

3. LIMITATIONS ON THE DERIVATIVE WORKS RIGHT

Page 771. Number the QUESTION as Question 1 and add the following new question:

2. "VidAngel, Inc. operates an online streaming service that removes objectionable content from movies and television shows. VidAngel purchases physical discs containing copyrighted movies and television shows [and then] decrypts the discs to 'rip' a digital copy to a computer . . . After decryption, VidAngel creates 'intermediate files,' converting them to HTTP Live Streaming format and breaking them into segments that can be tagged for over 80 categories of inappropriate content. Once tagged, the segments are encrypted and stored in cloud servers. . . . [A] customer selects at least one type of objectionable content to be filtered out of the work. VidAngel then streams the filtered work to the customer on 'any VidAngel-supported device, including Roku, Apple TV, Smart TV, Amazon Fire TV, Android, Chromecast, iPad/iPhone and desktop or laptop computers.' The work is streamed from the filtered segments stored in cloud servers, not from the original discs." *Disney Enterprises, Inc. v. VidAngel, Inc.*, 869 F.3d 848 (9th Cir. 2017). Are VidAngel's actions within the scope of section 110(11)? In particular, does the filtering of a motion picture's audiovisual content in a VidAngel stream occur "during a performance . . . from an authorized copy of the motion picture"? *See id.*

4. MORAL RIGHTS

a. FEDERAL PROTECTION OF MORAL RIGHTS

i. *What Is a "Work of Visual Art"?*

Page 788. Add after the carryover paragraph:

Although the building owner had cooperated with plaintiff Cohen in the installation of the graffiti art over the course of a decade, "[a]s soon as the Court denied the plaintiffs' application for a preliminary injunction, [the building owner] directed the whitewashing of virtually all the artwork on the 5Pointz site with rollers, spray machines, and buckets of white paint." *Cohen v. G&M Realty LP*, 2018 WL 851374 (E.D.N.Y. 2018). The graffiti artists' VARA claims proceeded to trial. The court rejected the defendants' argument that VARA did not apply to temporary works, and then found that 45 of 49 works that had been whitewashed had achieved "recognized stature" to qualify for protection under VARA and that the defendants had violated the plaintiffs' VARA rights by intentionally destroying those works. The court declined to award actual damages, concluding that the plaintiffs "failed to establish a reliable market value for their work." *Id.* However, in awarding statutory damages, the court found that the defendants had acted willfully and that all of the "relevant factors support the maximum award of statutory damages." *Id.* The court therefore awarded $150,000 for each of the 45 VARA-protected works destroyed, for a total of $6.75 million.

ii.   What Rights Does VARA Protect?

Page 806. At the end of subsection 6.B.4.ii, add the following REVIEW PROBLEM:

REVIEW PROBLEM

"Charging Bull," a 3-ton, 18-foot long bronze sculpture, created by Italian sculptor Arturo di Modica in 1989, stands on a traffic island in the Wall Street area of New York City. Di Modica intended the representational sculpture to celebrate the resurgent stock market following the downturns of the late 1980s. Di Modica's website explains that he "conceived of the Charging Bull as a way to celebrate the can-do spirit of America and especially New York, where people from all over the world could come regardless of their origin or circumstances, and through determination and hard work overcome every obstacle to become successful. It's this symbol of virility and courage." In 2017, to celebrate International Women's Day, State Street Global Advisors, a Boston investment firm, commissioned Kristen Visbal to create the sculpture "Fearless Girl," which depicts a determined-looking young girl, 4-feet tall, head held high and fists on hips. State Street installed "Fearless Girl" across from Di Modica's sculpture, giving the girl the appearance of staring down "Charging Bull." State Street asserts that its sculpture expresses "the power and potential of having more women in leadership." The mayor of New York City endorsed the statue as "standing up to fear, standing up to power, being able to find in yourself the strength to do what's right." Di Modica disagrees: he laments that "Fearless Girl" has distorted the message of "Charging Bull," turning it from one about "freedom in the world, peace, strength, power and love," into one of menace. Di Modica claims "Fearless Girl" infringes his rights under federal copyright law, and demands its removal. He seeks your advice. What title 17 rights may he assert, and how likely is he to prevail?

Credit: Mark Lennihan/Associated Press,
https://www.nytimes.com/2017/04/12/nyregion/charging-bull-sculpture-
wall-street-fearless-girl.html.

C. THE RIGHT TO DISTRIBUTE COPIES AND PHONORECORDS UNDER § 106(3)

1. THE PURPOSE AND APPLICATION OF THE DISTRIBUTION RIGHT

Page 813. Number the existing QUESTION as Question 1 and insert new Question 2:

2. Amazon, the familiar online retailer, does not itself sell all of the products offered on its Amazon.com website. Many products listed on Amazon.com are offered by third parties. "When a third-party seller uses Amazon's website to sell a product, the seller provides information regarding the product, such as a product description, images[, and price]." *Milo & Gabby LLC v. Amazon.com, Inc.*, 2017 WL 2258605 (Fed. Cir. 2017).

Amazon also offers third-party sellers a service called "Fulfillment by Amazon," which allows third-party sellers to take advantage of Amazon's logistical network. When using this service, a third-party seller sends its product to an Amazon fulfillment center, where Amazon stores the product. If a customer buys the product from the third-party seller, Amazon pulls the product off the shelf, packages it, and ships it to the customer on behalf of the seller. . . .

Third-party sellers using the Fulfillment by Amazon service maintain full ownership of the products stored by Amazon. The third-party seller using this service can remove its stock at any time by requesting that Amazon return the product to the third-party seller.

Id. Your client Pat Plaintiff has discovered a third-party seller listing unauthorized copies of Pat's copyrighted work on Amazon.com. The third party is using the Fulfillment by Amazon service. Does Pat have a claim against Amazon for violating Pat's § 106(3) distribution right? See *id.*

D. RIGHTS OF PUBLIC PERFORMANCE AND DISPLAY UNDER § 106(4), (5), (6)

2. "PUBLIC" PERFORMANCES UNDER THE 1976 ACT

Page 894. Add at the end of the *Editors' Note*:

In March 2017, the Ninth Circuit ruled that the service was not eligible for the Section 111 license. 851 F.3d 1002 (9th Cir. 2017). The court found the statute ambiguous, and, finding the Copyright Office's interpretation "persuasive and reasonable," deferred to the Office's position that Internet-based retransmission services are not cable systems under Section 111 because a provider must be "an inherently localized transmission media of limited availability to qualify as a cable system." *Id.* at 1012 (quoting 62 Fed.Reg. 18,707).

4. THE DIGITAL PERFORMANCE RIGHT IN SOUND RECORDINGS . . . AND ITS LIMITATIONS

b. PUBLIC PERFORMANCES OF PRE-1972 SOUND RECORDINGS

Pages 918–920. Replace the current section with the following:

Recall that only sound recordings fixed on or after February 15, 1972, are subject to *federal* copyright law. *See supra*, page 553. When Congress granted federal copyright to sound recordings, it did so only prospectively, and expressly left state protection for existing sound recordings unpreempted by federal copyright law until Feb. 15, 2067. 17 U.S.C. § 301(c). At the time that Congress granted federal protection to sound recordings, some states offered creators of sound recordings some protection against those who produced "bootleg" copies of such sound recordings, but not much other protection was available.

In 2014, federal district courts in California and New York confronted the question of whether those states' laws granted an exclusive public performance right in pre-1972 sound recordings. *Flo & Eddie, Inc. v. Sirius XM Radio, Inc.*, 112 U.S.P.Q.2d 1307 (C.D. Cal. 2014); *Flo & Eddie, Inc. v. Sirius XM Radio, Inc.*, 62 F.Supp.3d 325 (S.D.N.Y. 2014). Flo & Eddie owns sound recordings made in the 1960s by the rock group The Turtles, including the hit "Happy Together." The company sued Sirius XM Radio, alleging, *inter alia*, that playing those sound recordings on its satellite radio service violated Flo & Eddie's public performance rights in the sound recordings. Each court ruled that the law of its respective state provided owners of pre-1972 sound recordings with the exclusive right to publicly perform their sound recordings, at least by satellite transmission

The question in each case was one of first impression. The California decision was based on a 1982 state statute granting "[t]he author of an original work of authorship consisting of a sound recording initially fixed prior to February 15, 1972 . . . an exclusive ownership interest therein until February 15, 2047, as against all persons . . . " Cal. Civ. Code § 980(a)(2). The court concluded that this "exclusive ownership interest" includes the exclusive right to publicly perform the sound recording. The New York decision was based on a prediction of how the New York Court of Appeals would interpret that state's common law protection for sound recordings (since such protection is purely common law, rather than statutory, and since no New York court had addressed the issue of public performance rights).

By contrast, a federal court in Florida, noting the absence of either a pertinent statute or caselaw, declined to "creat[e] a new property right in Florida as opposed to interpreting the law," and therefore ruled against the existence of a common law public performance right in sound recordings in Florida. *Flo & Eddie, Inc. v. Sirius XM Radio, Inc.*, 114 U.S.P.Q.2d 1997 (S.D. Fla. 2015); *accord Alticor Inc. v. UMG Recordings, Inc.*, 117 U.S.P.Q.2d 1134 (M.D. Fla. 2015).

All three decisions were appealed, to the Ninth, Second, and Eleventh Circuits, respectively, and each circuit certified the question of whether state law grants pre-1972 sound recordings the right of public performance to the highest state court in California, New York, and Florida, respectively. *Flo & Eddie, Inc. v. Pandora Media, Inc.*, 851 F.3d 950 (9th Cir. 2017); *Flo & Eddie, Inc. v. Sirius XM Radio, Inc.*, 821 F.3d 265, 272 (2d Cir. 2016); *Flo & Eddie, Inc. v. Sirius XM Radio, Inc.*, 827 F.3d 1016 (11th Cir. 2016).

The New York Court of Appeals concluded that "New York common-law copyright does not recognize a right of public performance for creators of sound recordings." 70 N.E.3d 936, 937 (N.Y. 2016). Reviewing state caselaw, the court concluded that "New York's common-law copyright has never recognized a right of public performance for pre-1972 sound recordings. Because the consequences of doing so could be extensive and far-reaching, and there are many competing interests at state, which we are not equipped to address, we decline to create such a right for the first time now." *Id.* at 949. The Second Circuit therefore reversed the district court's ruling in favor of the copyright owners. 849 F.3d 14 (2d Cir. 2017).

The Supreme Court of Florida similarly concluded that "Florida common law has never previously recognized an exclusive right of public performance for sound recordings" and that because of the impact that recognizing such a right would have, "[t]o recognize such a right for the first time today would be an inherently legislative task." 229 So.3d 305,

315–16 (Fla. 2017). Therefore, the court ruled that Florida common law does not recognize such a right. *Id.* at 319. Consequently, the Eleventh Circuit affirmed the district court's ruling in favor of Sirius XM. 709 Fed.Appx. 661 (2018).

The California supreme court has not yet ruled.

A federal court in Illinois has ruled that that state's common-law copyright protects only unpublished works, and that the broadcast or sale of a phonorecord of a sound recordings constituted a publication of that sound recording that ended common-law copyright protection. *Sheridan v. iHeartMedia, Inc.*, 255 F.Supp.3d 767 (N.D. Ill. 2017). (Other cases asserting a state-law public performance right, including cases involving other state's laws, have been stayed pending the appeals in the circuit courts. *See, e.g., Sheridan v. iHeartMedia, Inc.*, 2016 WL 1059268 (D.N.J. 2016).)

Does the California decision simply put pre-1972 sound recordings on an even footing with later, federally copyrighted sound recordings? The limited federal public performance right for sound recordings in § 106(6), first granted by Congress in 1995, gives copyright owners the right to control public performance of their works by satellite transmission as long as the transmission is digital. But that control is subject to the statutory license under § 114(d) if the satellite transmitting service qualifies for the license. Will such a statutory license be available under California law for compliant satellite radio transmitters?

Will rulings that pre-1972 sound recordings enjoy a state-law right of public performance be limited to satellite radio transmissions, or will they apply to other types of *digital* audio transmissions, such as webcasting? If the state performance right applies to webcasting, will online transmitting services be able to secure the right to transmit pre-1972 sound recordings through a statutory licensing procedure similar to § 114? If not, how might that shape which music gets played online?

Is there any reason to think that the decisions are limited to *digital* transmissions (which were, of course, essentially unknown at the time Congress granted copyright to sound recordings in 1972, and when California adopted § 980(a)(2) in 1982)? If not, do the decisions apply to over-the-air transmissions by terrestrial radio stations? (Recall that those radio transmissions incur no public performance liability under federal copyright law, either because they are not digital (and therefore not within the scope of § 106(6)) or because if they are digital they are exempt under § 114(d)(1).) If the California decision extends to public performance by radio, has every radio station that played a sound recording from before 1972 over the air violated the sound recording owner's state public performance right in California since 1982? Can you offer any explanation why for more than 30 years sound recording copyright owners in California never asserted that any radio station in the state that played pre-1972 recordings was infringing on their common-law copyright? (Consider the evolving economics of sound recording copyright.)

Finally, while the limited federal public performance right in sound recordings in § 106(6) extends only to *transmissions*, the general public performance right in § 106(4) also covers nontransmitted performances that occur in public or semi-public places. Given a decision recognizing that the owners of state common law rights in sound recordings own a "public performance" right, is there any reason that decision would not apply to discotheques, restaurants, bars, and retail establishments that play records on their premises? Again, can you explain the lack of enforcement against such establishments for three decades or more?

If a pre-1972 sound recording is remastered after February 15, 1972, does the remastering produce a derivative sound recording subject to federal copyright protection? If so, is the public performance of that derivative sound recording governed by federal law? By state law? By both? *See ABS Entertainment, Inc. v. CBS Corp.*, 119 U.S.P.Q.2d 1152 (C.D. Cal. 2016).

5. THE RIGHT OF PUBLIC DISPLAY

Page 930. After the QUESTIONS, add the following new case:

Goldman v. Breitbart News Network, LLC

302 F.Supp.3d 585 (S.D.N.Y. 2018)

■ FORREST, DISTRICT JUDGE.

When the Copyright Act was amended in 1976, the words "tweet," "viral," and "embed" invoked thoughts of a bird, a disease, and a reporter. Decades later, these same terms have taken on new meanings as the centerpieces of an interconnected world wide web in which images are shared with dizzying speed over the course of any given news day. That technology and terminology change means that, from time to time, questions of copyright law will not be altogether clear. In answering questions with previously uncontemplated technologies, however, the Court must not be distracted by new terms or new forms of content, but turn instead to familiar guiding principles of copyright. In this copyright infringement case, concerning a candid photograph of a famous sports figure, the Court must construe how images shown on one website but stored on another website's server implicate an owner's exclusive display right.

Today, many websites embed Twitter posts into their own content; for those familiar with digital news or other content, this is common knowledge. Here, plaintiff Justin Goldman's copyrighted photo of Tom Brady went "viral"—rapidly moving from Snapchat to Reddit to Twitter—and finally, made its way onto the websites of the defendants, who embedded the Tweet alongside articles they wrote about Tom Brady actively helping the Boston Celtics recruit basketball player Kevin Durant.

Plaintiff, claiming he never publicly released or licensed his photograph, filed suit against the defendant websites, claiming a violation of his exclusive right to display his photo, under § 106(5) of the Copyright Act.

With the consent of the parties, this Court divided the litigation into two phases—the first to determine whether defendants' actions violate the exclusive right to display a work (here an embedded Tweet), and the second to deal with all remaining issues, such as the liability (or non-liability) for other defendants and any defenses that have been raised.

Defendants filed a motion for partial Summary Judgment on October 5, 2017. The Court heard oral argument on January 16, 2018.

Having carefully considered the embedding issue, this Court concludes, for the reasons discussed below, that when defendants caused the embedded Tweets to appear on their websites, their actions violated plaintiff's exclusive display right; the fact that the image was hosted on a server owned and operated by an unrelated third party (Twitter) does not shield them from this result.

Accordingly, defendants' motion for partial Summary Judgment is DENIED. Partial Summary Judgment is GRANTED to the plaintiff.

I. FACTUAL BACKGROUND

The parties agree that the principal issue briefed on this motion is a legal one and amenable to summary judgment. The following facts are materially undisputed and all inferences are drawn in favor of the plaintiff.

A. The Tom Brady Photo

On July 2, 2016, plaintiff Justin Goldman snapped a photograph of Tom Brady (the "Photo"), Danny Ainge, and others on the street in East Hampton. Shortly thereafter, he uploaded the photograph to his Snapchat Story.[1] The Photo then went "viral," traveling through several levels of social media platforms—and finally onto Twitter, where it was uploaded by several users, including Cassidy Hubbarth (@cassidyhubbarth), Bobby Manning (@RealBobManning), Rob H (@rch111), and Travis Singleton (@SneakerReporter). These uploads onto Twitter are referred to as "Tweets."

Defendants in this case are online news outlets and blogs who published articles featuring the Photo. Each of defendants' websites prominently featured the Photo by "embedding" the Tweet into articles they wrote over the course of the next forty-eight hours; the articles were all focused on the issue of whether the Boston Celtics would successfully

---

[1]   Snapchat is a social media platform where users share photographs and messages; a Snapchat story is a series of photos a user posts—each photo is available for twenty-four hours only.

recruit basketball player Kevin Durant, and if Tom Brady would help to seal the deal.

It is undisputed that plaintiff holds the copyright to the Photo.

B. Embedding

None of the defendant websites copied and saved the Photo onto their own servers. Rather, they made the Photo visible in their articles through a technical process known as "embedding." Some background is helpful to an understanding of the embedding process.

A webpage is made up of a series of instructions usually written by coders in Hypertext Markup Language ("HTML"). These instructions are saved to a server (a computer connected to the internet), and when a user wishes to view a webpage, his or her computer's browser connects with the server, at which point the HTML code previously written by the coder instructs the browser on how to arrange the webpage on the user's computer. The HTML code can allow for the arrangement of text and/or images on a page and can also include photographs. When including a photograph on a web page, the HTML code instructs the browser how and where to place the photograph. Importantly for this case, the HTML code could instruct the browser either to retrieve the photograph from the webpage's own server or to retrieve it from a third-party server.

"Embedding" an image on a webpage is the act of a coder intentionally adding a specific "embed" code to the HTML instructions that incorporates an image, hosted on a third-party server, onto a webpage. To embed an image, the coder or web designer would add an "embed code" to the HTML instructions; this code directs the browser to the third-party server to retrieve the image. An embedded image will then hyperlink (that is, create a link from one place in a hypertext document to another in a different document) to the third-party website. The result: a seamlessly integrated webpage, a mix of text and images, although the underlying images may be hosted in varying locations. Most social media sites—Facebook, Twitter, and YouTube, for example— provide code that coders and web designers can easily copy in order to enable embedding on their own webpages.

Here, it is undisputed that none of the defendant websites actually downloaded the Photo from Twitter, copied it, and stored it on their own servers. Rather, each defendant website merely embedded the Photo, by including the necessary embed code in their HTML instructions. As a result, all of defendants' websites included articles about the meeting between Tom Brady and the Celtics, with the full-size Photo visible without the user having to click on a hyperlink, or a thumbnail, in order to view the Photo.

II. LEGAL PRINCIPLES

B. The Copyright Act

"From its beginning, the law of copyright has developed in response to significant changes in technology." *Sony Corp. of America v. Universal City Studios, Inc.*, 464 U.S. 417, 430 (1984). Copyright protections "subsists . . . in original works of authorship fixed in any tangible medium of expression." 17 U.S.C. § 102(a). The Copyright Act of 1976, enacted in response to changing technology, gives a copyright owner several "exclusive rights," including the exclusive right to "display the copyrighted work publicly." 17 U.S.C. § 106(5). To display a work, under the Act, is to "show a copy of it, either directly or by means of a film, slide, television image, or *any other device or process.*" 17 U.S.C. § 101 (emphasis added). The Act's Transmit Clause defines that exclusive right as including the right to "transmit or otherwise communicate . . . a display of the work . . . to the public, by means of any device or process." *Id.* It further defines "device or process" as "one now known or later developed." *Id.*

A review of the legislative history reveals that the drafters of the 1976 Amendments intended copyright protection to broadly encompass new, and not yet understood, technologies. Indeed, on the first page of the House Report, the drafters proclaimed that the Amendments were necessary in part because "technical advances have generated new industries and new methods for the reproduction and dissemination of copyrighted works;" furthermore, Congress did "not intend to freeze the scope of copyrightable subject matter at the present stage of communications technology." H.R. Rep. 94–1476, 47, 51 (1976).

Specifically, in considering the display right, Congress cast a very wide net, intending to include "*[e]ach and every method* by which the images . . . comprising a . . . display are picked up and conveyed," assuming that they reach the public. Id. at 64 (emphasis added). It further noted that " 'display' would include the projection of an image on a screen or other surface *by any method*, the transmission of an image by electronic or other means, and the showing of an image on a cathode ray tube, or similar viewing apparatus connected with any sort of *information storage and retrieval system.*" Id. (emphasis added). Indeed, an infringement of the display right could occur "if the image were transmitted by *any method* (by closed or open circuit television, for example, *or by a computer system*) from one place to members of the public elsewhere." *Id.* at 80 (emphasis added).

The Register of Copyrights testified during hearings that preceded the passage of the Act: "[T]he definition [of the display right] is intended to cover every transmission, retransmission, or other communication of [the image]," beyond the originating source that might store the image, but including "any other transmitter who picks up his signals and passes them on." *H. Comm. On the Judiciary, 89th Cong., Copyright Law Revision Part 6: Supplementary Report of the Register of Copyrights on the General Revision of the U.S. Copyright Law: 1965 Revision Bill*, at 25 (Comm. Print. 1965). He highlighted the importance of the display right in light of changing technology, specifically warning that "information storage and retrieval devices . . . *when linked together by communication satellites or other means* . . . could eventually provide libraries and individuals throughout the world with access to a single copy of a work by transmission of electronic images" and therefore that "a basic right of public exhibition should be expressly recognized in the statute." *Id.* at 20 (emphasis added).

C. American Broadcasting Cos., Inc. v. Aereo, Inc.

The Supreme Court most recently considered the intersection of novel technologies and the Copyright Act in the *Aereo* decision, rendered in 2014. A*merican Broadcasting Cos., Inc. v. Aereo, Inc.*, ___ U.S. ___, 134 S.Ct. 2498 (2014). The issue in *Aereo* was the performance right; the Court was deciding whether Aereo "infringed this exclusive right by selling its subscribers a technologically complex service that allows them to watch television programs over the Internet at about the same time as the programs are broadcast over the air." *Id.* at 2503. Aereo charged a monthly fee to allow subscribers to watch broadcast television programming over the internet; it maintained a vast number of servers and antennas in a central warehouse. When a user wanted to watch a program, he would visit Aereo's website and select a show; in turn, Aereo's servers would select an antenna, tune it to the on-air broadcast, and transmit it via the internet to the subscriber. Aereo argued that since the user chose the programs and Aereo's technology merely responded to the user's choice, it was the user and not Aereo who was in fact "transmitting" the performance.

The Court rejected this analysis, comparing Aereo to the cable companies that parts of the 1976 Amendments were intended to reach. When comparing cable technology (where the signals "lurked behind the screen") to Aereo's technology (controlled by a click on a website), the Court stated: "[T]his difference means nothing to the subscriber. It means nothing to the broadcaster. We do not see how this single difference, invisible to subscriber and broadcaster alike, could transform a system that is for all practical purposes a traditional cable system into 'a copy shop that provides its patrons with a library card.' " *Id.* at 2507.

Even the dissent, which would have found no liability based on the lack of Aereo's volition in choosing which programming to make available, stated that where the alleged infringer plays no role in selecting the content, it cannot be held directly liable when a customer makes an infringing copy: "Aereo does not 'perform' for the sole and simple reason that it does not make the choice of content." *Id.* at 2514 (Scalia, J., dissenting).

D. The "Server Test"

Defendants urge this Court to define the scope of the display right in terms of what they refer to as the "Server Test." According to defendants, it is "well settled" law and the facts of this case call for its application. As set forth below, the Court does not view the Server Test as the correct application of the law with regard to the facts here. Nevertheless, it is useful to briefly chronicle the body of law that has developed in that area and explain why it is inapplicable.

[The court reviewed the Ninth Circuit's decision in *Perfect 10, Inc. v. Amazon.com, Inc.,* 508 F.3d 1146 (9th Cir. 2007) (*"Perfect 10 II"*).]

Defendants here argue that *Perfect 10* is part of an "unbroken line of authority" on which this Court should rely in determining broadly whether a copyright owner's display right has been violated. Outside of the Ninth Circuit, however, the Server Test has not been widely adopted. Even a quick survey reveals that the case law in this area is somewhat scattered. Of the other Circuits, only the Seventh Circuit has weighed in thus far—in *Flava Works, Inc. v. Gunter,* 689 F.3d 754 (7th Cir. 2012), the question before the court was whether the defendant was a *contributory* infringer. Defendant in that case, a "social bookmarker," whose service involved enabling individuals who share interests to point each other towards online materials (in this case, videos) that cater towards that taste, through embedding the code for the video onto its website. The videos remained hosted on the original servers. As with Perfect 10, upon arriving on defendant's website, thumbnails would appear; after clicking on one, the user would retrieve content from plaintiff's website. The *Flava* Court found that defendants were not contributory infringers; the question of direct infringement was never reached. The lower court, however, had opined that "[t]o the extent that *Perfect 10* can be read to stand for the proposition that inline linking can never cause a display of images or videos that would give rise to a claim of direct copyright infringement, *we respectfully disagree. In our view, a website's servers need not actually store a copy of the work in order to 'display' it."* *Flava Works, Inc. v. Gunter,* 2011 WL 3876910, at *4 (N.D. Ill. Sept. 1, 2011), *rev'd on other grounds,* 689 F.3d 754 (7th Cir. 2012) (emphasis added).

Four courts in this District have discussed the Server Test and *Perfect 10's* holding; none adopted the Server Test for the display right. [Three of those cases involved the distribution right, not the display right.]

Only the fourth case in this District, *Capitol Records, LLC v. ReDigi Inc.,* 934 F.Supp.2d 640 (S.D.N.Y. 2013) squarely dealt with the § 106(5) display right. There, however, the court did no more than offer a simple factual statement, "The Ninth Circuit has held that the display of a photographic image on a computer *may* implicate the display right, though infringement hinges, *in part*, on where the image was hosted." *Id.* at 652 (emphasis added). It then proceeded to deny summary judgment based on material disputes as to the content of the allegedly infringing issues. *Id.*

. . .

Only a handful of other district courts have considered the issue. . . . [I] n The *Leader's Institute, LLC v. Jackson*, 2017 WL 5629514 (N.D. Tex. Nov. 22, 2017), at issue on summary judgment was, *inter alia*, whether plaintiffs infringed defendant's exclusive display rights by "framing" defendant's websites. The court rejected *Perfect 10*, holding that by "framing the defendant's copyrighted works, the plaintiffs impermissibly displayed the works to the public." *Id.* at *10. It distinguished *Perfect 10* on its facts, noting that, "[U]nlike Google, [plaintiffs' website] did not merely provide a link by which users could access [defendant's] content but instead displayed [defendant's] content as if it were its own." *Id.* at *11. It further stated: "[T]o the extent *Perfect 10* makes actual possession of a copy a necessary condition to violating a copyright owner's exclusive right to display the copyrighted works, the Court respectfully disagrees with the Ninth Circuit. . . . The text of the Copyright Act does not make actual possession of a work a prerequisite for infringement." *Id.*

In sum, this Court is aware of only three decisions outside of the Ninth Circuit considering the display right in light of Perfect 10; one from the Seventh Circuit which adopted the Server Test for contributory liability, one from the Southern District which stated as a factual matter only that *Perfect 10* existed, and one from the Northern District of Texas rejecting *Perfect 10*.

III. DISCUSSION

Defendants' argument is simple—they have framed the issue as one in which the physical location and/or possession of an allegedly infringing image determines liability under the § 106(5) exclusive display right. Defendants argue that—despite the seamless presentation of the Brady Photo on their webpages—they simply provided "instructions" for the user to navigate to a third-party server on which the photo resided. According to defendants, merely providing instructions does not constitute a "display" by the defendants as a matter of law. They maintain that *Perfect 10*'s Server Test is settled law that should determine the outcome of this case.

Plaintiff maintains both 1) that to apply the Server Test leads to results incongruous with the purposes and text of the Copyright Act; and 2) even if the Server Test is rightfully applied in a case such as *Perfect 10*, or another case in which the user takes a volitional action of his own to display an image, it is inappropriate in cases such as those here, where the user takes no action to "display" the image. He and his amici caution that to adopt the Server Test broadly would have a "devastating" economic impact on photography and visual artwork licensing industries, noting that it would "eliminate" the incentives for websites to pay licensing fees, and thus "deprive content creators of the resources necessary to invest in further creation."

The Court agrees with plaintiff. The plain language of the Copyright Act, the legislative history undergirding its enactment, and subsequent Supreme Court jurisprudence provide no basis for a rule that allows the physical location or possession of an image to determine who may or may not have "displayed" a work within the meaning of the Copyright Act. Moreover, the Court agrees that there are critical factual distinctions between *Perfect 10* and this case such that, even if the Second Circuit were to find the Server Test consistent with the Copyright Act, it would be inapplicable here.

A. The Copyright Act

Nowhere does the Copyright Act suggest that possession of an image is necessary in order to display it. Indeed, the purpose and language of the Act support the opposite view. The definitions in § 101 are illuminating. First, to display a work publicly means to "to transmit . . . a . . . display of the work . . . by means of any device or process." 17 USC § 101. To transmit a display is to "communicate it by any device or process whereby images or sounds are received beyond the place from which they are sent." *Id.* (emphasis added). Devices and processes are further defined to mean ones "now known or later developed." *Id.* This is plainly drafted with the intent to sweep broadly.

Here, defendants' websites actively took steps to "display" the image. A review of just a few of the declarations proffered by defendants illustrates the point. For defendant Heavy.com:

> [I]n order to embed the SneakerReporter Tweet, Heavy.com navigated to Twitter and copied the SneakerReporter Tweet's URL. Heavy.com then used out of the box content management functionality provided by WordPress to embed the SneakerReporter Tweet within the Heavy.com Article.

Defendant Boston Herald "pasted a code line into its blog/article that contains Twitter HTML instructions."

Defendant The Big Lead submitted a declaration in which the managing editor stated, "My entering the URL for the RealBobManningTweet into the field for embedded content in the CMS [content management system] caused this URL to be inserted into embedding code that became part of the HTML code for the Big Lead Article."

Defendant Gannett submitted a declaration in which the Vice President stated that:

> [I]f I wanted that web page to *display* a photo that a third party user had posted to a site like Twitter, I could do so without me ever having to make a copy of the photo. I would simply include in my HTML code some additional coding containing a link to

the URL of the Twitter page where the photo appeared. (emphasis added).

It is clear, therefore, that each and every defendant itself took active steps to put a process in place that resulted in a transmission of the photos so that they could be visibly shown. Most directly this was accomplished by the act of including the code in the overall design of their webpage; that is, embedding. Properly understood, the steps necessary to embed a Tweet are accomplished by the defendant website; these steps constitute a process. The plain language of the Copyright Act calls for no more.

Indeed, and as discussed above, the Copyright Act's authors intended to include "each and every method by which images . . . comprising a . . . display are picked up and conveyed;" moreover they went as far as to note that an infringement of the display right could occur "if the image were transmitted by *any method* (. . . for example, by a computer system) from one place to members of the public elsewhere." H.R. Rep. 94–1476, 64, 70 (1976). Persuasive as well is the warning of the Register of Copyrights that a "basic right of public exhibition" was necessary to the 1976 Amendments precisely because "information storage and retrieval devices . . . when linked together by communication satellites or other means . . . could eventually provide libraries and individuals throughout the world with access to a single copy or a work by transmission of electronic images." H. Comm. On the Judiciary, 89th Cong., *Copyright Law Revision Part 6: Supplementary Report of the Register of Copyrights on the General Revision of the U.S. Copyright Law: 1965 Revision Bill*, at 25 (Comm. Print. 1965).

In sum, this Court sees nothing in either the text or purpose of the Copyright Act suggesting that physical possession of an image is a necessary element to its display for purposes of the Act.

B. *Aereo*'s Impact

Moreover, though the Supreme Court has only weighed in obliquely on the issue, its language in *Aereo* is instructive. At heart, the Court's holding eschewed the notion that Aereo should be absolved of liability based upon purely technical distinctions—in the end, Aereo was held to have transmitted the performances, despite its argument that it was the user clicking a button, and not any volitional act of Aereo itself, that did the performing. The language the Court used there to describe invisible technological details applies equally well here: "This difference means nothing to the subscriber. It means nothing to the broadcaster. We do not see how this single difference, *invisible to subscriber and broadcaster alike*, could transform a system that is for all practical purposes a traditional cable system into a 'copy shop that provides patrons with a library card.' " *Aereo*, 134 S.Ct. at 2507.

Of course, in *Aereo* there was no argument about the physical location of the antennae, which were without dispute located in Aereo's warehouses; similarly there was no dispute that Aereo's servers saved data from the on-air broadcasts onto its own hard drives. On the other hand, Aereo was arguably a more passive participant in transmitting the performance right than is a user in the case here—who has no choice in what is displayed to him when he navigates to one of defendant's webpages. Furthermore, the principles that undergird the *Aereo* decision—chief among them that mere technical distinctions invisible to the user should not be the lynchpin on which copyright liability lies—apply with equal vigor here.

As noted above, even the dissent implies that *were* Aereo to engage in any sort of curatorial process as to content, that liability might lie: "In sum, Aereo does not perform for the *sole and simple reason* that it does not make the choice of content." *Id.* at 2514 (Scalia, J., dissenting). This adds credence to the notion that where, as here, defendants are choosing the content which will be displayed, that they would indeed be displaying.

In sum, this Court reads *Aereo*, while not directly on point, as strongly supporting plaintiff's argument that liability should not hinge on invisible, technical processes imperceptible to the viewer.

C. *Perfect 10*

The Court declines defendants' invitation to apply *Perfect 10*'s Server Test for two reasons. First, this Court is skeptical that *Perfect 10* correctly interprets the display right of the Copyright Act. As stated above, this Court finds no indication in the text or legislative history of the Act that possessing a copy of an infringing image is a prerequisite to displaying it. The Ninth Circuit's analysis hinged, however, on making a "copy" of the image to be displayed—which copy would be stored on the server. It stated that its holding did not "erroneously collapse the display right in section 106(5) into the reproduction right in 106(1)." *Perfect 10 II*, 508 F.3d at 1161. But indeed, that appears to be exactly what was done.

The Copyright Act, however, provides several clues that this is not what was intended. In several distinct parts of the Act, it contemplates infringers who would not be in possession of copies—for example in Section 110(5)(A) which exempts "small commercial establishments whose proprietors merely bring onto their premises standard radio or television equipment and turn it on for their customer's enjoyment" from liability. H.R. Rep. No. 94–1476 at 87 (1976). That these establishments require an exemption, despite the fact that to turn on the radio or television is not to make or store a copy, is strong evidence that a copy need not be made in order to display an image.

Second, even if it correctly interprets the Act, to the degree that defendants interpret *Perfect 10* as standing for a *broadly-construed* Server Test, focusing on the physical location of allegedly infringing images, this Court disagrees. Rather, *Perfect 10* was heavily informed by two factors—the fact that the defendant operated a search engine, and the fact that the user made an active choice to click on an image before it was displayed—that suggest that such a broad reading is neither appropriate nor desirable.

In *Perfect 10*, the district court's Opinion, while not strictly cabining its adoption of the Server Test to a search engine like Google, nevertheless relied heavily on that fact in its analysis. It stated, for example, that adopting the Server Test "will merely preclude *search engines* from being held directly liable for in-line linking and or framing infringing contents stored on third-party websites." *Perfect 10 I*, 416 F.Supp.2d at 844 (emphasis added). It went on: "*Merely to index the web so that users can more readily find the information they seek* should not constitute direct infringement. . . ." *Id.* (emphasis added). On appeal, the Ninth Circuit began its statement of the case by saying, "we consider a copyright owner's efforts to stop an *Internet search engine* from facilitating access to infringing images." *Perfect 10 II*, 508 F.3d at 1154.

In addition, the role of the user was paramount in the *Perfect 10* case—the district court found that users who view the full-size images "*after clicking* on one of the thumbnails" are "engaged in a *direct* connection with third-party websites, which are themselves responsible for transferring content." *Perfect 10 I*, 416 F.Supp.2d at 843.

In this Court's view, these distinctions are critical. In *Perfect 10*, Google's search engine provided a service whereby the user navigated from webpage to webpage, with Google's assistance. This is manifestly not the same as opening up a favorite blog or website to find a full color image awaiting the user, whether he or she asked for it, looked for it, clicked on it, or not. Both the nature of Google Search Engine, as compared to the defendant websites, and the volitional act taken by users of the services, provide a sharp contrast to the facts at hand.

In sum, the Court here does *not* apply the Server Test. It is neither appropriate to the specific facts of this case, nor, this Court believes, adequately grounded in the text of the Copyright Act. It therefore does not and should not control the outcome here.

D. Defenses

Defendants warn that to find for plaintiff here would "cause a tremendous chilling effect on the core functionality of the web." (ECF No. 121, Defs.' Mem. of Law in Supp. at 35) (quoting *Perfect 10 I*, 416 F.Supp.2d at 840). Their amici warn that not adopting the Server Test here would "radically change linking practices, and thereby transform the Internet as we know it."

The Court does not view the results of its decision as having such dire consequences. Certainly, given a number as of yet unresolved strong defenses to liability separate from this issue, numerous viable claims should not follow.

In this case, there are genuine questions about whether plaintiff effectively released his image into the public domain when he posted it to his Snapchat account. Indeed, in many cases there are likely to be factual questions as to licensing and authorization. There is also a very serious and strong fair use defense, a defense under the Digital Millennium Copyright Act, and limitations on damages from innocent infringement.

In sum, for all the reasons discussed above, the Court DENIES defendants' motion for partial summary judgment and GRANTS partial summary judgment to the plaintiff.

. . .

QUESTIONS

1. Some have argued that hyperlinks no more "display" copyrighted works than do footnotes or library catalog call numbers, which simply supply locational information. How persuasive is the metaphor? While it may be true that a "simple" link fulfills a function limited to sending the user to another site that will in turn provide information about the location of a particular piece of content, embedded links such as those involved in *Goldman v. Breitbart* do more than provide locational information—they instead serve up content directly to the user, stripping away the need to navigate through the source website to access the targeted work. In other words, would it not be more correct to characterize such links not only as fulfilling the function of a "library's card index" by identifying the location of a piece of content, but also as taking the metaphorical book off the library's shelf, placing the book in the recipient's hands, and turning to a particular page?

2. Had the defendants right-clicked on the source image and pasted it into their own websites, there would be no doubt that the defendants engaged in prima facie infringing acts of reproduction and public display. By embedding the links to the source image, the defendants avoided reproducing the image, but the view of the image that defendants offer their users is the same as if defendants had physically incorporated a copy of the image; from the viewer's experience, "it makes no difference" whether the image was cut-and-pasted, or embedded. What is the legal basis for requiring not only that the defendant "show a copy" (see sec. 101 definition of to display), but that the defendant *possess* the copy that she shows? Does the requirement that the person making a public display by transmission "transmit" the display explain the difference?

3. Is the court's analysis limited to links that embed images, as the defendants' did? What if you find a photo on a third party's website, copy the URL for the website (or photo), paste the URL into an email message as a hyperlink and send the email message to all of your classmates, many of whom, upon receiving the email, click on the hyperlink and view the photo when the third-party website transmits the image file to your classmates' computers? Didn't you "[take] active steps to put a process in place that resulted in a transmission of the photos so they could be visibly shown," as the court describes the defendants' conduct? Under the court's reasoning, isn't that enough to conclude your actions constitute a public display of the photo? Is the same thing true if you post a hyperlink to the photo on your blog or webpage?

CHAPTER 7

FAIR USE

A. BACKGROUND

Page 951. Insert a new NOTE before Section B.

PROCEDURAL ISSUES

Courts often characterize fair use as a "mixed question of law and fact," a denomination that has the effect of reviewing the district court's findings under a *de novo*, rather than a clearly erroneous, standard of review. What if a jury decided whether or not defendant's acts were fair use? How should a court review those findings? The Court of Appeals for the Federal Circuit, standing in for the Ninth Circuit, in *Oracle Am., Inc. v. Google LLC*, 886 F.3d 1179 (Fed. Cir. 2018), varied the standard of review based on its characterization of the kind of question the jury was deciding.

B. Standards of Review

Before turning to a consideration of the four statutory factors and any relevant underlying factual determinations, we first address the standard of review we are to employ in that consideration. While this section of most appellate opinions presents easily resolvable questions, like much else in the fair use context, that is not completely the case here.

There are several components to this inquiry. First, which aspects of the fair use determination are legal in nature and which are factual? Particularly, is the ultimate question of fair use a legal inquiry which is to be reviewed de novo? Second, what factual questions are involved in the fair use determination and under what standard are those determinations to be reviewed? Finally, though neither party addresses the question in detail, we consider what, if any, aspects of the fair use determination are for the jury to decide.

The Supreme Court has said that fair use is a mixed question of law and fact. [Citation].

The Supreme Court has recently explained how we are to determine what the standard of review should be in connection with any mixed question of law and fact. Specifically, the Court made clear that an appellate court is to break mixed questions into their component parts and to review each under the appropriate standard of review.... The Court found that there were three components to that inquiry: (1) determining the legal standard governing the question posed and what types of historical facts are relevant to that standard; (2) finding what the historical facts in the case at hand are; and (3) assessing whether the historical facts found satisfy the legal test governing the question to be answered.

As the Court explained, the first of these three is a purely legal question to be reviewed de novo on appeal and the second involves factual questions which "are reviewable only for clear error." The third is what the Court characterized as the "mixed question."

Importantly, the Court noted that "[m]ixed questions are not all alike." The Court then held that "the standard of review for a mixed question all depends—on whether answering it entails primarily legal or factual work." Where applying the law to the historical facts "involves developing auxiliary legal principles of use in other cases—appellate courts should typically review a decision de novo." But where the mixed question requires immersion in case-specific factual issues that are so narrow as to "utterly resist generalization," the mixed question review is to be deferential. Ultimately, the Court found that review of the mixed question at issue in that bankruptcy context should be deferential because de novo review of the question would do little to "clarify legal principles or provide guidance to other courts resolving other disputes."

While this may be the first time the Supreme Court has so clearly explained how appellate courts are to analyze mixed questions of law and fact, it is not the first time the Supreme Court has told us how to analyze the particular mixed question of law and fact at issue here. In other words, while the Supreme Court has not previously broken the fair use inquiry into its three analytical components as expressly as it did the question in [the above-quoted decision], it has made clear that both the first and third of those components are subject to de novo review.

In *Harper & Row*, the Court explained that, "[w]here the district court has found facts sufficient to evaluate each of the statutory factors, an appellate court 'need not remand for further factfinding but may conclude as a matter of law that the challenged use does not qualify as a fair use of the copyrighted work.' " [Citation] The Ninth Circuit has resolved the question in the same way. Where fair use is resolved on summary judgment, the Ninth Circuit reviews the district court's ultimate determination de novo. . . . That court has explained that, "as fair use is a mixed question of fact and law, so long as the record is 'sufficient to evaluate each of the statutory factors,' we may reweigh on appeal the inferences to be drawn from that record.' " [Citations]

This treatment of the ultimate question posed when a fair use defense is raised makes sense. The fair use question entails, . . . a primarily legal exercise. It requires a court to assess the inferences to be drawn from the historical facts found in light of the legal standards outlined in the statute and relevant case law and to determine what conclusion those inferences dictate. Because, as noted below, the historical facts in a fair use inquiry are generally few, generally similar from case to case, and rarely debated, resolution of what any set of facts means to the fair use determination definitely does not "resist generalization." [Citation] Instead, the exercise of assessing whether a use is fair in one case will help guide resolution of that question in all future cases.

For these reasons, we conclude that whether the court applied the correct legal standard to the fair use inquiry is a question we review de novo, whether the findings relating to any relevant historical facts were correct are questions which we review with deference, and whether the use at issue is ultimately a fair one is something we also review de novo.

. . .The Supreme Court has described "historical facts" as "a recital of external events." [Citations.] In the fair use context, historical facts include the "origin, history, content, and defendant's use" of the copyrighted work. [Citations.] When asked at oral argument to identify historical facts relevant to the fair use inquiry, counsel for Oracle agreed that they are the "who, what, where, when, how, [and] how much." Google did not dispute this characterization. This is, in part, because, in most fair use cases, defendants concede that they have used the copyrighted work, and "there is rarely dispute over the history, content, or origin of the copyrighted work." [Citations.]

While some courts once treated the entire question of fair use as factual, and, thus, a question to be sent to the jury, that is not the modern view. Since *Harper & Row*, the Ninth Circuit has described fair use as an "equitable defense." [Citation.] Indeed, the Supreme Court referred to fair use as "an equitable rule of reason" in *Harper & Row*. 471 U.S. at 560. Congress did the same when it codified the doctrine of fair use in 1976. [Citation.] If fair use is equitable in nature, it would seem to be a question for the judge, not the jury, to decide, even when there are factual disputes regarding its application. [Citation.] In that instance, it would be the judge's factual determinations that would receive a deferential review—being assessed for clear error on the record before the court.

That said, the Supreme Court has never clarified whether and to what extent the jury is to play a role in the fair use analysis. *Harper & Row* involved an appeal from a *bench* trial where the district court concluded that the use of the copyrighted material was not a fair use. [Citation.] The Court, thus, had no reason to discuss a jury determination of fair use and has not since taken an opportunity to do so.

Perhaps because of this silence, even after *Harper & Row*, several courts—including the Ninth Circuit—have continued to accept the fact that the question of fair use may go to a jury, albeit without analysis of why it may. [Citations.]

The Ninth Circuit has clarified, however, that the jury role in this context is limited to determining disputed "historical facts," not the inferences or conclusions to be drawn from those facts. *See Fisher [v. Dees]*, 794 F.2d [432] at 436. In *Fisher*, for example, the court explained that "[n]o material historical facts are at issue in this case. The parties dispute only the ultimate conclusions to be drawn from the admitted facts. Because, under *Harper & Row*, these judgments are legal in nature, we can make them without usurping the function of the jury." [Citations.]. Accordingly, while inferences from the four-factor analysis and the ultimate question of fair use are "legal in nature," in the Ninth Circuit, disputed historical facts represent questions for the jury. *Fisher*, 794 F.2d at 436. Where there are no disputed material historical facts, fair use can be decided by the court alone. *Id.*

Despite this case law, all aspects of Google's fair use defense went to the jury with neither party arguing that it should not. Thus, the jury was asked not just what the historical facts were, but what the implications of those facts were for the fair use defense. During the first appeal, Google argued to this court that there were disputed issues of material historical fact relevant to its fair use defense. As discussed below, the parties stipulated—or at least ceased to dispute—some of those facts, and presented the remaining disputed historical facts to the jury on remand. The jury returned a verdict in favor of Google on its fair use defense. Because the verdict form—though captioned as a "special verdict"—did not ask the jury to articulate its fact findings in any detail, we must assume that the jury resolved all factual issues relating to the historical facts in favor of the verdict. Despite the posture of the fair use finding, we must break that finding into its constituent parts. We must then review the subsidiary and controverted findings of historical fact for substantial evidence. [Citations.]

B. APPLICATION OF FAIR USE DOCTRINE TO CREATION OF NEW WORKS

Page 970. Insert before QUESTIONS:

Lombardo v. Dr. Seuss Ents., 279 F. Supp. 3d 497 (S.D.N.Y. 2017). The author of *Who's Holiday*, a parodic reimagining of the *How the Grinch Stole Christmas* characters in later life, obtained a declaratory judgment of fair use. The court described plaintiff's work as follows:

Who's Holiday is a one-actress 75-minute comedic play featuring a rather down-and-out 45 year-old version of Cindy-Lou Who. The Play takes place at Cindy-Lou's 1970s era trailer in the hills of Mount Crumpit. Cindy-Lou speaks to the audience only in rhyming couplets that are clearly intended to evoke the work of Dr. Seuss. While waiting for guests to arrive for her Christmas party, Cindy-Lou tells the audience the story of her life, beginning with her first encounter with the Grinch at the age of two. Throughout the Play, as she shares her history, Cindy-Lou drinks hard alcohol, abuses prescription pills, and smokes a substance she identifies as "Who Hash," which she describes as just "like a prescription" which keeps her in check to avoid a "conniption." She engages in this self-medication following her realization that none of the guests she invited to her party is likely to attend, as they keep calling throughout the Play to cancel.

As Cindy-Lou recounts her initial encounter with the Grinch and his subsequent change of heart, paralleling the plot of the original *Grinch*, she incorporates age-inappropriate language and details that do not appear in the original work. ("I watched for a while as he was stealin' our shit / Then I cooed by mistake and he saw me. That twit."); ("How would I know he was evil or crass? / He gave me some water. Then patted my ass."). After recounting the plot of the original *Grinch*, Cindy-Lou goes on to tell the audience—using rhymes involving bawdy, ribald innuendo—that she became friends with the Grinch during her school-age years, and that she engaged in sexual intercourse with the Grinch upon turning eighteen. Cindy-Lou refers to the size of the Grinch's genitalia growing "three sizes that day." After learning that she is pregnant, Cindy-Lou informs the Grinch, who asks her to marry him. Over her parents' protestation ("When I told my parents they weren't pleased in the least / I mean, who wants their baby girl deflowered by a beast."), Cindy-Lou marries the Grinch, moves into his cave at the top of Mount Crumpit, and gives birth to their child ("With the fur and the paws it looked just like its Daddy / With no who dilly attached, I named the kid Patti.").

As the years go by, Cindy-Lou and the Grinch's relationship begins to sour as they struggle with issues such as unemployment, access to health care, lack of heat, and hunger. One day, Cindy-Lou discovers that the family dog Max has frozen to death, and she decides to cook his carcass in order to feed her family. When the Grinch discovers what his dinner is made of, he attempts to physically abuse Cindy-Lou. During the ensuing scuffle, the Grinch falls off the edge of a cliff and dies. Following the Grinch's death, Cindy-Lou is arrested, convicted and incarcerated, and her daughter is put into foster care. After describing how her time in prison ultimately made her stronger and wiser, Cindy-Lou eventually finds out that all of her guests have declined to attend her party and begins to cry. It then dawns on her that she can celebrate Christmas with the audience instead. After singing a few Christmas songs, the door bells rings. Cindy-Lou expects it to be a local prankster, but it turns out to be her daughter, Patti.

Turning to the fair use analysis, the Court continued:

The key question I must therefore resolve, is whether the Play comments on *Grinch* by imitating and ridiculing its characteristic style for comic effect, or, as defendant contends, merely exploits the characters, style and themes of *Grinch* in order "to avoid the drudgery in working up something fresh." Defendant argues that the Play "does not poke fun of the Seussian rhyming style," but instead usurps that style in order to sell a commercial work. . . . The Play recontextualizes *Grinch's* easily-recognizable plot and rhyming style by placing Cindy-Lou Who—a symbol of childhood innocence and naiveté— in outlandish, profanity-laden, adult-themed scenarios involving topics such as poverty, teen-age pregnancy, drug and alcohol abuse, prison culture, and murder. In so doing, the Play subverts the expectations of the Seussian genre, and lampoons the *Grinch* by making Cindy-Lou's naiveté, Who-Ville's endlessly-smiling, problem-free citizens, and Dr. Seuss' rhyming innocence, all appear ridiculous.

. . .

[T]he Play does much more than just insert the characters from *Grinch* into a dark, updated setting. By parodying those characters and setting, the Play "adds something new" and "alters the [original] with new expression, meaning, [and] message." [citation] The Play, as a parody, qualifies as a transformative work. *See Abilene Music*, 320 F. Supp. 2d at 89 ("[D]eciding that the new work is a parody necessarily entails finding that the new work is transformative.").

The court also found economic harm unlikely:

[T]here is virtually no possibility that consumers will go see the Play in lieu of reading Grinch or watching an authorized derivative work, such as the 2000 film Dr. Seuss' *How the Grinch Stole Christmas*. Grinch is a children's book intended for an all-ages audience, whereas the Play is a bawdy, off-color parody of Grinch that is clearly intended for adult audiences. . . . The Play is not an unauthorized sequel of Grinch, and given the clear differences in tone and content, it is unreasonable to assume that audiences might confuse the Play for a theatrical version of Grinch, or that the Play would usurp the market for Grinch.

Page 970. Add new Questions 3 and 4.

3. Suppose *Lombardo* had been decided by a district court in the 11th Circuit, and suppose you were arguing an appeal. How would you distinguish *Lombardo* from *Suntrust*? Would it matter?

4. Why isn't *Who's Holiday* an "unauthorized sequel of Grinch"? What difference would it make? Cf. *Salinger v. Colting*, *infra* main casebook at p. 1257.

C. APPLICATION OF FAIR USE DOCTRINE TO NEW TECHNOLOGIES

2. DIGITAL COPYING BY COMMERCIAL INTERMEDIARIES

Page 1105–1112. Replace excerpt of district court opinion in *Fox News Network, LLC v. TVEyes, Inc.*, 43 F.Supp.3d 379 (S.D.N.Y. 2014) with the following:

Fox News Network, LLC v. TVEyes, Inc.

883 F.3d 169 (2d Cir. 2018).

■ JACOBS, CIRCUIT JUDGE:

In this copyright infringement suit, defendant TVEyes, Inc. ("TVEyes") offers a service that enables its clients to easily locate and view segments of televised video programming that are responsive to the clients' interests. It does so by continuously recording vast quantities of television programming, compiling the recorded broadcasts into a database that is text-searchable (based primarily on the closed-captioned text copied from the broadcasts), and allowing its clients to search for and watch (up to) ten-minute video clips that mention terms of interest to the clients. Plaintiff Fox News Network, LLC ("Fox"), which has sued TVEyes in the United States District Court for the Southern District of New York, does not challenge the creation of the text-searchable database but alleges that TVEyes infringed Fox's copyrights by re-distributing Fox's copied audiovisual content, thereby enabling TVEyes's clients to access that content without Fox's permission. The principal question on appeal is whether TVEyes's enabling of its clients to watch Fox's programming is protected by the doctrine of fair use.

The district court held that fewer than all of the functions of TVEyes's service constitute a fair use. Specifically, the district court deemed a fair use the functions enabling clients of TVEyes to search for videos by term, to watch the resulting videos, and to archive the videos on the TVEyes servers; but the court held that certain other functions were not a fair use, such as those enabling TVEyes's clients to download videos to their computers, to freely e-mail videos to others, or to watch videos after searching for them by date, time, and channel (rather than by keyword). The district court therefore dismissed Fox's challenge to important functions of TVEyes's service, but also held that TVEyes was liable to Fox for copyright infringement on account of other functions of that service. A permanent injunction limited various aspects of TVEyes's service.

This appeal shares features with our decision in Authors Guild v. Google, Inc., 804 F.3d 202 (2d Cir. 2015) ("Google Books"). That case held that Google's creation of a text-searchable database of millions of books (including books under copyright) was a fair use because Google's service was "transformative" and because integral features protected the rights of copyright holders. However, we cautioned that the case "test[ed] the boundaries of fair use." Google Books, 804 F.3d at 206. We conclude that defendant TVEyes has exceeded those bounds.

TVEyes's re-distribution of Fox's audiovisual content serves a transformative purpose in that it enables TVEyes's clients to isolate from the vast corpus of Fox's content the material that is responsive to their interests, and to access that material in a convenient manner. But because that re-distribution makes available virtually all of Fox's copyrighted audiovisual content—including all of the Fox content that TVEyes's clients wish to see and hear—and because it deprives Fox of revenue that properly belongs to the copyright holder, TVEyes has failed to show that the product it offers to its clients can be justified as a fair use.

Accordingly, we reverse the order of the district court to the extent it held that some of the challenged TVEyes functions constituted a fair use. . . .

I

TVEyes is a for-profit media company. It offers a service that allows its clients to efficiently sort through vast quantities of television content in order to find clips that discuss items of interest to them. For example, a client in marketing or public relations interested in how a particular product is faring in the media can use the TVEyes service to find, watch, and share clips of recent television broadcasts that mention that product.

The service works this way. TVEyes records essentially all television broadcasts as they happen, drawing from more than 1,400 channels, recording 24 hours a day, every day. By copying the closed-captioned text that accompanies the content it records (and utilizing speech-to-text software when necessary), TVEyes creates a text-searchable transcript of the words spoken in each video. The videos and transcripts are consolidated into a database. A client inputs a search term and gets a list of video clips that mention the term. A click on a thumbnail image of a clip plays the video, beginning fourteen seconds before the search term was spoken, and displays a segment of the transcript with the search term highlighted. The parties dispute the quality of the clips. Fox contends that the clips are high definition; TVEyes contends that the clips are grainier than the original broadcasts. The clips can be played for no more than ten minutes, but a user can play an unlimited number of clips. To prevent clients from watching entire programs, TVEyes (during the course of this litigation) implemented a device that is claimed to prevent clients from viewing consecutive segments. The parties dispute whether this measure is effective.

TVEyes's service has ancillary functions. A TVEyes client may "archive" videos permanently on the TVEyes servers and may download videos directly to the client's computer. These services are useful because

TVEyes otherwise deletes captured content after thirty-two days. Clients can also email the clips for viewing by others, including those who are not TVEyes clients. And clients can search for videos by date, time, and channel (rather than by keyword). The parties dispute whether clients can watch live broadcasts on TVEyes.

A TVEyes subscription costs approximately $500 per month, is available for business and professional use, and is not offered to private consumers for personal use. Clients include journalists, government and political organizations, law enforcement, the military, for-profit companies, and non-profits.

TVEyes asserts that it restricts its clients' use of its content in various ways. For example, clients are required to sign a contract that limits their use of clips to "internal purposes only" and are warned upon downloading a clip that it is to be used for only "internal review, analysis or research." Fox contends that these safeguards are ineffective and disputes the assertion by TVEyes that its service is primarily used for "internal" research and analysis.

Fox claims that at some point TVEyes unsuccessfully approached it to procure a license to use Fox programming. Fox demanded that TVEyes stop using its programming; when TVEyes refused, litigation ensued. The lawsuit focuses on nineteen copyrighted Fox broadcasts. The legal question is whether TVEyes has a "fair use" defense to Fox's copyright infringement claims.

. . .

It is useful to analyze separately distinct functions of the secondary use (i.e., the use by TVEyes of Fox's copyrighted material), considering whether each independent function is a fair use. See *Google Books*, 804 F.3d at 216–18. TVEyes has two core offerings: the "Search function" and the "Watch function." The Search function allows clients to identify videos that contain keywords of interest. The Watch function allows TVEyes clients to view up to ten-minute, unaltered video clips of copyrighted content. Fox does not challenge the Search function on appeal. Fox's challenge is to the Watch function, and we determine that its inclusion renders TVEyes's package of services unprotected by the fair use doctrine.

Turning to the Watch function, we next consider each of the four factors listed in § 107.

A

In considering the first statutory factor—the "purpose and character" of the secondary use, . . . [b]oth parties rely most heavily on *Google Books*, which provides the starting point for analysis.

. . .

We held that Google's copying served a transformative purpose because it created a text-searchable database that "communicate[d] something new and different from the original." "[T]he result of a word search is different in purpose, character, expression, meaning, and message from the page (and the book) from which it is drawn."

We also held that the "snippet view" of unaltered, copyrighted text "add[ed] important value to the basic transformative search function" by allowing users to verify that the list of books returned by the database was responsive to the user's search. . . .

TVEyes's copying of Fox's content for use in the Watch function is similarly transformative insofar as it enables users to isolate, from an ocean of programming, material that is responsive to their interests and needs, and to access that material with targeted precision. It enables nearly instant access to a subset of material—and to information about the material—that would otherwise be irretrievable, or else retrievable only through prohibitively inconvenient or inefficient means.

Sony Corporation of America vs. Universal City Studios, Inc. is instructive. In *Sony*, a television customer, who (by virtue of owning a television set) had acquired authorization to watch a program when it was broadcast, recorded it in order to watch it instead at a later, more convenient time. That was held to be a fair use. While *Sony* was decided before "transformative" became a term of art, the apparent reasoning was that a secondary use may be a fair use if it utilizes technology to achieve the transformative purpose of improving the efficiency of delivering content without unreasonably encroaching on the commercial entitlements of the rights holder.

The Watch function certainly qualifies as technology that achieves the transformative purpose of enhancing efficiency: it enables TVEyes's clients to view all of the Fox programming that (over the prior thirty-two days) discussed a particular topic of interest to them, without having to monitor thirty-two days of programming in order to catch each relevant discussion; and it eliminates the clients' need even to view entire programs, because the ten most relevant minutes are presented to them. Much like the television customer in *Sony*, TVEyes clients can view the Fox programming they want at a time and place that is convenient to them, rather than at the time and place of broadcast. For these reasons, TVEyes's Watch function is at least somewhat transformative.

The first statutory factor also implicates considerations distinct from whether the secondary use is transformative. In particular, Fox argues that the "commercial nature" of TVEyes's copying (its sale of access to Fox's content) weighs against a finding of fair use.

The commercial nature of a secondary use weighs against a finding of fair use. [Citation] And it does so especially when, as here, the transformative character of the secondary use is modest. . . . The Watch function has only a modest transformative character because, notwithstanding the transformative manner in which it delivers content, it essentially republishes that content unaltered from its original form, with no "new expression, meaning or message." *HathiTrust*, 755 F.3d at 96 [further citations omitted] The clients of TVEyes use Fox's news broadcasts for the same purpose that authorized Fox viewers use those broadcasts—the purpose of learning the information reported.

The first statutory factor therefore favors TVEyes, albeit slightly.

B

The second statutory factor is "the nature of the copyrighted work." This factor "has rarely played a significant role in the determination of a fair use dispute," and it plays no significant role here. *Google Books*, 804 F.3d at 220.

TVEyes presses the argument that, since facts are not copyrightable, the factual nature of Fox's content militates in favor of a finding of fair use. We have rejected this argument: "Those who report the news undoubtedly create factual works. It cannot seriously be argued that, for that reason, others may freely copy and re-disseminate news reports." *Id.* at 220.

C

The third statutory factor is "the amount and substantiality of the portion used in relation to the copyrighted work as a whole." The relevant consideration is the amount of copyrighted material made available to the public rather than the amount of material used by the copier. *Google Books*, 804 F.3d at 222.

This factor clearly favors Fox because TVEyes makes available virtually the entirety of the Fox programming that TVEyes users want to see and hear. While "courts have rejected any categorical rule that a copying of the entirety cannot be a fair use," "a finding of fair use is [less] likely . . . when the copying is extensive, or encompasses the most important parts of the original." *Id.* at 221. In this respect, the TVEyes Watch function is radically dissimilar to the service at issue in Google Books.

Google's snippet function was designed to ensure that users could see only a very small piece of a book's contents. Each snippet was three lines of text, constituting approximately one-eighth of a page; a viewer could see at most three snippets per book for any searched term, and no more than one per page. Users were prevented from performing repeated searches to find multiple snippets that could be compiled into a coherent block of text. Approximately 22% of a book's text was "blacklist[ed]": no snippet could be shown from those pages. *Id.* at 222. And snippets were not available at all for such books as dictionaries or cookbooks, in which a snippet might convey all the information that a searcher was likely to need. While the snippets allowed a user to judge whether a book was responsive to the user's needs, they were abbreviated to ensure that it would be nearly impossible for a user to see a meaningful exposition of what the author originally intended to convey to readers.

TVEyes redistributes Fox's news programming in ten-minute clips, which—given the brevity of the average news segment on a particular topic—likely provide TVEyes's users with all of the Fox programming that they seek and the entirety of the message conveyed by Fox to authorized viewers of the original. Cf. *Harper & Row Publishers, Inc. v. Nation Enterprises*, 471 U.S. 539, 564–65 (1985) (finding no fair use when the copying involved only about 300 words, but the portion copied was "the heart of the book"). TVEyes's use of Fox's content is therefore both "extensive" and inclusive of all that is "important" from the copyrighted work. *Google Books*, 804 F.3d at 221.

D

The fourth statutory factor is "the effect of the [secondary] use upon the potential market for or value of the copyrighted work." This factor is "undoubtedly the single most important element of fair use." *Harper & Row Publishers, Inc. v. Nation Enters.*, 471 U.S. 539, 566 (1985). It "focuses on whether the copy brings to the marketplace a competing substitute for the original, or its derivative, so as to deprive the rights holder of significant revenues because of the likelihood that potential purchasers may opt to acquire the copy in preference to the original." *Google Books*, 804 F.3d at 223. Critically, it requires consideration of "not only the . . . market harm caused by the particular actions of the alleged infringer," but also the market harm that would result from "unrestricted and widespread conduct of the [same] sort." *Campbell*, 510 U.S. at 590 (internal quotation marks and alteration omitted).

TVEyes argues that its service poses little risk of being a "competing substitute" for Fox's offerings. *Google Books*, 804 F.3d at 223. Fox argues that TVEyes undercuts Fox's ability to profit from licensing searchable access to its copyrighted content to third parties. Fox has much the stronger point.

. . . Even if a use does infringe an exclusive right, "[o]nly an impact on potential licensing revenues for traditional, reasonable, or likely to be developed markets should be legally cognizable when evaluating a secondary use's effect upon the potential market for or value of the copyrighted work." *Texaco*, 60 F.3d at 930 (internal quotation marks omitted).

. . . The success of the TVEyes business model demonstrates that deep-pocketed consumers are willing to pay well for a service that allows them to search for and view selected television clips, and that this market is worth millions of dollars in the aggregate. Consequently, there is a plausibly exploitable market for such access to televised content, and it is proper to consider whether TVEyes displaces potential Fox revenues when TVEyes allows its clients to watch Fox's copyrighted content without Fox's permission.

Such displacement does occur. Since the ability to re-distribute Fox's content in the manner that TVEyes does is clearly of value to TVEyes, it (or a similar service) should be willing to pay Fox for the right to offer the content. By providing Fox's content to TVEyes clients without payment to Fox, TVEyes is in effect depriving Fox of licensing revenues from TVEyes or from similar entities. And Fox itself might wish to exploit the market for such a service rather than license it to others. TVEyes has thus "usurp[ed] a market that properly belongs to the copyright-holder." *Kirkwood*, 150 F.3d at 110. It is of no moment that TVEyes allegedly approached Fox for a license but was rebuffed: the failure to strike a deal satisfactory to both parties does not give TVEyes the right to copy Fox's copyrighted material without payment.

In short, by selling access to Fox's audiovisual content without a license, TVEyes deprives Fox of revenues to which Fox is entitled as the copyright holder. Therefore, the fourth factor favors Fox.

E

To ascertain whether TVEyes's service is protected as a fair use, the final step is to weigh the four statutory factors together, along with any other relevant considerations. . . .

We conclude that TVEyes's service is not justifiable as a fair use. As to the first factor, TVEyes's Watch function is at least somewhat transformative in that it renders convenient and efficient access to a subset of content; however, because the function does little if anything to change the content itself or the purpose for which the content is used, its transformative character is modest at best. Accordingly—and because the service at issue is commercial—the first factor favors TVEyes only slightly. The second factor is neutral in this case. The third factor strongly favors Fox because the Watch function allows TVEyes's clients to see and hear virtually all of the Fox programming that they wish. And the fourth factor favors Fox as well because TVEyes has usurped a function for which Fox is entitled to demand compensation under a licensing agreement.

At bottom, TVEyes is unlawfully profiting off the work of others by commercially re-distributing all of that work that a viewer wishes to use, without payment or license. Having weighed the required factors, we conclude that the balance strongly favors Fox and defeats the defense of fair use.

. . .

■ KAPLAN, DISTRICT JUDGE,* concurring:

I concur in the result as well as part I, the preamble to part II, and parts II.B, III and IV of the majority opinion. With great respect for my learned and distinguished colleagues, however, I do not join in their characterization of TVEyes' Watch function as "somewhat transformative." . . .

---

*   Lewis A. Kaplan, United States District Judge for the Southern District of New York, sitting by designation.

. . . In view of the majority's expression of its opinion that the Watch function is "somewhat transformative," I feel compelled to express my own doubts regarding that conclusion. . . .

[T]he majority's justification for concluding that the Watch function is "somewhat transformative" is that it "improve[s] the efficiency of delivering content."

. . .

Even on the majority's view that TVEyes' Watch function substantially improves the efficiency with which TVEyes customers can access Fox copyrighted broadcasts of possible interest, it does no more than repackage and deliver the original works. It adds no new information, no new aesthetics, and no new insights or understandings. I therefore doubt that it is transformative. Indeed, I regard *Infinity Broadcast Corp. v. Kirkwood* as having settled the question whether a use is transformative simply because it is more efficient or convenient than what preceded it.

In that case, the defendant, Kirkwood, offered a service through which a Kirkwood customer, regardless of its physical location, could dial a Kirkwood device over a phone line, tune to the radio station of its choice in any of the nation's 10 largest radio markets, and listen to the broadcast of its chosen station. Kirkwood marketed the service to "radio stations, advertisers, talent scouts, and others" for purposes such as "auditioning on-air talent, verifying the broadcast of commercials, and listing to a station's programming format and feel." No doubt Kirkwood's service was convenient and efficiency-enhancing. It enabled interested clients who, by reason of distance, could not receive the radio stations of interest to them to (a) access those stations through Kirkwood, (b) listen to their broadcasts over telephone lines and (c) do so for reasons that, at least in many cases, had nothing to do with the purposes for which local listeners tuned their radios to their stations of choice. Nevertheless, this Court rejected Kirkwood's fair use defense, stating that there was a "total absence of transformativeness" in Kirkwood's retransmission of the broadcasts. And the Watch function at issue here is essentially indistinguishable in principle.

We rejected the argument that convenience of accessing copyrighted material is a transformative purpose in *American Geophysical Union, et al. v. Texaco* as well. That involved photocopying of scientific journal articles for use in laboratories. Texaco there argued that "its conversion of the individual [journal] articles through photocopying into a form more easily used in a laboratory might constitute transformative use." Notwithstanding the fact that the photocopies often were more convenient or efficient than, for example, buying, borrowing, shelving and carrying about bound volumes of journals, we wrote that "Texaco's photocopying merely transforms the material object embodying the intangible article that is the copyrighted original work. Texaco's making of copies cannot properly be regarded as a transformative use of the copyrighted material."

Also closely aligned with this case are others that dealt with technologies relating to digitized music, mp3s, and music sharing. Defendants in those cases argued that their technologies should be considered fair use because they permitted "space-shifting"—they allowed users to store music in different, more convenient forms that allowed them to listen to it in venues more desirable to them. In other words, the technology enhanced efficiency and convenience. But courts presented with this argument either rejected the idea that space-shifting is a transformative purpose or considered the space-shifting argument relevant only to the question of the commercial nature of the use.

These cases support my inclination to conclude that a technological means that delivers copies of copyrighted material to a secondary user more quickly, efficiently or conveniently does not render the distribution of those copies transformative, at least standing alone.

. . .

Page 1112. Delete Questions 1–3. Renumber Question 4 as Question 1 and add the following new Questions.

2. The majority stated that: "While *Sony* was decided before "transformative" became a term of art, the apparent reasoning was that a secondary use may be a fair use if it utilizes technology to achieve the transformative purpose of improving the efficiency of delivering content without unreasonably encroaching on the commercial entitlements of the rights holder." Judge Kaplan, in a portion of his concurrence reproduced *infra* this Supplement (page 62), challenged *Sony*'s authority for the proposition that enhancing convenience could be a fair use purpose under the first factor. We will return to that issue in the next subsection of this chapter.

3. What is "transformative" (even "modestly") about "improving the efficiency of delivering content"? Would it follow that a defendant who is able more efficiently to provide unauthorized copies to the public than the author can supply lawful copies, has engaged in a "transformative use" under the first factor? Does the endorsement of efficient delivery simply favor well-resourced defendants?

4. Consider Question 2, page 1104, main casebook. Notwithstanding *TVEyes*' capacious concept of transformativeness, does the court's emphasis on economic harm redress the concern that once a court found a use to be transformative, all the other factors would align in favor of fair use?

3.   COPYING BY END USERS

Page 1119. Add new Question 6.

6. In *Fox News v. TVEyes*, *supra* this Supplement, the Second Circuit panel majority indicated that *Sony* provided authority for the proposition that "improving the efficiency of delivering content" was a transformative purpose (*avant la lettre*). Does Justice Stevens' opinion, particularly n. 40, support the transformativeness of efficient content delivery? Consider in this regard, Judge Kaplan's rejoinder to the *TVEyes* majority:

> The majority here reads *Sony* as reasoning "that a secondary use may be a fair use if it utilizes transformative technology to improve the efficiency of delivering content." But *Sony* was decided before Judge Leval's article introduced the concept of transformative use or purpose into the copyright lexicon. I thus find what *Sony* teaches about transformative purpose, if anything, to be less than perfectly clear. I certainly do not find within *Sony* the idea that efficiency-enhancing technology is transformative.
>
> The efficiency enhancement at issue in *Sony* was "time-shifting"— the use by a consumer of a Betamax device to record a broadcast so that the consumer could watch that show at a later, presumably more convenient, time. The Court asked whether time-shifting was a substantial noninfringing use; the answer to that question determined whether Sony could be liable for contributory infringement. It was in that context that the Court found that unauthorized time shifting—consumers recording copyrighted shows without authorization to watch the shows once at a later time—was "not necessarily infringing."
>
> The Court's discussion of time-shifting focused on the non-commercial nature of in-home recording . . .
>
> Perhaps the Court in *Sony* would have found efficiency-enhancing technology to be transformative for that reason alone had that argument been put to it. But I see no indication of that in the opinion. Rather, *Sony* turned on the question whether "time-shifting," on the facts presented in that case, was a commercial use that affected the broadcasters' ability to make a profit in the market. And the Court so concluded without considering, at least explicitly, whether the recordings served a purpose different from the original broadcasts. In fact, the Court said that "timeshifting merely enables a viewer to see such a work which he had been invited to witness." In other words, time-shifting allows a user to do exactly that which the user could have done with the original: watch the show for whatever entertainment, informational or other purpose it serves. No new purpose had been added. So I hesitate to conclude that *Sony* mandates, or even suggests, the idea that efficiency-enhancing technology is transformative.
>
> My hesitation in this regard is strengthened by this Court's subsequent treatment of *Sony*. No prior opinion of this Court says, or even suggests, that *Sony* stands for the proposition that time-shifting in particular, or efficiency-enhancing delivery technology in general, is transformative. In *Swatch Group Management Services Ltd v. Bloomberg L.P.*, we described *Sony* as a decision "finding a *non-transformative* use to be a fair use." *Infinity Broadcast Corp.* described *Sony*'s discussion of time-shifting as a

"determin[ation] that time-shifting of television programs by consumers in their homes was a non-commercial use." Indeed, as noted, we there held that an efficiency promoting technology was not transformative and gave no sign that *Sony* was relevant to that conclusion.

Similarly, *Authors Guild, Inc. v. HathiTrust* and *Google Books* cite *Sony* for various principles, but never for the proposition that efficiency-enhancing technology is transformative, despite that idea's obvious potential application in those cases. Because *HathiTrust* and *Google Books* so clearly confront an issue closely related to that here, I see as instructive their omission of the idea that *Sony* declared efficiency-enhancing delivery technology to be transformative. I would join those cases in declining to construe *Sony* as offering significant guidance regarding transformative use.

In sum, *Sony*'s relevance to transformative use is, at best, unclear. I decline to join in the majority's novel interpretation of *Sony*.

CHAPTER 8

SECONDARY LIABILITY

B. FACILITATION OF INFRINGEMENT BY OTHERS

Page 1182. Insert following new decision after the QUESTIONS.

Universal City Studios v TickBox TV, 2018 U.S. Dist. LEXIS 40756 (C.D. Cal. Jan 30 2018). The TickBox company makes an eponymous device that enables users to perform many of the functions of a computer or tablet on their television set or other monitor, including browsing the internet and streaming media content through applications. It also operates a website offering "live chat" technical support,

> Upon connecting the Device to a television and the internet, a user is prompted by on-screen pictures and messages directing her to download and install software that will ultimately allow the user to view online content on their television screen via the Device. Once the relevant software is installed, upon turning on the Device and the television, a user will see a TickBox home page where he may choose among eight clickable options: (1) Welcome to TickBox TV; (2) WATCH MOVIES TV SPORTS; (3) Select your Theme; (4) Android Apps; (5) Live TV; (6) Settings; (7) OneClick Webinar; and (8) Support.
>
> . . .
>
> **D. Accessing Infringing Content with TickBox's Device**
>
> Device users are able to access unauthorized versions of copyrighted content through their selected themes. . . . When a user selects one of the content categories, for example "TV SHOWS," a list of installed streaming addons that provide access to that category is shown at the bottom of the screen. In the picture above, the featured addons are "Elysium," "UK Turk," "Maverick," "Gurzil," "Covenant," and "Poseidon." These addons allow a user to access film and television content available at disparate internet locations. They allow a user to search for specific titles or to browse by other criteria, such as genre or films currently in theaters. They compile lists of sources for a selected title, and allow the user to select a source. If the selected source is unavailable, the addon automatically tries others. The addon plays the selected content . . ., allowing the user to control the content (e.g., pause, rewind, fast-forward) within his selected theme.

A user who selects the "Covenant" addon would be presented with a menu offering, among other things, "Movies," "TV Shows," and "Search." If the user selects "Movies," he will be brought to another screen that presents different categories of movies, such as "Most Popular," "Box Office," and "In Theaters," . . . When a user selects a category, he will be presented with a list of movies that fall within the particular category. For example, on November 22, 2017, [plaintiffs' expert] selected the "In Theaters" category and accessed a list of recently released movie titles (along with year of release and running time) that were still (at least in an authorized manner) being shown exclusively in theaters. . . .

Once the user clicks on a title, he is informed that Covenant is searching for "providers" of that particular title, and then is shown how many sources have been located and their quality. For example, [plaintiffs' expert] clicked on Fox's Murder on the Orient Express, and Covenant located versions of the film in varying quality (e.g., 4K, 1080p, 720p, and standard definition), from 179 sources . . . Once the compilation process (which generally takes less than a minute) is complete, the user receives a list of providers from which to stream the selected title along with information about the quality of each version. If the first entry a user selects does not work, Covenant will automatically try other options until it locates a functional version. Once a functional link is located, Covenant will play the selected title . . .

E. TickBox's Advertising and Customer Support

Plaintiffs have compiled a variety of TickBox advertising and promotional material and support-related communications with Device users to bolster their argument that TickBox has actively encouraged copyright infringement.

Advertising. TickBox has advertised its Device as a way to "cut the cord" if "you're sick of paying high monthly fees and expensive bills for your regular cable . . . and premium cable channels like HBO and SHOWTIME. . . [o]r if you're tired of wasting money with online streaming services like Netflix, Hulu, or Amazon Prime. . ." In the same advertisement, it directed prospective customers to "[s]imply plug the Tickbox TV [the Device] into your current television and enjoy unlimited access to ALL the hottest TV shows, Hollywood blockbusters and LIVE sporting events in one convenient little device . . . ABSOLUTELY FREE." [Other advertisements emphasized access to "virtually any television show or Hollywood movie" without having to pay rental fees or monthly subscriptions.]

Customer support. TickBox's website and its Device home page contain links for technical and other customer support, which provide information that would assist an untrained user in accessing unauthorized copyrighted material. . . . TickBox's website also has a "Frequently Asked Questions" page. On that page, TickBox advises customers that they may "of course" "still [use] Amazon Video, Netflix or Hulu on" the Device, but that "within a few days of using [the Device] you will find you no longer need those subscriptions." On another question-and-answer page, TickBox advises customers that they "can see almost every movie and TV series ever made" and "can even access movies and shows that are still on Demand and episodes of TV that were just aired," and "will never need to pay to watch any of them."

. . .

2. Acts of Infringement

. . .

TickBox argues that it simply "offers a computer, onto which users can voluntarily install legitimate or illegitimate software" and that the "product about which Plaintiffs complain is third-party software which can be downloaded onto a myriad of devices, and which [TickBox] neither created nor supplies." . . . In *Grokster*, the Court held that "where evidence goes beyond a product's characteristics or the knowledge that it may be put to infringing uses, and shows statements or actions directed to promoting infringement, *Sony*'s staple-article rule will not preclude liability." *Grokster*, 545 U.S. at 935. Thus, the fact that the Device is just a "computer" that can be used for infringing and noninfringing purposes does not insulate TickBox from liability if (as discussed further below) the Device is actually used for infringing purposes and TickBox encourages such use.

TickBox also emphasizes that the themes through which Device users are able to access (via addons such as Covenant) copyrighted content "are not the [Device], and . . . have absolutely nothing to do with Defendant." But the evidentiary record establishes that, at least prior to Plaintiffs' filing of the Motion, TickBox preloaded the Device with third-party themes that provided easy access to copyrighted content and actually directed Device users to "install a theme" in order to gain access to the (since renamed) "WATCH MOVIES TV SPORTS" option on the home screen. TickBox has also instructed its customers to try the "Wookie Theme" when other themes were not functioning well. In short, TickBox's behavior was hardly passive with respect to the themes.

[TickBox argued that its customers' acts of viewing, but not downloading, infringing copies were not themselves copyright-infringing acts, and that TickBox could not be held liable for facilitating non infringing acts. The court, however, ruled that] defendant's device or service is funneling users to third parties that are directly infringing upon the plaintiffs' exclusive rights under the Copyright Act (i.e., displaying copyrighted images or broadcasting copyrighted video content). . . . Absent viewers, including Device users, the third-party streamers of video content would have no audience to broadcast unauthorized versions of Plaintiffs' (and others') copyrighted works to, and thus would not be infringing upon Plaintiffs' public performance rights. But there is an audience, and the Device (via the preinstalled themes and the addons within those themes), by aggregating various unauthorized sources of copyrighted work and simplifying the process of accessing that work, undoubtedly enlarges that audience and thereby enlarges the scope of the infringement. . . .

3. An object of promoting the device's use to infringe copyright

[The court ruled that TickBox's advertisements and customer service constituted intentional inducement. Regarding the *Grokster* filtering and business plan factors, the court held that] TickBox does not dispute that the Device is devoid of any mechanisms to curb users' access to infringing content. Given the presence of affirmative inducement-related activity, in the form of advertisements and customer support, the lack of any filtering mechanisms "underscores [TickBox's] intentional facilitation" of infringement. . . . TickBox argues that it "does not profit if its users access unauthorized content." TickBox ignores the fact that many customers would presumably not have purchased the Device in the first place if they had not been convinced that they would be able to use it to access unauthorized content. Accordingly, the fact that TickBox undoubtedly sold more Devices than it otherwise would have as a result of affirmatively advertising it as a means of accessing unauthorized content underscores TickBox's illicit intent.

C. SECONDARY LIABILITY OF INTERNET SERVICE PROVIDERS

2. SERVICE PROVIDER LIABILITY UNDER THE STATUTORY SAFE HARBORS

Page 1187. Insert after carry-over paragraph:

General prerequisite for application of safe harbors: Repeat infringer policy

To qualify for safe harbors, service providers of all kinds must have adopted and reasonably implemented . . . a policy that provides for the termination in appropriate circumstances of subscribers and account holders of the service provider's system or network who are repeat infringers," 17 U.S.C. sec. 512(i)(1)(A). Several recent decisions have interpreted the requirements for a repeat infringer policy. In **BMG Rights Mgmt. (US) LLC v. Cox Communs., Inc.,** 881 F.3d 293 (4th Cir. 2018), the defendant "conduit ISP" provided internet access to its subscribers. Plaintiffs charged that several of Cox's subscribers participated in unauthorized BitTorrent file-sharing networks, and that Cox had failed to exclude them from its service. Cox contended that the statutory term "repeat infringers" must mean subscribers whom courts had repeatedly held to have infringed copyrights.

Cox's agreement with its subscribers reserves the right to suspend or terminate subscribers who use Cox's service "to post, copy, transmit, or disseminate any content that infringes the patents, copyrights . . . or proprietary rights of any party." To enforce that agreement and protect itself from liability, however, Cox created only a very limited automated system to process notifications of alleged infringement received from copyright owners. Cox's automated system rests on a thirteen-strike policy that determines the action to be taken based on how many notices Cox has previously received regarding infringement by a particular subscriber. The first notice alleging a subscriber's infringement produces no action from Cox. The second through seventh notices result in warning emails from Cox to the subscriber. After the eighth and ninth notices, Cox limits the subscriber's Internet access to a single webpage that contains a warning, but the subscriber can reactivate complete service by clicking an acknowledgement. After the tenth and eleventh notices, Cox suspends services, requiring the subscriber to call a technician, who, after explaining the reason for suspension and advising removal of infringing content, reactivates service. After the twelfth notice, the subscriber is suspended and directed to a specialized technician, who, after another warning to cease infringing conduct, reactivates service. After the thirteenth notice, the subscriber is again suspended, and, for the first time, considered for termination. Cox never automatically terminates a subscriber.

The effectiveness of Cox's thirteen-strike policy as a deterrent to copyright infringement has several additional limitations. Cox restricts the number of notices it will process from any copyright holder or agent in one day; any notice received after this limit has been met does not count in Cox's graduated response escalation. Cox also counts only one notice per subscriber per day. And Cox resets a subscriber's thirteen-strike counter every six months.

. . .

Cox's principal contention is that "repeat infringers" means adjudicated repeat infringers: people who have been held liable by a court for multiple instances of copyright infringement. Cox asserts that it complied with § 512(i)(1)(A)'s requirement and is therefore entitled to the § 512(a) DMCA safe harbor because BMG did not show that Cox failed to terminate any adjudicated infringers. BMG responds that Cox's interpretation of "repeat infringers" is contrary to "the DMCA's plain terms."

Because the statute does not define the term "repeat infringers," to resolve that question, we turn first to the term's ordinary meaning. [Citation.] The ordinary meaning of an infringer is "[s]omeone who interferes with one of the exclusive rights of a . . . copyright" holder—in short, one who infringes a copyright. Infringer, Black's Law Dictionary 902 (10th ed. 2014). A repeat infringer, then, is one who infringes a copyright more than once.

Cox contends that because the repeat infringer provision uses the term "infringer" without modifiers such as "alleged" or "claimed" that appear elsewhere in the DMCA, "infringer" must mean "adjudicated infringer." But the DMCA's use of phrases like "alleged infringer" in other portions of the statute indicates only that the term "infringer" alone must mean something different than "alleged infringer," otherwise, the word "alleged" would be superfluous. Using the ordinary meaning of "infringer," however, fully accords with this principle: someone who actually infringes a copyright differs from someone who has merely allegedly infringed a copyright, because an allegation could be false. The need to differentiate the terms "infringer" and "alleged infringer" thus does not mandate Cox's proposed definition.

Moreover, other provisions of the Copyright Act use the term "infringer" (and similar terms) to refer to all who engage in infringing activity, not just the narrow subset of those who have been so adjudicated by a court. For example, § 501(a), which creates a civil cause of action for copyright owners, states that "[a]nyone who violates any of the exclusive rights of the copyright owner" provided for in the statute "is an *infringer* of the copyright or right of the author." 17 U.S.C. § 501(a) (emphasis added).

Similarly, the DMCA itself provides that ISPs who store copyrighted material are generally not liable for removing "material or activity *claimed to be infringing* or based on facts or circumstances from which *infringing activity is apparent*, regardless of whether the material or activity is *ultimately determined to be infringing*." Id. § 512(g)(1) (emphases added). This provision expressly distinguishes among three categories of activity: activity merely "claimed to be infringing," actual "infringing activity" (as is apparent from "facts or circumstances"), and activity "ultimately determined to be infringing." The distinction between "infringing activity" and activity "ultimately determined to be infringing" in § 512(g) shelters ISPs from being liable for taking down material that is "infringing," even if no court "ultimately determine[s]" that it is infringing—because, for example, the copyright holder simply does not file a lawsuit against the person who uploaded the infringing material. As this provision illustrates, Congress knew how to expressly refer to adjudicated infringement, but did not do so in the repeat infringer provision. See also id. § 512(b)(2)(E)(i) (addressing circumstance in which "a court has ordered that . . . material be removed"). That suggests the term "infringer" in § 512(i) is not limited to adjudicated infringers.

The legislative history of the repeat infringer provision supports this conclusion. Both the House Commerce and Senate Judiciary Committee Reports explained that "those who repeatedly or flagrantly abuse their access to the Internet through disrespect for the intellectual property rights of others should know that there is a realistic threat of losing that access." H.R. Rep. No. 105–551, pt. 2, at 61 (1998); S. Rep. No. 105–190, at 52 (1998). This passage makes clear that if persons "abuse their access to the Internet through disrespect for the intellectual property rights of others"—that is, if they infringe copyrights—they should face a "realistic threat of losing" their Internet access. The passage does not suggest that they should risk losing Internet access only once they have been sued in court and found liable for multiple instances of infringement. Indeed, the risk of losing one's Internet access would hardly constitute a "realistic threat" capable of deterring infringement if that punishment applied only to those already subject to civil penalties and legal fees as adjudicated infringers.

The only circuit to expressly consider the definition of a "repeat infringer" in the DMCA has defined it to mean "someone who interferes with one of the exclusive rights of a copyright" "again or repeatedly." EMI Christian Music Grp., Inc. v. MP3tunes, LLC, 844 F.3d 79, 89 (2d Cir. 2016) (alterations, internal quotation marks, and citations omitted); accord, e.g., Ellison v. Robertson, 357 F.3d 1072, 1080 (9th Cir. 2004) (finding material dispute of fact as to whether ISP was entitled to invoke safe harbor provision because there was "ample evidence" that ISP did not terminate "repeat infringers," but not suggesting that the infringing subscribers were adjudicated infringers); In re Aimster Copyright Litig., 334 F.3d 643, 655 (7th Cir. 2003) (finding ISP ineligible for safe harbor defense where ISP "invited" "the use of its service by 'repeat infringers,'" but not discussing any evidence that users were adjudicated infringers). Cox does not cite a single case adopting its contrary view that only adjudicated infringers can be "repeat infringers" for purposes of the DMCA.

Accordingly, we reject Cox's argument that the term "repeat infringers" in § 512(i) is limited to adjudicated infringers.

B.

Section 512(i) thus requires that, to obtain the benefit of the *DMCA* safe harbor, Cox must have reasonably implemented "a policy that provides for the termination in appropriate circumstances" of its subscribers who repeatedly infringe copyrights. We are mindful of the need to afford ISPs flexibility in crafting repeat infringer policies, and of the difficulty of determining when it is "appropriate" to terminate a person's access to the Internet. At a minimum, however, an ISP has not "reasonably implemented" a repeat infringer policy if the ISP fails to enforce the terms of its policy in any meaningful fashion. [Citations.] Here, Cox formally adopted a repeat infringer "policy," but, both before and after September 2012, made every effort to avoid reasonably implementing that policy. Indeed, in carrying out its thirteen-strike process, Cox very clearly determined not to terminate subscribers who in fact repeatedly violated the policy. . . . Cox *never* terminated a subscriber for infringement without reactivating them. . . .

The evidence shows that Cox *always* reactivated subscribers after termination, regardless of its knowledge of the subscriber's infringement. Cox did not, for example, advise employees *not* to reactivate a subscriber if the employees had reliable information regarding the subscriber's repeat infringement. An ISP cannot claim the protections of the *DMCA* safe harbor provisions merely by terminating customers as a symbolic gesture before indiscriminately reactivating them within a short timeframe.

EMI Christian Music Group v. MP3Tunes, 844 F.3d 79 (2d Cir. 2016), cited in *BMG v. Cox Comms.* addressed a different limiting construction of the repeat infringer policy requirement, The Second Circuit reversed a grant of summary judgment in favor of MP3Tunes, a locker service for storing digital music, and sideload.com, which allowed users to search for free, and often infringing, music on the internet. The district court had accepted defendant's contention that the statute required termination only of willful infringers.

In addressing [the repeat infringer] argument, we answer two questions: first, whether certain MP3tunes users qualified as "repeat infringers"; and second, if so, whether MP3tunes reasonably implemented a policy directed at them.

We begin with the first question. The District Court held that "[t]he purpose of subsection 512(i) is to deny protection to websites that tolerate users who flagrantly disrespect copyrights." *Capitol Records*, 821 F.Supp.2d at 637. For the purposes of § 512(i)(1)(A), it defined a "repeat infringer" as a user who posts or uploads infringing content "to the internet for the world to experience or copy" knowing that the conduct infringes another's copyright. In contrast, the District Court believed, a user who downloads or copies "songs from third-party sites for their personal entertainment" could not be a "repeat infringer."[4] The District Court thus concluded that only users who upload infringing content are "blatant infringers that internet service providers are obligated to ban from their websites."

We reject this definition of a "repeat infringer," which finds no support in the text, structure, or legislative history of the DMCA.

Starting with the text, we note that the DMCA does not itself define "repeat infringers." But "where a statute does not define a term, we give the term its ordinary meaning." [citation]. In this context, we take "repeat" to mean "a person who does something . . . again or repeatedly," *Oxford English Dictionary* (3d ed. 2009), while an "infringer" is "[s]omeone who interferes with one of the exclusive rights of a . . . copyright," *Infringer, Black's Law Dictionary* (10th ed. 2014). Copyright infringement is a strict liability offense in the sense that a plaintiff is not required to prove unlawful intent or culpability, and a user does not have to share copyrighted works in order to infringe a copyright. In the context of this case, all it took to be a "repeat infringer" was to repeatedly upload or download copyrighted material for personal use.

We turn next to the structure and context of the DMCA, interpreting the term "repeat infringer" against the backdrop of the statute as a whole. It is important to recall that the DMCA imposes certain requirements on *service providers* in exchange for limitations on liability. It would make little sense to link that limitation on liability to the knowledge of *users*. Indeed, the DMCA explicitly relieves service providers from having to affirmatively monitor their users for infringement—something that would likely be required should MP3tunes have to ascertain its users' knowledge.

---

[4] The District Court explained that, unlike users who upload infringing content, users who download "content for their personal use and are otherwise oblivious to the copyrights of others . . . like MP3tunes users who sideload content to their lockers for personal use, do not know for certain whether the material they download violates the copyrights of others." *Id.*

The legislative history also confirms our view that the District Court's definition of "repeat infringer" as limited to willful infringement is too narrow. The Senate and House reports accompanying the DMCA recognize a difference between inadvertent and willful infringement. But both reports also assert that a "repeat infringer" requirement is meant to deter those "who repeatedly *or* flagrantly abuse their access to the Internet through disrespect for the intellectual property rights of others." S. Rep. 105–190, at 52 (1998); H.R. Rep. 105–551(II), at 61 (1998) (emphasis added). In other words, the legislative history of the DMCA indicates that a "repeat infringer" does not need to know of the infringing nature of its online activities.

Finally, none of our sister circuits has adopted the District Court's definition of "repeat infringer" to include only those who willfully infringe copyrights. To the contrary, the Seventh Circuit has suggested that the term covers users of file-sharing services who are "ignorant or more commonly disdainful of copyright." *See In re Aimster Copyright Litig.*, 334 F.3d 643, 645 (7th Cir. 2003).

Our view of what Congress meant by the term "repeat infringer" leads us to conclude that the District Court improperly granted summary judgment. Prior to trial, there was clearly enough disputed evidence relating to MP3tunes's policy regarding infringers to conclude that summary judgment was inappropriate. To show that it reasonably implemented such a policy, MP3tunes proffered evidence at the summary judgment stage that it terminated 153 users who shared locker passwords. In response, though, the plaintiffs demonstrated that MP3tunes did not even try to connect known infringing activity of which it became aware through takedown notices to users who repeatedly [sideloaded files and created links to that infringing content in the sideload.com index.

Furthermore, the plaintiffs presented evidence that MP3tunes executives were encouraged to and did personally sideload songs from blatantly infringing websites. The same executives made the songs available to sideload.com users. There was also evidence that MP3tunes was capable of cataloging the sideloads of each MP3tunes user. A jury could reasonably infer from that evidence that MP3tunes actually knew of specific repeat infringers and failed to take action.

A reasonable jury alternatively could have determined that MP3tunes consciously avoided knowing about specific repeat infringers using its services, even though the infringement was rampant and obvious. In *Viacom*, we held that "the willful blindness doctrine may be applied, in appropriate circumstances, to demonstrate knowledge or awareness of specific instances of infringement under the DMCA." 676 F.3d at 35. Thus, at trial the plaintiffs could prevail by demonstrating that MP3tunes's failure to track users who created links to infringing content identified on takedown notices or who copied files from those links evidenced its willful blindness to the repeat infringing activity of its users.

Our conclusion that the District Court improperly granted partial summary judgment to MP3tunes on the basis of its policy regarding "repeat infringers" is not inconsistent with the DMCA's provision declaring "that safe harbor protection cannot be conditioned on 'a service provider monitoring its service or affirmatively seeking facts indicating infringing activity.'" *Id.* at 41 (quoting 17 U.S.C. § 512(m)(1)). Based on the available evidence, a reasonable jury could have concluded that it was reasonable for MP3tunes to track users who repeatedly created links to infringing content in the sideload.com index or who copied files from those links. *See Aimster*, 334 F.3d at 655 ("The common element of [DMCA] safe harbors is that the service provider must do what it can reasonably be asked to do to prevent the use of its service by 'repeat infringers.'"). After all, MP3tunes had already tracked and removed 153 users "who allowed others to access their lockers and copy music files without authorization," *Capitol Records*, 821 F.Supp.2d at 639; by comparison, requiring MP3tunes to extend that policy to users who sideloaded infringing content may not be an unreasonably burdensome request. Furthermore, doing so would not require MP3tunes to "monitor" or "affirmatively seek facts" about infringing activity in a manner inconsistent with § 512(m)(1) because it already had adequate information at its disposal in the form of takedown notices provided by EMI as to which links were allegedly infringing. MP3tunes would simply have had to make use of information already within its possession and connect that information to known users. While the defendants could yet make the case at trial that it was unreasonable under the circumstances to ask MP3tunes to identify users who repeatedly infringed plaintiffs' copyrights by sideloading music files, no evidence available at the summary judgment stage compelled that conclusion as a matter of law.

By contrast, in **Ventura Content, Ltd. v. Motherless, Inc.,** 885 F.3d 597 (9th Cir. 2018), the Ninth Circuit ruled that defendant Motherless, a website that hosted pornographic videos, satisfied the requirements of section 512(i) despite the absence of a formal repeat infringer policy, and notwithstanding the apparently haphazard implementation of the unwritten policy:

The details of the termination policy are not written down. However, the statute does not say that the policy details must be written, just that the site must inform subscribers of "a policy" of terminating repeat infringers in appropriate circumstances. Motherless consists only of Lange and a few independent contractors, and Lange alone determines when to terminate repeat infringers. A company might need a written policy to tell its employees or independent contractors what to do if there were a significant number of them, but Motherless is not such a firm. Small operations in many industries often do not have written policies because the owners who would formulate the policies are also the ones who execute it. There might not have been a need for anything in writing. So the lack of a detailed written policy is not by itself fatal to safe harbor eligibility. Neither is the fact that Motherless did not publicize its internal criteria.

Lange described how he applies Motherless's repeat infringer policy in his deposition testimony. He testified that he excludes infringing material by looking for an identifying watermark in the corner, the usual way owners identify their copyrighted material. If he receives a DMCA takedown notice (the form designated in subsection (c)(3)(A)), he also uses "hashing" software so that copies of the image or clip will be removed and will be screened out if anyone tries to post them again. Ordinarily, he will not terminate a user because of one takedown notice, but he will if there are two or more, which is to say, "repeated" instances of infringement. He might make a "gut decision" to terminate a user after the first DMCA notice (that is, a user who is not a repeat infringer) if there are multiple infringing pictures or videos identified in the notice, though that is not his usual practice. Motherless has received over 3,000 DMCA takedown notices. Lange does not keep a written list of subscribers whose submissions generated DMCA notices, but he saves each of the takedown notices and can track the number of times each user's content has been deleted in response, as well as the date of and reason (e.g., copyright infringement, child pornography) for each deletion. In deciding to terminate a user, he considers the account's history, as well as his memory and judgment. He is especially careful to look for and screen out material from one producer who threatened to sue him for infringement.

. . .

Various factors may bear on whether a service provider has "adopted and reasonably implemented" its policy for terminating, "in appropriate circumstances," repeat infringers. Certain factors work in favor of the service provider, including:

a DMCA log, . . .; blocking a subscriber's name and email address from uploads; putting email addresses from terminated accounts on a banned list; and prohibiting a banned user from reopening a terminated account. Other factors cut against the service provider, including: changing the email address to which takedown notices are sent without providing notice of the change; participating in copyright infringement; allowing terminated users to rejoin the site; and refusing to terminate known repeat infringers. Congress did not require that, to be eligible for safe harbor, a provider must maintain a logbook of infringers which it consults whenever it receives a DMCA notice. Congress required that the provider reasonably implement a policy of terminating repeat infringers, and the use of such a logbook and procedure would be good evidence that it did.

We conclude that on this record, there was no triable issue of fact as to whether Motherless, when it infringed on Ventura's copyrighted material, had "adopted and reasonably implemented" its policy of terminating repeat infringers "in appropriate circumstances." No trier of fact could conclude from the evidence in the record that Motherless had failed to reasonably implement a repeat infringer policy.

As the district court pointed out, there is a paucity of proven failures to terminate. Safe harbor eligibility does not require perfection, just "reasonable" implementation of the policy "in appropriate circumstances." Eligibility for the safe harbor is not lost just because some repeat infringers may have slipped through the provider's net for screening them out and terminating their access. The evidence in the record shows that Motherless terminated between 1,320 and 1,980 users for alleged copyright infringement and that only nine alleged repeat infringers had slipped through. Of those nine, only six were before Ventura filed its lawsuit, and only four of the six had been the subject of more than one DMCA notice. That suggests that less than one repeat infringer in 100,000 active users was missed. If that is the extent of failure, there could be no genuine issue of material fact as to whether Motherless "reasonably implemented" its termination policy. Congress used the word "reasonable" to modify "implemented," so the phrase cannot be construed to require perfect implementation.

Ventura points out that one of Motherless's biggest uploaders, Kristy7187, was not terminated until Motherless had received a fourth DMCA-compliant notice on a Kristy7187 upload. It may be hard to imagine how a site with so many subscribers and uploads could have so few repeat infringers, and how it could screen so effectively. Motherless does not even have an automated log of subscribers whose uploads generated DMCA notices. And since the policy is little more than Lange's multifactor judgment based largely on his recollection of DMCA notices, it may be hard to imagine how it could work so well. It is tempting, perhaps, to say that a policy is not "reasonably" implemented if it does not include both a database of users whose uploads have generated DMCA notices and some automated means of catching them if they do it again. But the statute does not require that. It modifies the termination requirement with the phrase "appropriate circumstances" in addition to the word "reasonable." And as the district court held, the evidence in the record allows for only one conclusion: that Motherless succeeded in reasonably implementing its policy of terminating repeated infringers. . . . The number of repeat infringers who escaped termination, at least as the record shows, is a tiny number and a minuscule percentage of users.

Doubt that Motherless really does have a "policy" of terminating repeat infringers that is "reasonably implemented" is unavoidable in light of unsystematic and casual implementation. But doubt is not evidence. Ventura has presented no evidence to establish a genuine issue of fact as to whether Motherless failed to reasonably implement its policy. Motherless, however, has met its burden. The absence of any significant number of repeat infringers who escaped termination compels the conclusion that a trier of fact could not conclude, on the record before us, that Motherless failed to meet the repeat infringer eligibility requirement for safe harbor. Motherless and Lange are therefore entitled to claim the protection of the safe harbor.

Requirements by type of service provider

[Return to introductory note on p. 1187, deleting first word in paragraph ("Thus,")]

Page 1241. Insert the following two case squibs after *Columbia Pictures v. Fung*:

Mavrix Photographs, LLC v. LiveJournal, Inc., 853 F.3d 1020 (9th Cir. 2017). Mavrix is a photo company specializing in celebrity images that it sells to magazines. LiveJournal is a social media platform. It allows users to create and run thematic "communities" in which they post and comment on content related to the theme. LiveJournal set up unpaid administrator roles to run its communities. "Moderators" review posts submitted by users to ensure compliance with the rules;

"maintainers" review and delete posts and have the authority to remove moderators and users from the community. ONTD (Oh No, They Didn't!) is LiveJournal's most popular community. It has nine moderators, and six maintainers. In addition, in order to

> exercise more control over ONTD so that it could generate advertising revenue from the popular community[,] LiveJournal hired a then active moderator, Brendan Delzer, to serve as the community's full time "primary leader." By hiring Delzer, LiveJournal intended to "take over" ONTD, grow the site, and run ads on it.
>
> As the "primary leader," Delzer instructs ONTD moderators on the content they should approve and selects and removes moderators on the basis of their performance. Delzer also continues to perform moderator work, reviewing and approving posts alongside the other moderators whom he oversees. While Delzer is paid and expected to work full time, the other moderators are "free to leave and go and volunteer their time in any way they see fit."

Mavrix brought an infringement action against LiveJournal, claiming that its images had appeared without authorization on the ONTD site, and that Delzer and the moderators and maintainers were LiveJournal's agents, disqualifying LiveJournal from sheltering under the section 512(c) safe harbor for user-posted content. Mavrix also contended that its photographs bore watermarks that should have alerted LiveJournal that the photos were proprietary. Accordingly, Mavrix urged, LiveJournal had actual or red flag knowledge that the postings were infringing. The District Court granted summary judgment to LiveJournal on the grounds that unpaid moderators were not agents of LiveJournal, and that LiveJournal lacked knowledge of infringement because Mavrix had not sent it take-down notices. The Ninth Circuit reversed on both grounds. Regarding the first, it held that genuine issues of material fact existed as to whether the moderators were LiveJournal's agents. The Court then turned to LiveJournal's actual or red flag knowledge:

> A copyright holder's failure to notify the service provider of infringement through the notice and takedown procedure, as Mavrix failed to do here, "strip[s] it of the most powerful evidence of [actual] knowledge." [Citation.] Such evidence is powerful, but not conclusive, towards showing that a service provider lacked actual knowledge. The district court held that LiveJournal lacked actual knowledge of the infringing nature of Mavrix's photographs solely on the basis of Mavrix's failure to notify LiveJournal of the infringements. This was an incomplete assessment of the issue. To fully assess actual knowledge, the fact finder should also assess a service provider's subjective knowledge of the infringing nature of the posts. Although Delzer

does not remember approving the posts and for this reason can be said to lack actual knowledge, Mavrix has not had the opportunity to depose the moderators to determine their subjective knowledge. On remand, the fact finder should determine whether LiveJournal, through its agents, had actual knowledge of the infringing nature of the posts.

In the event the fact finder determines that LiveJournal lacked actual knowledge of the infringements, it must then assess whether LiveJournal lacked red flag knowledge. Red flag knowledge arises when a service provider is "aware of facts that would have made the specific infringement 'objectively' obvious to a reasonable person." *Fung*, 710 F.3d at 1043 (quoting *YouTube*, 676 F.3d at 31); see also *UMG Recordings, Inc. v. Veoh Networks Inc.*, 665 F. Supp. 2d 1099, 1111 (C.D. Cal. 2009) (describing red flag knowledge as a "high bar"). The infringement must be immediately apparent to a non-expert. See *Veoh Networks Inc.*, 665 F. Supp. 2d at 1108; H.R. Rep. 105–551, pt. 2 at 58 (1998) (explaining that infringements must be "apparent from even a brief and casual viewing"). Some of the photographs at issue in this case contained either a generic watermark or a watermark containing Mavrix's website, "Mavrixonline.com."

To determine whether LiveJournal had red flag knowledge, the fact finder should assess if it would be objectively obvious to a reasonable person that material bearing a generic watermark or a watermark referring to a service provider's website was infringing.

Mavrix also charged that LiveJournal's control over the user postings and its profits from the ONTD barred a section 512(c) defense.

The district court concluded that LiveJournal did not have high levels of control such that it had "something more" than the right and ability to remove or block access to material posted on ONTD. LiveJournal's rules instruct users on the substance and infringement of their posts. The moderators screen for content and other guidelines such as infringement. Nearly two-thirds of submitted posts are rejected, including on substantive grounds. ONTD maintains a list of sources that have complained about infringement from which users should not submit posts. LiveJournal went so far as to use a tool to automatically block any posts from one source. In determining whether LiveJournal had the right and ability to control infringements, the fact finder must assess whether LiveJournal's extensive review process, infringement list, and blocker tool constituted high levels of control to show "something more."

LiveJournal must also show that it did not derive a financial benefit from infringement that it had the right and ability to control. See 17 U.S.C. § 512(c)(1)(B). "In determining whether the financial benefit criterion is satisfied, courts should take a common-sense, fact-based approach, not a formalistic one." S. Rep. No. 105–190, at 44 (1998). The financial benefit need not be substantial or a large proportion of the service provider's revenue. [Citation.] In *Fung*, we held that a financial benefit was shown when "there was a vast amount of infringing material on [the service provider's] websites . . . supporting an inference that [the service provider's] revenue stream is predicated on the broad availability of infringing materials for [its] users, thereby attracting advertisers." 710 F.3d at 1045. On the other hand, the service provider in that case "promoted advertising by pointing to infringing activity" and "attracted primarily visitors who were seeking to engage in infringing activity, as that is mostly what occurred on [the service provider's] sites." *Id.*

LiveJournal derives revenue from advertising based on the number of views ONTD receives. Mavrix presented evidence showing that approximately 84% of posts on ONTD contain infringing material, although LiveJournal contested the validity of this evidence. The fact finder should determine whether LiveJournal financially benefitted from infringement that it had the right and ability to control.

EMI Christian Music Group v. MP3Tunes, 844 F.3d 79 (2d Cir. 2016). In addition to its analysis of the statutory requirement of a repeat infringer policy, *supra* this Supplement (page 72), the Second Circuit addressed MP3Tunes' red flag knowledge of its users' infringements, and reversed the district court on this ground as well.

We turn next to the District Court's determination that the jury's finding of red-flag knowledge or willful blindness with respect to certain categories of songs was wrong as a matter of law. . . . At trial, the plaintiffs contended that MP3tunes was "aware of facts or circumstances from which infringing activity was apparent"—or in other words had "red-flag knowledge" or willful blindness, *see Viacom*, 676 F.3d at 31, 35, with respect to several categories of songs. The jury found that MP3tunes had knowledge as to four categories of files: (1) those stored on domains identified in takedown notices as having ten or more infringing files; (2) sideloads of MP3s before January 2007; (3) certain sideloads by MP3tunes executives; and (4) works by the Beatles. The District Court upheld the jury's finding of red-flag knowledge with respect to certain songs and subsets of songs but granted the defendants judgment as a matter of law as to two categories of songs that are the subject of our review: MP3s from major labels issued before 2007, and all songs by the Beatles.

We have already explained that the DMCA does not impose "an amorphous obligation to take commercially reasonable steps in response to a generalized awareness of infringement." *Viacom*, 676 F.3d at 31 (quotation marks omitted). Accordingly, "[o]n the issue of disqualifying knowledge . . . the burden falls on the copyright owner to demonstrate that the service provider acquired knowledge of the infringement, or of facts and circumstances from which infringing activity was obvious, and failed to promptly take down the infringing matter, thus forfeiting its right to the safe harbor." *Capitol Records, LLC v. Vimeo, LLC*, 826 F.3d 78, 95 (2d Cir. 2016). In other words, a copyright owner must point to a defendant's "actual knowledge or awareness of facts or circumstances that indicate specific and identifiable instances of infringement." *Viacom*, 676 F.3d at 32.

With this principle in mind, we conclude that the trial evidence in this case, viewed in the light most favorable to the plaintiffs, showed that MP3tunes and Robertson knew that major music labels generally had not even authorized their music to be distributed in the format most widely available on sideload.com, let alone authorized it to be shared on the internet. In particular, Robertson apparently knew that major record labels had not offered songs in MP3 format until 2007. In January 2007, in connection with MP3tunes's MP3 sale model, for example, Robertson admitted that "popular acts have never before sold tracks in MP3 formats." With respect to MP3s sideloaded before 2007, therefore, the jury reasonably could have concluded that MP3tunes and Robertson were aware of "facts and circumstances that make infringement obvious." *Vimeo*, 826 F.3d at 98.

What prompted the District Court to conclude otherwise? In granting judgment as a matter of law to the defendants on this issue, the District Court explained that barring MP3tunes from the DMCA safe harbor "would require Defendants to actively conduct routine searches and eliminate material likely to be infringing." *Capitol Records, Inc. v. MP3tunes LLC*, 48 F.Supp.3d 703, 716 (S.D.N.Y. 2014). It therefore understandably concluded that imposing such a duty clashed with the DMCA's "express . . . disavowal of a duty to affirmatively monitor." *Id.* Under the circumstances of this case, we respectfully disagree with the District Court's assessment, primarily for two reasons.

First, the jury was clearly instructed, and we presume it understood, that MP3tunes had no continuing, affirmative duty to monitor its servers for infringement. The jury could comply with that instruction and still find that MP3tunes was required to disable access to pre-2007 songs by "act[ing] expeditiously to remove, or disable access to" the pre-2007 songs "upon obtaining such knowledge or awareness." 17 U.S.C. § 512(c)(1)(A)(iii). There was evidence at trial that MP3tunes could disable access. Indeed, an expert testified that searching through libraries of MP3 songs was a common function of MP3tunes's business. The jury was therefore permitted to conclude that a time-limited, targeted duty—even if encompassing a large number of songs—does not give rise to an "amorphous" duty to monitor in contravention of the DMCA. *Viacom*, 676 F.3d at 31; *see also id.* at 34 (suggesting that a reasonable jury could find red-flag knowledge with respect to groups of clips). The same is true of the Beatles songs. The jury heard evidence that Robertson knew there had been no *legal* online distribution of Beatles tracks before 2010, other than one track used within a video game. Robertson further admitted that he authored a 2009 e-mail that showed he was aware of the plaintiffs' position that "[the] Beatles have never authorized their songs to be available digitally." And MP3tunes was made aware through user emails that Beatles songs such as "Strawberry Fields Forever" were on sideload.com's index. The jury could have reasonably concluded that MP3tunes had red-flag knowledge of, or was willfully blind to, the infringing nature of the Beatles tracks on its servers and failed to "act[ ] expeditiously" to remove them. 17 U.S.C. § 512(c)(1)(A)(iii).

Second, the jury could reasonably have found that MP3tunes conceived of and was designed to facilitate infringement based in part on evidence presented at trial that MP3tunes "actively encourage[ed] infringement" and that Robertson and MP3tunes executives "personally used [sideload.com] to download infringing material." *Columbia Pictures Indus., Inc. v. Fung*, 710 F.3d 1020, 1043 (9th Cir. 2013). Although such evidence might not alone support a separate finding of red-flag knowledge or willful blindness as to users, *see Vimeo*, 826 F.3d at 99, the jury could certainly rely on it in deciding whether MP3tunes was entitled to the DMCA safe harbor, *see Fung*, 710 F.3d at 1040 (holding that "aspects of the inducing behavior that give rise to liability are relevant to the operation of some of the DMCA safe harbors and can, in some circumstances, preclude their application"). Indeed, the jury could reasonably have understood Robertson to have admitted on cross-examination that sideload.com "was premised on the notion that everything that was on the internet that was not locked down could be sideloaded into the site." And in editing sideload.com's Frequently Asked Questions ("FAQs"), Robertson emphasized that the site should tell users that its music is "legal to download" because "[s]ideload.com does not store any music, but rather links to files publicly available [in] other places on the net."

For these reasons, we reverse the District Court's ruling vacating the jury verdict with respect to red-flag knowledge and willful blindness for pre-2007 MP3s and Beatles songs.

Page 1249. Before QUESTIONS, add the following text to *Lenz v. Universal Music Corp.*

On June 6, 2018, the parties settled the case. See Anandashankar Mazumdar, *Suit Over Dancing Baby YouTube Video Settled After 11 Years*, 96 PATENT, TRADEMARK & COPYRIGHT J. 160 (June 8, 2018).

Page 1253. Insert after the final paragraph on the page:

In January 2017, CCI announced that it was discontinuing the Copyright Alert System. See Anandashankar Mazumdar, *Copyright Alert System Outpaced by Tech But Set Example of Cooperation*, 93 PATENT, TRADEMARK & COPYRIGHT J. 3071 (Feb. 10, 2017).

CHAPTER 9

ENFORCEMENT OF COPYRIGHT

A. REMEDIES

2. DAMAGES

b. STATUTORY DAMAGES

Page 1297. Add a new Question 9:

9. Does the general remedial principle that precludes a plaintiff from recovering damages that could have been avoided through the plaintiff's reasonable efforts to mitigate damages apply when a copyright infringement plaintiff seeks to recover statutory damages for the infringement? Compare *Energy Intelligence Group, Inc. v. Kanye Anderson Capital Advisors, LP*, 2018 WL 2048896 (S.D. Tex. 2018) with *Energy Intelligence Group, Inc. v. CHS McPherson Refinery, Inc.*, 300 F.Supp.3d 1356 (D. Kan. 2018); *Purzel Video GmbH v. Smoak*, 11 F.Supp.3d 1020 (D. Colo. 2014).

4. PROCEDURAL ISSUES

b. STANDING

Page 1321. Add at the end of the carryover paragraph:

See also *John Wiley & Sons, Inc. v. DRK Photo*, 882 F.3d 394 (2d Cir. 2018) (concluding that Copyright Act does not confer standing to sue for infringement on a party to whom copyright owner has assigned the bare right to bring suit where that party is not a legal or beneficial owner of any of the section 106 exclusive rights).

B. TECHNOLOGICAL PROTECTION MEASURES

1. PROTECTION AGAINST CIRCUMVENTION

b. EXCEPTIONS AND LIMITATIONS

i. *Statutory Scheme*

Page 1368. Add before QUESTIONS:

In June 2017, the Copyright Office initiated the seventh Rulemaking, which will determine classes of works, if any, to be exempted from October 2018 to October 2021. 82 Fed.Reg. 29,804 (Jun. 30, 2017). The Office announced a streamlined procedure for considering petitions to renew current exemptions; the procedure allows the Office to make a de novo assessment of the prior evidence for an exemption, rather than requiring submission of a new evidentiary record. *Id.* at 29,805–

29,807. In October 2017, the Office recommended readopting all of the existing exemptions, and initiated the public comment and public hearing process on newly proposed exemptions. 82 Fed. Reg. 49,500 (Oct. 26, 2017).

CHAPTER 11

INTERNATIONAL DIMENSIONS OF COPYRIGHT

D. U.S.-BASED COPYRIGHT ACTIONS WITH AN INTERNATIONAL DIMENSION

1. PROTECTION OF ALIEN AUTHORS

Page 1501. Add new Question 1. Renumber Questions 1–4 as 2–5.

1. The Berne Convention mandates national treatment for foreign Berne Union authors. But it also requires member states' whose domestic law does not conform to Berne substantive minima to provide those protections for foreign authors, even if domestic authors do not enjoy those rights. See Berne Conv. art. 5(1): "Authors shall enjoy, in respect of works for which they are protected under this Convention, in countries of the Union other than the country of origin, the rights which their respective laws do now or may hereafter grant to their nationals, *as well as the rights specially granted by this Convention*" (emphasis supplied). The United States, however, has declared that the Berne Convention is not self-executing; its protections must be implemented into domestic law, see Berne Convention Implementation Act of 1988, Pub L. 100–568, 102 Stat. 2853. Section 4(a)(3) of the BCIA states: "No right or interest in a work eligible for protection under this title may be claimed by virtue of . . . the provisions of the Berne Convention. . . . Any rights in a work eligible for protection under this title that derive from this title . . . shall not be expanded or reduced by virtue of . . . the provisions of the Berne Convention." As a result, in the U.S. a foreign author will receive national treatment, but no more, even if U.S. law falls short of Convention norms. For example, there is no remedy in the U.S. for violations of moral rights within the scope of the Berne Convention, but for which U.S. law does not provide. See *Fahmy v. Jay-Z*, 891 F.3d 823 (9th Cir. 2018) (albeit incorrectly stating that the Berne Convention requires only national treatment).

3. JURISDICTION OF U.S. COURTS TO ADJUDICATE COPYRIGHT CLAIMS PRESENTING AN EXTRATERRITORIAL ELEMENT

Page 1519. Insert at end of paragraph before the paragraph referencing *Monroig v. RMM Records & Video Corp.*:

By contrast, in **Triple Up Ltd. v. Youku Tudou Inc.,** 235 F.Supp.3d 15 (D.D.C. 2017), *aff'd.* 2018 U.S. App. LEXIS 19699 (D.C. Cir. July 17, 2018) (unpublished), the court declined to find personal jurisdiction over a Mandarin-language Chinese website, 99% of whose viewers are located outside the United States, when a U.S. user (an investigator for plaintiff) was able to stream one of plaintiff's films that Youku had not been authorized to display in the United States. Although Youku uses geoblocking to restrict access to licensed videos based on the viewer's geographic location, Plaintiff contended that Youku's failure to use geoblocking to limit access from the United States to user-posted videos constituted "purposeful availment" of the benefits of a U.S. forum. The court rejected the claim:

> Triple Up's proposed rule—which equates a failure to geoblock with purposeful availment—would effectively mandate geoblocking for any website operator wishing to avoid suit in the United States. To say the least, such a rule would carry significant policy implications reaching beyond the scope of this lawsuit, [citation], and, indeed, could limit U.S. residents' access to what is appropriately called the World Wide Web. Perhaps, in the future, geoblocking will become sufficiently widespread that a failure to use it will be considered "purposeful" and assigned jurisdictional significance. But Triple Up provides no factual basis for the Court to conclude that this is the case now . . .

4. WHEN U.S. COURTS EXERCISE JURISDICTION OVER CLAIMS PRESENTING EXTRATERRITORIAL ELEMENTS, WHAT LAW APPLIES

a. TO DETERMINE COPYRIGHT OWNERSHIP OF A FOREIGN WORK

Page 1529. Add new Questions 6 and 7:

6. An Italian composer enters into a contract with an Italian music publisher to compose a theme song for an Italian film. The broadly-worded contract does not explicitly grant the publisher rights in derivative versions of the song. Some years later, the same composer enters into a contract in the United States to provide a theme song for a U.S. film (the song became "Mah Nah Mah Nah" and the film was the *Muppets Movie*). The Italian publisher contends that the song is largely recycled from the prior composition, and therefore comes within the scope of the rights the composer granted to the Italian publisher. The composer rejoins that the contract should be interpreted narrowly under principles of Italian law to reserve rights in reworked versions to the composer. The Italian publisher argues that U.S. law applies to the scope of the grant of rights because the alleged infringement concerns a U.S. exploitation. Which law applies? See *Creazioni Artistiche Musicali, S.r.l. v. Carlin Am., Inc.*, 121 U.S.P.Q.2D (BNA) 1324, 2016 WL 7507757 (Dec. 30, 2016).

7. An Italian composer is commissioned to compose a soundtrack for a film. Thirty-five years later he serves a notice of termination of his grant of rights respecting the US exploitation of his compositions. The grantee opposes on the ground that the compositions are works made for hire, and therefore exempt from the section 203 termination right. The parties dispute whether Italian law vests economic rights in commissioning parties in a manner equivalent to US works made for hire. The parties do not dispute that under Italian copyright law, the creator of the commissioned work retains authorship status and enjoys moral rights in her contributions to a cinematographic work. Is the creator's continued ownership of moral rights relevant to the equivalence of commissioned works under Italian law to commissioned works made for hire under US law? See *Ennio Morricone Music Inc. v. Bixio Music Group Ltd.* 124 U.S.P.Q.2D (BNA) 1541 (S.D.N.Y. October 6, 2017), *appeal pending*.

b. TO INFRINGEMENTS OCCURRING, AT LEAST IN PART, BEYOND U.S. BORDERS

Page 1537. Add the following after *Shropshire v. Canning*:

In *Shropshire v. Canning*, there was no extraterritorial application of U.S. copyright law because the defendant sent the unauthorized video to YouTube, where it was reproduced and publicly displayed from servers located in the U.S. In addition, members of the U.S. public would be viewing the video. Does it make a difference if the point of departure of the public performance or display is located outside the U.S.? In **Spanski Enters. v. Telewizja Polska, S.A.,** 883 F.3d 904 (D.C. Cir. 2018) the court held that U.S. law applied to transmissions originating offshore (from a website located in Poland), when the transmissions entity, who had previously granted the plaintiff exclusive North American transmission rights, failed to geoblock its communications, thus making them accessible in the U.S.

> In late 2011, Spanski's attorneys discovered that certain TVP Polonia content was not properly geoblocked, leaving it available to North and South American internet users through TV Polska's video-on-demand system. This content included fifty-one individual episodes that Spanski had registered with the United States Copyright Office and in which it held valid and exclusive United States copyrights. . . .

> [TV Polska] argues that because its conduct occurred exclusively in Poland, imposing [U.S.] Copyright Act liability on the basis of that conduct would amount to an impermissible extraterritorial application of the Act. . . .

> Whether an infringing performance that originates abroad but that ultimately reaches viewers in the United States can be actionable under the Copyright Act is a question of first impression in the federal appellate courts.

> The Supreme Court recently described "a two-step framework for analyzing" whether a statutory violation that, at least in part, takes place abroad gives rise to liability. *RJR Nabisco, Inc. v. European Community*, 136 S. Ct. 2090, 2101 (2016). A court first asks "whether the statute gives a clear, affirmative

indication that it applies extraterritorially." *Id.* Here, the parties agree that the Copyright Act has no extraterritorial application, and we assume they are correct. [Citations.] We therefore move to the second step, which requires us to determine whether this case, notwithstanding its extraterritorial elements, "involves a permissible domestic application" of the Copyright Act. *RJR Nabisco*, 136 S. Ct. at 2101. "[W]e do this," the Court has explained, "by looking to the statute's 'focus,' " *id.*, described as "the objects of the statute's solicitude," or what it is "that the statute seeks to 'regulate' " or protect, [citation]. "If the conduct relevant to the statute's focus occurred in the United States, then the case involves a permissible domestic application even if other conduct occurred abroad; but if the conduct relevant to the focus occurred in a foreign country, then the case involves an impermissible extraterritorial application regardless of any other conduct that occurred in U.S. territory." *RJR Nabisco*, 136 S. Ct. at 2101.

. . .

Guided by the Supreme Court's methodology, we identify the "conduct relevant to the [Copyright Act's] focus," *RJR Nabisco*, 136 S. Ct. at 2101, by asking precisely what it is that the Act regulates. The answer is clear: the Act grants copyright holders several "exclusive rights"—among them, the right "to perform [a] copyrighted work publicly," 17 U.S.C. § 106(4)—and effectuates those rights by prohibiting "infringement," or the "violat[ion]" of those "exclusive rights," id. § 501. The Copyright Act "focuses," then, on policing infringement or, put another way, on protecting the exclusivity of the rights it guarantees. Here, although it was in Poland that TV Polska uploaded and digitally formatted the fifty-one episodes, the infringing performances—and consequent violation of Spanski's copyrights—occurred on the computer screens in the United States on which the episodes' "images" were "show[n]." Id. § 101. Accordingly, because "the conduct relevant to the statute's focus occurred in the United States," this case "involves a permissible domestic application" of the Copyright Act, "even if other conduct occurred abroad." *RJR Nabisco*, 136 S. Ct. at 2101.

Characterizing the statute's focus differently, TV Polska points to *Aereo*'s discussion of the Act's 1976 amendments as establishing that "the 'focus' of the Copyright Act's public performance provisions is prohibition of unauthorized retransmissions by cable TV systems." Reply Br. 16. TV Polska misunderstands the "focus" inquiry: instead of asking what components of an otherwise actionable statutory violation must occur within the United States to bring it within the Act's domestic sweep, . . . Given our conclusion that TV Polska's broadcasts would have been actionable had they been entirely domestic, the relevant question is whether the ultimate performance of those broadcasts on computer screens in the United States was "relevant to [the Copyright Act's] focus." *RJR Nabisco*, 136 S. Ct. at 2101. TV Polska offers no reason to question our understanding that it was.

Alternatively, TV Polska argues that even if the Copyright Act's focus includes, as we have concluded, the infringing performance itself, *Aereo* establishes that its performance occurred abroad. As TV Polska sees it, *Aereo*'s observation that under the Act "both the broadcaster and the viewer of a television program 'perform'" that program, Aereo, 134 S. Ct. at 2506, means that, in the context of an international transmission, there are two performances—one by the broadcaster at the foreign point of origin and one by the user at the domestic point of reception. TV Polska overreads *Aereo*, which asks only whether Aereo performed "when a subscriber watche[d] a show using Aereo's system." Under TV Polska's reading, a broadcaster would commit an infringing performance merely by transmitting a copyrighted work into the void, regardless of whether those transmissions ever result in the work's "images" being "show[n]" to even a single viewer. 17 U.S.C. § 101. Given that the Act defines "perform" (in relevant part) to require such a showing, see id., we think *Aereo* is better read to establish only that a broadcaster and a viewer can both be liable for the same performance, i.e., the infringing display of copyrighted images on the viewer's screen. In this case, the infringing performance occurred in the United States.

Congress had good reason to allow domestic copyright holders to enforce their rights against foreign broadcasters who direct infringing performances into the United States. Given the ease of transnational internet transmissions, a statutory scheme that affords copyright holders no protection from such broadcasters would leave the door open to widespread infringement, rendering copyright in works capable of online transmission largely nugatory.

In its amicus brief, the United States offers two examples that helpfully illustrate this point. First, it points out that under such a scheme, "large-scale criminal copyright pirates could avoid United States copyright liability simply by locating their servers outside the United States." Second, "television stations in San Diego and El Paso could eliminate the need to obtain U.S. copyright licenses simply by moving their broadcast antennae to Tijuana and Ciudad Juarez." We agree with the United States that "Congress could not have intended the public-performance right to be susceptible to such ready evasion."

TV Polska offers little response to these troubling consequences of its position, claiming only that foreign enforcement authorities can address such cases. But nothing in the Copyright Act even hints that Congress intended to rely on the uncertain cooperation of foreign governments to ensure that copyright holders are able to enjoy their exclusive statutory rights while in the United States. Nor do we see any relevance to the Supreme Court's statement in *RJR Nabisco, Inc. v. European Community*, 136 S. Ct. 2090 (2016), that "a potential for international controversy . . . militates against recognizing foreign-injury claims without clear direction from Congress. The violation of a copyright holder's exclusive performance right inside the United States, after all, represents a domestic injury.

TV Polska argues that even if the government's concerns are well taken, they lose their force in situations where, as here, the foreign infringers "are lawful copyright owners in their home countries," or where, again as here, the domestic copyright holder is protected by contract and so need not invoke statutory law to protect its interests. TV Polska, however, offers no legal grounding for these proposed distinctions. Nor do we see any logical connection between the scope of a broadcaster and copyright holder's respective rights and the question of whether the direction of an infringing performance into the United States from abroad is domestic or extraterritorial.

Attempting to turn the table on the United States, TV Polska argues that treating its conduct as a domestic violation of the Copyright Act would leave any casual internet user anywhere in the world open to liability for uploading copyrighted content to a foreign website whenever anyone in the United States happens to stumble upon it. Indeed, given that "intent is not an element of [copyright] infringement," [citation], TV Polska argues, liability could attach where, even though a foreign website owner conscientiously geoblocks the copyrighted material it posts to its website, an American user manages to circumvent the territorial restrictions and views the content domestically. Although we have no occasion to prejudge such situations, we note that foreign defendants in such cases may well have alternative defenses against liability, such as a lack of proximate causation between the foreign conduct and the domestic performance or an American court's lack of personal jurisdiction over the foreign infringer. [citation] For present purposes, we need hold only that a foreign broadcaster that, as here, directs infringing performances into the United States from abroad commits a domestic violation of the Copyright Act.

Finally, the decisions TV Polska cites for the proposition that "acts committed abroad cannot form the basis for a U.S.

copyright infringement suit," hold nothing of the sort. Instead, they indicate only that infringements that, unlike the performances at issue here, occur abroad cannot in most cases generate Copyright Act liability. See *Subafilms*, 24 F.3d at 1098 (extraterritoriality doctrine barred liability for distribution of allegedly infringing videos abroad); *Luar Music Corp. v. Universal Music Group, Inc.*, 861 F. Supp. 2d 30, 38–40 (D.P.R. 2012) (extraterritoriality doctrine barred liability for releasing an allegedly infringing sound recording abroad). Indeed, Spanski and the United States point to multiple district court decisions holding, as do we, that an infringing performance that originates abroad but terminates in the United States constitutes a domestic Copyright Act violation. See, e.g., *Crunchyroll, Inc. v. Pledge*, No. C 11–2334, 2014 U.S. Dist. LEXIS 47033, 2014 WL 1347492, at *17 (N.D. Cal. Mar. 31, 2014) (defendant who copied and uploaded copyrighted television episodes while in United Kingdom could be liable where those episodes were transmitted to United States viewers); *United Feature Syndicate, Inc. v. Miller Features Syndicate, Inc.*, 216 F. Supp. 2d 198, 225 (S.D.N.Y. 2002) (rejecting Canadian website owner's extraterritoriality defense because infringing material posted on the site was viewed in the United States).

In passing the Copyright Act, Congress bestowed on copyright holders a specific set of rights. Holding foreign actors liable for conduct that results in the domestic infringement of those rights effectuates the Act's guarantees and fully coheres with principles of extraterritoriality as articulated by the Supreme Court.

QUESTION

In *Triple Up Ltd. v. Youku Tudou Inc.*, *supra* this Supplement (page 88), the D.C. district court ruled that failure to geoblock did not make an offshore website operator subject to personal jurisdiction in the U.S. In *Spanski*, failure to geoblock justified application of U.S. law to transmissions received in the U.S. Can you reconcile the two decisions?

APPENDIX A

THE COPYRIGHT ACT OF 1976

Public Law 94–553, 90 Stat. 2541, as amended through June 30, 2016

TITLE 17—COPYRIGHTS

CHAPTER 1.—SUBJECT MATTER AND SCOPE OF COPYRIGHT

Sec. 101.   Definitions

Except as otherwise provided in this title, as used in this title, the following terms and their variant forms mean the following:

An "anonymous work" is a work on the copies or phonorecords of which no natural person is identified as author.

An "architectural work" is the design of a building as embodied in any tangible medium of expression, including a building, architectural plans, or drawings. The work includes the overall form as well as the arrangement and composition of spaces and elements in the design, but does not include individual standard features.

"Audiovisual works" are works that consist of a series of related images which are intrinsically intended to be shown by the use of machines or devices such as projectors, viewers, or electronic equipment, together with accompanying sounds, if any, regardless of the nature of the material objects, such as films or tapes, in which the works are embodied.

The "Berne Convention" is the Convention for the Protection of Literary and Artistic Works, signed at Berne, Switzerland, on September 9, 1886, and all acts, protocols, and revisions thereto.

The "best edition" of a work is the edition, published in the United States at any time before the date of deposit, that the Library of Congress determines to be most suitable for its purposes.

A person's "children" are that person's immediate offspring, whether legitimate or not, and any children legally adopted by that person.

A "collective work" is a work, such as a periodical issue, anthology, or encyclopedia, in which a number of contributions, constituting separate and independent works in themselves, are assembled into a collective whole.

A "compilation" is a work formed by the collection and assembling of preexisting materials or of data that are selected, coordinated, or arranged in such a way that the resulting work as a whole constitutes an original work of authorship. The term "compilation" includes collective works.

A "computer program" is a set of statements or instructions to be used directly or indirectly in a computer in order to bring about a certain result.

"Copies" are material objects, other than phonorecords, in which a work is fixed by any method now known or later developed, and from which the work can be perceived, reproduced, or otherwise communicated, either directly or with the aid of a machine or device. The term "copies" includes the material object, other than a phonorecord, in which the work is first fixed.

"Copyright owner", with respect to any one of the exclusive rights comprised in a copyright, refers to the owner of that particular right.

A "Copyright Royalty Judge" is a Copyright Royalty Judge appointed under section 802 of this title, and includes any individual serving as an interim Copyright Royalty Judge under such section.

A work is "created" when it is fixed in a copy or phonorecord for the first time; where a work is prepared over a period of time, the portion of it that has been fixed at any particular time constitutes the work as of that time, and where the work has been prepared in different versions, each version constitutes a separate work.

A "derivative work" is a work based upon one or more preexisting works, such as a translation, musical arrangement, dramatization, fictionalization, motion picture version, sound recording, art reproduction, abridgment, condensation, or any other form in which a work may be recast, transformed, or adapted. A work consisting of editorial revisions, annotations, elaborations, or other modifications which, as a whole, represent an original work of authorship, is a "derivative work".

A "device", "machine", or "process" is one now known or later developed.

A "digital transmission" is a transmission in whole or in part in a digital or other non-analog format.

To "display" a work means to show a copy of it, either directly or by means of a film, slide, television image, or any other device or process or, in the case of a motion picture or other audiovisual work, to show individual images nonsequentially.

An "establishment" is a store, shop, or any similar place of business open to the general public for the primary purpose of selling goods or services in which the majority of the gross square feet of space that is nonresidential is used for that purpose, and in which nondramatic musical works are performed publicly.

The term "financial gain" includes receipt, or expectation of receipt, of anything of value, including the receipt of other copyrighted works.

A work is "fixed" in a tangible medium of expression when its embodiment in a copy or phonorecord, by or under the authority of the author, is sufficiently permanent or stable to permit it to be perceived, reproduced, or otherwise communicated for a period of more than transitory duration. A work consisting of sounds, images, or both, that are being transmitted, is "fixed" for purposes of this title if a fixation of the work is being made simultaneously with its transmission.

A "food service or drinking establishment" is a restaurant, inn, bar, tavern, or any other similar place of business in which the public or patrons assemble for the primary purpose of being served food or drink, in which the majority of the gross square feet of space that is nonresidential is used for that purpose, and in which nondramatic musical works are performed publicly.

The "Geneva Phonograms Convention" is the Convention for the Protection of Producers of Phonograms Against Unauthorized Duplication of Their Phonograms, concluded at Geneva, Switzerland, on October 29, 1971.

The "gross square feet of space" of an establishment means the entire interior space of that establishment, and any adjoining outdoor space used to serve patrons, whether on a seasonal basis or otherwise.

The terms "including" and "such as" are illustrative and not limitative.

An "international agreement" is—

(1) the Universal Copyright Convention;

(2) the Geneva Phonograms Convention;

(3) the Berne Convention;

(4) the WTO Agreement;

(5) the WIPO Copyright Treaty;

(6) the WIPO Performances and Phonograms Treaty; and

(7) any other copyright treaty to which the United States is a party.

A "joint work" is a work prepared by two or more authors with the intention that their contributions be merged into inseparable or interdependent parts of a unitary whole.

"Literary works" are works, other than audiovisual works, expressed in words, numbers, or other verbal or numerical symbols or indicia, regardless of the nature of the material objects, such as books, periodicals, manuscripts, phonorecords, film, tapes, disks, or cards, in which they are embodied.

The term "motion picture exhibition facility" means a movie theater, screening room, or other venue that is being used primarily for the exhibition of a copyrighted motion picture, if such exhibition is open to the public or is made to an assembled group of viewers outside of a normal circle of a family and its social acquaintances.

"Motion pictures" are audiovisual works consisting of a series of related images which, when shown in succession, impart an impression of motion, together with accompanying sounds, if any.

To "perform" a work means to recite, render, play, dance, or act it, either directly or by means of any device or process or, in the case of a motion picture or other audiovisual work, to show its images in any sequence or to make the sounds accompanying it audible.

A "performing rights society" is an association, corporation, or other entity that licenses the public performance of nondramatic musical works on behalf of copyright owners of such works, such as the American Society of Composers, Authors and Publishers (ASCAP), Broadcast Music, Inc. (BMI), and SESAC, Inc.

"Phonorecords" are material objects in which sounds, other than those accompanying a motion picture or other audiovisual work, are fixed by any method now known or later developed, and from which the sounds can be perceived, reproduced, or otherwise communicated, either directly or with the aid of a machine or device. The term "phonorecords" includes the material object in which the sounds are first fixed.

"Pictorial, graphic, and sculptural works" include two-dimensional and three-dimensional works of fine, graphic, and applied art, photographs, prints and art reproductions, maps, globes, charts, diagrams, models, and technical drawings, including architectural plans. Such works shall include works of artistic craftsmanship insofar as their form but not their mechanical or utilitarian aspects are concerned; the design of a useful article, as defined in this section, shall be considered a pictorial, graphic, or sculptural work only if, and only to the extent that, such design incorporates pictorial, graphic, or sculptural features that can be identified separately from, and are capable of existing independently of, the utilitarian aspects of the article.

For purposes of section 513, a "proprietor" is an individual, corporation, partnership, or other entity, as the case may be, that owns an establishment or a food service or drinking establishment, except that no owner or operator of a radio or television station licensed by the Federal Communications Commission, cable system or satellite carrier, cable or satellite carrier service or programmer, provider of online services or network access or the operator of facilities therefor, telecommunications company, or any other such audio or audiovisual service or programmer now known or as may be developed in the future, commercial subscription music service, or owner or operator of any other transmission service, shall under any circumstances be deemed to be a proprietor.

A "pseudonymous work" is a work on the copies or phonorecords of which the author is identified under a fictitious name.

"Publication" is the distribution of copies or phonorecords of a work to the public by sale or other transfer of ownership, or by rental, lease, or lending. The offering to distribute copies or phonorecords to a group of persons for purposes of further distribution, public performance, or public display, constitutes publication. A public performance or display of a work does not of itself constitute publication.

To perform or display a work "publicly" means—

(1) to perform or display it at a place open to the public or at any place where a substantial number of persons outside of a normal circle of a family and its social acquaintances is gathered; or

(2) to transmit or otherwise communicate a performance or display of the work to a place specified by clause (1) or to the public, by means of any device or process, whether the members of the public capable of receiving the performance or display receive it in the same place or in separate places and at the same time or at different times.

"Registration," for purposes of sections 205(c)(2), 405, 406, 410(d), 411, 412, and 506(e), means a registration of a claim in the original or the renewed and extended term of copyright.

"Sound recordings" are works that result from the fixation of a series of musical, spoken, or other sounds, but not including the sounds accompanying a motion picture or other audiovisual work, regardless of the nature of the material objects, such as disks, tapes, or other phonorecords, in which they are embodied.

"State" includes the District of Columbia and the Commonwealth of Puerto Rico, and any territories to which this title is made applicable by an Act of Congress.

A "transfer of copyright ownership" is an assignment, mortgage, exclusive license, or any other conveyance, alienation, or hypothecation of a copyright or of any of the exclusive rights comprised in a copyright, whether or not it is limited in time or place of effect, but not including a nonexclusive license.

A "transmission program" is a body of material that, as an aggregate, has been produced for the sole purpose of transmission to the public in sequence and as a unit.

To "transmit" a performance or display is to communicate it by any device or process whereby images or sounds are received beyond the place from which they are sent.

A "treaty party" is a country or intergovernmental organization other than the United States that is a party to an international agreement.

The "United States", when used in a geographical sense, comprises the several States, the District of Columbia and the Commonwealth of Puerto Rico, and the organized territories under the jurisdiction of the United States Government.

For purposes of section 411, a work is a "United States work" only if—

(1) in the case of a published work, the work is first published—

(A) in the United States;

(B) simultaneously in the United States and another treaty party or parties, whose law grants a term of copyright protection that is the same as or longer than the term provided in the United States;

(C) simultaneously in the United States and a foreign nation that is not a treaty party; or

(D) in a foreign nation that is not a treaty party, and all of the authors of the work are nationals, domiciliaries, or habitual residents of, or in the case of an audiovisual work legal entities with headquarters in, the United States;

(2) in the case of an unpublished work, all the authors of the work are nationals, domiciliaries, or habitual residents of the United States, or, in the case of an unpublished audiovisual work, all the authors are legal entities with headquarters in the United States; or

(3) in the case of a pictorial, graphic, or sculptural work incorporated in a building or structure, the building or structure is located in the United States.

A "useful article" is an article having an intrinsic utilitarian function that is not merely to portray the appearance of the article or to convey information. An article that is normally a part of a useful article is considered a "useful article".

The author's "widow" or "widower" is the author's surviving spouse under the law of the author's domicile at the time of his or her death, whether or not the spouse has later remarried.

The "WIPO Copyright Treaty" is the WIPO Copyright Treaty concluded at Geneva, Switzerland, on December 20, 1996.

The "WIPO Performance and Phonograms Treaty" is the WIPO Performances and Phonograms Treaty concluded at Geneva, Switzerland, on December 20, 1996.

A "work of visual art" is—

(1) a painting, drawing, print, or sculpture, existing in a single copy, in a limited edition of 200 copies or fewer that are signed and consecutively numbered by the author, or, in the case of a sculpture, in multiple cast, carved, or fabricated sculptures of 200 or fewer that are consecutively numbered by the author and bear the signature or other identifying mark of the author; or

(2) a still photographic image produced for exhibition purposes only, existing in a single copy that is signed by the author, or in a

limited edition of 200 copies or fewer that are signed and consecutively numbered by the author.

A work of visual art does not include—

(A)(i) any poster, map, globe, chart, technical drawing, diagram, model, applied art, motion picture or other audiovisual work, book, magazine, newspaper, periodical, data base, electronic information service, electronic publication, or similar publication;

(ii) any merchandising item or advertising, promotional, descriptive, covering, or packaging material or container;

(iii) any portion or part of any item described in clause (i) or (ii);

(B) any work made for hire; or

(C) any work not subject to copyright protection under this title.

A "work of the United States Government" is a work prepared by an officer or employee of the United States Government as part of that person's official duties.

A "work made for hire" is—

(1) a work prepared by an employee within the scope of his or her employment; or

(2) a work specially ordered or commissioned for use as a contribution to a collective work, as a part of a motion picture or other audiovisual work, as a translation, as a supplementary work, as a compilation, as an instructional text, as a test, as answer material for a test, or as an atlas, if the parties expressly agree in a written instrument signed by them that the work shall be considered a work made for hire. For the purpose of the foregoing sentence, a "supplementary work" is a work prepared for publication as a secondary adjunct to a work by another author for the purpose of introducing, concluding, illustrating, explaining, revising, commenting upon, or assisting in the use of the other work, such as forewords, afterwords, pictorial illustrations, maps, charts, tables, editorial notes, musical arrangements, answer material for tests, bibliographies, appendixes, and indexes, and an "instructional text" is a literary, pictorial, or graphic work prepared for publication and with the purpose of use in systematic instructional activities.

In determining whether any work is eligible to be considered a work made for hire under paragraph (2), neither the amendment contained in section 1011(d) of the Intellectual Property and Communications Omnibus Reform Act of 1999, as enacted by section 1000(a)(9) of Public Law 106–113, nor the deletion of the words added by that amendment—

(A) shall be considered or otherwise given any legal significance, or

(B) shall be interpreted to indicate congressional approval or disapproval of, or acquiescence in, any judicial determination,

by the courts or the Copyright Office. Paragraph (2) shall be interpreted as if both section 2(a)(1) of the Work Made For Hire and Copyright Corrections Act of 2000 and section 1011(d) of the Intellectual Property and Communications Omnibus Reform Act of 1999, as enacted by section 1000(a)(9) of Public Law 106–113, were never enacted, and without regard to any inaction or awareness by the Congress at any time of any judicial determinations.

The terms "WTO Agreement" and "WTO member country" have the meanings given those terms in paragraphs (9) and (10), respectively, of section 2 of the Uruguay Round Agreements Act.

Sec. 102.   Subject Matter of Copyright: In General

(a) Copyright protection subsists, in accordance with this title, in original works of authorship fixed in any tangible medium of expression, now known or later developed, from which they can be perceived, reproduced, or otherwise communicated, either directly or with the aid of a machine or device. Works of authorship include the following categories:

(1) literary works;

(2) musical works, including any accompanying words;

(3) dramatic works, including any accompanying music;

(4) pantomimes and choreographic works;

(5) pictorial, graphic, and sculptural works;

(6) motion pictures and other audiovisual works;

(7) sound recordings; and

(8) architectural works.[a]

(b) In no case does copyright protection for an original work of authorship extend to any idea, procedure, process, system, method of operation, concept, principle, or discovery, regardless of the form in which it is described, explained, illustrated, or embodied in such work.

---

[a] The Architectural Works Copyright Protection Act, Title VII of Pub.L. 101–650, 104 Stat. 5089 (1990), enacted Dec. 1, 1990, further provides:

Sec. 706.   Effective Date.

The amendments made by this title apply to—

(1) any architectural work created on or after the date of the enactment of this Act; and

(2) any architectural work that, on the date of the enactment of this Act, is unconstructed and embodied in unpublished plans or drawings, except that protection for such architectural work under title 17, United States Code, by virtue of the amendments made by this title, shall terminate on December 31, 2002, unless the work is constructed by that date.

Sec. 103. Subject Matter of Copyright: Compilations and Derivative Works

(a) The subject matter of copyright as specified by section 102 includes compilations and derivative works, but protection for a work employing preexisting material in which copyright subsists does not extend to any part of the work in which such material has been used unlawfully.

(b) The copyright in a compilation or derivative work extends only to the material contributed by the author of such work, as distinguished from the preexisting material employed in the work, and does not imply any exclusive right in the preexisting material. The copyright in such work is independent of, and does not affect or enlarge the scope, duration, ownership, or subsistence of, any copyright protection in the preexisting material.

Sec. 104. Subject Matter of Copyright: National Origin

(a) Unpublished Works.—The works specified by sections 102 and 103, while unpublished, are subject to protection under this title without regard to the nationality or domicile of the author.

(b) Published Works.—The works specified by sections 102 and 103, when published, are subject to protection under this title if—

(1) on the date of first publication, one or more of the authors is a national or domiciliary of the United States, or is a national, domiciliary, or sovereign authority of a treaty party, or is a stateless person, wherever that person may be domiciled; or

(2) the work is first published in the United States or in a foreign nation that, on the date of first publication, is a treaty party; or

(3) the work is a sound recording that was first fixed in a treaty party; or

(4) the work is a pictorial, graphic, or sculptural work that is incorporated in a building or other structure, or an architectural work that is embodied in a building and the building or structure is located in the United States or a treaty party; or

(5) the work is first published by the United Nations or any of its specialized agencies, or by the Organization of American States; or

(6) the work comes within the scope of a Presidential proclamation. Whenever the President finds that a particular foreign nation extends, to works by authors who are nationals or domiciliaries of the United States or to works that are first published in the United States, copyright protection on substantially the same basis as that on which the foreign nation extends protection to works of its own nationals and domiciliaries and works first published in that nation, the President may by proclamation extend protection under this title to works of which one or more of the authors is, on

the date of first publication, a national, domiciliary, or sovereign authority of that nation, or which was first published in that nation. The President may revise, suspend, or revoke any such proclamation or impose any conditions or limitations on protection under a proclamation.

For purposes of paragraph (2), a work that is published in the United States or a treaty party within 30 days after publication in a foreign nation that is not a treaty party shall be considered to be first published in the United States or such treaty party, as the case may be.

(c) Effect of Berne Convention.—No right or interest in a work eligible for protection under this title may be claimed by virtue of, or in reliance upon, the provisions of the Berne Convention, or the adherence of the United States thereto. Any rights in a work eligible for protection under this title that derive from this title, other Federal or State statutes, or the common law, shall not be expanded or reduced by virtue of, or in reliance upon, the provisions of the Berne Convention, or the adherence of the United States thereto.

(d) Effect of Phonograms Treatises.—Notwithstanding the provisions of subsection (b), no works other than sound recordings shall be eligible for protection under this title solely by virtue of the adherence of the United States to the Geneva Phonograms Convention or the WIPO Performances and Phonograms Treaty.

Sec. 104A. Subject Matter of Copyright: Copyright in Restored Works

(a) Automatic Protection and Term.—

(1) Term.—

(A) Copyright subsists, in accordance with this section, in restored works, and vests automatically on the date of restoration.

(B) Any work in which copyright is restored under this section shall subsist for the remainder of the term of copyright that the work would have otherwise been granted in the United States if the work never entered the public domain in the United States.

(2) Exception.—Any work in which the copyright was ever owned or administered by the Alien Property Custodian and in which the restored copyright would be owned by a government or instrumentality thereof, is not a restored work.

(b) Ownership of Restored Copyright.—A restored work vests initially in the author or initial rightholder of the work as determined by the law of the source country of the work.

(c) Filing of Notice of Intent to Enforce Restored Copyright Against Reliance Parties.—On or after the date of restoration, any person who owns a copyright in a restored work or an exclusive right therein may file with the Copyright Office a notice of intent to enforce that person's copyright or exclusive right or may serve such a notice directly on a reliance party. Acceptance of a notice by the Copyright Office is effective as to any reliance parties but shall not create a presumption of the validity of any of the facts stated therein. Service on a reliance party is effective as to that reliance party and any other reliance parties with actual knowledge of such service and of the contents of that notice.

(d) Remedies for Infringement of Restored Copyrights.—

(1) Enforcement of copyright in restored works in the absence of a reliance party.—As against any party who is not a reliance party, the remedies provided in chapter 5 of this title shall be available on or after the date of restoration of a restored copyright with respect to an act of infringement of the restored copyright that is commenced on or after the date of restoration.

(2) Enforcement of copyright in restored works as against reliance parties.—As against a reliance party, except to the extent provided in paragraphs (3) and (4), the remedies provided in chapter 5 of this title shall be available, with respect to an act of infringement of a restored copyright, on or after the date of restoration of the restored copyright if the requirements of either of the following subparagraphs are met:

(A)(i) The owner of the restored copyright (or such owner's agent) or the owner of an exclusive right therein (or such owner's agent) files with the Copyright Office, during the 24-month period beginning on the date of restoration, a notice of intent to enforce the restored copyright; and

(ii)(I) the act of infringement commenced after the end of the 12-month period beginning on the date of publication of the notice in the Federal Register;

(II) the act of infringement commenced before the end of the 12-month period described in subclause (I) and continued after the end of that 12-month period, in which case remedies shall be available only for infringement occurring after the end of that 12-month period; or

(III) copies or phonorecords of a work in which copyright has been restored under this section are made after publication of the notice of intent in the Federal Register.

(B)(i) The owner of the restored copyright (or such owner's agent) or the owner of an exclusive right therein (or such owner's agent) serves upon a reliance party a notice of intent to enforce a restored copyright; and (ii)(I) the act of infringement commenced after the end of the 12-month period beginning on the date the notice of intent is received;

(II) the act of infringement commenced before the end of the 12-month period described in subclause (I) and continued after the end of that 12-month period, in which case remedies shall be available only for the infringement occurring after the end of that 12-month period; or

(III) copies or phonorecords of a work in which copyright has been restored under this section are made after receipt of the notice of intent.

In the event that notice is provided under both subparagraphs (A) and (B), the 12-month period referred to in such subparagraphs shall run from the earlier of publication or service of notice.

(3) Existing derivative works.—(A) In the case of a derivative work that is based upon a restored work and is created—

(i) before the date of the enactment of the Uruguay Round Agreements Act, if the source country of the restored work is an eligible country on such date, or

(ii) before the date on which the source country of the restored work becomes an eligible country, if that country is not an eligible country on such date of enactment,

a reliance party may continue to exploit that derivative work for the duration of the restored copyright if the reliance party pays to the owner of the restored copyright reasonable compensation for conduct which would be subject to a remedy for infringement but for the provisions of this paragraph.

(B) In the absence of an agreement between the parties, the amount of such compensation shall be determined by an action in United States district court, and shall reflect any harm to the actual or potential market for or value of the restored work from the reliance party's continued exploitation of the work, as well as compensation for the relative contributions of expression of the author of the restored work and the reliance party to the derivative work.

(4) Commencement of infringement for reliance parties.—For purposes of section 412, in the case of reliance parties, infringement shall be deemed to have commenced before registration when acts which would have constituted infringement had the restored work been subject to copyright were commenced before the date of restoration.

(e) Notices of Intent to Enforce a Restored Copyright.—

(1) Notices of intent filed with the Copyright Office.—

(A)(i) A notice of intent filed with the Copyright Office to enforce a restored copyright shall be signed by the owner of the restored copyright or the owner of an exclusive right therein, who files the notice under subsection (d)(2)(A)(i) (hereafter in this paragraph referred to as the "owner"), or by the owner's agent, shall identify the title of the restored work, and shall include an English translation of the title and any other alternative titles known to the owner by which the restored work may be identified, and an address and telephone number at which the owner may be contacted. If the notice is signed by an agent, the agency relationship must have been constituted in a writing signed by the owner before the filing of the notice. The Copyright Office may specifically require in regulations other information to be included in the notice, but failure to provide such other information shall not invalidate the notice or be a basis for refusal to list the restored work in the Federal Register.

(ii) If a work in which copyright is restored has no formal title, it shall be described in the notice of intent in detail sufficient to identify it.

(iii) Minor errors or omissions may be corrected by further notice at any time after the notice of intent is filed. Notices of corrections for such minor errors or omissions shall be accepted after the period established in subsection (d)(2)(A)(i). Notices shall be published in the Federal Register pursuant to subparagraph (B).

(B)(i) The Register of Copyrights shall publish in the Federal Register, commencing not later than 4 months after the date of restoration for a particular nation and every 4 months thereafter for a period of 2 years, lists identifying restored works and the ownership thereof if a notice of intent to enforce a restored copyright has been filed.

(ii) Not less than 1 list containing all notices of intent to enforce shall be maintained in the Public Information Office of the Copyright Office and shall be available for public inspection and copying during regular business hours pursuant to sections 705 and 708.

(C) The Register of Copyrights is authorized to fix reasonable fees based on the costs of receipt, processing, recording, and publication of notices of intent to enforce a restored copyright and corrections thereto.

(D)(i) Not later than 90 days before the date the Agreement on Trade-Related Aspects of Intellectual Property referred to in section 101(d)(15) of the Uruguay Round Agreements Act enters into force with respect to the United States, the Copyright Office shall issue and publish in the Federal Register regulations governing the filing under this subsection of notices of intent to enforce a restored copyright.

(ii) Such regulations shall permit owners of restored copyrights to file simultaneously for registration of the restored copyright.

(2) Notices of intent served on a reliance party.—

(A) Notices of intent to enforce a restored copyright may be served on a reliance party at any time after the date of restoration of the restored copyright.

(B) Notices of intent to enforce a restored copyright served on a reliance party shall be signed by the owner or the owner's agent, shall identify the restored work and the work in which the restored work is used, if any, in detail sufficient to identify them, and shall include an English translation of the title, any other alternative titles known to the owner by which the work may be identified, the use or uses to which the owner objects, and an address and telephone number at which the reliance party may contact the owner. If the notice is signed by an agent, the agency relationship must have been constituted in writing and signed by the owner before service of the notice.

(3) Effect of material false statements.—Any material false statement knowingly made with respect to any restored copyright identified in any notice of intent shall make void all claims and assertions made with respect to such restored copyright.

(f) Immunity From Warranty and Related Liability.—

(1) In general.—Any person who warrants, promises, or guarantees that a work does not violate an exclusive right granted in section 106 shall not be liable for legal, equitable, arbitral, or administrative relief if the warranty, promise, or guarantee is breached by virtue of the restoration of copyright under this section, if such warranty, promise, or guarantee is made before January 1, 1995.

(2) Performances.—No person shall be required to perform any act if such performance is made infringing by virtue of the restoration of copyright under the provisions of this section, if the obligation to perform was undertaken before January 1, 1995.

(g) Proclamation of Copyright Restoration.—Whenever the President finds that a particular foreign nation extends, to works by authors who are nationals or domiciliaries of the United States, restored copyright protection on substantially the same basis as provided under this section, the President may by proclamation extend restored protection provided under this section to any work—

(1) of which one or more of the authors is, on the date of first publication, a national, domiciliary, or sovereign authority of that nation; or

(2) which was first published in that nation. The President may revise, suspend, or revoke any such proclamation or impose any conditions or limitations on protection under such a proclamation.

(h) Definitions.—For purposes of this section and section 109(a):

(1) The term "date of adherence or proclamation" means the earlier of the date on which a foreign nation which, as of the date the WTO Agreement enters into force with respect to the United States, is not a nation adhering to the Berne Convention or a WTO member country, becomes—

(A) a nation adhering to the Berne Convention;

(B) a WTO member country;

(C) a nation adhering to the WIPO Copyright Treaty;

(D) a nation adhering to the WIPO Performance and Phonograms Treaty; or

(E) subject to a Presidential proclamation under subsection (g).

(2) The "date of restoration" of a restored copyright is—

(A) January 1, 1996, if the source country of the restored work is a nation adhering to the Berne Convention or a WTO member country on such date, or

(B) the date of adherence or proclamation, in the case of any other source country of the restored work.

(3) The term "eligible country" means a nation, other than the United States, that—

(A) becomes a WTO member country after the date of the enactment of the Uruguay Round Agreements Act;

(B) on such date of enactment is, or after such date of enactment becomes, a nation adhering to the Berne Convention;

(C) adheres to the WIPO Copyright Treaty;

(D) adheres to the WIPO Performance and Phonograms Treaty; or

(E) after such date of enactment becomes subject to a proclamation under subsection (g).

(4) The term "reliance party" means any person who—

(A) with respect to a particular work, engages in acts, before the source country of that work becomes an eligible country, which would have violated section 106 if the restored work had been subject to copyright protection, and who, after the source country becomes an eligible country, continues to engage in such acts;

(B) before the source country of a particular work becomes an eligible country, makes or acquires 1 or more copies or phonorecords of that work; or

(C) as the result of the sale or other disposition of a derivative work covered under subsection (d)(3), or significant assets of a person described in subparagraph (A) or (B), is a successor, assignee, or licensee of that person.

(5) The term "restored copyright" means copyright in a restored work under this section.

(6) The term "restored work" means an original work of authorship that—

(A) is protected under subsection (a);

(B) is not in the public domain in its source country through expiration of term of protection;

(C) is in the public domain in the United States due to—

(i) noncompliance with formalities imposed at any time by United States copyright law, including failure of renewal, lack of proper notice, or failure to comply with any manufacturing requirements;

(ii) lack of subject matter protection in the case of sound recordings fixed before February 15, 1972; or

(iii) lack of national eligibility;

(D) has at least one author or rightholder who was, at the time the work was created, a national or domiciliary of an eligible country, and if published, was first published in an eligible country and not published in the United States during the 30-day period following publication in such eligible country; and

(E) if the source country for the work is an eligible country solely by virtue of its adherence to the WIPO Performance and Phonograms Treaty, is a sound recording.

(7) The term "rightholder" means the person—

(A) who, with respect to a sound recording, first fixes a sound recording with authorization, or

(B) who has acquired rights from the person described in subparagraph (A) by means of any conveyance or by operation of law.

(8) The "source country" of a restored work is—

(A) a nation other than the United States;

(B) in the case of an unpublished work—

(i) the eligible country in which the author or rightholder is a national or domiciliary, or, if a restored work has more than 1 author or rightholder, of which the majority of foreign authors or rightholders are nationals or domiciliaries; or

(ii) if the majority of authors or rightholders are not foreign, the nation other than the United States which has the most significant contacts with the work; and

(C) in the case of a published work—

(i) the eligible country in which the work is first published, or

(ii) if the restored work is published on the same day in 2 or more eligible countries, the eligible country which has the most significant contacts with the work.

Sec. 105.   Subject Matter of Copyright: United States Government Works

Copyright protection under this title is not available for any work of the United States Government, but the United States Government is not precluded from receiving and holding copyrights transferred to it by assignment, bequest, or otherwise.

Sec. 106.   Exclusive Rights in Copyrighted Works

Subject to sections 107 through 122, the owner of copyright under this title has the exclusive rights to do and to authorize any of the following:

(1) to reproduce the copyrighted work in copies or phonorecords;

(2) to prepare derivative works based upon the copyrighted work;

(3) to distribute copies or phonorecords of the copyrighted work to the public by sale or other transfer of ownership, or by rental, lease, or lending;

(4) in the case of literary, musical, dramatic, and choreographic works, pantomimes, and motion pictures and other audiovisual works, to perform the copyrighted work publicly;

(5) in the case of literary, musical, dramatic, and choreographic works, pantomimes, and pictorial, graphic, or sculptural works, including the individual images of a motion picture or other audiovisual work, to display the copyrighted work publicly; and

(6) in the case of sound recordings, to perform the copyrighted work publicly by means of a digital audio transmission.

Sec. 106A. Rights of Certain Authors to Attribution and Integrity

(a) Rights of Attribution and Integrity.—Subject to section 107 and independent of the exclusive rights provided in section 106, the author of a work of visual art—

(1) shall have the right—

(A) to claim authorship of that work, and

(B) to prevent the use of his or her name as the author of any work of visual art which he or she did not create;

(2) shall have the right to prevent the use of his or her name as the author of the work of visual art in the event of a distortion, mutilation, or other modification of the work which would be prejudicial to his or her honor or reputation; and

(3) subject to the limitations set forth in section 113(d), shall have the right—

(A) to prevent any intentional distortion, mutilation, or other modification of that work which would be prejudicial to his or her honor or reputation, and any intentional distortion, mutilation, or modification of that work is a violation of that right, and

(B) to prevent any destruction of a work of recognized stature, and any intentional or grossly negligent destruction of that work is a violation of that right.

(b) Scope and Exercise of Rights.—Only the author of a work of visual art has the rights conferred by subsection (a) in that work, whether or not the author is the copyright owner. The authors of a joint work of visual art are coowners of the rights conferred by subsection (a) in that work.

(c) Exceptions.—

(1) The modification of a work of visual art which is a result of the passage of time or the inherent nature of the materials is not distortion, mutilation, or other modification described in subsection (a)(3)(A).

(2) The modification of a work of visual art which is the result of conservation, or of the public presentation, including lighting and placement, of the work is not a destruction, distortion, mutilation, or other modification described in subsection (a)(3) unless the modification is caused by gross negligence.

(3) The rights described in paragraphs (1) and (2) of subsection (a) shall not apply to any reproduction, depiction, portrayal, or other use of a work in, upon, or in any connection with any item described in subparagraph (A) or (B) of the definition of "work of visual art" in section 101, and any such reproduction, depiction, portrayal, or other

use of a work is not a destruction, distortion, mutilation, or other modification described in paragraph (3) of subsection (a).

(d) Duration of Rights.—

(1) With respect to works of visual art created on or after the effective date set forth in section 9(a) of the Visual Artists Rights Act of 1990, the rights conferred by subsection (a) shall endure for a term consisting of the life of the author.

(2) With respect to works of visual art created before the effective date set forth in section 9(a) of the Visual Artists Rights Act of 1990, but title to which has not, as of such effective date, been transferred from the author, the rights conferred by subsection (a) shall be coextensive with, and shall expire at the same time as, the rights conferred by section 106.

(3) In the case of a joint work prepared by two or more authors, the rights conferred by subsection (a) shall endure for a term consisting of the life of the last surviving author.

(4) All terms of the right conferred by subsection (a) run to the end of the calendar year in which they would otherwise expire.

(e) Transfer and Waiver.—

(1) The rights conferred by subsection (a) may not be transferred, but those rights may be waived if the author expressly agrees to such waiver in a written instrument signed by the author. Such instrument shall specifically identify the work, and uses of that work, to which the waiver applies, and the waiver shall apply only to the work and uses so identified. In the case of a joint work prepared by two or more authors, a waiver of rights under this paragraph made by one such author waives such rights for all such authors.

(2) Ownership of the rights conferred by subsection (a) with respect to a work of visual art is distinct from ownership of any copy of that work, or of a copyright or any exclusive right under a copyright in that work. Transfer of ownership of any copy of a work of visual art, or of a copyright or any exclusive right under a copyright, shall not constitute a waiver of the rights conferred by subsection (a). Except as may otherwise be agreed by the author in a written instrument signed by the author, a waiver of the rights conferred by subsection (a) with respect to a work of visual art shall not constitute a transfer of ownership of any copy of that work, or of ownership of a copyright or of any exclusive right under a copyright in that work.[b]

---

[b]   The Visual Artists Rights Act of 1990, Title VI of Pub.L. 101–650, 104 Stat. 5089 (1990), enacted Dec. 1, 1990, further provides:

SEC. 610.   EFFECTIVE DATE.

Sec. 107.   Limitations on Exclusive Rights: Fair Use

Notwithstanding the provisions of sections 106 and 106A, the fair use of a copyrighted work, including such use by reproduction in copies or phonorecords or by any other means specified by that section, for purposes such as criticism, comment, news reporting, teaching (including multiple copies for classroom use), scholarship, or research, is not an infringement of copyright. In determining whether the use made of a work in any particular case is a fair use the factors to be considered shall include—

> (1) the purpose and character of the use, including whether such use is of a commercial nature or is for nonprofit educational purposes;

> (2) the nature of the copyrighted work;

> (3) the amount and substantiality of the portion used in relation to the copyrighted work as a whole; and

> (4) the effect of the use upon the potential market for or value of the copyrighted work.

The fact that a work is unpublished shall not itself bar a finding of fair use if such finding is made upon consideration of all the above factors.

Sec. 108.   Limitations on Exclusive Rights: Reproduction by Libraries and Archives

(a) Except as otherwise provided in this title and notwithstanding the provisions of section 106, it is not an infringement of copyright for a library or archives, or any of its employees acting within the scope of their employment, to reproduce no more than one copy or phonorecord of a work, except as provided in subsections (b) and (c), or to distribute such copy or phonorecord, under the conditions specified by this section, if—

> (1) the reproduction or distribution is made without any purpose of direct or indirect commercial advantage;

> (2) the collections of the library or archives are (i) open to the public, or (ii) available not only to researchers affiliated with the library or archives or with the institution of which it is a part, but also to other persons doing research in a specialized field; and

> (3) the reproduction or distribution of the work includes a notice of copyright that appears on the copy or phonorecord that is

---

(a) In General.—Subject to subsection (b) and except as provided in subsection (c), this title and the amendments made by this title take effect 6 months after the date of the enactment of this Act.

(b) Applicability.—The rights created by section 106A of title 17, United States Code, shall apply to—

> (1) works created before the effective date set forth in subsection (a) but title to which has not, as of such effective date, been transferred from the author, and

> (2) works created on or after such effective date, but shall not apply to any destruction, distortion, mutilation, or other modification (as described in section 106A(a)(3) of such title) of any work which occurred before such effective date.

reproduced under the provisions of this section, or includes a legend stating that the work may be protected by copyright if no such notice can be found on the copy or phonorecord that is reproduced under the provisions of this section.

(b) The rights of reproduction and distribution under this section apply to three copies or phonorecords of an unpublished work duplicated solely for purposes of preservation and security or for deposit for research use in another library or archives of the type described by clause (2) of subsection (a), if—

(1) the copy or phonorecord reproduced is currently in the collections of the library or archives; and

(2) any such copy or phonorecord that is reproduced in digital format is not otherwise distributed in that format and is not made available to the public in that format outside the premises of the library or archives.

(c) The right of reproduction under this section applies to three copies or phonorecords of a published work duplicated solely for the purpose of replacement of a copy or phonorecord that is damaged, deteriorating, lost, or stolen, or of the existing format in which the work is stored has become obsolete, if—

(1) the library or archives has, after a reasonable effort, determined that an unused replacement cannot be obtained at a fair price; and

(2) any such copy or phonorecord that is reproduced in digital format is not made available to the public in that format outside the premises of the library or archives in lawful possession of such copy.

For purposes of this subsection, a format shall be considered obsolete if the machine or device necessary to render perceptible a work stored in that format is no longer manufactured or is no longer reasonably available in the commercial marketplace.

(d) The rights of reproduction and distribution under this section apply to a copy, made from the collection of a library or archives where the user makes his or her request or from that of another library or archives, of no more than one article or other contribution to a copyrighted collection or periodical issue, or to a copy or phonorecord of a small part of any other copyrighted work, if—

(1) the copy or phonorecord becomes the property of the user, and the library or archives has had no notice that the copy or phonorecord would be used for any purpose other than private study, scholarship, or research; and

(2) the library or archives displays prominently, at the place where orders are accepted, and includes on its order form, a warning of copyright in accordance with requirements that the Register of Copyrights shall prescribe by regulation.

(e) The rights of reproduction and distribution under this section apply to the entire work, or to a substantial part of it, made from the collection of a library or archives where the user makes his or her request or from that of another library or archives, if the library or archives has first determined, on the basis of a reasonable investigation, that a copy, or phonorecord of the copyrighted work cannot be obtained at a fair price, if—

(1) the copy or phonorecord becomes the property of the user, and the library or archives has had no notice that the copy or phonorecord would be used for any purpose other than private study, scholarship, or research; and

(2) the library or archives displays prominently, at the place where orders are accepted, and includes on its order form, a warning of copyright in accordance with requirements that the Register of Copyrights shall prescribe by regulation.

(f) Nothing in this section—

(1) shall be construed to impose liability for copyright infringement upon a library or archives or its employees for the unsupervised use of reproducing equipment located on its premises: *Provided,* That such equipment displays a notice that the making of a copy may be subject to the copyright law;

(2) excuses a person who uses such reproducing equipment or who requests a copy or phonorecord under subsection (d) from liability for copyright infringement for any such act, or for any later use of such copy or phonorecord, if it exceeds fair use as provided by section 107;

(3) shall be construed to limit the reproduction and distribution by lending of a limited number of copies and excerpts by a library or archives of an audiovisual news program, subject to clauses (1), (2), and (3) of subsection (a); or

(4) in any way affects the right of fair use as provided by section 107, or any contractual obligations assumed at any time by the library or archives when it obtained a copy or phonorecord of a work in its collections.

(g) The rights of reproduction and distribution under this section extend to the isolated and unrelated reproduction or distribution of a single copy or phonorecord of the same material on separate occasions, but do not extend to cases where the library or archives, or its employee—

(1) is aware or has substantial reason to believe that it is engaging in the related or concerted reproduction or distribution of multiple copies or phonorecords of the same material, whether made on one occasion or over a period of time, and whether intended for aggregate use by one or more individuals or for separate use by the individual members of a group; or

(2) engages in the systematic reproduction or distribution of single or multiple copies or phonorecords of material described in subsection (d): *Provided,* That nothing in this clause prevents a library or archives from participating in interlibrary arrangements that do not have, as their purpose or effect, that the library or archives receiving such copies or phonorecords for distribution does so in such aggregate quantities as to substitute for a subscription to or purchase of such work.

(h)(1) For purposes of this section, during the last 20 years of any term of copyright of a published work, a library or archives, including a nonprofit educational institution that functions as such, may reproduce, distribute, display, or perform in facsimile or digital form a copy or phonorecord of such work, or portions thereof, for purposes of preservation, scholarship, or research, if such library or archives has first determined, on the basis of a reasonable investigation, that none of the conditions set forth in subparagraphs (A), (B), and (C) of paragraph (2) apply.

(2) No reproduction, distribution, display, or performance is authorized under this subsection if—

(A) the work is subject to normal commercial exploitation;

(B) a copy or phonorecord of the work can be obtained at a reasonable price; or

(C) the copyright owner or its agent provides notice pursuant to regulations promulgated by the Register of Copyrights that either of the conditions set forth in subparagraphs (A) and (B) applies.

(3) The exemption provided in this subsection does not apply to any subsequent uses by users other than such library or archives.

(i) The rights of reproduction and distribution under this section do not apply to a musical work, a pictorial, graphic or sculptural work, or a motion picture or other audiovisual work other than an audiovisual work dealing with news, except that no such limitation shall apply with respect to rights granted by subsections (b), (c), and (h), or with respect to pictorial or graphic works published as illustrations, diagrams, or similar adjuncts to works of which copies are reproduced or distributed in accordance with subsections (d) and (e).

Sec. 109.   Limitations on Exclusive Rights: Effect of Transfer of Particular Copy or Phonorecord

(a) Notwithstanding the provisions of section 106(3), the owner of a particular copy or phonorecord lawfully made under this title, or any person authorized by such owner, is entitled, without the authority of the copyright owner, to sell or otherwise dispose of the possession of that copy or phonorecord. Notwithstanding the preceding sentence, copies or phonorecords of works subject to restored copyright under section 104A that are manufactured before the date of restoration of copyright or, with respect to reliance parties, before publication or service of notice under section 104A(e), may be sold or otherwise disposed of without the authorization of the owner of the restored copyright for purposes of direct or indirect commercial advantage only during the 12-month period beginning on—

> (1) the date of the publication in the Federal Register of the notice of intent filed with the Copyright Office under section 104A(d)(2)(A), or

> (2) the date of the receipt of actual notice served under section 104A(d)(2)(B),

whichever occurs first.

(b)(1)(A) Notwithstanding the provisions of subsection (a), unless authorized by the owners of copyright in the sound recording or the owner of copyright in a computer program (including any tape, disk, or other medium embodying such program), and in the case of a sound recording in the musical works embodied therein, neither the owner of a particular phonorecord nor any person in possession of a particular copy of a computer program (including any tape, disk, or other medium embodying such program), may, for the purposes of direct or indirect commercial advantage, dispose of, or authorize the disposal of, the possession of that phonorecord or computer program (including any tape, disk, or other medium embodying such program) by rental, lease, or lending, or by any other act or practice in the nature of rental, lease, or lending. Nothing in the preceding sentence shall apply to the rental, lease, or lending of a phonorecord for nonprofit purposes by a nonprofit library or nonprofit educational institution. The transfer of possession of a lawfully made copy of a computer program by a nonprofit educational institution to another nonprofit educational institution or to faculty, staff, and students does not constitute rental, lease, or lending for direct or indirect commercial purposes under this subsection.

(B) This subsection does not apply to—

> (i) a computer program which is embodied in a machine or product and which cannot be copied during the ordinary operation or use of the machine or product; or

> (ii) a computer program embodied in or used in conjunction with a limited purpose computer that is designed for playing video games and may be designed for other purposes.

(C) Nothing in this subsection affects any provision of chapter 9 of this title.

(2)(A) Nothing in this subsection shall apply to the lending of a computer program for nonprofit purposes by a nonprofit library, if each copy of a computer program which is lent by such library has affixed to the packaging containing the program a warning of copyright in accordance with requirements that the Register of Copyrights shall prescribe by regulation.

(B) Not later than three years after the date of the enactment of the Computer Software Rental Amendments Act of 1990, and at such times thereafter as the Register of Copyrights considers appropriate, the Register of Copyrights, after consultation with representatives of copyright owners and librarians, shall submit to the Congress a report stating whether this paragraph has achieved its intended purpose of maintaining the integrity of the copyright system while providing nonprofit libraries the capability to fulfill their function. Such report shall advise the Congress as to any information or recommendations that the Register of Copyrights considers necessary to carry out the purposes of this subsection.

(3) Nothing in this subsection shall affect any provision of the antitrust laws. For purposes of the preceding sentence, "antitrust laws" has the meaning given that term in the first section of the Clayton Act and includes section 5 of the Federal Trade Commission Act to the extent that section relates to unfair methods of competition.

(4) Any person who distributes a phonorecord[c] or a copy of a computer program[d] (including any tape, disk, or other medium embodying such program) in violation of paragraph (1) is an infringer of copyright under section 501 of this title and is subject to the remedies set forth in sections 502, 503, 504 and 505. Such violation shall not be a criminal offense under section 506 or cause such person to be subject to the criminal penalties set forth in section 2319 of title 18.

(c) Notwithstanding the provisions of section 106(5), the owner of a particular copy lawfully made under this title, or any person authorized

[c] The Record Rental Amendment, Pub.L. 98–450, 98 Stat. 1727 (1984), enacted Oct. 4, 1984, concludes as follows:

Sec. 4. (a) The amendments made by this Act shall take effect on the date of the enactment of this Act.

(b) The provisions of section 109(b) of title 17, United States Code, as added by section 2 of this Act, shall not affect the right of an owner of a particular phonorecord of a sound recording, who acquired such ownership before the date of the enactment of this Act, to dispose of the possession of that particular phonorecord on or after such date of enactment in any manner permitted by section 109 of title 17, United States Code, as in effect on the day before the date of the enactment of this Act.

[d] The Computer Software Rental Amendments Act of 1990, Title VIII of Pub.L. 101–650, 104 Stat. 5089 (1990), enacted Dec. 1, 1990, further provides:

(a) In General.—Subject to subsection (b), this title and the amendments made in section 802 shall take effect on the date of the enactment of this Act. The amendment made by section 803 [adding § 109(e)] shall take effect one year after such date of enactment.

(b) Prospective Application.—Section 109(b) of title 17, United States Code, as amended by section 802 of this Act, shall not affect the right of a person in possession of a particular copy of a computer program, who acquired such copy before the date of the enactment of this Act, to dispose of the possession of that copy on or after such date of enactment in any manner permitted by section 109 of title 17, United States Code, as in effect on the day before such date of enactment.

(c) Termination.—The amendments made by section 803 [adding § 109(e)] shall not apply to public performances or displays that occur on or after October 1, 1995.

by such owner, is entitled, without the authority of the copyright owner, to display that copy publicly, either directly or by the projection of no more than one image at a time, to viewers present at the place where the copy is located.

(d) The privileges prescribed by subsections (a) and (c) do not, unless authorized by the copyright owner, extend to any person who has acquired possession of the copy or phonorecord from the copyright owner, by rental, lease, loan, or otherwise, without acquiring ownership of it.

(e) Notwithstanding the provisions of sections 106(4) and 106(5), in the case of an electronic audiovisual game intended for use in coin-operated equipment, the owner of a particular copy of such a game lawfully made under this title, is entitled, without the authority of the copyright owner of the game, to publicly perform or display that game in coin-operated equipment, except that this subsection shall not apply to any work of authorship embodied in the audiovisual game if the copyright owner of the electronic audiovisual game is not also the copyright owner of the work of authorship.

Sec. 110. Limitations on Exclusive Rights: Exemption of Certain Performances and Displays

Notwithstanding the provisions of section 106, the following are not infringements of copyright:

(1) performance or display of a work by instructors or pupils in the course of face-to-face teaching activities of a nonprofit educational institution, in a classroom or similar place devoted to instruction, unless, in the case of a motion picture or other audiovisual work, the performance, or the display of individual images, is given by means of a copy that was not lawfully made under this title, and that the person responsible for the performance knew or had reason to believe was not lawfully made;

(2) except with respect to a work produced or marketed primarily for performance or display as part of mediated instructional activities transmitted via digital networks, or a performance or display that is given by means of a copy or phonorecord that is not lawfully made and acquired under this title, and the transmitting government body or accredited nonprofit educational institution knew or had reason to believe was not lawfully made and acquired, the performance of a nondramatic literary or musical work or reasonable and limited portions of any other work, or display of a work in an amount comparable to that which is typically displayed in the course of a live classroom session, by or in the course of a transmission, if—

(A) the performance or display is made by, at the direction of, or under the actual supervision of an instructor as an integral part of a class session offered as a regular part of the systematic mediated instructional activities of a governmental body or an accredited nonprofit educational institution;

(B) the performance or display is directly related and of material assistance to the teaching content of the transmission;

(C) the transmission is made solely for, and, to the extent technologically feasible, the reception of such transmission is limited to—

(i) students officially enrolled in the course for which the transmission is made; or

(ii) officers or employees of governmental bodies as a part of their official duties or employment; and

(D) the transmitting body or institution—

(i) institutes policies regarding copyright, provides informational materials to faculty, students, and relevant staff members that accurately describe, and promote compliance with, the laws of the United States relating to copyright, and provides notice to students that materials used in connection with the course may be subject to copyright protection; and

(ii) in the case of digital transmissions—

(I) applies technological measures that reasonably prevent—

(aa) retention of the work in accessible form by recipients of the transmission from the transmitting body or institution for longer than the class session; and

(bb) unauthorized further dissemination of the work in accessible form by such recipients to others; and

(II) does not engage in conduct that could reasonably be expected to interfere with technological measures used by copyright owners to prevent such retention or unauthorized further dissemination;

(3) performance of a nondramatic literary or musical work or of a dramatico-musical work of a religious nature, or display of a work, in the course of services at a place of worship or other religious assembly;

(4) performance of a nondramatic literary or musical work otherwise than in a transmission to the public, without any purpose of direct or indirect commercial advantage and without payment of any fee or other compensation for the performance to any of its performers, promoters, or organizers, if—

(A) there is no direct or indirect admission charge; or

(B) the proceeds, after deducting the reasonable costs of producing the performance, are used exclusively for educational, religious, or charitable purposes and not for private financial gain, except where the copyright owner has served notice of objection to the performance under the following conditions:

(i) the notice shall be in writing and signed by the copyright owner or such owner's duly authorized agent; and

(ii) the notice shall be served on the person responsible for the performance at least seven days before the date of the performance, and shall state the reasons for the objection; and

(iii) the notice shall comply, in form, content, and manner of service, with requirements that the Register of Copyrights shall prescribe by regulation;

(5)(A) except as provided in subparagraph (B), communication of a transmission embodying a performance or display of a work by the public reception of the transmission on a single receiving apparatus of a kind commonly used in private homes, unless—

(i) a direct charge is made to see or hear the transmission; or

(ii) the transmission thus received is further transmitted to the public;

(B) communication by an establishment of a transmission or retransmission embodying a performance or display of a nondramatic musical work intended to be received by the general public, originated by a radio or television broadcast station licensed as such by the Federal Communications Commission, or, if an audiovisual transmission, by a cable system or satellite carrier, if—

(i) in the case of an establishment other than a food service or drinking establishment, either the establishment in which the communication occurs has less than 2,000 gross square feet of space (excluding space used for customer parking and for no other purpose), or the establishment in which the communication occurs has 2,000 or more gross square feet of space (excluding space used for customer parking and for no other purpose) and—

(I) if the performance is by audio means only, the performance is communicated by means of a total of not more than 6 loudspeakers, of which not more than 4 loudspeakers are located in any 1 room or adjoining outdoor space; or

(II) if the performance or display is by audiovisual means, any visual portion of the performance or display is communicated by means of a total of not more than 4 audiovisual devices, of which not more than 1 audiovisual device is located in any 1 room, and no such audiovisual device has a diagonal screen size greater than 55 inches, and any audio portion of the performance or display is communicated by means of a total of not more than 6 loudspeakers, of which not more than 4 loudspeakers are located in any 1 room or adjoining outdoor space;

(ii) in the case of a food service or drinking establishment, either the establishment in which the communication occurs has less than 3,750 gross square feet of space (excluding space used for customer parking and for no other purpose), or the establishment in which the communication occurs has 3,750 gross square feet of space or more (excluding space used for customer parking and for no other purpose) and—

(I) if the performance is by audio means only, the performance is communicated by means of a total of not more than 6 loudspeakers, of which not more than 4 loudspeakers are located in any 1 room or adjoining outdoor space; or

(II) if the performance or display is by audiovisual means, any visual portion of the performance or display is communicated by means of a total of not more than 4 audiovisual devices, of which not more than one audiovisual device is located in any 1 room, and no such audiovisual device has a diagonal screen size greater than 55 inches, and any audio portion of the performance or display is communicated by means of a total of not more than 6 loudspeakers, of which not more than 4 loudspeakers are located in any 1 room or adjoining outdoor space;

(iii) no direct charge is made to see or hear the transmission or retransmission;

(iv) the transmission or retransmission is not further transmitted beyond the establishment where it is received; and

(v) the transmission or retransmission is licensed by the copyright owner of the work so publicly performed or displayed;

(6) performance of a nondramatic musical work by a governmental body or a nonprofit agricultural or horticultural organization, in the course of an annual agricultural or horticultural fair or exhibition conducted by such body or organization; the exemption provided by this clause shall extend to any liability for copyright infringement that would otherwise be imposed on such body or organization, under doctrines of vicarious liability or related infringement, for a performance by a concessionnaire, business

establishment, or other person at such fair or exhibition, but shall not excuse any such person from liability for the performance;

(7) performance of a nondramatic musical work by a vending establishment open to the public at large without any direct or indirect admission charge, where the sole purpose of the performance is to promote the retail sale of copies or phonorecords of the work, or of the audiovisual or other devices utilized in such performance, and the performance is not transmitted beyond the place where the establishment is located and is within the immediate area where the sale is occurring;

(8) performance of a nondramatic literary work, by or in the course of a transmission specifically designed for and primarily directed to blind or other handicapped persons who are unable to read normal printed material as a result of their handicap, or deaf or other handicapped persons who are unable to hear the aural signals accompanying a transmission of visual signals, if the performance is made without any purpose of direct or indirect commercial advantage and its transmission is made through the facilities of: (i) a governmental body; or (ii) a noncommercial educational broadcast station (as defined in section 397 of title 47); or (iii) a radio subcarrier authorization (as defined in 47 CFR 73.293–73.295 and 73.593–73.595); or (iv) a cable system (as defined in section 111(f));

(9) performance on a single occasion of a dramatic literary work published at least ten years before the date of the performance, by or in the course of a transmission specifically designed for and primarily directed to blind or other handicapped persons who are unable to read normal printed material as a result of their handicap, if the performance is made without any purpose of direct or indirect commercial advantage and its transmission is made through the facilities of a radio subcarrier authorization referred to in clause (8)(iii), *Provided,* That the provisions of this clause shall not be applicable to more than one performance of the same work by the same performers or under the auspices of the same organization;

(10) notwithstanding paragraph (4), the following is not an infringement of copyright: performance of a nondramatic literary or musical work in the course of a social function which is organized and promoted by a nonprofit veterans' organization or a nonprofit fraternal organization to which the general public is not invited, but not including the invitees of the organizations, if the proceeds from the performance, after deducting the reasonable costs of producing the performance, are used exclusively for charitable purposes and not for financial gain. For purposes of this section the social functions of any college or university fraternity or sorority shall not be included unless the social function is held solely to raise funds for a specific charitable purpose; and

(11) the making imperceptible, by or at the direction of a member of a private household, of limited portions of audio or video content of a motion picture, during a performance in or transmitted to that household for private home viewing, from an authorized copy of the motion picture, or the creation or provision of a computer program or other technology that enables such making imperceptible and that is designed and marketed to be used, at the direction of a member of a private household, for such making imperceptible, if no fixed copy of the altered version of the motion picture is created by such computer program or other technology.

The exemptions provided under paragraph (5) shall not be taken into account in any administrative, judicial, or other governmental proceeding to set or adjust the royalties payable to copyright owners for the public performance or display of their works. Royalties payable to copyright owners for any public performance or display of their works other than such performances or displays as are exempted under paragraph (5) shall not be diminished in any respect as a result of such exemption

In paragraph (2), the term "mediated instructional activities" with respect to the performance or display of a work by digital transmission under this section refers to activities that use such work as an integral part of the class experience, controlled by or under the actual supervision of the instructor and analogous to the type of performance or display that would take place in a live classroom setting. The term does not refer to activities that use, in one or more class sessions of a single course, such works as textbooks, course packs, or other material in any media, copies or phonorecords of which are typically purchased or acquired by the students in higher education for their independent use and retention or are typically purchased or acquired for elementary and secondary students for their possession and independent use.

For purposes of paragraph (2), accreditation—

(A) with respect to an institution providing post-secondary education, shall be as determined by a regional or national accrediting agency recognized by the Council on Higher Education Accreditation or the United States Department of Education; and

(B) with respect to an institution providing elementary or secondary education, shall be as recognized by the applicable state certification or licensing procedures.

For purposes of paragraph (2), no governmental body or accredited nonprofit educational institution shall be liable for infringement by reason of the transient or temporary storage of material carried out through the automatic technical process of a digital transmission of the performance or display of that material as authorized under paragraph (2). No such material stored on the system or network controlled or operated by the transmitting body or institution under this paragraph shall be maintained on such system or network in a manner ordinarily accessible to anyone other than anticipated recipients. No such copy shall be maintained on the system or network in a manner ordinarily accessible to such anticipated recipients for a longer period than is reasonably necessary to facilitate the transmissions for which it was made.

For purposes of paragraph (11), the term "making imperceptible" does not include the addition of audio or video content that is performed or displayed over or in place of existing content in a motion picture.

Nothing in paragraph (11) shall be construed to imply further rights under section 106 of this title, or to have any effect on defenses or limitations on rights granted under any other section of this title or under any other paragraph of this section.

Sec. 111. Limitations on Exclusive Rights: Secondary Transmissions of Broadcast Programming by Cable

(a) Certain Secondary Transmissions Exempted.—The secondary transmission of a performance or display of a work embodied in a primary transmission is not an infringement of copyright if—

(1) the secondary transmission is not made by a cable system, and consists entirely of the relaying, by the management of a hotel, apartment house, or similar establishment, of signals transmitted by a broadcast station licensed by the Federal Communications Commission, within the local service area of such station, to the private lodgings of guests or residents of such establishment, and no direct charge is made to see or hear the secondary transmission; or

(2) the secondary transmission is made solely for the purpose and under the conditions specified by paragraph (2) of section 110; or

(3) the secondary transmission is made by any carrier who has no direct or indirect control over the content or selection of the primary transmission or over the particular recipients of the secondary transmission, and whose activities with respect to the secondary transmission consist solely of providing wires, cables, or other communications channels for the use of others: Provided, That the provisions of this paragraph extend only to the activities of said carrier with respect to secondary transmissions and do not exempt from liability the activities of others with respect to their own primary or secondary transmissions;

(4) the secondary transmission is made by a satellite carrier pursuant to a statutory license under section 119 or section 122;

(5) the secondary transmission is not made by a cable system but is made by a governmental body, or other nonprofit organization, without any purpose of direct or indirect commercial advantage, and without charge to the recipients of the secondary transmission other

than assessments necessary to defray the actual and reasonable costs of maintaining and operating the secondary transmission service.

(b) Secondary Transmission of Primary Transmission to Controlled Group.—Notwithstanding the provisions of subsections (a) and (c), the secondary transmission to the public of a performance or display of a work embodied in a primary transmission is actionable as an act of infringement under section 501, and is fully subject to the remedies provided by sections 502 through 506, if the primary transmission is not made for reception by the public at large but is controlled and limited to reception by particular members of the public: Provided, however, That such secondary transmission is not actionable as an act of infringement if—

(1) the primary transmission is made by a broadcast station licensed by the Federal Communications Commission; and

(2) the carriage of the signals comprising the secondary transmission is required under the rules, regulations, or authorizations of the Federal Communications Commission; and

(3) the signal of the primary transmitter is not altered or changed in any way by the secondary transmitter.

(c) Secondary Transmissions by Cable Systems.—

(1) Subject to the provisions of paragraphs (2), (3), and (4) of this subsection and section 114(d), secondary transmissions to the public by a cable system of a performance or display of a work embodied in a primary transmission made by a broadcast station licensed by the Federal Communications Commission or by an appropriate governmental authority of Canada or Mexico shall be subject to statutory licensing upon compliance with the requirements of subsection (d) where the carriage of the signals comprising the secondary transmission is permissible under the rules, regulations, or authorizations of the Federal Communications Commission.

(2) Notwithstanding the provisions of paragraph (1) of this subsection, the willful or repeated secondary transmission to the public by a cable system of a primary transmission made by a broadcast station licensed by the Federal Communications Commission or by an appropriate governmental authority of Canada or Mexico and embodying a performance or display of a work is actionable as an act of infringement under section 501, and is fully subject to the remedies provided by sections 502 through 506, in the following cases:

(A) where the carriage of the signals comprising the secondary transmission is not permissible under the rules, regulations, or authorizations of the Federal Communications Commission; or

(B) where the cable system has not deposited the statement of account and royalty fee required by subsection (d).

(3) Notwithstanding the provisions of paragraph (1) of this subsection and subject to the provisions of subsection (e) of this section, the secondary transmission to the public by a cable system of a performance or display of a work embodied in a primary transmission made by a broadcast station licensed by the Federal Communications Commission or by an appropriate governmental authority of Canada or Mexico is actionable as an act of infringement under section 501, and is fully subject to the remedies provided by sections 502 through 506 and section 510, if the content of the particular program in which the performance or display is embodied, or any commercial advertising or station announcements transmitted by the primary transmitter during, or immediately before or after, the transmission of such program, is in any way willfully altered by the cable system through changes, deletions, or additions, except for the alteration, deletion, or substitution of commercial advertisements performed by those engaged in television commercial advertising market research: Provided, That the research company has obtained the prior consent of the advertiser who has purchased the original commercial advertisement, the television station broadcasting that commercial advertisement, and the cable system performing the secondary transmission: And provided further, That such commercial alteration, deletion, or substitution is not performed for the purpose of deriving income from the sale of that commercial time.

(4) Notwithstanding the provisions of paragraph (1) of this subsection, the secondary transmission to the public by a cable system of a performance or display of a work embodied in a primary transmission made by a broadcast station licensed by an appropriate governmental authority of Canada or Mexico is actionable as an act of infringement under section 501, and is fully subject to the remedies provided by sections 502 through 506, if (A) with respect to Canadian signals, the community of the cable system is located more than 150 miles from the United States-Canadian border and is also located south of the forty-second parallel of latitude, or (B) with respect to Mexican signals, the secondary transmission is made by a cable system which received the primary transmission by means other than direct interception of a free space radio wave emitted by such broadcast television station, unless prior to April 15, 1976, such cable system was actually carrying, or was specifically authorized to carry, the signal of such foreign station on the system pursuant to the rules, regulations, or authorizations of the Federal Communications Commission.

(d) Statutory License for Secondary Transmissions by Cable Systems.—

(1) Statement of Account and Royalty Fees.—Subject to paragraph (5), a cable system whose secondary transmissions have been subject to statutory licensing under subsection (c) shall, on a semiannual basis, deposit with the Register of Copyrights, in accordance with requirements that the Register shall prescribe by regulation the following:

(A) A statement of account, covering the six months next preceding, specifying the number of channels on which the cable system made secondary transmissions to its subscribers, the names and locations of all primary transmitters whose transmissions were further transmitted by the cable system, the total number of subscribers, the gross amounts paid to the cable system for the basic service of providing secondary transmissions of primary broadcast transmitters, and such other data as the Register of Copyrights may from time to time prescribe by regulation. In determining the total number of subscribers and the gross amounts paid to the cable system for the basic service of providing secondary transmissions of primary broadcast transmitters, the system shall not include subscribers and amounts collected from subscribers receiving secondary transmissions pursuant to section 119. Such statement shall also include a special statement of account covering any non-network television programming that was carried by the cable system in whole or in part beyond the local service area of the primary transmitter, under rules, regulations, or authorizations of the Federal Communications Commission permitting the substitution or addition of signals under certain circumstances, together with logs showing the times, dates, stations, and programs involved in such substituted or added carriage.

(B) Except in the case of a cable system whose royalty fee is specified in subparagraph (E) or (F), a total royalty fee payable to copyright owners pursuant to paragraph (3) for the period covered by the statement, computed on the basis of specified percentages of the gross receipts from subscribers to the cable service during such period for the basic service of providing secondary transmissions of primary broadcast transmitters, as follows:

(i) 1.064 percent of such gross receipts for the privilege of further transmitting, beyond the local service area of such primary transmitter, any non-network programming of a primary transmitter in whole or in part, such amount to be applied against the fee, if any, payable pursuant to clauses (ii) through (iv);

(ii) 1.064 percent of such gross receipts for the first distant signal equivalent;

(iii) 0.701 percent of such gross receipts for each of the second, third, and fourth distant signal equivalents; and

(iv) 0.330 percent of such gross receipts for the fifth distant signal equivalent and each distant signal equivalent thereafter.

(C) In computing amounts under clauses (ii) through (iv) of subparagraph (B)—

(i) any fraction of a distant signal equivalent shall be computed at its fractional value;

(ii) in the case of any cable system located partly within and partly outside of the local service area of a primary transmitter, gross receipts shall be limited to those gross receipts derived from subscribers located outside of the local service area of such primary transmitter; and

(iii) if a cable system provides a secondary transmission of a primary transmitter to some but not all communities served by that cable system—

(I) the gross receipts and the distant signal equivalent values for such secondary transmission shall be derived solely on the basis of the subscribers in those communities where the cable system provides such secondary transmission; and

(II) the total royalty fee for the period paid by such system shall not be less than the royalty fee calculated under subparagraph (B)(i) multiplied by the gross receipts from all subscribers to the system.

(D) A cable system that, on a statement submitted before the date of the enactment of the Satellite Television Extension and Localism Act of 2010, computed its royalty fee consistent with the methodology under subparagraph (C)(iii), or that amends a statement filed before such date of enactment to compute the royalty fee due using such methodology, shall not be subject to an action for infringement, or eligible for any royalty refund or offset, arising out of its use of such methodology on such statement.

(E) If the actual gross receipts paid by subscribers to a cable system for the period covered by the statement for the basic service of providing secondary transmissions of primary broadcast transmitters are $263,800 or less—

(i) gross receipts of the cable system for the purpose of this paragraph shall be computed by subtracting from such actual gross receipts the amount by which $263,800 exceeds such actual gross receipts, except that in no case shall a cable system's gross receipts be reduced to less than $10,400; and

(ii) the royalty fee payable under this paragraph to copyright owners pursuant to paragraph (3) shall be 0.5 percent, regardless of the number of distant signal equivalents, if any.

(F) If the actual gross receipts paid by subscribers to a cable system for the period covered by the statement for the basic service of providing secondary transmissions of primary broadcast transmitters are more than $263,800 but less than $527,600, the royalty fee payable under this paragraph to copyright owners pursuant to paragraph (3) shall be—

(i) 0.5 percent of any gross receipts up to $263,800, regardless of the number of distant signal equivalents, if any; and

(ii) 1 percent of any gross receipts in excess of $263,800, but less than $527,600, regardless of the number of distant signal equivalents, if any.

(G) A filing fee, as determined by the Register of Copyrights pursuant to section 708(a).

(2) Handling of Fees.—The Register of Copyrights shall receive all fees (including the filing fee specified in paragraph (1)(G)) deposited under this section and, after deducting the reasonable costs incurred by the Copyright Office under this section, shall deposit the balance in the Treasury of the United States, in such manner as the Secretary of the Treasury directs. All funds held by the Secretary of the Treasury shall be invested in interest-bearing United States securities for later distribution with interest by the Librarian of Congress upon authorization by the Copyright Royalty Judges.

(3) Distribution of Royalty Fees to Copyright Owners.— The royalty fees thus deposited shall, in accordance with the procedures provided by paragraph (4), be distributed to those among the following copyright owners who claim that their works were the subject of secondary transmissions by cable systems during the relevant semiannual period:

(A) Any such owner whose work was included in a secondary transmission made by a cable system of a non-network television program in whole or in part beyond the local service area of the primary transmitter.

(B) Any such owner whose work was included in a secondary transmission identified in a special statement of account deposited under paragraph (1)(A).

(C) Any such owner whose work was included in non-network programming consisting exclusively of aural signals carried by a cable system in whole or in part beyond the local service area of the primary transmitter of such programs.

(4) Procedures for Royalty Fee Distribution.—The royalty fees thus deposited shall be distributed in accordance with the following procedures:

(A) During the month of July in each year, every person claiming to be entitled to statutory license fees for secondary transmissions shall file a claim with the Copyright Royalty Judges, in accordance with requirements that the Copyright Royalty Judges shall prescribe by regulation. Notwithstanding any provisions of the antitrust laws, for purposes of this clause any claimants may agree among themselves as to the proportionate division of statutory licensing fees among them, may lump their claims together and file them jointly or as a single claim, or may designate a common agent to receive payment on their behalf.

(B) After the first day of August of each year, the Copyright Royalty Judges shall determine whether there exists a controversy concerning the distribution of royalty fees. If the Copyright Royalty Judges determine that no such controversy exists, the Copyright Royalty Judges shall authorize the Librarian of Congress to proceed to distribute such fees to the copyright owners entitled to receive them, or to their designated agents, subject to the deduction of reasonable administrative costs under this section. If the Copyright Royalty Judges find the existence of a controversy, the Copyright Royalty Judges shall, pursuant to chapter 8 of this title, conduct a proceeding to determine the distribution of royalty fees.

(C) During the pendency of any proceeding under this subsection, the Copyright Royalty Judges shall have the discretion to authorize the Librarian of Congress to proceed to distribute any amounts that are not in controversy.

(5) 3.75 Percent Rate and Syndicated Exclusivity Surcharge Not Applicable to Multicast Streams.—The royalty rates specified in sections 256.2(c) and 256.2(d) of title 37, Code of Federal Regulations (commonly referred to as the "3.75 percent rate" and the "syndicated exclusivity surcharge", respectively), as in effect on the date of the enactment of the Satellite Television Extension and Localism Act of 2010, as such rates may be adjusted, or such sections redesignated, thereafter by the Copyright Royalty Judges, shall not apply to the secondary transmission of a multicast stream.

(6) Verification of Accounts and Fee Payments.—The Register of Copyrights shall issue regulations to provide for the confidential verification by copyright owners whose works were embodied in the secondary transmissions of primary transmissions pursuant to this section of the information reported on the semiannual statements of account filed under this subsection for accounting periods beginning on or after January 1, 2010, in order that the auditor designated under subparagraph (A) is able to confirm the correctness of the calculations and royalty payments reported therein. The regulations shall—

(A) establish procedures for the designation of a qualified independent auditor—

(i)   with exclusive authority to request verification of such a statement of account on behalf of all copyright owners whose works were the subject of secondary transmissions of primary transmissions by the cable system (that deposited the statement) during the accounting period covered by the statement; and

(ii) who is not an officer, employee, or agent of any such copyright owner for any purpose other than such audit;

(B) establish procedures for safeguarding all non-public financial and business information provided under this paragraph;

(C)(i)   require a consultation period for the independent auditor to review its conclusions with a designee of the cable system;

(ii) establish a mechanism for the cable system to remedy any errors identified in the auditor's report and to cure any underpayment identified; and

(iii) provide an opportunity to remedy any disputed facts or conclusions;

(D) limit the frequency of requests for verification for a particular cable system and the number of audits that a multiple system operator can be required to undergo in a single year; and

(E) permit requests for verification of a statement of account to be made only within 3 years after the last day of the year in which the statement of account is filed.

(7) Acceptance of Additional Deposits.—Any royalty fee payments received by the Copyright Office from cable systems for the secondary transmission of primary transmissions that are in addition to the payments calculated and deposited in accordance with this subsection shall be deemed to have been deposited for the particular accounting period for which they are received and shall be distributed as specified under this subsection.

(e) Nonsimultaneous Secondary Transmissions by Cable Systems.—

(1) Notwithstanding those provisions of the subsection (f)(2) relating to nonsimultaneous secondary transmissions by a cable system, any such transmissions are actionable as an act of infringement under section 501, and are fully subject to the remedies provided by sections 502 through 506 and section 510, unless—

(A) the program on the videotape is transmitted no more than one time to the cable system's subscribers;

(B) the copyrighted program, episode, or motion picture videotape, including the commercials contained within such program, episode, or picture, is transmitted without deletion or editing;

(C) an owner or officer of the cable system (i) prevents the duplication of the videotape while in the possession of the system, (ii) prevents unauthorized duplication while in the possession of the facility making the videotape for the system if the system owns or controls the facility, or takes reasonable precautions to prevent such duplication if it does not own or control the facility, (iii) takes adequate precautions to prevent duplication while the tape is being transported, and (iv) subject to paragraph (2), erases or destroys, or causes the erasure or destruction of, the videotape;

(D) within forty-five days after the end of each calendar quarter, an owner or officer of the cable system executes an affidavit attesting (i) to the steps and precautions taken to prevent duplication of the videotape, and (ii) subject to paragraph (2), to the erasure or destruction of all videotapes made or used during such quarter;

(E) such owner or officer places or causes each such affidavit, and affidavits received pursuant to paragraph (2)(C), to be placed in a file, open to public inspection, at such system's main office in the community where the transmission is made or in the nearest community where such system maintains an office; and

(F) the nonsimultaneous transmission is one that the cable system would be authorized to transmit under the rules, regulations, and authorizations of the Federal Communications Commission in effect at the time of the nonsimultaneous transmission if the transmission had been made simultaneously, except that this subparagraph shall not apply to inadvertent or accidental transmissions.

(2) If a cable system transfers to any person a videotape of a program nonsimultaneously transmitted by it, such transfer is actionable as an act of infringement under section 501, and is fully

subject to the remedies provided by sections 502 through 506, except that, pursuant to a written, nonprofit contract providing for the equitable sharing of the costs of such videotape and its transfer, a videotape nonsimultaneously transmitted by it, in accordance with paragraph (1), may be transferred by one cable system in Alaska to another system in Alaska, by one cable system in Hawaii permitted to make such nonsimultaneous transmissions to another such cable system in Hawaii, or by one cable system in Guam, the Northern Mariana Islands, the Federated States of Micronesia, the Republic of Palau, or the Republic of the Marshall Islands, to another cable system in any of those five entities, if—

(A) each such contract is available for public inspection in the offices of the cable systems involved, and a copy of such contract is filed, within thirty days after such contract is entered into, with the Copyright Office (which Office shall make each such contract available for public inspection);

(B) the cable system to which the videotape is transferred complies with paragraph (1)(A), (B), (C)(i), (iii), and (iv), and (D) through (F); and

(C) such system provides a copy of the affidavit required to be made in accordance with paragraph (1)(D) to each cable system making a previous nonsimultaneous transmission of the same videotape.

(3) This subsection shall not be construed to supersede the exclusivity protection provisions of any existing agreement, or any such agreement hereafter entered into, between a cable system and a television broadcast station in the area in which the cable system is located, or a network with which such station is affiliated.

(4) As used in this subsection, the term "videotape" means the reproduction of the images and sounds of a program or programs broadcast by a television broadcast station licensed by the Federal Communications Commission, regardless of the nature of the material objects, such as tapes or films, in which the reproduction is embodied.

(f) **Definitions.**—As used in this section, the following terms mean the following:

(1) **Primary Transmission.**—A "primary transmission" is a transmission made to the public by a transmitting facility whose signals are being received and further transmitted by a secondary transmission service, regardless of where or when the performance or display was first transmitted. In the case of a television broadcast station, the primary stream and any multicast streams transmitted by the station constitute primary transmissions.

(2) **Secondary Transmission.**—A "secondary transmission" is the further transmitting of a primary transmission

simultaneously with the primary transmission, or nonsimultaneously with the primary transmission if by a cable system not located in whole or in part within the boundary of the forty-eight contiguous States, Hawaii, or Puerto Rico: Provided, however, That a nonsimultaneous further transmission by a cable system located in Hawaii of a primary transmission shall be deemed to be a secondary transmission if the carriage of the television broadcast signal comprising such further transmission is permissible under the rules, regulations, or authorizations of the Federal Communications Commission.

(3) Cable System.—A "cable system" is a facility, located in any State, territory, trust territory, or possession of the United States, that in whole or in part receives signals transmitted or programs broadcast by one or more television broadcast stations licensed by the Federal Communications Commission, and makes secondary transmissions of such signals or programs by wires, cables, microwave, or other communications channels to subscribing members of the public who pay for such service. For purposes of determining the royalty fee under subsection (d)(1), two or more cable systems in contiguous communities under common ownership or control or operating from one headend shall be considered as one system.

(4) Local Service Area of a Primary Transmitter.—The "local service area of a primary transmitter", in the case of both the primary stream and any multicast streams transmitted by a primary transmitter that is a television broadcast station, comprises the area where such primary transmitter could have insisted upon its signal being retransmitted by a cable system pursuant to the rules, regulations, and authorizations of the Federal Communications Commission in effect on April 15, 1976, or such station's television market as defined in section 76.55(e) of title 47, Code of Federal Regulations (as in effect on September 18, 1993), or any modifications to such television market made, on or after September 18, 1993, pursuant to section 76.55(e) or 76.59 of title 47, Code of Federal Regulations, or within the noise-limited contour as defined in § 73.622(e)(1) of title 47, Code of Federal Regulations, or in the case of a television broadcast station licensed by an appropriate governmental authority of Canada or Mexico, the area in which it would be entitled to insist upon its signal being retransmitted if it were a television broadcast station subject to such rules, regulations, and authorizations. In the case of a low power television station, as defined by the rules and regulations of the Federal Communications Commission, the "local service area of a primary transmitter" comprises the designated market area, as defined in section 122(j)(2)(C), that encompasses the community of license of such station and any community that is located outside such designated market area that is either wholly or partially within 20 miles of the transmitter site, or in the case of such a station located in a standard metropolitan statistical area which has one of the 50 largest populations of all standard metropolitan statistical areas (based on the 1980 decennial census of population taken by the Secretary of Commerce), wholly or partially within 20 miles of such transmitter site. The "local service area of a primary transmitter", in the case of a radio broadcast station, comprises the primary service area of such station, pursuant to the rules and regulations of the Federal Communications Commission.

(5) Distant Signal Equivalent.—

(A) In General.—Except as provided under subparagraph (B), a "distant signal equivalent"—

(i) is the value assigned to the secondary transmission of any non-network television programming carried by a cable system in whole or in part beyond the local service area of the primary transmitter of such programming; and

(ii) is computed by assigning a value of one to each primary stream and to each multicast stream (other than a simulcast) that is an independent station, and by assigning a value of one-quarter to each primary stream and to each multicast stream (other than a simulcast) that is a network station or a noncommercial educational station.

(B) Exceptions.—The values for independent, network, and noncommercial educational stations specified in subparagraph (A) are subject to the following:

(i) Where the rules and regulations of the Federal Communications Commission require a cable system to omit the further transmission of a particular program and such rules and regulations also permit the substitution of another program embodying a performance or display of a work in place of the omitted transmission, or where such rules and regulations in effect on the date of the enactment of the Copyright Act of 1976 permit a cable system, at its election, to effect such omission and substitution of a nonlive program or to carry additional programs not transmitted by primary transmitters within whose local service area the cable system is located, no value shall be assigned for the substituted or additional program.

(ii) Where the rules, regulations, or authorizations of the Federal Communications Commission in effect on the date of the enactment of the Copyright Act of 1976 permit a cable system, at its election, to omit the further transmission of a particular program and such rules, regulations, or authorizations also permit the substitution of another program embodying a performance or display of a work in place of the omitted transmission, the value assigned for the substituted or additional program shall be, in the case of a live program, the value of one full distant signal equivalent multiplied by a fraction that has as its numerator the number of days in the year in which such substitution occurs and as its denominator the number of days in the year.

(iii) In the case of the secondary transmission of a primary transmitter that is a television broadcast station pursuant to the late-night or specialty programming rules of the Federal Communications Commission, or the secondary transmission of a primary transmitter that is a television broadcast station on a part-time basis where full-time carriage is not possible because the cable system lacks the activated channel capacity to retransmit on a full-time basis all signals that it is authorized to carry, the values for independent, network, and noncommercial educational stations set forth in subparagraph (A), as the case may be, shall be multiplied by a fraction that is equal to the ratio of the broadcast hours of such primary transmitter retransmitted by the cable system to the total broadcast hours of the primary transmitter.

(iv) No value shall be assigned for the secondary transmission of the primary stream or any multicast streams of a primary transmitter that is a television broadcast station in any community that is within the local service area of the primary transmitter.

(6) Network Station.—

(A) Treatment of Primary Stream.—The term "network station" shall be applied to a primary stream of a television broadcast station that is owned or operated by, or affiliated with, one or more of the television networks in the United States providing nationwide transmissions, and that transmits a substantial part of the programming supplied by such networks for a substantial part of the primary stream's typical broadcast day.

(B) Treatment of Multicast Streams.—The term "network station" shall be applied to a multicast stream on which a television broadcast station transmits all or substantially all of the programming of an interconnected program service that—

(i)   is owned or operated by, or affiliated with, one or more of the television networks described in subparagraph (A); and

(ii) offers programming on a regular basis for 15 or more hours per week to at least 25 of the affiliated television licensees of the interconnected program service in 10 or more States.

(7) Independent Station.—The term "independent station" shall be applied to the primary stream or a multicast stream of a television broadcast station that is not a network station or a noncommercial educational station.

(8) Noncommercial Educational Station.—The term "noncommercial educational station" shall be applied to the primary stream or a multicast stream of a television broadcast station that is a noncommercial educational broadcast station as defined in section 397 of the Communications Act of 1934, as in effect on the date of the enactment of the Satellite Television Extension and Localism Act of 2010.

(9) Primary Stream.—A "primary stream" is—

(A) the single digital stream of programming that, before June 12, 2009, was substantially duplicating the programming transmitted by the television broadcast station as an analog signal; or

(B) if there is no stream described in subparagraph (A), then the single digital stream of programming transmitted by the television broadcast station for the longest period of time.

(10) Primary Transmitter.—A "primary transmitter" is a television or radio broadcast station licensed by the Federal Communications Commission, or by an appropriate governmental authority of Canada or Mexico, that makes primary transmissions to the public.

(11) Multicast Stream.—A "multicast stream" is a digital stream of programming that is transmitted by a television broadcast station and is not the station's primary stream.

(12) Simulcast.—A "simulcast" is a multicast stream of a television broadcast station that duplicates the programming transmitted by the primary stream or another multicast stream of such station.

(13) Subscriber; Subscribe.—

(A) Subscriber.—The term "subscriber" means a person or entity that receives a secondary transmission service from a cable system and pays a fee for the service, directly or indirectly, to the cable system.

(B) Subscribe.—The term "subscribe" means to elect to become a subscriber.

Sec. 112. Limitations on Exclusive Rights: Ephemeral Recordings

(a)(1) Notwithstanding the provisions of section 106, and except in the case of a motion picture or other audiovisual work, it is not an infringement of copyright for a transmitting organization entitled to transmit to the public a performance or display of a work, under a license, including a statutory license under section 114(f), or transfer of the copyright or under the limitations on exclusive rights in sound recordings specified by section 114(a), or for a transmitting organization that is a broadcast radio or television station licensed as such by the Federal Communications Commission and that makes a broadcast transmission of a performance of a sound recording in a digital format on a nonsubscription basis, to make no more than one copy or phonorecord of a particular transmission program embodying the performance or display, if—

(A) the copy or phonorecord is retained and used solely by the transmitting organization that made it, and no further copies or phonorecords are reproduced from it; and

(B) the copy or phonorecord is used solely for the transmitting organization's own transmissions within its local service area, or for purposes of archival preservation or security; and

(C) unless preserved exclusively for archival purposes, the copy or phonorecord is destroyed within six months from the date the transmission program was first transmitted to the public.

(2) In a case in which a transmitting organization entitled to make a copy or phonorecord under paragraph (1) in connection with the transmission to the public of a performance or display of a work is prevented from making such copy or phonorecord by reason of the application by the copyright owner of technical measures that prevent the reproduction of the work, the copyright owner shall make available to the transmitting organization the necessary means for permitting the making of such copy or phonorecord as permitted under that paragraph, if it is technologically feasible and economically reasonable for the copyright owner to do so. If the copyright owner fails to do so in a timely manner in light of the transmitting organization's reasonable business requirements, the transmitting organization shall not be liable for a violation of section 1201(a)(1) of this title for engaging in such activities as are necessary to make such copies or phonorecords as permitted under paragraph (1) of this subsection.

(b) Notwithstanding the provisions of section 106, it is not an infringement of copyright for a governmental body or other nonprofit organization entitled to transmit a performance or display of a work, under section 110(2) or under the limitations on exclusive rights in sound recordings specified by section 114(a), to make no more than thirty copies or phonorecords of a particular transmission program embodying the performance or display, if—

(1) no further copies or phonorecords are reproduced from the copies or phonorecords made under this clause; and

(2) except for one copy or phonorecord that may be preserved exclusively for archival purposes, the copies or phonorecords are destroyed within seven years from the date the transmission program was first transmitted to the public.

(c) Notwithstanding the provisions of section 106, it is not an infringement of copyright for a governmental body or other nonprofit organization to make for distribution no more than one copy or phonorecord, for each transmitting organization specified in clause (2) of this subsection, of a particular transmission program embodying a performance of a nondramatic musical work of a religious nature, or of a sound recording of such a musical work, if—

(1) there is no direct or indirect charge for making or distributing any such copies or phonorecords; and

(2) none of such copies or phonorecords is used for any performance other than a single transmission to the public by a transmitting organization entitled to transmit to the public a performance of the work under a license or transfer of the copyright; and

(3) except for one copy or phonorecord that may be preserved exclusively for archival purposes, the copies or phonorecords are all destroyed within one year from the date the transmission program was first transmitted to the public.

(d) Notwithstanding the provisions of section 106, it is not an infringement of copyright for a governmental body or other nonprofit organization entitled to transmit a performance of a work under section 110(8) to make no more than ten copies or phonorecords embodying the performance, or to permit the use of any such copy or phonorecord by any governmental body or nonprofit organization entitled to transmit a performance of a work under section 110(8), if—

(1) any such copy or phonorecord is retained and used solely by the organization that made it, or by a governmental body or nonprofit organization entitled to transmit a performance of a work under section 110(8), and no further copies or phonorecords are reproduced from it; and

(2) any such copy or phonorecord is used solely for transmissions authorized under section 110(8), or for purposes of archival preservation or security; and

(3) the governmental body or nonprofit organization permitting any use of any such copy or phonorecord by any governmental body

or nonprofit organization under this subsection does not make any charge for such use.

(e) Statutory license.—

(1) A transmitting organization entitled to transmit to the public a performance of a sound recording under the limitation on exclusive rights specified by section 114(d)(1)(C)(iv) or under a statutory license in accordance with section 114(f) is entitled to a statutory license, under the conditions specified by this subsection, to make no more than 1 phonorecord of the sound recording (unless the terms and conditions of the statutory license allow for more), if the following conditions are satisfied:

(A) The phonorecord is retained and used solely by the transmitting organization that made it, and no further phonorecords are reproduced from it.

(B) The phonorecord is used solely for the transmitting organization's own transmissions originating in the United States under a statutory license in accordance with section 114(f) or the limitation on exclusive rights specified by section 114(d)(1)(C)(iv).

(C) Unless preserved exclusively for purposes of archival preservation, the phonorecord is destroyed within 6 months from the date the sound recording was first transmitted to the public using the phonorecord.

(D) Phonorecords of the sound recording have been distributed to the public under the authority of the copyright owner or the copyright owner authorizes the transmitting entity to transmit the sound recording, and the transmitting entity makes the phonorecord under this subsection from a phonorecord lawfully made and acquired under the authority of the copyright owner.

(2) Notwithstanding any provision of the antitrust laws, any copyright owners of sound recordings and any transmitting organizations entitled to a statutory license under this subsection may negotiate and agree upon royalty rates and license terms and conditions for making phonorecords of such sound recordings under this section and the proportionate division of fees paid among copyright owners, and may designate common agents to negotiate, agree to, pay, or receive such royalty payments.

(3) Proceedings under chapter 8 shall determine reasonable rates and terms of royalty payments for the activities specified by paragraph (1) during the 5-year period beginning on January 1 of the second year following the year in which the proceedings are to be commenced, or such other period as the parties may agree. Such rates shall include a minimum fee for each type of service offered by transmitting organizations. Any copyright owners of sound recordings or any transmitting organizations entitled to a statutory license under this subsection may submit to the Copyright Royalty Judges licenses covering

such activities with respect to such sound recordings. The parties to each proceeding shall bear their own costs.

(4) The schedule of reasonable rates and terms determined by the Copyright Royalty Judges shall, subject to paragraph (5), be binding on all copyright owners of sound recordings and transmitting organizations entitled to a statutory license under this subsection during the 5-year period specified in paragraph (3), or such other period as the parties may agree. Such rates shall include a minimum fee for each type of service offered by transmitting organizations. The Copyright Royalty Judges shall establish rates that most clearly represent the fees that would have been negotiated in the marketplace between a willing buyer and a willing seller. In determining such rates and terms, the Copyright Royalty Judges shall base their decision on economic, competitive, and programming information presented by the parties, including—

(A) whether use of the service may substitute for or may promote the sales of phonorecords or otherwise interferes with or enhances the copyright owner's traditional streams of revenue; and

(B) the relative roles of the copyright owner and the transmitting organization in the copyrighted work and the service made available to the public with respect to relative creative contribution, technological contribution, capital investment, cost, and risk.

In establishing such rates and terms, the Copyright Royalty Judges may consider the rates and terms under voluntary license agreements described in paragraphs (2) and (3). The Copyright Royalty Judges shall also establish requirements by which copyright owners may receive reasonable notice of the use of their sound recordings under this section, and under which records of such use shall be kept and made available by transmitting organizations entitled to obtain a statutory license under this subsection.

(5) License agreements voluntarily negotiated at any time between 1 or more copyright owners of sound recordings and 1 or more transmitting organizations entitled to obtain a statutory license under this subsection shall be given effect in lieu of any decision by the Librarian of Congress or determination by the Copyright Royalty Judges.

(6)(A) Any person who wishes to make a phonorecord of a sound recording under a statutory license in accordance with this subsection may do so without infringing the exclusive right of the copyright owner of the sound recording under section 106(1)—

(i) by complying with such notice requirements as the Copyright Royalty Judges shall prescribe by regulation and by paying royalty fees in accordance with this subsection; or

(ii) if such royalty fees have not been set, by agreeing to pay such royalty fees as shall be determined in accordance with this subsection.

(B) Any royalty payments in arrears shall be made on or before the 20th day of the month next succeeding the month in which the royalty fees are set.

(7) If a transmitting organization entitled to make a phonorecord under this subsection is prevented from making such phonorecord by reason of the application by the copyright owner of technical measures that prevent the reproduction of the sound recording, the copyright owner shall make available to the transmitting organization the necessary means for permitting the making of such phonorecord as permitted under this subsection, if it is technologically feasible and economically reasonable for the copyright owner to do so. If the copyright owner fails to do so in a timely manner in light of the transmitting organization's reasonable business requirements, the transmitting organization shall not be liable for a violation of section 1201(a)(1) of this title for engaging in such activities as are necessary to make such phonorecords as permitted under this subsection.

(8) Nothing in this subsection annuls, limits, impairs, or otherwise affects in any way the existence or value of any of the exclusive rights of the copyright owners in a sound recording, except as otherwise provided in this subsection, or in a musical work, including the exclusive rights to reproduce and distribute a sound recording or musical work, including by means of a digital phonorecord delivery, under sections 106(1), 106(3), and 115, and the right to perform publicly a sound recording or musical work, including by means of a digital audio transmission, under sections 106(4) and 106(6).

(f)(1) Notwithstanding the provisions of section 106, and without limiting the application of subsection (b), it is not an infringement of copyright for a governmental body or other nonprofit educational institution entitled under section 110(2) to transmit a performance or display to make copies or phonorecords of a work that is in digital form and, solely to the extent permitted in paragraph (2), of a work that is in analog form, embodying the performance or display to be used for making transmissions authorized under section 110(2), if—

(A) such copies or phonorecords are retained and used solely by the body or institution that made them, and no further copies or phonorecords are reproduced from them, except as authorized under section 110(2); and

(B) such copies or phonorecords are used solely for transmissions authorized under section 110(2).

(2) This subsection does not authorize the conversion of print or other analog versions of works into digital formats, except that such conversion is permitted hereunder, only with respect to the amount of such works authorized to be performed or displayed under section 110(2), if—

(A) no digital version of the work is available to the institution; or

(B) the digital version of the work that is available to the institution is subject to technological protection measures that prevent its use for section 110(2).

(g) The transmission program embodied in a copy or phonorecord made under this section is not subject to protection as a derivative work under this title except with the express consent of the owners of copyright in the preexisting works employed in the program.

Sec. 113.   Scope of Exclusive Rights in Pictorial, Graphic, and Sculptural Works

(a) Subject to the provisions of subsections (b) and (c) of this section, the exclusive right to reproduce a copyrighted pictorial, graphic, or sculptural work in copies under section 106 includes the right to reproduce the work in or on any kind of article, whether useful or otherwise.

(b) This title does not afford, to the owner of copyright in a work that portrays a useful article as such, any greater or lesser rights with respect to the making, distribution, or display of the useful article so portrayed than those afforded to such works under the law, whether title 17 or the common law or statutes of a State, in effect on December 31, 1977, as held applicable and construed by a court in an action brought under this title.

(c) In the case of a work lawfully reproduced in useful articles that have been offered for sale or other distribution to the public, copyright does not include any right to prevent the making, distribution, or display of pictures or photographs of such articles in connection with advertisements or commentaries related to the distribution or display of such articles, or in connection with news reports.

(d)(1) In a case in which—

(A) a work of visual art has been incorporated in or made part of a building in such a way that removing the work from the building will cause the destruction, distortion, mutilation, or other modification of the work as described in section 106A(a)(3), and

(B) the author consented to the installation of the work in the building either before the effective date set forth in section 9(a) of the Visual Artists Rights Act of 1990, or in a written instrument executed on or after such effective date that is signed by the owner of the building and the author and that specifies that installation of the work may subject the work to destruction, distortion, mutilation, or other modification, by reason of its removal,

then the rights conferred by paragraphs (2) and (3) of section 106A(a) shall not apply.

(2) If the owner of a building wishes to remove a work of visual art which is a part of such building and which can be removed from the building without the destruction, distortion, mutilation, or other modification of the work as described in section 106A(a)(3), the author's rights under paragraphs (2) and (3) of section 106A(a) shall apply unless—

(A) the owner has made a diligent, good faith attempt without success to notify the author of the owner's intended action affecting the work of visual art, or

(B) the owner did provide such notice in writing and the person so notified failed, within 90 days after receiving such notice, either to remove the work or to pay for its removal.

For purposes of subparagraph (A), an owner shall be presumed to have made a diligent, good faith attempt to send notice if the owner sent such notice by registered mail to the author at the most recent address of the author that was recorded with the Register of Copyrights pursuant to paragraph (3). If the work is removed at the expense of the author, title to that copy of the work shall be deemed to be in the author.

(3) The Register of Copyrights shall establish a system of records whereby any author of a work of visual art that has been incorporated in or made part of a building, may record his identity and address with the Copyright Office. The Register shall also establish procedures under which any such author may update the information so recorded, and procedures under which owners of buildings may record with the Copyright Office evidence of their efforts to comply with this subsection.

Sec. 114.   Scope of Exclusive Rights in Sound Recordings

(a) The exclusive rights of the owner of copyright in a sound recording are limited to the rights specified by clauses (1), (2), (3) and (6) of section 106, and do not include any right of performance under section 106(4).

(b) The exclusive right of the owner of copyright in a sound recording under clause (1) of section 106 is limited to the right to duplicate the sound recording in the form of phonorecords or copies that directly or indirectly recapture the actual sounds fixed in the recording. The exclusive right of the owner of copyright in a sound recording under clause (2) of section 106 is limited to the right to prepare a derivative work in which the actual sounds fixed in the sound recording are rearranged, remixed, or otherwise altered in sequence or quality. The exclusive rights of the owner of copyright in a sound recording under clauses (1) and (2) of section 106 do not extend to the making or duplication of another sound recording that consists entirely of an independent fixation of other sounds, even though such sounds imitate or simulate those in the copyrighted sound recording. The exclusive rights of the owner of copyright in a sound recording under clauses (1), (2), and (3) of section 106 do not apply to sound recordings included in educational television and radio programs (as defined in section 397 of title 47) distributed or transmitted by or through public broadcasting entities (as defined by section 118(f)): Provided, That copies or phonorecords of said programs are not commercially distributed by or through public broadcasting entities to the general public.

(c) This section does not limit or impair the exclusive right to perform publicly, by means of a phonorecord, any of the works specified by section 106(4).

(d) **Limitations on Exclusive Right.**—Notwithstanding the provisions of section 106(6)—

(1) **Exempt transmissions and retransmissions.**—The performance of a sound recording publicly by means of a digital audio transmission, other than as a part of an interactive service, is not an infringement of section 106(6) if the performance is part of—

(A) a nonsubscription broadcast transmission;

(B) a retransmission of a nonsubscription broadcast transmission: *Provided,* That, in the case of a retransmission of a radio station's broadcast transmission—

(i) the radio station's broadcast transmission is not willfully or repeatedly retransmitted more than a radius of 150 miles from the site of the radio broadcast transmitter, however—

(I) the 150 mile limitation under this clause shall not apply when a nonsubscription broadcast transmission by a radio station licensed by the Federal Communications Commission is retransmitted on a nonsubscription basis by a terrestrial broadcast station, terrestrial translator, or terrestrial repeater licensed by the Federal Communications Commission; and

(II) in the case of a subscription retransmission of a nonsubscription broadcast retransmission covered by subclause (I), the 150 mile radius shall be measured from the transmitter site of such broadcast retransmitter;

(ii) the retransmission is of radio station broadcast transmissions that are—

(I) obtained by the retransmitter over the air;

(II) not electronically processed by the retransmitter to deliver separate and discrete signals; and

(III) retransmitted only within the local communities served by the retransmitter;

(iii) the radio station's broadcast transmission was being retransmitted to cable systems (as defined in section 111(f)) by a satellite carrier on January 1, 1995, and that retransmission was being retransmitted by cable systems as a separate and discrete signal, and the satellite carrier obtains the radio station's broadcast transmission in an analog format: *Provided,* That the broadcast transmission being retransmitted may embody the programming of no more than one radio station; or

(iv) the radio station's broadcast transmission is made by a noncommercial educational broadcast station funded on or after January 1, 1995, under section 396(k) of the Communications Act of 1934 (47 U.S.C. 396(k)), consists solely of noncommercial educational and cultural radio programs, and the retransmission, whether or not simultaneous, is a nonsubscription terrestrial broadcast retransmission; or

(C) a transmission that comes within any of the following categories—

(i) a prior or simultaneous transmission incidental to an exempt transmission, such as a feed received by and then retransmitted by an exempt transmitter: *Provided,* That such incidental transmissions do not include any subscription transmission directly for reception by members of the public;

(ii) a transmission within a business establishment, confined to its premises or the immediately surrounding vicinity;

(iii) a retransmission by any retransmitter, including a multichannel video programming distributor as defined in section 602(12) of the Communications Act of 1934 (47 U.S.C. 522(12)), of a transmission by a transmitter licensed to publicly perform the sound recording as a part of that transmission, if the retransmission is simultaneous with the licensed transmission and authorized by the transmitter; or

(iv) a transmission to a business establishment for use in the ordinary course of its business: *Provided,* That the business recipient does not retransmit the transmission outside of its premises or the immediately surrounding vicinity, and that the transmission does not exceed the sound recording performance complement. Nothing in this clause shall limit the scope of the exemption in clause (ii).

(2) Statutory licensing of certain transmissions.—The performance of a sound recording publicly by means of a subscription digital audio transmission not exempt under paragraph (1), an eligible nonsubscription transmission, or a transmission not exempt under paragraph (1) that is made by a preexisting satellite digital audio radio service shall be subject to statutory licensing, in accordance with subsection (f) if—

(A)(i) the transmission is not part of an interactive service;

(ii) except in the case of a transmission to a business establishment, the transmitting entity does not automatically and intentionally cause any device receiving the transmission to switch from one program channel to another; and

(iii) except as provided in section 1002(e), the transmission of the sound recording is accompanied, if technically feasible, by the information encoded in that sound recording, if any, by or under the authority of the copyright owner of that sound recording, that identifies the title of the sound recording, the featured recording artist who performs on the sound recording, and related information, including information concerning the underlying musical work and its writer;

(B) in the case of a subscription transmission not exempt under paragraph (1) that is made by a preexisting subscription service in the same transmission medium used by such service on July 31, 1998, or in the case of a transmission not exempt under paragraph (1) that is made by a preexisting satellite digital audio radio service—

(i) the transmission does not exceed the sound recording performance complement; and

(ii) the transmitting entity does not cause to be published by means of an advance program schedule or prior announcement the titles of the specific sound recordings or phonorecords embodying such sound recordings to be transmitted; and

(C) in the case of an eligible nonsubscription transmission or a subscription transmission not exempt under paragraph (1) that is made by a new subscription service or by a preexisting subscription service other than in the same transmission medium used by such service on July 31, 1998—

(i) the transmission does not exceed the sound recording performance complement, except that this requirement shall not apply in the case of a retransmission of a broadcast transmission if the retransmission is made by a transmitting entity that does not have the right or ability to control the programming of the broadcast station making the broadcast transmission, unless—

(I) the broadcast station makes broadcast transmissions—

(aa) in digital format that regularly exceed the sound recording performance complement; or

(bb) in analog format, a substantial portion of which, on a weekly basis, exceed the sound recording performance complement; and

(II) the sound recording copyright owner or its representative has notified the transmitting entity in writing that broadcast transmissions of the copyright owner's sound recordings exceed the sound recording performance complement as provided in this clause;

(ii) the transmitting entity does not cause to be published, or induce or facilitate the publication, by means of an advance program schedule or prior announcement, the titles

of the specific sound recordings to be transmitted, the phonorecords embodying such sound recordings, or, other than for illustrative purposes, the names of the featured recording artists, except that this clause does not disqualify a transmitting entity that makes a prior announcement that a particular artist will be featured within an unspecified future time period, and in the case of a retransmission of a broadcast transmission by a transmitting entity that does not have the right or ability to control the programming of the broadcast transmission, the requirement of this clause shall not apply to a prior oral announcement by the broadcast station, or to an advance program schedule published, induced, or facilitated by the broadcast station, if the transmitting entity does not have actual knowledge and has not received written notice from the copyright owner or its representative that the broadcast station publishes or induces or facilitates the publication of such advance program schedule, or if such advance program schedule is a schedule of classical music programming published by the broadcast station in the same manner as published by that broadcast station on or before September 30, 1998;

(iii) the transmission—

(I) is not part of an archived program of less than 5 hours duration;

(II) is not part of an archived program of 5 hours or greater in duration that is made available for a period exceeding 2 weeks;

(III) is not part of a continuous program which is of less than 3 hours duration; or

(IV) is not part of an identifiable program in which performances of sound recordings are rendered in a predetermined order, other than an archived or continuous program, that is transmitted at—

(aa) more than 3 times in any 2-week period that have been publicly announced in advance, in the case of a program of less than 1 hour in duration, or

(bb) more than 4 times in any 2-week period that have been publicly announced in advance, in the case of a program of 1 hour or more in duration,

except that the requirement of this subclause shall not apply in the case of a retransmission of a broadcast transmission by a transmitting entity that does not have the right or ability to control the programming of the broadcast transmission, unless the transmitting entity is given notice in writing by the copyright owner of the sound recording that the broadcast station makes broadcast transmissions that regularly violate such requirement;

(iv) the transmitting entity does not knowingly perform the sound recording, as part of a service that offers transmissions of visual images contemporaneously with transmissions of sound recordings, in a manner that is likely to cause confusion, to cause mistake, or to deceive, as to the affiliation, connection, or association of the copyright owner or featured recording artist with the transmitting entity or a particular product or service advertised by the transmitting entity, or as to the origin, sponsorship, or approval by the copyright owner or featured recording artist of the activities of the transmitting entity other than the performance of the sound recording itself;

(v) the transmitting entity cooperates to prevent, to the extent feasible without imposing substantial costs or burdens, a transmission recipient or any other person or entity from automatically scanning the transmitting entity's transmissions alone or together with transmissions by other transmitting entities in order to select a particular sound recording to be transmitted to the transmission recipient, except that the requirement of this clause shall not apply to a satellite digital audio service that is in operation, or that is licensed by the Federal Communications Commission, on or before July 31, 1998;

(vi) the transmitting entity takes no affirmative steps to cause or induce the making of a phonorecord by the transmission recipient, and if the technology used by the transmitting entity enables the transmitting entity to limit the making by the transmission recipient of phonorecords of the transmission directly in a digital format, the transmitting entity sets such technology to limit such making of phonorecords to the extent permitted by such technology;

(vii) phonorecords of the sound recording have been distributed to the public under the authority of the copyright owner or the copyright owner authorizes the transmitting entity to transmit the sound recording, and the transmitting entity makes the transmission from a phonorecord lawfully made under the authority of the copyright owner, except that the requirement of this clause shall not apply to a retransmission of a broadcast transmission by a transmitting entity that does not have the right or ability to control the programming of the broadcast transmission, unless the transmitting entity is given notice in writing by the copyright owner of the sound recording that the broadcast station makes broadcast transmissions that regularly violate such requirement;

(viii) the transmitting entity accommodates and does not interfere with the transmission of technical measures that are widely used by sound recording copyright owners to identify or protect copyrighted works, and that are technically feasible of being transmitted by the transmitting entity without imposing substantial costs on the transmitting entity or resulting in perceptible aural or visual degradation of the digital signal, except that the requirement of this clause shall not apply to a satellite digital audio service that is in operation, or that is licensed under the authority of the Federal Communications Commission, on or before July 31, 1998, to the extent that such service has designed, developed, or made commitments to procure equipment or technology that is not compatible with such technical measures before such technical measures are widely adopted by sound recording copyright owners; and

(ix) the transmitting entity identifies in textual data the sound recording during, but not before, the time it is performed, including the title of the sound recording, the title of the phonorecord embodying such sound recording, if any, and the featured recording artist, in a manner to permit it to be displayed to the transmission recipient by the device or technology intended for receiving the service provided by the transmitting entity, except that the obligation in this clause shall not take effect until 1 year after the date of the enactment of the Digital Millennium Copyright Act and shall not apply in the case of a retransmission of a broadcast transmission by a transmitting entity that does not have the right or ability to control the programming of the broadcast transmission, or in the case in which devices or technology intended for receiving the service provided by the transmitting entity that have the capability to display such textual data are not common in the marketplace.

(3) Licenses for transmissions by interactive services.—

(A) No interactive service shall be granted an exclusive license under section 106(6) for the performance of a sound recording publicly by means of digital audio transmission for a period in excess of 12 months, except that with respect to an exclusive license granted to an interactive service by a licensor that holds the copyright to 1,000 or fewer sound recordings, the period of such license shall not exceed 24 months: *Provided, however,* That the grantee of such exclusive license shall be ineligible to receive another exclusive license for the performance of that sound recording for a period of 13 months from the expiration of the prior exclusive license.

(B) The limitation set forth in subparagraph (A) of this paragraph shall not apply if—

(i) the licensor has granted and there remain in effect licenses under section 106(6) for the public performance of sound recordings by means of digital audio transmission by at least 5 different interactive services: *Provided, however,* That each such license must be for a minimum of 10 percent of the copyrighted sound recordings owned by the licensor that have been licensed to interactive services, but in no event less than 50 sound recordings; or

(ii) the exclusive license is granted to perform publicly up to 45 seconds of a sound recording and the sole purpose of the performance is to promote the distribution or performance of that sound recording.

(C) Notwithstanding the grant of an exclusive or nonexclusive license of the right of public performance under section 106(6), an interactive service may not publicly perform a sound recording unless a license has been granted for the public performance of any copyrighted musical work contained in the sound recording: *Provided,* That such license to publicly perform the copyrighted musical work may be granted either by a performing rights society representing the copyright owner or by the copyright owner.

(D) The performance of a sound recording by means of a retransmission of a digital audio transmission is not an infringement of section 106(6) if—

(i) the retransmission is of a transmission by an interactive service licensed to publicly perform the sound recording to a particular member of the public as part of that transmission; and

(ii) the retransmission is simultaneous with the licensed transmission, authorized by the transmitter, and limited to that particular member of the public intended by the interactive service to be the recipient of the transmission.

(E) For the purposes of this paragraph—

(i) a "licensor" shall include the licensing entity and any other entity under any material degree of common ownership, management, or control that owns copyrights in sound recordings; and

(ii) a "performing rights society" is an association or corporation that licenses the public performance of nondramatic musical works on behalf of the copyright owner, such as the American Society of Composers, Authors and Publishers, Broadcast Music, Inc., and SESAC, Inc.

(4) Rights not otherwise limited.—

(A) Except as expressly provided in this section, this section does not limit or impair the exclusive right to perform a sound recording publicly by means of a digital audio transmission under section 106(6).

(B) Nothing in this section annuls or limits in any way—

(i) the exclusive right to publicly perform a musical work, including by means of a digital audio transmission, under section 106(4);

(ii) the exclusive rights in a sound recording or the musical work embodied therein under sections 106(1), 106(2) and 106(3); or

(iii) any other rights under any other clause of section 106, or remedies available under this title, as such rights or remedies exist either before or after the date of enactment of the Digital Performance Right in Sound Recordings Act of 1995.

(C) Any limitations in this section on the exclusive right under section 106(6) apply only to the exclusive right under section 106(6) and not to any other exclusive rights under section 106. Nothing in this section shall be construed to annul, limit, impair or otherwise affect in any way the ability of the owner of a copyright in a sound recording to exercise the rights under sections 106(1), 106(2) and 106(3), or to obtain the remedies available under this title pursuant to such rights, as such rights and remedies exist either before or after the date of enactment of the Digital Performance Right in Sound Recordings Act of 1995.

(e) Authority for Negotiations.—

(1) Notwithstanding any provision of the antitrust laws, in negotiating statutory licenses in accordance with subsection (f), any copyright owners of sound recordings and any entities performing sound recordings affected by this section may negotiate and agree upon the royalty rates and license terms and conditions for the performance of such sound recordings and the proportionate division of fees paid among copyright owners, and may designate common agents on a nonexclusive basis to negotiate, agree to, pay, or receive payments.

(2) For licenses granted under section 106(6), other than statutory licenses, such as for performances by interactive services or performances that exceed the sound recording performance complement—

(A) copyright owners of sound recordings affected by this section may designate common agents to act on their behalf to grant licenses and receive and remit royalty payments: *Provided,* That each copyright owner shall establish the royalty rates and material license terms and conditions unilaterally, that is, not in agreement, combination, or concert with other copyright owners of sound recordings; and

(B) entities performing sound recordings affected by this section may designate common agents to act on their behalf to obtain licenses and collect and pay royalty fees: *Provided,* That each entity performing sound recordings shall determine the royalty rates and material license terms and conditions unilaterally, that is, not in agreement, combination, or concert with other entities performing sound recordings.

(f) Licenses for Certain Nonexempt Transmissions.—

(1)(A) Proceedings under chapter 8 shall determine reasonable rates and terms of royalty payments for subscription transmissions by preexisting subscription services and transmissions by preexisting satellite digital audio radio services specified by subsection (d)(2) during the 5-year period beginning on January 1 of the second year following the year in which the proceedings are to be commenced, except in the case of a different transitional period provided under section 6(b)(3) of the Copyright Royalty and Distribution Reform Act of 2004, or such other period as the parties may agree. Such terms and rates shall distinguish among the different types of digital audio transmission services then in operation. Any copyright owners of sound recordings, preexisting subscription services, or preexisting satellite digital audio radio services may submit to the Copyright Royalty Judges licenses covering such subscription transmissions with respect to such sound recordings. The parties to each proceeding shall bear their own costs.

(B) The schedule of reasonable rates and terms determined by the Copyright Royalty Judges shall, subject to paragraph (3), be binding on all copyright owners of sound recordings and entities performing sound recordings affected by this paragraph during the 5-year period specified in subparagraph (A), a transitional period provided under section 6(b)(3) of the Copyright Royalty and Distribution Reform Act of 2004, or such other period as the parties may agree. In establishing rates and terms for preexisting subscription services and preexisting satellite digital audio radio services, in addition to the objectives set forth in section 801(b)(1), the Copyright Royalty Judges may consider the rates and terms for comparable types of subscription digital audio transmission services and comparable circumstances under voluntary license agreements described in subparagraph (A).

(C) The procedures under subparagraphs (A) and (B) also shall be initiated pursuant to a petition filed by any copyright owners of sound recordings, any preexisting subscription services, or any preexisting satellite digital audio radio services indicating that a new type of subscription digital audio transmission service on which sound recordings are performed is or is about to become operational, for the purpose of determining reasonable terms and rates of royalty payments with respect to such new type of transmission service for the period beginning with the inception of such new type of service and ending on the date on which the royalty rates and terms for subscription digital audio transmission services most recently determined under subparagraph (A) or (B) and chapter 8 expire, or such other period as the parties may agree.

(2)(A) Proceedings under chapter 8 shall determine reasonable rates and terms of royalty payments for public performances of sound recordings by means of eligible nonsubscription transmission services and new subscription services specified by subsection (d)(2) during the 5-year period beginning on January 1 of the second year following the year in which the proceedings are to be commenced, except in the case of a different transitional period provided under section 6(b)(3) of the Copyright Royalty and Distribution Reform Act of 2004, or such other period as the parties may agree. Such rates and terms shall distinguish among the different types of eligible nonsubscription transmission services and new subscription services then in operation and shall include a minimum fee for each such type of service. Any copyright owners of sound recordings or any entities performing sound recordings affected by this paragraph may submit to the Copyright Royalty Judges licenses covering such eligible nonsubscription transmissions and new subscription services with respect to such sound recordings. The parties to each proceeding shall bear their own costs.

(B) The schedule of reasonable rates and terms determined by the Copyright Royalty Judges shall, subject to paragraph (3), be binding on all copyright owners of sound recordings and entities performing sound recordings affected by this paragraph during the 5-year period specified in subparagraph (A), a transitional period provided under section 6(b)(3) of the Copyright Royalty and Distribution Reform Act of 2004, or such other period as the parties may agree. Such rates and terms shall distinguish among the different types of eligible nonsubscription transmission services then in operation and shall include a minimum fee for each such type of service, such differences to be based on criteria including, but not limited to, the quantity and nature of the use of sound recordings and the degree to which use of the service may substitute for or may promote the purchase of phonorecords by consumers. In establishing rates and terms for transmissions by eligible nonsubscription services and new subscription services, the Copyright Royalty Judges shall establish rates and terms that most clearly represent the rates and terms that would have been negotiated in the marketplace between a willing buyer and a willing seller. In determining such rates and terms, the Copyright Royalty Judges shall base their decision on economic, competitive and programming information presented by the parties, including—

    (i) whether use of the service may substitute for or may promote the sales of phonorecords or otherwise may interfere with or may enhance the sound recording copyright owner's other streams of revenue from its sound recordings; and

    (ii) the relative roles of the copyright owner and the transmitting entity in the copyrighted work and the service made available to the public with respect to relative creative contribution, technological contribution, capital investment, cost, and risk.

In establishing such rates and terms, the Copyright Royalty Judges may consider the rates and terms for comparable types of digital audio transmission services and comparable circumstances under voluntary license agreements described in subparagraph (A).

(C) The procedures under subparagraphs (A) and (B) shall also be initiated pursuant to a petition filed by any copyright owners of sound recordings or any eligible nonsubscription service or new subscription service indicating that a new type of eligible nonsubscription service or new subscription service on which sound recordings are performed is or is about to become operational, for the purpose of determining reasonable terms and rates of royalty payments with respect to such new type of service for the period beginning with the inception of such new type of service and ending on the date on which the royalty rates and terms for eligible nonsubscription services and new subscription services, as the case may be, most recently determined under subparagraph (A) or (B) and chapter 8 expire, or such other period as the parties may agree.

(3) License agreements voluntarily negotiated at any time between 1 or more copyright owners of sound recordings and 1 or more entities performing sound recordings shall be given effect in lieu of any decision by the Librarian of Congress or determination by the Copyright Royalty Judges.

(4)(A) The Copyright Royalty Judges shall also establish requirements by which copyright owners may receive reasonable notice of the use of their sound recordings under this section, and under which records of such use shall be kept and made available by entities performing sound recordings. The notice and recordkeeping rules in effect on the day before the effective date of the Copyright Royalty and Distribution Reform Act of 2004 shall remain in effect unless and until new regulations are promulgated by the Copyright Royalty Judges. If new regulations are promulgated under this subparagraph, the Copyright Royalty Judges shall take into account the substance and effect of the rules in effect on the day before the effective date of the Copyright Royalty and Distribution Reform Act of 2004 and shall, to the extent practicable, avoid significant disruption of the functions of any designated agent authorized to collect and distribute royalty fees.

(B) Any person who wishes to perform a sound recording publicly by means of a transmission eligible for statutory licensing under this subsection may do so without infringing the exclusive right of the copyright owner of the sound recording—

(i) by complying with such notice requirements as the Copyright Royalty Judges shall prescribe by regulation and by paying royalty fees in accordance with this subsection; or

(ii) if such royalty fees have not been set, by agreeing to pay such royalty fees as shall be determined in accordance with this subsection.

(C) Any royalty payments in arrears shall be made on or before the twentieth day of the month next succeeding the month in which the royalty fees are set.

(5)(A) Notwithstanding section 112(e) and the other provisions of this subsection, the receiving agent may enter into agreements for the reproduction and performance of sound recordings under section 112(e) and this section by any one or more commercial webcasters or noncommercial webcasters for a period of not more than 11 years beginning on January 1, 2005, that, once published in the Federal Register pursuant to subparagraph (B), shall be binding on all copyright owners of sound recordings and other persons entitled to payment under this section, in lieu of any determination by the Copyright Royalty Judges. Any such agreement for commercial webcasters may include provisions for payment of royalties on the basis of a percentage of revenue or expenses, or both, and include a minimum fee. Any such agreement may include other terms and conditions, including requirements by which copyright owners may receive notice of the use of their sound recordings and under which records of such use shall be kept and made available by commercial webcasters or noncommercial webcasters. The receiving agent shall be under no obligation to negotiate any such agreement. The receiving agent shall have no obligation to any copyright owner of sound recordings or any other person entitled to payment under this section in negotiating any such agreement, and no liability to any copyright owner of sound recordings or any other person entitled to payment under this section for having entered into such agreement.

(B) The Copyright Office shall cause to be published in the Federal Register any agreement entered into pursuant to subparagraph (A). Such publication shall include a statement containing the substance of subparagraph (C). Such agreements shall not be included in the Code of Federal Regulations. Thereafter, the terms of such agreement shall be available, as an option, to any commercial webcaster or noncommercial webcaster meeting the eligibility conditions of such agreement.

(C) Neither subparagraph (A) nor any provisions of any agreement entered into pursuant to subparagraph (A), including any rate structure, fees, terms, conditions, or notice and recordkeeping requirements set forth therein, shall be admissible as evidence or otherwise taken into account in any administrative, judicial, or other government proceeding involving the setting or adjustment of the royalties payable for the public performance or reproduction in ephemeral phonorecords or copies of sound recordings, the determination of terms or conditions related thereto, or the establishment of notice or recordkeeping requirements by the Copyright Royalty Judges under paragraph (4) or section 112(e)(4). It is the intent of Congress that any royalty rates, rate structure, definitions, terms, conditions, or notice and recordkeeping requirements, included in such agreements shall be considered as a compromise motivated by the unique business, economic and political circumstances of webcasters, copyright owners, and performers rather than as matters that would have been negotiated in the marketplace between a willing buyer and a willing seller, or otherwise meet the objectives set forth in section 801(b). This subparagraph shall not apply to the extent that the receiving agent and a webcaster that is party to an agreement entered into pursuant to subparagraph (A) expressly authorize the submission of the agreement in a proceeding under this subsection.

(D) Nothing in the Webcaster Settlement Act of 2008, the Webcaster Settlement Act of 2009, or any agreement entered into pursuant to subparagraph (A) shall be taken into account by the United States Court of Appeals for the District of Columbia Circuit in its review of the determination by the Copyright Royalty Judges of May 1, 2007, of rates and terms for the digital performance of sound recordings and ephemeral recordings, pursuant to sections 112 and 114.

(E) As used in this paragraph—

(i) the term "noncommercial webcaster" means a webcaster that—

(I) is exempt from taxation under section 501 of the Internal Revenue Code of 1986 (26 U.S.C. 501);

(II) has applied in good faith to the Internal Revenue Service for exemption from taxation under section 501 of the Internal Revenue Code and has a commercially reasonable expectation that such exemption shall be granted; or

(III) is operated by a State or possession or any governmental entity or subordinate thereof, or by the United States or District of Columbia, for exclusively public purposes;

(ii) the term "receiving agent" shall have the meaning given that term in section 261.2 of title 37, Code of Federal Regulations, as published in the Federal Register on July 8, 2002; and

(iii) the term "webcaster" means a person or entity that has obtained a compulsory license under section 112 or 114 and the implementing regulations therefor

(F) The authority to make settlements pursuant to subparagraph (A) shall expire at 11:59 p.m. Eastern time on the 30th day after the date of the enactment of the Webcaster Settlement Act of 2009.

(g) Proceeds From Licensing of Transmissions.—

(1) Except in the case of a transmission licensed under a statutory license in accordance with subsection (f) of this section—

(A) a featured recording artist who performs on a sound recording that has been licensed for a transmission shall be entitled to receive payments from the copyright owner of the sound recording in accordance with the terms of the artist's contract; and

(B) a nonfeatured recording artist who performs on a sound recording that has been licensed for a transmission shall be entitled to receive payments from the copyright owner of the sound recording in accordance with the terms of the nonfeatured recording artist's applicable contract or other applicable agreement.

(2) An agent designated to distribute receipts from the licensing of transmissions in accordance with subsection (f) shall distribute such receipts as follows:

(A) 50 percent of the receipts shall be paid to the copyright owner of the exclusive right under section 106(6) of this title to publicly perform a sound recording by means of a digital audio transmission.

(B) 2 1/2 percent of the receipts shall be deposited in an escrow account managed by an independent administrator jointly appointed by copyright owners of sound recordings and the American Federation of Musicians (or any successor entity) to be distributed to nonfeatured musicians (whether or not members of the American Federation of Musicians) who have performed on sound recordings.

(C) 2 1/2 percent of the receipts shall be deposited in an escrow account managed by an independent administrator jointly appointed by copyright owners of sound recordings and the American Federation of Television and Radio Artists (or any successor entity) to be distributed to nonfeatured vocalists (whether or not members of the American Federation of Television and Radio Artists) who have performed on sound recordings.

(D) 45 percent of the receipts shall be paid, on a per sound recording basis, to the recording artist or artists featured on such sound recording (or the persons conveying rights in the artists' performance in the sound recordings).

(3) A nonprofit agent designated to distribute receipts from the licensing of transmissions in accordance with subsection (f) may deduct from any of its receipts, prior to the distribution of such receipts to any person or entity entitled thereto other than copyright owners and performers who have elected to receive royalties from another designated agent and have notified such nonprofit agent in writing of such election, the reasonable costs of such agent incurred after November 1, 1995, in—

(A) the administration of the collection, distribution, and calculation of the royalties;

(B) the settlement of disputes relating to the collection and calculation of the royalties; and

(C) the licensing and enforcement of rights with respect to the making of ephemeral recordings and performances subject to licensing under section 112 and this section, including those incurred in participating in negotiations or arbitration proceedings under section 112 and this section, except that all costs incurred relating to the section 112 ephemeral recordings right may only be deducted from the royalties received pursuant to section 112.

(4) Notwithstanding paragraph (3), any designated agent designated to distribute receipts from the licensing of transmissions in accordance with subsection (f) may deduct from any of its receipts, prior to the distribution of such receipts, the reasonable costs identified in paragraph (3) of such agent incurred after November 1, 1995, with respect to such copyright owners and performers who have entered with such agent a contractual relationship that specifies that such costs may be deducted from such royalty receipts.

(h) Licensing to Affiliates.—

(1) If the copyright owner of a sound recording licenses an affiliated entity the right to publicly perform a sound recording by means of a digital audio transmission under section 106(6), the copyright owner shall make the licensed sound recording available under section 106(6) on no less favorable terms and conditions to all bona fide entities that offer similar services, except that, if there are material differences in the scope of the requested license with respect to the type of service, the particular sound recordings licensed, the frequency of use, the number of subscribers served, or the duration, then the copyright owner may establish different terms and conditions for such other services.

(2) The limitation set forth in paragraph (1) of this subsection shall not apply in the case where the copyright owner of a sound recording licenses—

(A) an interactive service; or

(B) an entity to perform publicly up to 45 seconds of the sound recording and the sole purpose of the performance is to promote the distribution or performance of that sound recording.

(i) No Effect on Royalties for Underlying Works.—License fees payable for the public performance of sound recordings under section 106(6) shall not be taken into account in any administrative, judicial, or other governmental proceeding to set or adjust the royalties payable to copyright owners of musical works for the public performance of their works. It is the intent of Congress that royalties payable to copyright owners of musical works for the public performance of their works shall not be diminished in any respect as a result of the rights granted by section 106(6).

(j) Definitions.—As used in this section, the following terms have the following meanings:

(1) An "affiliated entity" is an entity engaging in digital audio transmissions covered by section 106(6), other than an interactive service, in which the licensor has any direct or indirect partnership or any ownership interest amounting to 5 percent or more of the outstanding voting or non-voting stock.

(2) An "archived program" is a predetermined program that is available repeatedly on the demand of the transmission recipient and that is performed in the same order from the beginning, except that an archived program shall not include a recorded event or broadcast transmission that makes no more than an incidental use of sound recordings, as long as such recorded event or broadcast transmission does not contain an entire sound recording or feature a particular sound recording.

(3) A "broadcast" transmission is a transmission made by a terrestrial broadcast station licensed as such by the Federal Communications Commission.

(4) A "continuous program" is a predetermined program that is continuously performed in the same order and that is accessed at a point in the program that is beyond the control of the transmission recipient.

(5) A "digital audio transmission" is a digital transmission as defined in section 101, that embodies the transmission of a sound recording. This term does not include the transmission of any audiovisual work.

(6) An "eligible nonsubscription transmission" is a noninteractive nonsubscription digital audio transmission not exempt under subsection (d)(1) that is made as part of a service that provides audio programming consisting, in whole or in part, of performances of sound recordings, including retransmissions of broadcast transmissions, if the primary purpose of the service is to provide to the public such audio or other entertainment programming, and the primary purpose of the service is not to sell, advertise, or promote particular products or services other than sound recordings, live concerts, or other music-related events.

(7) An "interactive service" is one that enables a member of the public to receive a transmission of a program specially created for the recipient, or on request, a transmission of a particular sound recording, whether or not as part of a program, which is selected by

or on behalf of the recipient. The ability of individuals to request that particular sound recordings be performed for reception by the public at large, or in the case of a subscription service, by all subscribers of the service, does not make a service interactive, if the programming on each channel of the service does not substantially consist of sound recordings that are performed within 1 hour of the request or at a time designated by either the transmitting entity or the individual making such request. If an entity offers both interactive and noninteractive services (either concurrently or at different times), the noninteractive component shall not be treated as part of an interactive service.

(8) A "new subscription service" is a service that performs sound recordings by means of noninteractive subscription digital audio transmissions and that is not a preexisting subscription service or a preexisting satellite digital audio radio service.

(9) A "nonsubscription" transmission is any transmission that is not a subscription transmission.

(10) A "preexisting satellite digital audio radio service" is a subscription satellite digital audio radio service provided pursuant to a satellite digital audio radio service license issued by the Federal Communications Commission on or before July 31, 1998, and any renewal of such license to the extent of the scope of the original license, and may include a limited number of sample channels representative of the subscription service that are made available on a nonsubscription basis in order to promote the subscription service.

(11) A "preexisting subscription service" is a service that performs sound recordings by means of noninteractive audio-only subscription digital audio transmissions, which was in existence and was making such transmissions to the public for a fee on or before July 31, 1998, and may include a limited number of sample channels representative of the subscription service that are made available on a nonsubscription basis in order to promote the subscription service.

(12) A "retransmission" is a further transmission of an initial transmission, and includes any further retransmission of the same transmission. Except as provided in this section, a transmission qualifies as a "retransmission" only if it is simultaneous with the initial transmission. Nothing in this definition shall be construed to exempt a transmission that fails to satisfy a separate element required to qualify for an exemption under section 114(d)(1).

(13) The "sound recording performance complement" is the transmission during any 3-hour period, on a particular channel used by a transmitting entity, of no more than—

(A) 3 different selections of sound recordings from any one phonorecord lawfully distributed for public performance or sale in the United States, if no more than 2 such selections are transmitted consecutively; or

    (B) 4 different selections of sound recordings—

        (i) by the same featured recording artist; or

        (ii) from any set or compilation of phonorecords lawfully distributed together as a unit for public performance or sale in the United States,

if no more than three such selections are transmitted consecutively:

Provided, That the transmission of selections in excess of the numerical limits provided for in clauses (A) and (B) from multiple phonorecords shall nonetheless qualify as a sound recording performance complement if the programming of the multiple phonorecords was not willfully intended to avoid the numerical limitations prescribed in such clauses.

    (14) A "subscription" transmission is a transmission that is controlled and limited to particular recipients, and for which consideration is required to be paid or otherwise given by or on behalf of the recipient to receive the transmission or a package of transmissions including the transmission.

    (15) A "transmission" is either an initial transmission or a retransmission.

Sec. 115.   Scope of Exclusive Rights in Nondramatic Musical Works: Compulsory License for Making and Distributing Phonorecords

In the case of nondramatic musical works, the exclusive rights provided by clauses (1) and (3) of section 106, to make and to distribute phonorecords of such works, are subject to compulsory licensing under the conditions specified by this section.

(a) Availability and Scope of Compulsory License.—

(1) When phonorecords of a nondramatic musical work have been distributed to the public in the United States under the authority of the copyright owner, any other person, including those who make phonorecords or digital phonorecord deliveries may, by complying with the provisions of this section, obtain a compulsory license to make and distribute phonorecords of the work. A person may obtain a compulsory license only if his or her primary purpose in making phonorecords is to distribute them to the public for private use, including by means of a digital phonorecord delivery. A person may not obtain a compulsory license for use of the work in the making of phonorecords duplicating a sound recording fixed by another, unless: (i) such sound recording was fixed lawfully; and (ii) the making of the phonorecords was authorized by the owner of copyright in the sound recording or, if the sound recording was fixed before February 15, 1972, by any person who fixed the sound recording pursuant to an express license from the owner of the copyright

in the musical work or pursuant to a valid compulsory license for use of such work in a sound recording.

(2) A compulsory license includes the privilege of making a musical arrangement of the work to the extent necessary to conform it to the style or manner of interpretation of the performance involved, but the arrangement shall not change the basic melody or fundamental character of the work, and shall not be subject to protection as a derivative work under this title, except with the express consent of the copyright owner.

(b) Notice of Intention to Obtain Compulsory License.—

(1) Any person who wishes to obtain a compulsory license under this section shall, before or within thirty days after making, and before distributing any phonorecords of the work, serve notice of intention to do so on the copyright owner. If the registration or other public records of the Copyright Office do not identify the copyright owner and include an address at which notice can be served, it shall be sufficient to file the notice of intention in the Copyright Office. The notice shall comply, in form, content, and manner of service, with requirements that the Register of Copyrights shall prescribe by regulation.

(2) Failure to serve or file the notice required by clause (1) forecloses the possibility of a compulsory license and, in the absence of a negotiated license, renders the making and distribution of phonorecords actionable as acts of infringement under section 501 and fully subject to the remedies provided by sections 502 through 506 and 509.

(c) Royalty Payable Under Compulsory License.—

(1) To be entitled to receive royalties under a compulsory license, the copyright owner must be identified in the registration or other public records of the Copyright Office. The owner is entitled to royalties for phonorecords made and distributed after being so identified, but is not entitled to recover for any phonorecords previously made and distributed.

(2) Except as provided by clause (1), the royalty under a compulsory license shall be payable for every phonorecord made and distributed in accordance with the license. For this purpose, and other than as provided in paragraph (3), a phonorecord is considered "distributed" if the person exercising the compulsory license has voluntarily and permanently parted with its possession. With respect to each work embodied in the phonorecord, the royalty shall be either two and three-fourths cents, or one-half of one cent per minute of playing time or fraction thereof, whichever amount is larger.[e]

(3)(A) A compulsory license under this section includes the right of the compulsory licensee to distribute or authorize the distribution of a phonorecord of a nondramatic musical work by means of a digital transmission which constitutes a digital phonorecord delivery, regardless

---

[e] The current royalty rate is set as provided in 37 C.F.R. § 385.3, at http://www.loc.gov/crb/laws/title37/index.htm

of whether the digital transmission is also a public performance of the sound recording under section 106(6) of this title or of any nondramatic musical work embodied therein under section 106(4) of this title. For every digital phonorecord delivery by or under the authority of the compulsory licensee—

(i) on or before December 31, 1997, the royalty payable by the compulsory licensee shall be the royalty prescribed under paragraph (2) and chapter 8 of this title; and

(ii) on or after January 1, 1998, the royalty payable by the compulsory licensee shall be the royalty prescribed under subparagraphs (B) through (E) and chapter 8 of this title.

(B) Notwithstanding any provision of the antitrust laws, any copyright owners of nondramatic musical works and any persons entitled to obtain a compulsory license under subsection (a)(1) may negotiate and agree upon the terms and rates of royalty payments under this section and the proportionate division of fees paid among copyright owners, and may designate common agents on a nonexclusive basis to negotiate, agree to, pay or receive such royalty payments. Such authority to negotiate the terms and rates of royalty payments includes, but is not limited to, the authority to negotiate the year during which the royalty rates prescribed under this subparagraph and subparagraphs (C) through (E) and chapter 8 of this title shall next be determined.

(C) Proceedings under chapter 8 shall determine reasonable rates and terms of royalty payments for the activities specified by this section during the period beginning with the effective date of such rates and terms, but not earlier than January 1 of the second year following the year in which the petition requesting the proceeding is filed, and ending on the effective date of successor rates and terms, or such other period as the parties may agree. Such terms and rates shall distinguish between (i) digital phonorecord deliveries where the reproduction or distribution of a phonorecord is incidental to the transmission which constitutes the digital phonorecord delivery, and (ii) digital phonorecord deliveries in general. Any copyright owners of nondramatic musical works and any persons entitled to obtain a compulsory license under subsection (a)(1) may submit to the Copyright Royalty Judges licenses covering such activities. The parties to each proceeding shall bear their own costs.

(D) The schedule of reasonable rates and terms determined by the Copyright Royalty Judges shall, subject to subparagraph (E), be binding on all copyright owners of nondramatic musical works and persons entitled to obtain a compulsory license under subsection (a)(1) during the period specified in subparagraph (C), such other period as may be determined pursuant to subparagraphs (B) and (C), or such other period as the parties may agree. Such terms and rates shall distinguish between (i) digital phonorecord deliveries where the reproduction or distribution of a phonorecord is incidental to the transmission which constitutes the digital phonorecord delivery, and (ii) digital phonorecord deliveries in general. In addition to the objectives set forth in section 801(b)(1), in establishing such rates and terms, the Copyright Royalty Judges may consider rates and terms under voluntary license agreements described in subparagraphs (B) and (C). The royalty rates payable for a compulsory license for a digital phonorecord delivery under this section shall be established de novo and no precedential effect shall be given to the amount of the royalty payable by a compulsory licensee for digital phonorecord deliveries on or before December 31, 1997. The Copyright Royalty Judges shall also establish requirements by which copyright owners may receive reasonable notice of the use of their works under this section, and under which records of such use shall be kept and made available by persons making digital phonorecord deliveries.

(E)(i) License agreements voluntarily negotiated at any time between one or more copyright owners of nondramatic musical works and one or more persons entitled to obtain a compulsory license under subsection (a)(1) shall be given effect in lieu of any determination by the Librarian of Congress and Copyright Royalty Judges. Subject to clause (ii), the royalty rates determined pursuant to subparagraph (C) and (D) shall be given effect as to digital phonorecord deliveries in lieu of any contrary royalty rates specified in a contract pursuant to which a recording artist who is the author of a nondramatic musical work grants a license under that person's exclusive rights in the musical work under paragraphs (1) and (3) of section 106 or commits another person to grant a license in that musical work under paragraphs (1) and (3) of section 106, to a person desiring to fix in a tangible medium of expression a sound recording embodying the musical work.

(ii) The second sentence of clause (i) shall not apply to—

(I) a contract entered into on or before June 22, 1995, and not modified thereafter for the purpose of reducing the royalty rates determined pursuant to subparagraph (C) and (D) or of increasing the number of musical works within the scope of the contract covered by the reduced rates, except if a contract entered into on or before June 22, 1995, is modified thereafter for the purpose of increasing the number of musical works within the scope of the contract, any contrary royalty rates specified in the contract shall be given effect in lieu of royalty rates determined pursuant to subparagraph (C) and (D) for the number of musical works within the scope of the contract as of June 22, 1995; and

(II) a contract entered into after the date that the sound recording is fixed in a tangible medium of expression substantially in a form intended for commercial release, if at the time the contract is entered into, the recording artist retains the right to grant licenses as to the musical work under paragraphs (1) and (3) of section 106.

(F) Except as provided in section 1002(e) of this title, a digital phonorecord delivery licensed under this paragraph shall be accompanied by the information encoded in the sound recording, if any, by or under the authority of the copyright owner of that sound recording, that identifies the title of the sound recording, the featured recording artist who performs on the sound recording, and related information, including information concerning the underlying musical work and its writer.

(G)(i) A digital phonorecord delivery of a sound recording is actionable as an act of infringement under section 501, and is fully subject to the remedies provided by sections 502 through 506, unless—

(I) the digital phonorecord delivery has been authorized by the copyright owner of the sound recording; and

(II) the owner of the copyright in the sound recording or the entity making the digital phonorecord delivery has obtained a compulsory license under this section or has otherwise been authorized by the copyright owner of the musical work to distribute or authorize the distribution, by means of a digital phonorecord delivery, of each musical work embodied in the sound recording.

(ii) Any cause of action under this subparagraph shall be in addition to those available to the owner of the copyright in the nondramatic musical work under subsection (c)(6) and section 106(4) and the owner of the copyright in the sound recording under section 106(6).

(H) The liability of the copyright owner of a sound recording for infringement of the copyright in a nondramatic musical work embodied in the sound recording shall be determined in accordance with applicable law, except that the owner of a copyright in a sound recording shall not be liable for a digital phonorecord delivery by a third party if the owner of the copyright in the sound recording does not license the distribution of a phonorecord of the nondramatic musical work.

(I) Nothing in section 1008 shall be construed to prevent the exercise of the rights and remedies allowed by this paragraph, paragraph (6), and chapter 5 in the event of a digital phonorecord delivery, except that no action alleging infringement of copyright may be brought under this title against a manufacturer, importer or distributor of a digital audio recording device, a digital audio recording medium, an analog recording device, or an analog recording medium, or against a consumer, based on the actions described in such section.

(J) Nothing in this section annuls or limits (i) the exclusive right to publicly perform a sound recording or the musical work embodied therein, including by means of a digital transmission, under sections 106(4) and 106(6), (ii) except for compulsory licensing under the conditions specified by this section, the exclusive rights to reproduce and distribute the sound recording and the musical work embodied therein under sections 106(1) and 106(3), including by means of a digital phonorecord delivery, or (iii) any other rights under any other provision of section 106, or remedies available under this title, as such rights or remedies exist either before or after the date of enactment of the Digital Performance Right in Sound Recordings Act of 1995.

(K) The provisions of this section concerning digital phonorecord deliveries shall not apply to any exempt transmissions or retransmissions under section 114(d)(1). The exemptions created in section 114(d)(1) do not expand or reduce the rights of copyright owners under section 106(1) through (5) with respect to such transmissions and retransmissions.

(4) A compulsory license under this section includes the right of the maker of a phonorecord of a nondramatic musical work under subsection (a)(1) to distribute or authorize distribution of such phonorecord by rental, lease, or lending (or by acts or practices in the nature of rental, lease, or lending). In addition to any royalty payable under clause (2) and chapter 8 of this title, a royalty shall be payable by the compulsory licensee for every act of distribution of a phonorecord by or in the nature of rental, lease, or lending, by or under the authority of the compulsory licensee. With respect to each nondramatic, musical work embodied in the phonorecord, the royalty shall be a proportion of the revenue received by the compulsory licensee from every such act of distribution of the phonorecord under this clause equal to the proportion of the revenue received by the compulsory licensee from distribution of the phonorecord under clause (2) that is payable by a compulsory licensee under that clause and under chapter 8. The Register of Copyrights shall issue regulations to carry out the purpose of this clause.

(5) Royalty payments shall be made on or before the twentieth day of each month and shall include all royalties for the month next preceding. Each monthly payment shall be made under oath and shall comply with requirements that the Register of Copyrights shall prescribe by regulation. The Register shall also prescribe regulations under which detailed cumulative annual statements of account, certified by a certified public accountant, shall be filed for every compulsory license under this section. The regulations covering both the monthly and the annual statements of account shall prescribe the form, content, and manner of certification with respect to the number of records made and the number of records distributed.

(6) If the copyright owner does not receive the monthly payment and the monthly and annual statements of account when due, the owner may give written notice to the licensee that, unless the default is remedied within thirty days from the date of the notice, the compulsory license will be automatically terminated. Such termination renders either the making or the distribution, or both, of all phonorecords for which the royalty has not been paid, actionable as acts of infringement under

section 501 and fully subject to the remedies provided by sections 502 through 506.

(d) Definition.—As used in this section, the following term has the following meaning: A "digital phonorecord delivery" is each individual delivery of a phonorecord by digital transmission of a sound recording which results in a specifically identifiable reproduction by or for any transmission recipient of a phonorecord of that sound recording, regardless of whether the digital transmission is also a public performance of the sound recording or any nondramatic musical work embodied therein. A digital phonorecord delivery does not result from a real-time, non-interactive subscription transmission of a sound recording where no reproduction of the sound recording or the musical work embodied therein is made from the inception of the transmission through to its receipt by the transmission recipient in order to make the sound recording audible.

Sec. 116.   Negotiated Licenses for Public Performances by Means of Coin-Operated Phonorecord Players

(a) Applicability of Section.—This section applies to any nondramatic musical work embodied in a phonorecord.

(b) Negotiated Licenses.—

(1) Authority for Negotiations.—Any owners of copyright in works to which this section applies and any operators of coin-operated phonorecord players may negotiate and agree upon the terms and rates of royalty payments for the performance of such works and the proportionate division of fees paid among copyright owners, and may designate common agents to negotiate, agree to, pay, or receive such royalty payments.

(2) Chapter 8 Proceeding.—Parties not subject to such a negotiation may have the terms and rates and the division of fees described in paragraph (1) determined in a proceeding in accordance with the provisions of chapter 8.

(c) License Agreements Superior to Determinations by Copyright Royalty Judges.—License agreements between one or more copyright owners and one or more operators of coin-operated phonorecord players, which are negotiated in accordance with subsection (b), shall be given effect in lieu of any otherwise applicable determination by the Copyright Royalty Judges.

(d) Definitions.—As used in this section, the following terms mean the following:

(1) A "coin-operated phonorecord player" is a machine or device that—

(A) is employed solely for the performance of nondramatic musical works by means of phonorecords upon being activated by the insertion of coins, currency, tokens, or other monetary units or their equivalent;

(B) is located in an establishment making no direct or indirect charge for admission;

(C) is accompanied by a list which is comprised of the titles of all the musical works available for performance on it, and is affixed to the phonorecord player or posted in the establishment in a prominent position where it can be readily examined by the public; and

(D) affords a choice of works available for performance and permits the choice to be made by the patrons of the establishment in which it is located.

(2) An "operator" is any person who, alone or jointly with others—

(A) owns a coin-operated phonorecord player;

(B) has the power to make a coin-operated phonorecord player available for placement in an establishment for purposes of public performance; or

(C) has the power to exercise primary control over the selection of the musical works made available for public performance on a coin-operated phonorecord player.

Sec. 117. Limitations on Exclusive Rights: Computer Programs

(a) Making of Additional Copy or Adaptation by Owner of Copy.—Notwithstanding the provisions of section 106, it is not an infringement for the owner of a copy of a computer program to make or authorize the making of another copy or adaptation of that computer program provided:

(1) that such a new copy or adaptation is created as an essential step in the utilization of the computer program in conjunction with a machine and that it is used in no other manner, or

(2) that such new copy or adaptation is for archival purposes only and that all archival copies are destroyed in the event that continued possession of the computer program should cease to be rightful.

(b) Leases, Sale, or Other Transfer of Additional Copy or Adaptation.—Any exact copies prepared in accordance with the provisions of this section may be leased, sold, or otherwise transferred, along with the copy from which such copies were prepared, only as part of the lease, sale, or other transfer of all rights in the program. Adaptations so prepared may be transferred only with the authorization of the copyright owner.

(c) Machine Maintenance or Repair.—Notwithstanding the provisions of section 106, it is not an infringement for the owner or lessee of a machine to make or authorize the making of a copy of a computer program if such copy is made solely by virtue of the activation of a machine that lawfully contains an authorized copy of the computer program, for purposes only of maintenance or repair of that machine, if—

(1) such new copy is used in no other manner and is destroyed immediately after the maintenance or repair is completed; and

(2) with respect to any computer program or part thereof that is not necessary for that machine to be activated, such program or part thereof is not accessed or used other than to make such new copy by virtue of the activation of the machine.

(d) Definitions.—For purposes of this section—

(1) the "maintenance" of a machine is the servicing of the machine in order to make it work in accordance with its original specifications and any changes to those specifications authorized for that machine; and

(2) the "repair" of a machine is the restoring of the machine to the state of working in accordance with its original specifications and any changes to those specifications authorized for that machine.

Sec. 118.   Scope of Exclusive Rights: Use of Certain Works in Connection With Noncommercial Broadcasting

(a) The exclusive rights provided by section 106 shall, with respect to the works specified by subsection (b) and the activities specified by subsection (d), be subject to the conditions and limitations prescribed by this section.

(b) Notwithstanding any provision of the antitrust laws, any owners of copyright in published nondramatic musical works and published pictorial, graphic, and sculptural works and any public broadcasting entities, respectively, may negotiate and agree upon the terms and rates of royalty payments and the proportionate division of fees paid among various copyright owners, and may designate common agents to negotiate, agree to, pay, or receive payments.

(1) Any owner of copyright in a work specified in this subsection or any public broadcasting entity may submit to the Copyright Royalty Judges proposed licenses covering such activities with respect to such works.

(2) License agreements voluntarily negotiated at any time between one or more copyright owners and one or more public broadcasting entities shall be given effect in lieu of any determination by the Librarian of Congress or the Copyright Royalty Judges, if copies of such agreements are filed with the Copyright Royalty Judges within 30 days of execution in accordance with regulations that the Copyright Royalty Judges shall issue.

(3) Voluntary negotiation proceedings initiated pursuant to a petition filed under section 804(a) for the purpose of determining a schedule of terms and rates of royalty payments by public broadcasting entities to owners of copyright in works specified by this subsection and the proportionate division of fees paid among various copyright owners shall cover the 5-year period beginning on January 1 of the second year following the year in which the petition is filed. The parties to each negotiation proceeding shall bear their own costs. In establishing such rates and terms the Copyright Royalty Judges may consider the rates for comparable circumstances under voluntary license agreements negotiated as provided in paragraph (2) or (3). The Copyright Royalty Judges shall also establish requirements by which copyright owners may receive reasonable notice of the use of their works under this section, and under which records of such use shall be kept by public broadcasting entities.

(4) In the absence of license agreements negotiated under paragraph (2) or (3), the Copyright Royalty Judges shall, pursuant to chapter 8, conduct a proceeding to determine and publish in the Federal Register a schedule of rates and terms which, subject to paragraph (2), shall be binding on all owners of copyright in works specified by this subsection and public broadcasting entities, regardless of whether such copyright owners have submitted proposals to the Copyright Royalty Judges.

(c) Subject to the terms of any voluntary license agreements that have been negotiated as provided by subsection (b)(2) or (3), a public broadcasting entity may, upon compliance with the provisions of this section, including the rates and terms established by the Copyright Royalty Judges under subsection (b)(4), engage in the following activities with respect to published nondramatic musical works and published pictorial, graphic, and sculptural works:

(1) performance or display of a work by or in the course of a transmission made by a noncommercial educational broadcast station referred to in subsection (f); and

(2) production of a transmission program, reproduction of copies or phonorecords of such a transmission program, and distribution of such copies or phonorecords, where such production, reproduction, or distribution is made by a nonprofit institution or organization solely for the purpose of transmissions specified in paragraph (1); and

(3) the making of reproductions by a governmental body or a nonprofit institution of a transmission program simultaneously with its transmission as specified in paragraph (1), and the performance or display of the contents of such program under the conditions specified by paragraph (1) of section 110, but only if the reproductions are used for performances or displays for a period of

no more than seven days from the date of the transmission specified in paragraph (1), and are destroyed before or at the end of such period. No person supplying, in accordance with paragraph (2), a reproduction of a transmission program to governmental bodies or nonprofit institutions under this paragraph shall have any liability as a result of failure of such body or institution to destroy such reproduction: *Provided,* That it shall have notified such body or institution of the requirement for such destruction pursuant to this paragraph: *And provided further,* That if such body or institution itself fails to destroy such reproduction it shall be deemed to have infringed.

(d) Except as expressly provided in this subsection, this section shall have no applicability to works other than those specified in subsection (b). Owners of copyright in nondramatic literary works and public broadcasting entities may, during the course of voluntary negotiations, agree among themselves, respectively, as to the terms and rates of royalty payments without liability under the antitrust laws. Any such terms and rates of royalty payments shall be effective upon filing with the Copyright Royalty Judges, in accordance with regulations that the Copyright Royalty Judges shall prescribe as provided in section 803(b)(6).

(e) Nothing in this section shall be construed to permit, beyond the limits of fair use as provided by section 107, the unauthorized dramatization of a nondramatic musical work, the production of a transmission program drawn to any substantial extent from a published compilation of pictorial, graphic, or sculptural works, or the unauthorized use of any portion of an audiovisual work.

(f) As used in this section, the term "public broadcasting entity" means a noncommercial educational broadcast station as defined in section 397 of title 47 and any nonprofit institution or organization engaged in the activities described in paragraph (2) of subsection (c).

Sec. 119.   Limitations   on   Exclusive   Rights: Secondary Transmissions of Distant Television Programming by Satellite

(a) Secondary Transmissions by Satellite Carriers.—

(1) **Non-network Stations.**—Subject to the provisions of paragraphs (4), (5), and (7) of this subsection and section 114(d), secondary transmissions of a performance or display of a work embodied in a primary transmission made by a non-network station shall be subject to statutory licensing under this section if the secondary transmission is made by a satellite carrier to the public for private home viewing or for viewing in a commercial establishment, with regard to secondary transmissions the satellite carrier is in compliance with the rules, regulations, or authorizations of the Federal Communications Commission governing the carriage of television broadcast station signals, and the carrier makes a direct or indirect charge for each retransmission service to each subscriber

receiving the secondary transmission or to a distributor that has contracted with the carrier for direct or indirect delivery of the secondary transmission to the public for private home viewing or for viewing in a commercial establishment.

(2) Network Stations.—

(A) In General.—Subject to the provisions of subparagraph (B) of this paragraph and paragraphs (4), (5), (6), and (7) of this subsection and section 114(d), secondary transmissions of a performance or display of a work embodied in a primary transmission made by a network station shall be subject to statutory licensing under this section if the secondary transmission is made by a satellite carrier to the public for private home viewing, with regard to secondary transmissions the satellite carrier is in compliance with the rules, regulations, or authorizations of the Federal Communications Commission governing the carriage of television broadcast station signals, and the carrier makes a direct or indirect charge for such retransmission service to each subscriber receiving the secondary transmission.

(B) Secondary Transmissions to Unserved Households.—

(i) In General.—The statutory license provided for in subparagraph (A) shall be limited to secondary transmissions of the signals of no more than two network stations in a single day for each television network to persons who reside in unserved households.

(ii) Accurate Determinations of Eligibility.—

(I) Accurate Predictive Model.—In determining presumptively whether a person resides in an unserved household under subsection (d)(10)(A), a court shall rely on the Individual Location Longley-Rice model set forth by the Federal Communications Commission in Docket No. 98–201, as that model may be amended by the Commission over time under section 339(c)(3) of the Communications Act of 1934 to increase the accuracy of that model.

(II) Accurate Measurements.—For purposes of site measurements to determine whether a person resides in an unserved household under subsection (d)(10)(A), a court shall rely on section 339(c)(4) of the Communications Act of 1934.

(III) Accurate Predictive Model With Respect to Digital Signals.—Notwithstanding subclause (I), in determining presumptively whether a person resides in an unserved household under subsection (d)(10)(A) with respect to digital signals, a court shall rely on a predictive model set forth by the Federal Communications Commission pursuant to a rulemaking as provided in section 339(c)(3) of the Communications Act of 1934 (47 U.S.C. 339(c)(3)), as that model may be amended by the Commission over time under such section to increase the accuracy of that model. Until such time as the Commission sets forth such model, a court shall rely on the predictive model as recommended by the Commission with respect to digital signals in its Report to Congress in ET Docket No. 05–182, FCC 05–199 (released December 9, 2005).

(iii) C-band Exemption to Unserved Households.—

(I) In General.—The limitations of clause (i) shall not apply to any secondary transmissions by C-band services of network stations that a subscriber to C-band service received before any termination of such secondary transmissions before October 31, 1999.

(II) Definition.—In this clause, the term "C-band service" means a service that is licensed by the Federal Communications Commission and operates in the Fixed Satellite Service under part 25 of title 47, Code of Federal Regulations.

(C) Submission of Subscriber Lists to Networks.—

(i) Initial Lists.—A satellite carrier that makes secondary transmissions of a primary transmission made by a network station pursuant to subparagraph (A) shall, not later than 90 days after commencing such secondary transmissions, submit to the network that owns or is affiliated with the network station a list identifying (by name and address, including street or rural route number, city, State, and 9-digit zip code) all subscribers to which the satellite carrier makes secondary transmissions of that primary transmission to subscribers in unserved households.

(ii) Monthly Lists.—After the submission of the initial lists under clause (i), the satellite carrier shall, not later than the 15th of each month, submit to the network a list, aggregated by designated market area, identifying (by name and address, including street or rural route number, city, State, and 9-digit zip code) any persons who have been added or dropped as subscribers under clause (i) since the last submission under this subparagraph.

(iii) **Use of Subscriber Information.**—Subscriber information submitted by a satellite carrier under this subparagraph may be used only for purposes of monitoring compliance by the satellite carrier with this subsection.

(iv) **Applicability.**—The submission requirements of this subparagraph shall apply to a satellite carrier only if the network to which the submissions are to be made places on file with the Register of Copyrights a document identifying the name and address of the person to whom such submissions are to be made. The Register shall maintain for public inspection a file of all such documents.

(3) **Statutory License Where Retransmissions into Local Market Available.**—

(A) **Rules for Subscribers to Signals Under Subsection (e)**—

(i) **For Those Receiving Distant Signals.**—In the case of a subscriber of a satellite carrier who is eligible to receive the secondary transmission of the primary transmission of a network station solely by reason of subsection (e) (in this subparagraph referred to as a "distant signal"), and who, as of October 1, 2004, is receiving the distant signal of that network station, the following shall apply:

(I) In a case in which the satellite carrier makes available to the subscriber the secondary transmission of the primary transmission of a local network station affiliated with the same television network pursuant to the statutory license under section 122, the statutory license under paragraph (2) shall apply only to secondary transmissions by that satellite carrier to that subscriber of the distant signal of a station affiliated with the same television network—

(aa) if, within 60 days after receiving the notice of the satellite carrier under section 338(h)(1) of the Communications Act of 1934, the subscriber elects to retain the distant signal; but

(bb) only until such time as the subscriber elects to receive such local signal.

(II) Notwithstanding subclause (I), the statutory license under paragraph (2) shall not apply with respect to any subscriber who is eligible to receive the distant signal of a television network station solely by reason of subsection (e), unless the satellite carrier, within 60 days after the date of the enactment of the Satellite Home Viewer Extension and Reauthorization

Act of 2004, submits to that television network a list, aggregated by designated market area (as defined in section 122(j)(2)(C)), that—

　　(aa) identifies that subscriber by name and address (street or rural route number, city, State, and zip code) and specifies the distant signals received by the subscriber; and

　　(bb) states, to the best of the satellite carrier's knowledge and belief, after having made diligent and good faith inquiries, that the subscriber is eligible under subsection (e) to receive the distant signals.

(ii) For Those Not Receiving Distant Signals.—In the case of any subscriber of a satellite carrier who is eligible to receive the distant signal of a network station solely by reason of subsection (e) and who did not receive a distant signal of a station affiliated with the same network on October 1, 2004, the statutory license under paragraph (2) shall not apply to secondary transmissions by that satellite carrier to that subscriber of the distant signal of a station affiliated with the same network.

(B) Rules for Lawful Subscribers as of Date of Enactment of 2010 Act.—In the case of a subscriber of a satellite carrier who, on the day before the date of the enactment of the Satellite Television Extension and Localism Act of 2010, was lawfully receiving the secondary transmission of the primary transmission of a network station under the statutory license under paragraph (2) (in this subparagraph referred to as the "distant signal"), other than subscribers to whom subparagraph (A) applies, the statutory license under paragraph (2) shall apply to secondary transmissions by that satellite carrier to that subscriber of the distant signal of a station affiliated with the same television network, and the subscriber's household shall continue to be considered to be an unserved household with respect to such network, until such time as the subscriber elects to terminate such secondary transmissions, whether or not the subscriber elects to subscribe to receive the secondary transmission of the primary transmission of a local network station affiliated with the same network pursuant to the statutory license under section 122.

(C) Future Applicability.—

(i) When Local Signal Available at Time of Subscription.—The statutory license under paragraph (2) shall not apply to the secondary transmission by a satellite carrier of the primary transmission of a network station to a person who is not a subscriber lawfully receiving such secondary transmission as of the date of the enactment of the Satellite Television Extension and Localism Act of 2010 and, at the time such person seeks to subscribe to receive such secondary transmission, resides in a local market where the satellite carrier makes available to that person the secondary transmission of the primary transmission of a local network station affiliated with the same network pursuant to the statutory license under section 122.

(ii) When Local Signal Available After Subscription.—In the case of a subscriber who lawfully subscribes to and receives the secondary transmission by a satellite carrier of the primary transmission of a network station under the statutory license under paragraph (2) (in this clause referred to as the "distant signal") on or after the date of the enactment of the Satellite Television Extension and Localism Act of 2010, the statutory license under paragraph (2) shall apply to secondary transmissions by that satellite carrier to that subscriber of the distant signal of a station affiliated with the same television network, and the subscriber's household shall continue to be considered to be an unserved household with respect to such network, until such time as the subscriber elects to terminate such secondary transmissions, but only if such subscriber subscribes to the secondary transmission of the primary transmission of a local network station affiliated with the same network within 60 days after the satellite carrier makes available to the subscriber such secondary transmission of the primary transmission of such local network station.

(D) Other Provisions Not Affected.—This paragraph shall not affect the applicability of the statutory license to secondary transmissions to unserved households included under paragraph (11).

(E) Waiver.—A subscriber who is denied the secondary transmission of a network station under subparagraph (B) or (C) may request a waiver from such denial by submitting a request, through the subscriber's satellite carrier, to the network station in the local market affiliated with the same network where the subscriber is located. The network station shall accept or reject the subscriber's request for a waiver within 30 days after receipt of the request. If the network station fails to accept or reject the subscriber's request for a waiver within that 30-day period, that network station shall be deemed to agree to the waiver request. Unless specifically stated by the network station, a waiver that was granted before the date of the enactment of the Satellite Home Viewer Extension and Reauthorization Act of 2004 under section 339(c)(2) of the Communications Act of 1934 shall not constitute a waiver for purposes of this subparagraph.

(F) Available Defined.—For purposes of this paragraph, a satellite carrier makes available a secondary transmission of the primary transmission of a local station to a subscriber or person if the satellite carrier offers that secondary transmission to other subscribers who reside in the same 9-digit zip code as that subscriber or person.

(4) Noncompliance With Reporting and Payment Requirements.—Notwithstanding the provisions of paragraphs (1) and (2), the willful or repeated secondary transmission to the public by a satellite carrier of a primary transmission made by a non-network station or a network station and embodying a performance or display of a work is actionable as an act of infringement under section 501, and is fully subject to the remedies provided by sections 502 through 506, where the satellite carrier has not deposited the statement of account and royalty fee required by subsection (b), or has failed to make the submissions to networks required by paragraph (2)(C).

(5) Willful Alterations.—Notwithstanding the provisions of paragraphs (1) and (2), the secondary transmission to the public by a satellite carrier of a performance or display of a work embodied in a primary transmission made by a non-network station or a network station is actionable as an act of infringement under section 501, and is fully subject to the remedies provided by sections 502 through 506 and section 510, if the content of the particular program in which the performance or display is embodied, or any commercial advertising or station announcement transmitted by the primary transmitter during, or immediately before or after, the transmission of such program, is in any way willfully altered by the satellite carrier through changes, deletions, or additions, or is combined with programming from any other broadcast signal.

(6) Violation of Territorial Restrictions on Statutory License for Network Stations.—

(A) Individual Violations.—The willful or repeated secondary transmission by a satellite carrier of a primary transmission made by a network station and embodying a performance or display of a work to a subscriber who is not eligible to receive the transmission under this section is actionable as an act of infringement under section 501 and is fully subject to the remedies provided by sections 502 through 506, except that—

(i) no damages shall be awarded for such act of infringement if the satellite carrier took corrective action by promptly withdrawing service from the ineligible subscriber, and

(ii) any statutory damages shall not exceed $250 for such subscriber for each month during which the violation occurred.

(B) Pattern of Violations.—If a satellite carrier engages in a willful or repeated pattern or practice of delivering a primary transmission made by a network station and embodying a performance or display of a work to subscribers who are not eligible to receive the transmission under this section, then in addition to the remedies set forth in subparagraph (A)—

(i) if the pattern or practice has been carried out on a substantially nationwide basis, the court shall order a permanent injunction barring the secondary transmission by the satellite carrier, for private home viewing, of the primary transmissions of any primary network station affiliated with the same network, and the court may order statutory damages of not to exceed $2,500,000 for each 3-month period during which the pattern or practice was carried out; and

(ii) if the pattern or practice has been carried out on a local or regional basis, the court shall order a permanent injunction barring the secondary transmission, for private home viewing in that locality or region, by the satellite carrier of the primary transmissions of any primary network station affiliated with the same network, and the court may order statutory damages of not to exceed $2,500,000 for each 6-month period during which the pattern or practice was carried out.

(C) Previous Subscribers Excluded.—Subparagraphs (A) and (B) do not apply to secondary transmissions by a satellite carrier to persons who subscribed to receive such secondary transmissions from the satellite carrier or a distributor before November 16, 1988.

(D) Burden of Proof.—In any action brought under this paragraph, the satellite carrier shall have the burden of proving that its secondary transmission of a primary transmission by a network station is to a subscriber who is eligible to receive the secondary transmission under this section.

(E) Exception.—The secondary transmission by a satellite carrier of a performance or display of a work embodied in a primary transmission made by a network station to subscribers who do not reside in unserved households shall not be an act of infringement if—

(i) the station on May 1, 1991, was retransmitted by a satellite carrier and was not on that date owned or operated by or affiliated with a television network that offered interconnected program service on a regular basis for 15 or more hours per week to at least 25 affiliated television licensees in 10 or more States;

(ii) as of July 1, 1998, such station was retransmitted by a satellite carrier under the statutory license of this section; and

(iii) the station is not owned or operated by or affiliated with a television network that, as of January 1, 1995, offered interconnected program service on a regular basis for 15 or more hours per week to at least 25 affiliated television licensees in 10 or more States.

The court shall direct one half of any statutory damages ordered under clause (i) to be deposited with the Register of Copyrights for distribution to copyright owners pursuant to subsection (b). The Copyright Royalty Judges shall issue regulations establishing procedures for distributing such funds, on a proportional basis, to copyright owners whose works were included in the secondary transmissions that were the subject of the statutory damages.

(7) Discrimination by a Satellite Carrier.—Notwithstanding the provisions of paragraph (1), the willful or repeated secondary transmission to the public by a satellite carrier of a performance or display of a work embodied in a primary transmission made by a non-network station or a network station is actionable as an act of infringement under section 501, and is fully subject to the remedies provided by sections 502 through 506, if the satellite carrier unlawfully discriminates against a distributor.

(8) Geographic Limitation on Secondary Transmissions.—The statutory license created by this section shall apply only to secondary transmissions to households located in the United States.

(9) Loser Pays for Signal Intensity Measurement; Recovery of Measurement Costs in a Civil Action.—In any civil action filed relating to the eligibility of subscribing households as unserved households—

(A) a network station challenging such eligibility shall, within 60 days after receipt of the measurement results and a statement of such costs, reimburse the satellite carrier for any signal intensity measurement that is conducted by that carrier in response to a challenge by the network station and that establishes the household is an unserved household; and

(B) a satellite carrier shall, within 60 days after receipt of the measurement results and a statement of such costs, reimburse the network station challenging such eligibility for any signal intensity measurement that is conducted by that station and that establishes the household is not an unserved household.

(10) Inability to Conduct Measurement.—If a network station makes a reasonable attempt to conduct a site measurement of its signal at a subscriber's household and is denied access for the purpose of conducting the measurement, and is otherwise unable to conduct a measurement, the satellite carrier shall within 60 days notice thereof, terminate service of the station's network to that household.

(11) Service to Recreational Vehicles and Commercial Trucks.—

(A) Exemption.—

(i) In General.—For purposes of this subsection, and subject to clauses (ii) and (iii), the term "unserved household" shall include—

(I) recreational vehicles as defined in regulations of the Secretary of Housing and Urban Development under section 3282.8 of title 24, Code of Federal Regulations; and

(II) commercial trucks that qualify as commercial motor vehicles under regulations of the Secretary of Transportation under section 383.5 of title 49, Code of Federal Regulations.

(ii) Limitation.—Clause (i) shall apply only to a recreational vehicle or commercial truck if any satellite carrier that proposes to make a secondary transmission of a network station to the operator of such a recreational vehicle or commercial truck complies with the documentation requirements under subparagraphs (B) and (C).

(iii) Exclusion.—For purposes of this subparagraph, the terms "recreational vehicle" and "commercial truck" shall not include any fixed dwelling, whether a mobile home or otherwise.

(B) Documentation Requirements.—A recreational vehicle or commercial truck shall be deemed to be an unserved household beginning 10 days after the relevant satellite carrier provides to the network that owns or is affiliated with the network station that will be secondarily transmitted to the recreational vehicle or commercial truck the following documents:

(i) Declaration.—A signed declaration by the operator of the recreational vehicle or commercial truck that the satellite dish is permanently attached to the recreational vehicle or commercial truck, and will not be used to receive satellite programming at any fixed dwelling.

(ii) Registration.—In the case of a recreational vehicle, a copy of the current State vehicle registration for the recreational vehicle.

(iii) Registration and License.—In the case of a commercial truck, a copy of—

(I) the current State vehicle registration for the truck; and

(II) a copy of a valid, current commercial driver's license, as defined in regulations of the Secretary of Transportation under section 383 of title 49, Code of Federal Regulations, issued to the operator.

(C) Updated Documentation Requirements.—If a satellite carrier wishes to continue to make secondary transmissions to a recreational vehicle or commercial truck for more than a 2-year period, that carrier shall provide each network, upon request, with updated documentation in the form described under subparagraph (B) during the 90 days before expiration of that 2-year period.

(12) Statutory License Contingent on Compliance With FCC Rules and Remedial Steps.—Notwithstanding any other provision of this section, the willful or repeated secondary transmission to the public by a satellite carrier of a primary transmission embodying a performance or display of a work made by a broadcast station licensed by the Federal Communications Commission is actionable as an act of infringement under section 501, and is fully subject to the remedies provided by sections 502 through 506, if, at the time of such transmission, the satellite carrier is not in compliance with the rules, regulations, and authorizations of the Federal Communications Commission concerning the carriage of television broadcast station signals.

(13) Waivers.—A subscriber who is denied the secondary transmission of a signal of a network station under subsection (a)(2)(B) may request a waiver from such denial by submitting a request, through the subscriber's satellite carrier, to the network station asserting that the secondary transmission is prohibited. The network station shall accept or reject a subscriber's request for a waiver within 30 days after receipt of the request. If a television network station fails to accept or reject a subscriber's request for a waiver within the 30-day period after receipt of the request, that station shall be deemed to agree to the waiver request and have filed such written waiver. Unless specifically stated by the network station, a waiver that was granted before the date of the enactment of the Satellite Home Viewer Extension and Reauthorization Act of 2004 under section 339(c)(2) of the Communications Act of 1934, and that was in effect on such date of enactment, shall constitute a waiver for purposes of this paragraph.

(14) Restricted Transmission of Out-of-State Distant Network Signals into Certain Markets.—

(A) Out-of-State Network Affiliates.—Notwithstanding any other provision of this title, the statutory license in this subsection and subsection (b) shall not apply to any secondary transmission of the primary transmission of a network station located outside of the State of Alaska to any subscriber in that State to whom the secondary transmission of the primary transmission of a television station located in that State is made available by the satellite carrier pursuant to section 122.

(B) Exception.—The limitation in subparagraph (A) shall not apply to the secondary transmission of the primary transmission of a digital signal of a network station located outside of the State of Alaska if at the time that the secondary transmission is made, no television station licensed to a community in the State and affiliated with the same network makes primary transmissions of a digital signal.

(b) Deposit of Statements and Fees; Verification Procedures.—

(1) Deposits With the Register of Copyrights.—A satellite carrier whose secondary transmissions are subject to statutory licensing under subsection (a) shall, on a semiannual basis, deposit with the Register of Copyrights, in accordance with requirements that the Register shall prescribe by regulation—

(A) a statement of account, covering the preceding 6-month period, specifying the names and locations of all non-network stations and network stations whose signals were retransmitted, at any time during that period, to subscribers as described in subsections (a)(1) and (a)(2), the total number of subscribers that received such retransmissions, and such other data as the Register of Copyrights may from time to time prescribe by regulation;

(B) a royalty fee payable to copyright owners pursuant to paragraph (4) for that 6-month period, computed by multiplying the total number of subscribers receiving each secondary transmission of a primary stream or multicast stream of each non-network station or network station during each calendar year month by the appropriate rate in effect under this subsection; and

(C) a filing fee, as determined by the Register of Copyrights pursuant to section 708(a).

(2) Verification of Accounts and Fee Payments.—The Register of Copyrights shall issue regulations to permit interested parties to verify and audit the statements of account and royalty fees submitted by satellite carriers under this subsection.

(3) Investment of Fees.—The Register of Copyrights shall receive all fees (including the filing fee specified in paragraph (1)(C)) deposited under this section and, after deducting the reasonable costs incurred by the Copyright Office under this section (other than the costs deducted under paragraph (5)), shall deposit the balance in the Treasury of the United States, in such manner as the Secretary of the Treasury directs. All funds held by the Secretary of the Treasury shall be invested in interest-bearing securities of the United States for later distribution with interest by the Librarian of Congress as provided by this title.

(4) Persons to Whom Fees Are Distributed.—The royalty fees deposited under paragraph (3) shall, in accordance with the procedures provided by paragraph (5), be distributed to those copyright owners whose works were included in a secondary transmission made by a satellite carrier during the applicable 6-month accounting period and who file a claim with the Copyright Royalty Judges under paragraph (5).

(5) Procedures for Distribution.—The royalty fees deposited under paragraph (3) shall be distributed in accordance with the following procedures:

(A) Filing of Claims for Fees.—During the month of July in each year, each person claiming to be entitled to statutory license fees for secondary transmissions shall file a claim with the Copyright Royalty Judges, in accordance with requirements that the Copyright Royalty Judges shall prescribe by regulation. For purposes of this paragraph, any claimants may agree among themselves as to the proportionate division of statutory license fees among them, may lump their claims together and file them jointly or as a single claim, or may designate a common agent to receive payment on their behalf.

(B) Determination of Controversy; Distributions.—After the first day of August of each year, the Copyright Royalty Judges shall determine whether there exists a controversy concerning the distribution of royalty fees. If the Copyright Royalty Judges determine that no such controversy exists, the Copyright Royalty Judges shall authorize the Librarian of

Congress to proceed to distribute such fees to the copyright owners entitled to receive them, or to their designated agents, subject to the deduction of reasonable administrative costs under this section. If the Copyright Royalty Judges find the existence of a controversy, the Copyright Royalty Judges shall, pursuant to chapter 8 of this title, conduct a proceeding to determine the distribution of royalty fees.

(C) Withholding of Fees During Controversy.—During the pendency of any proceeding under this subsection, the Copyright Royalty Judges shall have the discretion to authorize the Librarian of Congress to proceed to distribute any amounts that are not in controversy.

(c) Adjustment of Royalty Fees.—

(1) Applicability and Determination of Royalty Fees for Signals.—

(A) Initial Fee.—The appropriate fee for purposes of determining the royalty fee under subsection (b)(1)(B) for the secondary transmission of the primary transmissions of network stations and non-network stations shall be the appropriate fee set forth in part 258 of title 37, Code of Federal Regulations, as in effect on July 1, 2009, as modified under this paragraph.

(B) Fee Set by Voluntary Negotiation.—On or before June 1, 2010, the Copyright Royalty Judges shall cause to be published in the Federal Register of the initiation of voluntary negotiation proceedings for the purpose of determining the royalty fee to be paid by satellite carriers for the secondary transmission of the primary transmissions of network stations and non-network stations under subsection (b)(1)(B).

(C) Negotiations.—Satellite carriers, distributors, and copyright owners entitled to royalty fees under this section shall negotiate in good faith in an effort to reach a voluntary agreement or agreements for the payment of royalty fees. Any such satellite carriers, distributors and copyright owners may at any time negotiate and agree to the royalty fee, and may designate common agents to negotiate, agree to, or pay such fees. If the parties fail to identify common agents, the Copyright Royalty Judges shall do so, after requesting recommendations from the parties to the negotiation proceeding. The parties to each negotiation proceeding shall bear the cost thereof.

(D) Agreements Binding on Parties; Filing of Agreements; Public Notice.—

(i) Voluntary Agreements; Filing.—Voluntary agreements negotiated at any time in accordance with this paragraph shall be binding upon all satellite carriers, distributors, and copyright owners that are parties thereto. Copies of such agreements shall be filed with the Copyright Office within 30 days after execution in accordance with regulations that the Register of Copyrights shall prescribe.

(ii) Procedure for Adoption of Fees.—

(I) Publication of Notice.—Within 10 days after publication in the Federal Register of a notice of the initiation of voluntary negotiation proceedings, parties who have reached a voluntary agreement may request that the royalty fees in that agreement be applied to all satellite carriers, distributors, and copyright owners without convening a proceeding under subparagraph (F).

(II) Public Notice of Fees.—Upon receiving a request under subclause (I), the Copyright Royalty Judges shall immediately provide public notice of the royalty fees from the voluntary agreement and afford parties an opportunity to state that they object to those fees.

(III)   Adoption of Fees.—The Copyright Royalty Judges shall adopt the royalty fees from the voluntary agreement for all satellite carriers, distributors, and copyright owners without convening the proceeding under subparagraph (F) unless a party with an intent to participate in that proceeding and a significant interest in the outcome of that proceeding objects under subclause (II).

(E) Period Agreement Is in Effect.—The obligation to pay the royalty fees established under a voluntary agreement which has been filed with the Copyright Royalty Judges in accordance with this paragraph shall become effective on the date specified in the agreement, and shall remain in effect until December 31, 2019, or in accordance with the terms of the agreement, whichever is later.

(F) Fee Set by Copyright Royalty Judges Proceeding.—

(i)   Notice of Initiation of the Proceeding.—On or before September 1, 2010, the Copyright Royalty Judges shall cause notice to be published in the Federal Register of the initiation of a proceeding for the purpose of determining the royalty fees to be paid for the secondary transmission of the primary transmissions of network stations and non-network stations under subsection (b)(1)(B) by satellite carriers and distributors—

(I) in the absence of a voluntary agreement filed in accordance with subparagraph (D) that establishes royalty fees to be paid by all satellite carriers and distributors; or

(II) if an objection to the fees from a voluntary agreement submitted for adoption by the Copyright Royalty Judges to apply to all satellite carriers, distributors, and copyright owners is received under subparagraph (D) from a party with an intent to participate in the proceeding and a significant interest in the outcome of that proceeding.

Such proceeding shall be conducted under chapter 8.

(ii) Establishment of Royalty Fees.—In determining royalty fees under this subparagraph, the Copyright Royalty Judges shall establish fees for the secondary transmissions of the primary transmissions of network stations and non-network stations that most clearly represent the fair market value of secondary transmissions, except that the Copyright Royalty Judges shall adjust royalty fees to account for the obligations of the parties under any applicable voluntary agreement filed with the Copyright Royalty Judges in accordance with subparagraph (D). In determining the fair market value, the Judges shall base their decision on economic, competitive, and programming information presented by the parties, including—

(I) the competitive environment in which such programming is distributed, the cost of similar signals in similar private and compulsory license marketplaces, and any special features and conditions of the retransmission marketplace;

(II) the economic impact of such fees on copyright owners and satellite carriers; and

(III) the impact on the continued availability of secondary transmissions to the public.

(iii) Effective Date for Decision of Copyright Royalty Judges.—The obligation to pay the royalty fees established under a determination that is made by the Copyright Royalty Judges in a proceeding under this paragraph shall be effective as of January 1, 2010.

(iv) Persons Subject to Royalty Fees.—The royalty fees referred to in clause (iii) shall be binding on all satellite carriers, distributors and copyright owners, who are not party to a voluntary agreement filed with the Copyright Office under subparagraph (D).

(2) Annual Royalty Fee Adjustment.—Effective January 1 of each year, the royalty fee payable under subsection (b)(1)(B) for the secondary transmission of the primary transmissions of network stations and non-network stations shall be adjusted by the Copyright Royalty Judges to reflect any changes occurring in the cost of living as determined by the most recent Consumer Price Index (for all consumers and for all items) published by the Secretary of Labor before December 1 of the preceding year. Notification of the adjusted fees shall be published in the Federal Register at least 25 days before January 1.

(d) Definitions.—As used in this section—

(1) Distributor.—The term "distributor" means an entity that contracts to distribute secondary transmissions from a satellite carrier and, either as a single channel or in a package with other programming, provides the secondary transmission either directly to individual subscribers or indirectly through other program distribution entities in accordance with the provisions of this section.

(2) Network Station.—The term "network station" means—

(A) a television station licensed by the Federal Communications Commission, including any translator station or terrestrial satellite station that rebroadcasts all or substantially all of the programming broadcast by a network station, that is owned or operated by, or affiliated with, one or more of the television networks in the United States that offer an interconnected program service on a regular basis for 15 or more hours per week to at least 25 of its affiliated television licensees in 10 or more States; or

(B) a noncommercial educational broadcast station (as defined in section 397 of the Communications Act of 1934);

except that the term does not include the signal of the Alaska Rural Communications Service, or any successor entity to that service.

(3) Primary Setwork station.—The term "primary network station" means a network station that broadcasts or rebroadcasts the basic programming service of a particular national network.

(4) Primary Transmission.—The term "primary transmission" has the meaning given that term in section 111(f) of this title.

(5) Private Home Viewing.—The term "private home viewing" means the viewing, for private use in a household by means of satellite reception equipment that is operated by an individual in that household and that serves only such household, of a secondary transmission delivered by a satellite carrier of a primary transmission of a television station licensed by the Federal Communications Commission.

(6) Satellite Carrier.—The term "satellite carrier" means an entity that uses the facilities of a satellite or satellite service licensed by the Federal Communications Commission and operates in the Fixed-Satellite Service under part 25 of title 47, Code of Federal Regulations, or the Direct Broadcast Satellite Service under part 100 of title 47, Code of Federal Regulations, to establish and operate a channel of communications for point-to-multipoint distribution of television station signals, and that owns or leases a capacity or service on a satellite in order to provide such point-to-multipoint distribution, except to the extent that such entity provides such distribution pursuant to tariff under the Communications Act of 1934, other than for private home viewing pursuant to this section.

(7) Secondary Transmission.—The term "secondary transmission" has the meaning given that term in section 111(f) of this title.

(8) Subscriber; Subscribe.—

(A) Subscriber.—The term "subscriber" means a person or entity that receives a secondary transmission service from a satellite carrier and pays a fee for the service, directly or indirectly, to the satellite carrier or to a distributor.

(B) Subscribe.—The term "subscribe" means to elect to become a subscriber.

(9) Non-network Station.—The term "non-network station" means a television station, other than a network station, licensed by the Federal Communications Commission, that is secondarily transmitted by a satellite carrier.

(10) Unserved Household.—The term "unserved household", with respect to a particular television network, means a household that—

(A) cannot receive, through the use of an antenna, an over-the-air signal containing the primary stream, or, on or after the qualifying date, the multicast stream, originating in that household's local market and affiliated with that network of—

(i) if the signal originates as an analog signal, Grade B intensity as defined by the Federal Communications Commission in section 73.683(a) of title 47, Code of Federal Regulations, as in effect on January 1, 1999; or

(ii) if the signal originates as a digital signal, intensity defined in the values for the digital television noise-limited service contour, as defined in regulations issued by the Federal Communications Commission (section 73.622(e) of title 47, Code of Federal Regulations), as such regulations may be amended from time to time;

(B) is subject to a waiver that meets the standards of subsection (a) (13), whether or not the waiver was granted before the date of the enactment of the Satellite Television Extension and Localism Act of 2010;

(C) is a subscriber to whom subsection (e) applies;

(D) is a subscriber to whom subsection (a)(11) applies; or

(E) is a subscriber to whom the exemption under subsection (a)(2)(B)(iii) applies.

(11) Local Market.—The term "local market" has the meaning given such term under section 122(j).

(12) Commercial Establishment.—The term "commercial establishment"—

(A) means an establishment used for commercial purposes, such as a bar, restaurant, private office, fitness club, oil rig, retail store, bank or other financial institution, supermarket, automobile or boat dealership, or any other establishment with a common business area; and

(B) does not include a multi-unit permanent or temporary dwelling where private home viewing occurs, such as a hotel, dormitory, hospital, apartment, condominium, or prison.

(13) Qualifying Date.—The term "qualifying date", for purposes of paragraph (10)(A), means—

(A) October 1, 2010, for multicast streams that exist on March 31, 2010; and

(B) January 1, 2011, for all other multicast streams.

(14) Multicast Stream.—The term "multicast stream" means a digital stream containing programming and program-related material affiliated with a television network, other than the primary stream.

(15) Primary Stream.—The term "primary stream" means—

(A) the single digital stream of programming as to which a television broadcast station has the right to mandatory carriage with a satellite carrier under the rules of the Federal Communications Commission in effect on July 1, 2009; or

(B) if there is no stream described in subparagraph (A), then either—

(i) the single digital stream of programming associated with the network last transmitted by the station as an analog signal; or

(ii) if there is no stream described in clause (i), then the single digital stream of programming affiliated with the network that, as of July 1, 2009, had been offered by the television broadcast station for the longest period of time.

(e) Moratorium on Copyright Liability.—Until December 31, 2019, a subscriber who does not receive a signal of Grade A intensity (as defined in the regulations of the Federal Communications Commission under section 73.683(a) of title 47, Code of Federal Regulations, as in effect on January 1, 1999, or predicted by the Federal Communications Commission using the Individual Location Longley-Rice methodology described by the Federal Communications Commission in Docket No. 98–201) of a local network television broadcast station shall remain eligible to receive signals of network stations affiliated with the same network, if that subscriber had satellite service of such network signal terminated after July 11, 1998, and before October 31, 1999, as required by this section, or received such service on October 31, 1999.

(f) Expedited Consideration by Justice Department of Voluntary Agreements to Provide Satellite Secondary Transmissions to Local Markets.—

    (1) In General.—In a case in which no satellite carrier makes available, to subscribers located in a local market, as defined in section 122(j)(2), the secondary transmission into that market of a primary transmission of one or more television broadcast stations licensed by the Federal Communications Commission, and two or more satellite carriers request a business review letter in accordance with section 50.6 of title 28, Code of Federal Regulations (as in effect on July 7, 2004), in order to assess the legality under the antitrust laws of proposed business conduct to make or carry out an agreement to provide such secondary transmission into such local market, the appropriate official of the Department of Justice shall respond to the request no later than 90 days after the date on which the request is received.

    (2) Definition.—For purposes of this subsection, the term "antitrust laws"—

        (A) has the meaning given that term in subsection (a) of the first section of the Clayton Act (15 U.S.C. 12(a)), except that such term includes section 5 of the Federal Trade Commission Act (15 U.S.C. 45) to the extent such section 5 applies to unfair methods of competition; and

        (B) includes any State law similar to the laws referred to in paragraph (1).

(g) Certain Waivers Granted to Providers of Local-into-Local Service to All DMAs.—

    (1) Injunction Waiver.—A court that issued an injunction pursuant to subsection (a)(7)(B) before the date of the enactment of this subsection shall waive such injunction if the court recognizes the entity against which the injunction was issued as a qualified carrier.

(2) Limited Temporary Waiver.—

(A) In General.—Upon a request made by a satellite carrier, a court that issued an injunction against such carrier under subsection (a)(7)(B) before the date of the enactment of this subsection shall waive such injunction with respect to the statutory license provided under subsection (a)(2) to the extent necessary to allow such carrier to make secondary transmissions of primary transmissions made by a network station to unserved households located in short markets in which such carrier was not providing local service pursuant to the license under section 122 as of December 31, 2009.

(B) Expiration of Temporary Waiver.—A temporary waiver of an injunction under subparagraph (A) shall expire after the end of the 120-day period beginning on the date such temporary waiver is issued unless extended for good cause by the court making the temporary waiver.

(C) Failure to Provide Local-into-Local Service to All DMAs.—

(i) Failure to Act Reasonably and in Good Faith.—If the court issuing a temporary waiver under subparagraph (A) determines that the satellite carrier that made the request for such waiver has failed to act reasonably or has failed to make a good faith effort to provide local-into-local service to all DMAs, such failure—

(I)   is actionable as an act of infringement under section 501 and the court may in its discretion impose the remedies provided for in sections 502 through 506 and subsection (a)(6)(B) of this section; and

(II) shall result in the termination of the waiver issued under subparagraph (A).

(ii) Failure to Provide Local-into-local Service.—If the court issuing a temporary waiver under subparagraph (A) determines that the satellite carrier that made the request for such waiver has failed to provide local-into-local service to all DMAs, but determines that the carrier acted reasonably and in good faith, the court may in its discretion impose financial penalties that reflect—

(I)   the degree of control the carrier had over the circumstances that resulted in the failure;

(II) the quality of the carrier's efforts to remedy the failure; and

(III) the severity and duration of any service interruption.

(D) Single Temporary Waiver Available.—An entity may only receive one temporary waiver under this paragraph.

(E) Short Market Defined.—For purposes of this paragraph, the term "short market" means a local market in which programming of one or more of the four most widely viewed television networks nationwide as measured on the date of the enactment of this subsection is not offered on the primary stream transmitted by any local television broadcast station.

(3) Establishment of Qualified Carrier Recognition.—

(A) Statement of Eligibility.—An entity seeking to be recognized as a qualified carrier under this subsection shall file a statement of eligibility with the court that imposed the injunction. A statement of eligibility must include—

(i)   an affidavit that the entity is providing local-into-local service to all DMAs;

(ii)   a motion for a waiver of the injunction;

(iii) a motion that the court appoint a special master under Rule 53 of the Federal Rules of Civil Procedure;

(iv) an agreement by the carrier to pay all expenses incurred by the special master under paragraph (4)(B)(ii); and

(v)   a certification issued pursuant to section 342(a) of Communications Act of 1934.

(B) Grant of Recognition as a Qualified Carrier.—Upon receipt of a statement of eligibility, the court shall recognize the entity as a qualified carrier and issue the waiver under paragraph (1). Upon motion pursuant to subparagraph (A)(iii), the court shall appoint a special master to conduct the examination and provide a report to the court as provided in paragraph (4)(B).

(C) Voluntary Termination.—At any time, an entity recognized as a qualified carrier may file a statement of voluntary termination with the court certifying that it no longer wishes to be recognized as a qualified carrier. Upon receipt of such statement, the court shall reinstate the injunction waived under paragraph (1).

(D) Loss of Recognition Prevents Future Recognition.—No entity may be recognized as a qualified carrier if such entity had previously been recognized as a qualified carrier and subsequently lost such recognition or voluntarily terminated such recognition under subparagraph (C).

(4) Qualified Carrier Obligations and Compliance.—

(A) Continuing Obligations.—

(i) In General.—An entity recognized as a qualified carrier shall continue to provide local-into-local service to all DMAs.

(ii) Cooperation With Compliance Examination.—An entity recognized as a qualified carrier shall fully cooperate with the special master appointed by the court under paragraph (3)(B) in an examination set forth in subparagraph (B).

(B) Qualified Carrier Compliance Examination.—

(i) Examination and Report.—A special master appointed by the court under paragraph (3)(B) shall conduct an examination of, and file a report on, the qualified carrier's compliance with the royalty payment and household eligibility requirements of the license under this section. The report shall address the qualified carrier's conduct during the period beginning on the date on which the qualified carrier is recognized as such under paragraph (3)(B) and ending on April 30, 2012.

(ii) Records of Qualified Carrier.—Beginning on the date that is one year after the date on which the qualified carrier is recognized as such under paragraph (3)(B), but not later than December 1, 2011, the qualified carrier shall provide the special master with all records that the special master considers to be directly pertinent to the following requirements under this section:

(I) Proper calculation and payment of royalties under the statutory license under this section.

(II) Provision of service under this license to eligible subscribers only.

(iii) Submission of Report.—The special master shall file the report required by clause (i) not later than July 24, 2012, with the court referred to in paragraph (1) that issued the injunction, and the court shall transmit a copy of the report to the Register of Copyrights, the Committees on the Judiciary and on Energy and Commerce of the House of Representatives, and the Committees on the Judiciary and on Commerce, Science, and Transportation of the Senate.

(iv) Evidence of Infringement.—The special master shall include in the report a statement of whether the examination by the special master indicated that there is substantial evidence that a copyright holder could bring a successful action under this section against the qualified carrier for infringement.

(v) **Subsequent Examination.**—If the special master's report includes a statement that its examination indicated the existence of substantial evidence that a copyright holder could bring a successful action under this section against the qualified carrier for infringement, the special master shall, not later than 6 months after the report under clause (i) is filed, initiate another examination of the qualified carrier's compliance with the royalty payment and household eligibility requirements of the license under this section since the last report was filed under clause (iii). The special master shall file a report on the results of the examination conducted under this clause with the court referred to in paragraph (1) that issued the injunction, and the court shall transmit a copy to the Register of Copyrights, the Committees on the Judiciary and on Energy and Commerce of the House of Representatives, and the Committees on the Judiciary and on Commerce, Science, and Transportation of the Senate. The report shall include a statement described in clause (iv).

(vi) **Compliance.**—Upon motion filed by an aggrieved copyright owner, the court recognizing an entity as a qualified carrier shall terminate such designation upon finding that the entity has failed to cooperate with an examination required by this subparagraph.

(vii) **Oversight.**—During the period of time that the special master is conducting an examination under this subparagraph, the Comptroller General shall monitor the degree to which the entity seeking to be recognized or recognized as a qualified carrier under paragraph (3) is complying with the special master's examination. The qualified carrier shall make available to the Comptroller General all records and individuals that the Comptroller General considers necessary to meet the Comptroller General's obligations under this clause. The Comptroller General shall report the results of the monitoring required by this clause to the Committees on the Judiciary and on Energy and Commerce of the House of Representatives and the Committees on the Judiciary and on Commerce, Science, and Transportation of the Senate at intervals of not less than six months during such period.

(C) **Affirmation.**—A qualified carrier shall file an affidavit with the district court and the Register of Copyrights

30 months after such status was granted stating that, to the best of the affiant's knowledge, it is in compliance with the requirements for a qualified carrier. The qualified carrier shall attach to its affidavit copies of all reports or orders issued by the court, the special master, and the Comptroller General.

(D) Compliance Determination.—Upon the motion of an aggrieved television broadcast station, the court recognizing an entity as a qualified carrier may make a determination of whether the entity is providing local-into-local service to all DMAs.

(E) Pleading Requirement.—In any motion brought under subparagraph (D), the party making such motion shall specify one or more designated market areas (as such term is defined in section 122(j)(2)(C)) for which the failure to provide service is being alleged, and, for each such designated market area, shall plead with particularity the circumstances of the alleged failure.

(F) Burden of Proof.—In any proceeding to make a determination under subparagraph (D), and with respect to a designated market area for which failure to provide service is alleged, the entity recognized as a qualified carrier shall have the burden of proving that the entity provided local-into-local service with a good quality satellite signal to at least 90 percent of the households in such designated market area (based on the most recent census data released by the United States Census Bureau) at the time and place alleged.

(5) Failure to Provide Service.—

(A) Penalties.—If the court recognizing an entity as a qualified carrier finds that such entity has willfully failed to provide local-into-local service to all DMAs, such finding shall result in the loss of recognition of the entity as a qualified carrier and the termination of the waiver provided under paragraph (1), and the court may, in its discretion—

(i)   treat such failure as an act of infringement under section 501, and subject such infringement to the remedies provided for in sections 502 through 506 and subsection (a)(6)(B) of this section; and

(ii) impose a fine of not less than $250,000 and not more than $5,000,000.

(B) Exception for Nonwillful Violation.—If the court determines that the failure to provide local-into-local service to all DMAs is nonwillful, the court may in its discretion impose financial penalties for noncompliance that reflect—

(i) the degree of control the entity had over the circumstances that resulted in the failure;

(ii) the quality of the entity's efforts to remedy the failure and restore service; and

(iii) the severity and duration of any service interruption.

(6) Penalties for Violations of License.—A court that finds, under subsection (a)(6)(A), that an entity recognized as a qualified carrier has willfully made a secondary transmission of a primary transmission made by a network station and embodying a performance or display of a work to a subscriber who is not eligible to receive the transmission under this section shall reinstate the injunction waived under paragraph (1), and the court may order statutory damages of not more than $2,500,000.

(7) Local-into-Local Service to All DMAs Defined.—For purposes of this subsection:

(A) In General.—An entity provides "local-into-local service to all DMAs" if the entity provides local service in all designated market areas (as such term is defined in section 122(j)(2)(C)) pursuant to the license under section 122.

(B) Household Coverage.—For purposes of subparagraph (A), an entity that makes available local-into-local service with a good quality satellite signal to at least 90 percent of the households in a designated market area based on the most recent census data released by the United States Census Bureau shall be considered to be providing local service to such designated market area.

(C) Good Quality Satellite Signal Defined.—The term "good quality satellite signal" has the meaning given such term under section 342(e)(2) of Communications Act of 1934.

(h) Termination of License.—This section shall cease to be effective on December 31, 2019.

Sec. 120.   Scope of Exclusive Rights in Architectural Works

(a) Pictorial Representations Permitted.—The copyright in an architectural work that has been constructed does not include the right to prevent the making, distributing, or public display of pictures, paintings, photographs, or other pictorial representations of the work, if the building in which the work is embodied is located in or ordinarily visible from a public place.

(b) Alterations to and Destruction of Buildings.—Notwithstanding the provisions of section 106(2), the owners of a building embodying an architectural work may, without the consent of the author or copyright owner of the architectural work, make or authorize the making of alterations to such building, and destroy or authorize the destruction of such building.

Sec. 121.   Limitations on Exclusive Rights: Reproduction for Blind or Other People with Disabilities

(a) Notwithstanding the provisions of section 106, it is not an infringement of copyright for an authorized entity to reproduce or to distribute copies or phonorecords of a previously published, nondramatic literary work if such copies or phonorecords are reproduced or distributed in specialized formats exclusively for use by blind or other persons with disabilities.

(b)(1) Copies or phonorecords to which this section applies shall—

(A) not be reproduced or distributed in a format other than a specialized format exclusively for use by blind or other persons with disabilities;

(B) bear a notice that any further reproduction or distribution in a format other than a specialized format is an infringement; and

(C) include a copyright notice identifying the copyright owner and the date of the original publication.

(2) The provisions of this subsection shall not apply to standardized, secure, or norm-referenced tests and related testing material, or to computer programs, except the portions thereof that are in conventional human language (including descriptions of pictorial works) and displayed to users in the ordinary course of using the computer programs.

(c) Notwithstanding the provisions of section 106, it is not an infringement of copyright for a publisher of print instructional materials for use in elementary or secondary schools to create and distribute to the National Instructional Materials Access Center copies of the electronic files described in sections 612(a)(23)(C), 613(a)(6), and section 674(e) of the Individuals with Disabilities Education Act that contain the contents of print instructional materials using the National Instructional Material Accessibility Standard (as defined in section 674(e)(3) of that Act), if—

(1) the inclusion of the contents of such print instructional materials is required by any State educational agency or local educational agency;

(2) the publisher had the right to publish such print instructional materials in print formats; and

(3) such copies are used solely for reproduction or distribution of the contents of such print instructional materials in specialized formats.

(d) For purposes of this section, the term—

(1) "authorized entity" means a nonprofit organization or a governmental agency that has a primary mission to provide specialized services relating to training, education, or adaptive

reading or information access needs of blind or other persons with disabilities;

(2) "blind or other persons with disabilities" means individuals who are eligible or who may qualify in accordance with the Act entitled "An Act to provide books for the adult blind", approved March 3, 1931 (2 U.S.C. 135a; 46 Stat. 1487) to receive books and other publications produced in specialized formats;

(3) "print instructional materials" has the meaning given under section 674(e)(3)(C) of the Individuals with Disabilities Education Act; and

(4) "specialized formats" means—

(A) braille, audio, or digital text which is exclusively for use by blind or other persons with disabilities; and

(B) with respect to print instructional materials, includes large print formats when such materials are distributed exclusively for use by blind or other persons with disabilities.

Sec. 122. Limitations on Exclusive Rights: Secondary Transmissions of Local Television Programming by Satellite

(a) Secondary Transmissions into Local Markets.—

(1) Secondary Transmissions of Television Broadcast Stations Within a Local Market.—A secondary transmission of a performance or display of a work embodied in a primary transmission of a television broadcast station into the station's local market shall be subject to statutory licensing under this section if—

(A) the secondary transmission is made by a satellite carrier to the public;

(B) with regard to secondary transmissions, the satellite carrier is in compliance with the rules, regulations, or authorizations of the Federal Communications Commission governing the carriage of television broadcast station signals; and

(C) the satellite carrier makes a direct or indirect charge for the secondary transmission to—

(i) each subscriber receiving the secondary transmission; or

(ii) a distributor that has contracted with the satellite carrier for direct or indirect delivery of the secondary transmission to the public.

(2) Significantly Viewed Stations.—

(A) In General.—A secondary transmission of a performance or display of a work embodied in a primary transmission of a television broadcast station to subscribers who receive secondary transmissions of primary transmissions under paragraph (1) shall be subject to statutory licensing under this paragraph if the secondary transmission is of the primary transmission of a network station or a non-network station to a subscriber who resides outside the station's local market but within a community in which the signal has been determined by the Federal Communications Commission to be significantly viewed in such community, pursuant to the rules, regulations, and authorizations of the Federal Communications Commission in effect on April 15, 1976, applicable to determining with respect to a cable system whether signals are significantly viewed in a community.

(B) Waiver.—A subscriber who is denied the secondary transmission of the primary transmission of a network station or a non-network station under subparagraph (A) may request a waiver from such denial by submitting a request, through the subscriber's satellite carrier, to the network station or non-network station in the local market affiliated with the same network or non-network where the subscriber is located. The network station or non-network station shall accept or reject the subscriber's request for a waiver within 30 days after receipt of the request. If the network station or non-network station fails to accept or reject the subscriber's request for a waiver within that 30-day period, that network station or non-network station shall be deemed to agree to the waiver request.

(3) Secondary   Transmission   of   Low   Power Programming.—

(A) In General.—Subject to subparagraphs (B) and (C), a secondary transmission of a performance or display of a work embodied in a primary transmission of a television broadcast station to subscribers who receive secondary transmissions of primary transmissions under paragraph (1) shall be subject to statutory licensing under this paragraph if the secondary transmission is of the primary transmission of a television broadcast station that is licensed as a low power television station, to a subscriber who resides within the same designated market area as the station that originates the transmission.

(B) No Applicability to Repeaters and Translators.— Secondary transmissions provided for in subparagraph (A) shall not apply to any low power television station that retransmits the programs and signals of another television station for more than 2 hours each day.

(C) No Impact on Other Secondary Transmissions Obligations.—A satellite carrier that makes secondary transmissions of a primary transmission of a low power television station under a statutory license provided under this section is not required, by reason of such secondary transmissions, to make any other secondary transmissions.

(4) Special Exceptions.—A secondary transmission of a performance or display of a work embodied in a primary transmission of a television broadcast station to subscribers who receive secondary transmissions of primary transmissions under paragraph (1) shall, if the secondary transmission is made by a satellite carrier that complies with the requirements of paragraph (1), be subject to statutory licensing under this paragraph as follows:

(A) States With Single Full-power Network Station.—In a State in which there is licensed by the Federal Communications Commission a single full-power station that was a network station on January 1, 1995, the statutory license provided for in this paragraph shall apply to the secondary transmission by a satellite carrier of the primary transmission of that station to any subscriber in a community that is located within that State and that is not within the first 50 television markets as listed in the regulations of the Commission as in effect on such date (47 C.F.R. 76.51).

(B) States With All Network Stations and Non-network Stations in Same Local Market.—In a State in which all network stations and non-network stations licensed by the Federal Communications Commission within that State as of January 1, 1995, are assigned to the same local market and that local market does not encompass all counties of that State, the statutory license provided under this paragraph shall apply to the secondary transmission by a satellite carrier of the primary transmissions of such station to all subscribers in the State who reside in a local market that is within the first 50 major television markets as listed in the regulations of the Commission as in effect on such date (section 76.51 of title 47, Code of Federal Regulations).

(C) Additional Stations.—In the case of that State in which are located 4 counties that—

(i) on January 1, 2004, were in local markets principally comprised of counties in another State, and

(ii) had a combined total of 41,340 television households, according to the U.S. Television Household Estimates by Nielsen Media Research for 2004,

the statutory license provided under this paragraph shall apply to secondary transmissions by a satellite carrier to subscribers in any such county of the primary transmissions of any network station located in that State, if the satellite carrier was making such secondary transmissions to any subscribers in that county on January 1, 2004.

(D) Certain Additional Stations.—If 2 adjacent counties in a single State are in a local market comprised principally of counties located in another State, the statutory license provided for in this paragraph shall apply to the secondary transmission by a satellite carrier to subscribers in those 2 counties of the primary transmissions of any network station located in the capital of the State in which such 2 counties are located, if—

    (i)   the 2 counties are located in a local market that is in the top 100 markets for the year 2003 according to Nielsen Media Research; and

    (ii)   the total number of television households in the 2 counties combined did not exceed 10,000 for the year 2003 according to Nielsen Media Research.

(E) Networks of Noncommercial Educational Broadcast Stations.—In the case of a system of three or more noncommercial educational broadcast stations licensed to a single State, public agency, or political, educational, or special purpose subdivision of a State, the statutory license provided for in this paragraph shall apply to the secondary transmission of the primary transmission of such system to any subscriber in any county or county equivalent within such State, if such subscriber is located in a designated market area that is not otherwise eligible to receive the secondary transmission of the primary transmission of a noncommercial educational broadcast station located within the State pursuant to paragraph (1).

(5) Applicability of Royalty Rates and Procedures.—The royalty rates and procedures under section 119(b) shall apply to the secondary transmissions to which the statutory license under paragraph (4) applies.

(b) Reporting Requirements.—

(1) Initial Lists.—A satellite carrier that makes secondary transmissions of a primary transmission made by a network station under subsection (a) shall, within 90 days after commencing such secondary transmissions, submit to the network that owns or is affiliated with the network station—

    (A)   a list identifying (by name in alphabetical order and street address, including county and 9-digit zip code) all subscribers to which the satellite carrier makes secondary transmissions of that primary transmission under subsection (a); and

    (B)   a separate list, aggregated by designated market area (by name and address, including street or rural route number, city, State, and 9-digit zip code), which shall indicate those subscribers being served pursuant to paragraph (2) of subsection (a).

(2) Subsequent Lists.—After the list is submitted under paragraph (1), the satellite carrier shall, on the 15th of each month, submit to the network—

(A) a list identifying (by name in alphabetical order and street address, including county and 9-digit zip code) any subscribers who have been added or dropped as subscribers since the last submission under this subsection; and

(B) a separate list, aggregated by designated market area (by name and street address, including street or rural route number, city, State, and 9-digit zip code), identifying those subscribers whose service pursuant to paragraph (2) of subsection (a) has been added or dropped since the last submission under this subsection.

(3) Use of Subscriber Information.—Subscriber information submitted by a satellite carrier under this subsection may be used only for the purposes of monitoring compliance by the satellite carrier with this section.

(4) Requirements of Networks.—The submission requirements of this subsection shall apply to a satellite carrier only if the network to which the submissions are to be made places on file with the Register of Copyrights a document identifying the name and address of the person to whom such submissions are to be made. The Register of Copyrights shall maintain for public inspection a file of all such documents.

(c) No Royalty Fee Required for Certain Secondary Transmissions.—A satellite carrier whose secondary transmissions are subject to statutory licensing under paragraphs (1), (2), and (3) of subsection (a) shall have no royalty obligation for such secondary transmissions.

(d) Noncompliance With Reporting and Regulatory Requirements.—Notwithstanding subsection (a), the willful or repeated secondary transmission to the public by a satellite carrier into the local market of a television broadcast station of a primary transmission embodying a performance or display of a work made by that television broadcast station is actionable as an act of infringement under section 501, and is fully subject to the remedies provided under sections 502 through 506, if the satellite carrier has not complied with the reporting requirements of subsection (b) or with the rules, regulations, and authorizations of the Federal Communications Commission concerning the carriage of television broadcast signals.

(e) Willful Alterations.—Notwithstanding subsection (a), the secondary transmission to the public by a satellite carrier into the local market of a television broadcast station of a performance or display of a work embodied in a primary transmission made by that television broadcast station is actionable as an act of infringement under section 501, and is fully subject to the remedies provided by sections 502 through 506 and section 510, if the content of the particular program in which the performance or display is embodied, or any commercial advertising or station announcement transmitted by the primary transmitter during, or immediately before or after, the transmission of such program, is in any way willfully altered by the satellite carrier through changes, deletions, or additions, or is combined with programming from any other broadcast signal.

(f) Violation of Territorial Restrictions on Statutory License for Television Broadcast Stations.—

(1) Individual Violations.—The willful or repeated secondary transmission to the public by a satellite carrier of a primary transmission embodying a performance or display of a work made by a television broadcast station to a subscriber who does not reside in that station's local market, and is not subject to statutory licensing under section 119, subject to statutory licensing by reason of paragraph (2)(A), (3), or (4) of subsection (a), or subject to a private licensing agreement, is actionable as an act of infringement under section 501 and is fully subject to the remedies provided by sections 502 through 506, except that—

(A) no damages shall be awarded for such act of infringement if the satellite carrier took corrective action by promptly withdrawing service from the ineligible subscriber; and

(B) any statutory damages shall not exceed $250 for such subscriber for each month during which the violation occurred.

(2) Pattern of Violations.—If a satellite carrier engages in a willful or repeated pattern or practice of secondarily transmitting to the public a primary transmission embodying a performance or display of a work made by a television broadcast station to subscribers who do not reside in that station's local market, and are not subject to statutory licensing under section 119, subject to statutory licensing by reason of paragraph (2)(A), (3), or (4) of subsection (a), or subject to a private licensing agreement, then in addition to the remedies under paragraph (1)—

(A) if the pattern or practice has been carried out on a substantially nationwide basis, the court—

(i) shall order a permanent injunction barring the secondary transmission by the satellite carrier of the primary transmissions of that television broadcast station (and if such television broadcast station is a network station, all other television broadcast stations affiliated with such network); and

(ii) may order statutory damages not exceeding $2,500,000 for each 6-month period during which the pattern or practice was carried out; and

(B) if the pattern or practice has been carried out on a local or regional basis with respect to more than one television broadcast station, the court—

(i) shall order a permanent injunction barring the secondary transmission in that locality or region by the satellite carrier of the primary transmissions of any television broadcast station; and

(ii) may order statutory damages not exceeding $2,500,000 for each 6-month period during which the pattern or practice was carried out.

(g) Burden of Proof.—In any action brought under subsection (f), the satellite carrier shall have the burden of proving that its secondary transmission of a primary transmission by a television broadcast station is made only to subscribers located within that station's local market or subscribers being served in compliance with section 119, paragraph (2)(A), (3), or (4) of subsection (a), or a private licensing agreement.

(h) Geographic Limitations on Secondary Transmissions.— The statutory license created by this section shall apply to secondary transmissions to locations in the United States.

(i) Exclusivity With Respect to Secondary Transmissions of Broadcast Stations by Satellite to Members of the Public.—No provision of section 111 or any other law (other than this section and section 119) shall be construed to contain any authorization, exemption, or license through which secondary transmissions by satellite carriers of programming contained in a primary transmission made by a television broadcast station may be made without obtaining the consent of the copyright owner.

(j) Definitions.—In this section—

(1) Distributor.—The term "distributor" means an entity that contracts to distribute secondary transmissions from a satellite carrier and, either as a single channel or in a package with other programming, provides the secondary transmission either directly to individual subscribers or indirectly through other program distribution entities.

(2) Local Market.—

(A) In General.—The term "local market", in the case of both commercial and noncommercial television broadcast stations, means the designated market area in which a station is located, and—

(i) in the case of a commercial television broadcast station, all commercial television broadcast stations licensed to a community within the same designated market area are within the same local market; and

(ii) in the case of a noncommercial educational television broadcast station, the market includes any station that is licensed to a community within the same designated market area as the noncommercial educational television broadcast station.

(B) County of License.—In addition to the area described in subparagraph (A), a station's local market includes the county in which the station's community of license is located.

(C) Designated Market Area.—For purposes of subparagraph (A), the term "designated market area" means a designated market area, as determined by Nielsen Media Research and published in the 1999–2000 Nielsen Station Index Directory and Nielsen Station Index United States Television Household Estimates or any successor publication.

(D) Certain Areas Outside of Any Designated Market Area.—Any census area, borough, or other area in the State of Alaska that is outside of a designated market area, as determined by Nielsen Media Research, shall be deemed to be part of one of the local markets in the State of Alaska. A satellite carrier may determine which local market in the State of Alaska will be deemed to be the relevant local market in connection with each subscriber in such census area, borough, or other area.

(E) Market Determination.—The local market of a commercial television broadcast station may be modified by the Federal Communications Commission in accordance with section 338(*l*) of the Communications Act of 1934 (47 U.S.C. 338).

(3) Low Power Television Station.—The term "low power television station" means a low power TV station as defined in section 74.701(f) of title 47, Code of Federal Regulations, as in effect on June 1, 2004. For purposes of this paragraph, the term 'low power television station' includes a low power television station that has been accorded primary status as a Class A television licensee under section 73.6001(a) of title 47, Code of Federal Regulations.

(4) Network Station; Non-network Station; Satellite Carrier; Secondary Transmission.—The terms "network station", "non-network station", "satellite carrier", and "secondary transmission" have the meanings given such terms under section 119(d).

(5) Noncommercial Educational Broadcast Station.—The term "noncommercial educational broadcast station" means a television broadcast station that is a noncommercial educational broadcast station as defined in section 397 of the Communications Act of 1934, as in effect on the date of the enactment of the Satellite Television Extension and Localism Act of 2010.

(6) Subscriber.—The term "subscriber" means a person or entity that receives a secondary transmission service from a satellite carrier and pays a fee for the service, directly or indirectly, to the satellite carrier or to a distributor.

(7) Television Broadcast Station.—The term "television broadcast station"—

(A) means an over-the-air, commercial or noncommercial television broadcast station licensed by the Federal Communications Commission under subpart E of part 73 of title 47, Code of Federal Regulations, except that such term does not include a low-power or translator television station; and

(B) includes a television broadcast station licensed by an appropriate governmental authority of Canada or Mexico if the station broadcasts primarily in the English language and is a network station as defined in section 119(d)(2)(A).

CHAPTER 2.—COPYRIGHT OWNERSHIP AND TRANSFER

Sec. 201.   Ownership of Copyright

(a) Initial Ownership.—Copyright in a work protected under this title vests initially in the author or authors of the work. The authors of a joint work are coowners of copyright in the work.

(b) Works Made for Hire.—In the case of a work made for hire, the employer or other person for whom the work was prepared is considered the author for purposes of this title, and, unless the parties have expressly agreed otherwise in a written instrument signed by them, owns all of the rights comprised in the copyright.

(c) Contributions to Collective Works.—Copyright in each separate contribution to a collective work is distinct from copyright in the collective work as a whole, and vests initially in the author of the contribution. In the absence of an express transfer of the copyright or of any rights under it, the owner of copyright in the collective work is presumed to have acquired only the privilege of reproducing and distributing the contribution as part of that particular collective work, any revision of that collective work, and any later collective work in the same series.

(d) Transfer of Ownership.—

(1) The ownership of a copyright may be transferred in whole or in part by any means of conveyance or by operation of law, and may be bequeathed by will or pass as personal property by the applicable laws of intestate succession.

(2) Any of the exclusive rights comprised in a copyright, including any subdivision of any of the rights specified by section 106, may be transferred as provided by clause (1) and owned separately. The owner of any particular exclusive right is entitled, to the extent of that right, to all of the protection and remedies accorded to the copyright owner by this title.

(e) Involuntary Transfer.—When an individual author's ownership of a copyright, or of any of the exclusive rights under a copyright, has not previously been transferred voluntarily by that individual author, no action by any governmental body or other official or organization purporting to seize, expropriate, transfer, or exercise rights of ownership with respect to the copyright, or any of the exclusive rights under a copyright, shall be given effect under this title, except as provided under Title 11.

Sec. 202. Ownership of Copyright as Distinct From Ownership of Material Object

Ownership of a copyright, or of any of the exclusive rights under a copyright, is distinct from ownership of any material object in which the work is embodied. Transfer of ownership of any material object, including the copy or phonorecord in which the work is first fixed, does not of itself convey any rights in the copyrighted work embodied in the object; nor, in the absence of an agreement, does transfer of ownership of a copyright or of any exclusive rights under a copyright convey property rights in any material object.

Sec. 203. Termination of Transfers and Licenses Granted by the Author

(a) Conditions for Termination.—In the case of any work other than a work made for hire, the exclusive or nonexclusive grant of a transfer or license of copyright or of any right under a copyright, executed by the author on or after January 1, 1978, otherwise than by will, is subject to termination under the following conditions:

(1) In the case of a grant executed by one author, termination of the grant may be effected by that author or, if the author is dead, by the person or persons who, under clause (2) of this subsection, own and are entitled to exercise a total of more than one-half of that author's termination interest. In the case of a grant executed by two or more authors of a joint work, termination of the grant may be

effected by a majority of the authors who executed it; if any of such authors is dead, the termination interest of any such author may be exercised as a unit by the person or persons who, under clause (2) of this subsection, own and are entitled to exercise a total of more than one-half of that author's interest.

(2) Where an author is dead, his or her termination interest is owned, and may be exercised, as follows:

(A) The widow or widower owns the author's entire termination interest unless there are any surviving children or grandchildren of the author, in which case the widow or widower owns one-half of the author's interest.

(B) The author's surviving children, and the surviving children of any dead child of the author, own the author's entire termination interest unless there is a widow or widower, in which case the ownership of one-half of the author's interest is divided among them.

(C) The rights of the author's children and grandchildren are in all cases divided among them and exercised on a per stirpes basis according to the number of such author's children represented; the share of the children of a dead child in a termination interest can be exercised only by the action of a majority of them.

(D) In the event that the author's widow or widower, children, and grandchildren are not living, the author's executor, administrator, personal representative, or trustee shall own the author's entire termination interest.

(3) Termination of the grant may be effected at any time during a period of five years beginning at the end of thirty-five years from the date of execution of the grant; or, if the grant covers the right of publication of the work, the period begins at the end of thirty-five years from the date of publication of the work under the grant or at the end of forty years from the date of execution of the grant, whichever term ends earlier.

(4) The termination shall be effected by serving an advance notice in writing, signed by the number and proportion of owners of termination interests required under clauses (1) and (2) of this subsection, or by their duly authorized agents, upon the grantee or the grantee's successor in title.

(A) The notice shall state the effective date of the termination, which shall fall within the five-year period specified by clause (3) of this subsection, and the notice shall be served not less than two or more than ten years before that date. A copy of the notice shall be recorded in the Copyright Office before the effective date of termination, as a condition to its taking effect.

(B) The notice shall comply, in form, content, and manner of service, with requirements that the Register of Copyrights shall prescribe by regulation.

(5) Termination of the grant may be effected notwithstanding any agreement to the contrary, including an agreement to make a will or to make any future grant.

(b) Effect of Termination.—Upon the effective date of termination, all rights under this title that were covered by the terminated grants revert to the author, authors, and other persons owning termination interests under clauses (1) and (2) of subsection (a), including those owners who did not join in signing the notice of termination under clause (4) of subsection (a), but with the following limitations:

(1) A derivative work prepared under authority of the grant before its termination may continue to be utilized under the terms of the grant after its termination, but this privilege does not extend to the preparation after the termination of other derivative works based upon the copyrighted work covered by the terminated grant.

(2) The future rights that will revert upon termination of the grant become vested on the date the notice of termination has been served as provided by clause (4) of subsection (a). The rights vest in the author, authors, and other persons named in, and in the proportionate shares provided by, clauses (1) and (2) of subsection (a).

(3) Subject to the provisions of clause (4) of this subsection, a further grant, or agreement to make a further grant, of any right covered by a terminated grant is valid only if it is signed by the same number and proportion of the owners, in whom the right has vested under clause (2) of this subsection, as are required to terminate the grant under clauses (1) and (2) of subsection (a). Such further grant or agreement is effective with respect to all of the persons in whom the right it covers has vested under clause (2) of this subsection, including those who did not join in signing it. If any person dies after rights under a terminated grant have vested in him or her, that person's legal representatives, legatees, or heirs at law represent him or her for purposes of this clause.

(4) A further grant, or agreement to make a further grant, of any right covered by a terminated grant is valid only if it is made after the effective date of the termination. As an exception, however, an agreement for such a further grant may be made between the persons provided by clause (3) of this subsection and the original grantee or such grantee's successor in title, after the notice of termination has been served as provided by clause (4) of subsection (a).

(5) Termination of a grant under this section affects only those rights covered by the grants that arise under this title, and in no way affects rights arising under any other Federal, State, or foreign laws.

(6) Unless and until termination is effected under this section, the grant, if it does not provide otherwise, continues in effect for the term of copyright provided by this title.

Sec. 204.   Execution of Transfers of Copyright Ownership

(a) A transfer of copyright ownership, other than by operation of law, is not valid unless an instrument of conveyance, or a note or memorandum of the transfer, is in writing and signed by the owner of the rights conveyed or such owner's duly authorized agent.

(b) A certificate of acknowledgement is not required for the validity of a transfer, but is prima facie evidence of the execution of the transfer if—

(1) in the case of a transfer executed in the United States, the certificate is issued by a person authorized to administer oaths within the United States; or

(2) in the case of a transfer executed in a foreign country, the certificate is issued by a diplomatic or consular officer of the United States, or by a person authorized to administer oaths whose authority is proved by a certificate of such an officer.

Sec. 205.   Recordation of Transfers and Other Documents

(a) Conditions for Recordation.—Any transfer of copyright ownership or other document pertaining to a copyright may be recorded in the Copyright Office if the document filed for recordation bears the actual signature of the person who executed it, or if it is accompanied by a sworn or official certification that it is a true copy of the original, signed document. A sworn official certification may be submitted to the Copyright Office electronically, pursuant to regulations established by the Register of Copyrights.

(b) Certificate of Recordation.—The Register of Copyrights shall, upon receipt of a document as provided by subsection (a) and of the fee provided by section 708, record the document and return it with a certificate of recordation.

(c) Recordation as Constructive Notice.—Recordation of a document in the Copyright Office gives all persons constructive notice of the facts stated in the recorded document, but only if—

(1) the document, or material attached to it, specifically identifies the work to which it pertains so that, after the document is indexed by the Register of Copyrights, it would be revealed by a reasonable search under the title or registration number of the work; and

(2) registration has been made for the work.

(d) Priority Between Conflicting Transfers.—As between two conflicting transfers, the one executed first prevails if it is recorded, in the manner required to give constructive notice under subsection (c), within one month after its execution in the United States or within two months after its execution outside the United States, or at any time before recordation in such manner of the later transfer. Otherwise the later transfer prevails if recorded first in such manner, and if taken in good faith, for valuable consideration or on the basis of a binding promise to pay royalties, and without notice of the earlier transfer.

(e) Priority Between Conflicting Transfer of Ownership and Nonexclusive License.—A nonexclusive license, whether recorded or not, prevails over a conflicting transfer of copyright ownership if the license is evidenced by a written instrument signed by the owner of the rights licensed or such owner's duly authorized agent; and if—

(1) the license was taken before execution of the transfer; or

(2) the license was taken in good faith before recordation of the transfer and without notice of it.

CHAPTER 3.—DURATION OF COPYRIGHT

Sec.

Sec. 301.   Preemption With Respect to Other Laws

(a) On and after January 1, 1978, all legal or equitable rights that are equivalent to any of the exclusive rights within the general scope of copyright as specified by section 106 in works of authorship that are fixed in a tangible medium of expression and come within the subject matter of copyright as specified by sections 102 and 103, whether created before or after that date and whether published or unpublished, are governed exclusively by this title. Thereafter, no person is entitled to any such right or equivalent right in any such work under the common law or statutes of any State.

(b) Nothing in this title annuls or limits any rights or remedies under the common law or statutes of any State with respect to—

(1) subject matter that does not come within the subject matter of copyright as specified by sections 102 and 103, including works of authorship not fixed in any tangible medium of expression; or

(2) any cause of action arising from undertakings commenced before January 1, 1978;

(3) activities violating legal or equitable rights that are not equivalent to any of the exclusive rights within the general scope of copyright as specified by section 106; or

(4) State and local landmarks, historic preservation, zoning, or building codes, relating to architectural works protected under section 102(a)(8).

(c) With respect to sound recordings fixed before February 15, 1972, any rights or remedies under the common law or statutes of any State shall not be annulled or limited by this title until February 15, 2067. The preemptive provisions of subsection (a) shall apply to any such rights and remedies pertaining to any cause of action arising from undertakings commenced on and after February 15, 2067. Notwithstanding the provisions of section 303, no sound recording fixed before February 15, 1972, shall be subject to copyright under this title before, on, or after February 15, 2067.

(d) Nothing in this title annuls or limits any rights or remedies under any other Federal statute.

(e) The scope of Federal preemption under this section is not affected by the adherence of the United States to the Berne Convention or the satisfaction of obligations of the United States thereunder.

(f)(1) On or after the effective date set forth in section 9(a) of the Visual Artists Rights Act of 1990, all legal or equitable rights that are equivalent to any of the rights conferred by section 106A with respect to works of visual art to which the rights conferred by section 106A apply are governed exclusively by section 106A and section 113(d) and the provisions of this title relating to such sections. Thereafter, no person is entitled to any such right or equivalent right in any work of visual art under the common law or statutes of any State.

(2) Nothing in paragraph (1) annuls or limits any rights or remedies under the common law or statutes of any State with respect to—

(A) any cause of action from undertakings commenced before the effective date set forth in section 9(a) of the Visual Artists Rights Act of 1990;

(B) activities violating legal or equitable rights that are not equivalent to any of the rights conferred by section 106A with respect to works of visual art; or

(C) activities violating legal or equitable rights which extend beyond the life of the author.

Sec. 302. Duration of Copyright: Works Created on or After January 1, 1978

(a) In General.—Copyright in a work created on or after January 1, 1978, subsists from its creation and, except as provided by the following subsections, endures for a term consisting of the life of the author and 70 years after the author's death.

(b) Joint Works.—In the case of a joint work prepared by two or more authors who did not work for hire, the copyright endures for a term consisting of the life of the last surviving author and 70 years after such last surviving author's death.

(c) Anonymous Works, Pseudonymous Works, and Works Made for Hire.—In the case of an anonymous work, a pseudonymous work, or a work made for hire, the copyright endures for a term of 95 years from the year of its first publication, or a term of 120 years from the year of its creation, whichever expires first. If, before the end of such term, the identity of one or more of the authors of an anonymous or pseudonymous work is revealed in the records of a registration made for that work under subsections (a) or (d) of section 408, or in the records provided by this subsection, the copyright in the work endures for the term specified by subsection (a) or (b), based on the life of the author or authors whose identity has been revealed. Any person having an interest in the copyright in an anonymous or pseudonymous work may at any time record, in records to be maintained by the Copyright Office for that purpose, a statement identifying one or more authors of the work; the statement shall also identify the person filing it, the nature of that person's interest, the source of the information recorded, and the particular work affected, and shall comply in form and content with requirements that the Register of Copyrights shall prescribe by regulation.

(d) Records Relating to Death of Authors.—Any person having an interest in a copyright may at any time record in the Copyright Office a statement of the date of death of the author of the copyrighted work, or a statement that the author is still living on a particular date. The statement shall identify the person filing it, the nature of that person's interest, and the source of the information recorded, and shall comply in form and content with requirements that the Register of Copyrights shall prescribe by regulation. The Register shall maintain current records of information relating to the death of authors of copyrighted works, based on such recorded statements and, to the extent the Register considers practicable, on data contained in any of the records of the Copyright Office or in other reference sources.

(e) Presumption as to Author's Death.—After a period of 95 years from the year of first publication of a work, or a period of 120 years from the year of its creation, whichever expires first, any person who obtains from the Copyright Office a certified report that the records provided by subsection (d) disclose nothing to indicate that the author of the work is living, or died less than 70 years before, is entitled to the benefit of a presumption that the author has been dead for at least 70 years. Reliance in good faith upon this presumption shall be a complete defense to any action for infringement under this title.

Sec. 303. Duration of Copyright: Works Created But Not Published or Copyrighted Before January 1, 1978

(a) Copyright in a work created before January 1, 1978, but not theretofore in the public domain or copyrighted, subsists from January 1, 1978, and endures for the term provided by section 302. In no case, however, shall the term of copyright in such a work expire before December 31, 2002; and, if the work is published on or before December 31, 2002, the term of copyright shall not expire before December 31, 2047.

(b) The distribution before January 1, 1978, of a phonorecord shall not for any purpose constitute a publication of any musical work, dramatic work, or literary work embodied therein.

Sec. 304. Duration of Copyright: Subsisting Copyrights

(a) Copyrights in Their First Term on January 1, 1978.—

(1)(A) Any copyright, the first term of which is subsisting on January 1, 1978, shall endure for 28 years from the date it was originally secured.

(B) In the case of—

(i) any posthumous work or of any periodical, cyclopedic, or other composite work upon which the copyright was originally secured by the proprietor thereof, or

(ii) any work copyrighted by a corporate body (otherwise than as assignee or licensee of the individual author) or by an employer for whom such work is made for hire,

the proprietor of such copyright shall be entitled to a renewal and extension of the copyright in such work for the further term of 67 years.

(C) In the case of any other copyrighted work, including a contribution by an individual author to a periodical or to a cyclopedic or other composite work—

(i) the author of such work, if the author is still living,

(ii) the widow, widower, or children of the author, if the author is not living,

(iii) the author's executors, if such author, widow, widower, or children are not living, or

(iv) the author's next of kin, in the absence of a will of the author,

shall be entitled to a renewal and extension of the copyright in such work for a further term of 67 years.

(2)(A) At the expiration of the original term of copyright in a work specified in paragraph (1)(B) of this subsection, the copyright shall endure for a renewed and extended further term of 67 years, which—

(i) if an application to register a claim to such further term has been made to the Copyright Office within 1 year before the expiration of the original term of copyright, and the claim is registered, shall vest, upon the beginning of such further term, in the proprietor of the copyright who is entitled to claim the renewal of copyright at the time the application is made; or

(ii) if no such application is made or the claim pursuant to such application is not registered, shall vest, upon the beginning of such further term, in the person or entity that was the proprietor of the copyright as of the last day of the original term of copyright.

(B) At the expiration of the original term of copyright in a work specified in paragraph (1)(C) of this subsection, the copyright shall endure for a renewed and extended further term of 67 years, which—

(i) if an application to register a claim to such further term has been made to the Copyright Office within 1 year before the expiration of the original term of copyright, and the claim is registered, shall vest, upon the beginning of such further term, in any person who is entitled under paragraph (1)(C) to the renewal and extension of the copyright at the time the application is made; or

(ii) if no such application is made or the claim pursuant to such application is not registered, shall vest, upon the beginning of such further term, in any person entitled under paragraph (1)(C), as of the last day of the original term of copyright, to the renewal and extension of the copyright.

(3)(A) An application to register a claim to the renewed and extended term of copyright in a work may be made to the Copyright Office—

(i) within 1 year before the expiration of the original term of copyright by any person entitled under paragraph (1)(B) or (C) to such further term of 67 years; and

(ii) at any time during the renewed and extended term by any person in whom such further term vested, under paragraph (2)(A) or (B), or by any successor or assign of such person, if the application is made in the name of such person.

(B) Such an application is not a condition of the renewal and extension of the copyright in a work for a further term of 67 years.

(4)(A) If an application to register a claim to the renewed and extended term of copyright in a work is not made within 1 year before the expiration of the original term of copyright in a work, or if the claim pursuant to such application is not registered, then a derivative work prepared under authority of a grant of a transfer or license of the copyright that is made before the expiration of the original term of copyright may continue to be used under the terms of the grant during the renewed and extended term of copyright without infringing the copyright, except that such use does not extend to the preparation during such renewed and extended term of other derivative works based upon the copyrighted work covered by such grant.

(B) If an application to register a claim to the renewed and extended term of copyright in a work is made within 1 year before its expiration, and the claim is registered, the certificate of such registration shall constitute prima facie evidence as to the validity of the copyright during its renewed and extended term and of the facts stated in the certificate. The evidentiary weight to be accorded the certificates of a registration of a renewed and extended term of copyright made after the end of that 1-year period shall be within the discretion of the court.*

(b) Copyrights in their Renewal Term at the Time of the Effective Date of the Sonny Bono Copyright Term Extension Act.—Any copyright still in its renewal term at the time that the Sonny Bono Copyright Term Extension Act becomes effective shall have a copyright term of 95 years from the date copyright was originally secured.

(c) Termination of Transfers and Licenses Covering Extended Renewal Term.—In the case of any copyright subsisting in either its first or renewal term on January 1, 1978, other than a copyright in a work made for hire, the exclusive or nonexclusive grant of a transfer or license of the renewal copyright or any right under it, executed before January 1, 1978, by any of the persons designated by subsection (a)(1)(C) of this section, otherwise than by will, is subject to termination under the following conditions:

---

*   Congress, in revising section 304(a) effective June 26, 1992, stated the following with respect to the effective date of this new renewal provision: "The amendments made by this section shall apply only to those copyrights secured between January 1, 1964, and December 31, 1977. Copyrights secured before January 1, 1964, shall be governed by the provisions of section 304(a) of title 17, United States Code, as in effect on the day before the effective date of this section." Pub. L. 102–307, § 102(g)(2). The text of section 304(a) as enacted in 1976, which thus governs works that were in their first term of copyright prior to January 1, 1964,and which thus would have to be renewed before the end of 1991, was as follows:

(a) Copyrights in their first term on January 1, 1978. Any copyright, the first term of which is subsisting on January 1, 1978, shall endure for twenty-eight years from the date it was originally secured: *Provided*, That in the case of any posthumous work or of any periodical, cyclopedic, or other composite work upon which the copyright was originally secured by the proprietor thereof, or of any work copyrighted by a corporate body (otherwise than as assignee or licensee of the individual author) or by an employer for whom such work is made for hire, the proprietor of such copyright shall be entitled to a renewal and extension of the copyright in such work for the further term of forty-seven years when application for such renewal and extension shall have been made to the Copyright Office and duly registered therein within one year prior to the expiration of the original term of copyright: *And provided further*, That in the case of any other copyrighted work, including a contribution by an individual author to a periodical or to a cyclopedic or other composite work, the author of such work, if still living, or the widow, widower, or children of the author, if the author be not living, or if such author, widow, widower, or children be not living, then the author's executors, or in the absence of a will, his or her next of kin shall be entitled to a renewal and extension of the copyright in such work for a further term of forty-seven years when application for such renewal and extension shall have been made to the Copyright Office and duly registered therein within one year prior to the expiration of the original term of copyright: *And provided further*, That in default of the registration of such application for renewal and extension, the copyright in any work shall terminate at the expiration of twenty-eight years from the date copyright was originally secured.

(1) In the case of a grant executed by a person or persons other than the author, termination of the grant may be effected by the surviving person or persons who executed it. In the case of a grant executed by one or more of the authors of the work, termination of the grant may be effected, to the extent of a particular author's share in the ownership of the renewal copyright, by the author who executed it or, if such author is dead, by the person or persons who, under clause (2) of this subsection, own and are entitled to exercise a total of more than one-half of that author's termination interest.

(2) Where an author is dead, his or her termination interest is owned, and may be exercised, as follows:

(A) The widow or widower owns the author's entire termination interest unless there are any surviving children or grandchildren of the author, in which case the widow or widower owns one-half of the author's interest.

(B) The author's surviving children, and the surviving children of any dead child of the author, own the author's entire termination interest unless there is a widow or widower, in which case the ownership of one-half of the author's interest is divided among them.

(C) The rights of the author's children and grandchildren are in all cases divided among them and exercised on a per stirpes basis according to the number of such author's children represented; the share of the children of a dead child in a termination interest can be exercised only by the action of a majority of them.

(D) In the event that the author's widow or widower, children, and grandchildren are not living, the author's executor, administrator, personal representative, or trustee shall own the author's entire termination interest.

(3) Termination of the grant may be effected at any time during a period of five years beginning at the end of fifty-six years from the date copyright was originally secured, or beginning on January 1, 1978, whichever is later.

(4) The termination shall be effected by serving an advance notice in writing upon the grantee or the grantee's successor in title. In the case of a grant executed by a person or persons other than the author, the notice shall be signed by all of those entitled to terminate the grant under clause (1) of this subsection, or by their duly authorized agents. In the case of a grant executed by one or more of the authors of the work, the notice as to any one author's share shall be signed by that author or his or her duly authorized agent or, if that author is dead, by the number and proportion of the owners of his or her termination interest required under clauses (1) and (2) of this subsection, or by their duly authorized agents.

(A) The notice shall state the effective date of the termination, which shall fall within the five-year period specified by clause (3) of this subsection, or, in the case of a termination under subsection (d), within the five-year period specified by subsection (d)(2), and the notice shall be served not less than two or more than ten years before that date. A copy of the notice shall be recorded in the Copyright Office before the effective date of termination, as a condition to its taking effect.

(B) The notice shall comply, in form, content, and manner of service, with requirements that the Register of Copyrights shall prescribe by regulation.

(5) Termination of the grant may be effected notwithstanding any agreement to the contrary, including an agreement to make a will or to make any future grant.

(6) In the case of a grant executed by a person or persons other than the author, all rights under this title that were covered by the terminated grant revert, upon the effective date of termination, to all of those entitled to terminate the grant under clause (1) of this subsection. In the case of a grant executed by one or more of the authors of the work, all of a particular author's rights under this title that were covered by the terminated grant revert, upon the effective date of termination, to that author or, if that author is dead, to the persons owning his or her termination interest under clause (2) of this subsection, including those owners who did not join in signing the notice of termination under clause (4) of this subsection. In all cases the reversion of rights is subject to the following limitations:

(A) A derivative work prepared under authority of the grant before its termination may continue to be utilized under the terms of the grant after its termination, but this privilege does not extend to the preparation after the termination of other derivative works based upon the copyrighted work covered by the terminated grant.

(B) The future rights that will revert upon termination of the grant become vested on the date the notice of termination has been served as provided by clause (4) of this subsection.

(C) Where the author's rights revert to two or more persons under clause (2) of this subsection, they shall vest in those persons in the proportionate shares provided by that clause. In such a case, and subject to the provisions of subclause (D) of this clause, a further grant, or agreement to make a further grant, of a particular author's share with respect to any right covered by a terminated grant is valid only if it is signed by the same number and proportion of the owners, in whom the right has vested under this clause, as are required to terminate the grant under clause (2) of this subsection. Such further grant or agreement is effective with respect to all of the persons in whom the right it covers has vested under this subclause, including those who did not join in signing it. If any person dies after rights under a terminated grant have vested in him or her, that person's legal representatives, legatees, or heirs at law represent him or her for purposes of this subclause.

(D) A further grant, or agreement to make a further grant, of any right covered by a terminated grant is valid only if it is made after the effective date of the termination. As an exception, however, an agreement for such a further grant may be made between the author or any of the persons provided by the first sentence of clause (6) of this subsection, or between the persons provided by subclause (C) of this clause, and the original grantee or such grantee's successor in title, after the notice of termination has been served as provided by clause (4) of this subsection.

(E) Termination of a grant under this subsection affects only those rights covered by the grant that arise under this title, and in no way affects rights arising under any other Federal, State, or foreign laws.

(F) Unless and until termination is effected under this subsection, the grant, if it does not provide otherwise, continues in effect for the remainder of the extended renewal term.

(d) Termination Rights Provided in Subsection (c) which have Expired On or Before the Effective Date of the Sonny Bono Copyright Term Extension Act.—In the case of any copyright other than a work made for hire, subsisting in its renewal term on the effective date of the Sonny Bono Copyright Term Extension Act for which the termination right provided in subsection (c) has expired by such date, where the author or owner of the termination right has not previously exercised such termination right, the exclusive or nonexclusive grant of a transfer or license of the renewal copyright or any right under it, executed before January 1, 1978, by any of the persons designated in subsection (a)(1)(C) of this section, other than by will, is subject to termination under the following conditions:

(1) The conditions specified in subsections (c)(1), (2), (4), (5), and (6) of this section apply to terminations of the last 20 years of copyright term as provided by the amendments made by the Sonny Bono Copyright Term Extension Act.

(2) Termination of the grant may be effected at any time during a period of 5 years beginning at the end of 75 years from the date copyright was originally secured.

Sec. 305.   Duration of Copyright: Terminal Date

All terms of copyright provided by sections 302 through 304 run to the end of the calendar year in which they would otherwise expire.

CHAPTER 4.—COPYRIGHT NOTICE, DEPOSIT, AND REGISTRATION

Sec. 401.   Notice of Copyright: Visually Perceptible Copies

(a) **General Provisions.**—Whenever a work protected under this title is published in the United States or elsewhere by authority of the copyright owner, a notice of copyright as provided by this section may be placed on publicly distributed copies from which the work can be visually perceived, either directly or with the aid of a machine or device.

(b) **Form of Notice.**—If a notice appears on the copies, it shall consist of the following three elements:

(1) the symbol © (the letter C in a circle), or the word "Copyright", or the abbreviation "Copr."; and

(2) the year of first publication of the work; in the case of compilations or derivative works incorporating previously published material, the year date of first publication of the compilation or derivative work is sufficient. The year date may be omitted where a pictorial, graphic, or sculptural work, with accompanying text matter, if any, is reproduced in or on greeting cards, postcards, stationery, jewelry, dolls, toys, or any useful articles; and

(3) the name of the owner of copyright in the work, or an abbreviation by which the name can be recognized, or a generally known alternative designation of the owner.

(c) **Position of Notice.**—The notice shall be affixed to the copies in such manner and location as to give reasonable notice of the claim of copyright. The Register of Copyrights shall prescribe by regulation, as examples, specific methods of affixation and positions of the notice on various types of works that will satisfy this requirement, but these specifications shall not be considered exhaustive.

(d) **Evidentiary Weight of Notice.**—If a notice of copyright in the form and position specified by this section appears on the published copy or copies to which a defendant in a copyright infringement suit had access, then no weight shall be given to such a defendant's interposition of a defense based on innocent infringement in mitigation of actual or statutory damages, except as provided in the last sentence of section 504(c)(2).

Sec. 402.   Notice   of   Copyright: Phonorecords   of   Sound Recordings

(a) General Provisions.—Whenever a sound recording protected under this title is published in the United States or elsewhere by authority of the copyright owner, a notice of copyright as provided by this section may be placed on publicly distributed phonorecords of the sound recording.

(b) Form of Notice.—If a notice appears on the phonorecords, it shall consist of the following three elements:

(1) the symbol ℗ (the letter P in a circle); and

(2) the year of first publication of the sound recording; and

(3) the name of the owner of copyright in the sound recording, or an abbreviation by which the name can be recognized, or a generally known alternative designation of the owner; if the producer of the sound recording is named on the phonorecord labels or containers, and if no other name appears in conjunction with the notice, the producer's name shall be considered a part of the notice.

(c) Position of Notice.—The notice shall be placed on the surface of the phonorecord, or on the phonorecord label or container, in such manner and location as to give reasonable notice of the claim of copyright.

(d) Evidentiary Weight of Notice.—If a notice of copyright in the form and position specified by this section appears on the published phonorecord or phonorecords to which a defendant in a copyright infringement suit had access, then no weight shall be given to such a defendant's interposition of a defense based on innocent infringement in mitigation of actual or statutory damages, except as provided in the last sentence of section 504(c)(2).

Sec. 403.   Notice   of   Copyright: Publications   Incorporating United States Government Works

Sections 401(d) and 402(d) shall not apply to a work published in copies or phonorecords consisting predominantly of one or more works of the United States Government unless the notice of copyright appearing on the published copies or phonorecords to which a defendant in the copyright

infringement suit had access includes a statement identifying, either affirmatively or negatively, those portions of the copies or phonorecords embodying any work or works protected under this title.

Sec. 404.   Notice of Copyright: Contributions to Collective Works

(a) A separate contribution to a collective work may bear its own notice of copyright, as provided by sections 401 through 403. However, a single notice applicable to the collective work as a whole is sufficient to invoke the provisions of section 401(d) or 402(d), as applicable with respect to the separate contributions it contains (not including advertisements inserted on behalf of persons other than the owner of copyright in the collective work), regardless of the ownership of copyright in the contributions and whether or not they have been previously published.

(b) With respect to copies and phonorecords publicly distributed by authority of the copyright owner before the effective date of the Berne Convention Implementation Act of 1988, where the person named in a single notice applicable to a collective work as a whole is not the owner of copyright in a separate contribution that does not bear its own notice, the case is governed by the provisions of section 406(a).

Sec. 405.   Notice of Copyright: Omission of Notice on Certain Copies and Phonorecords

(a) **Effect of Omission on Copyright.**—With respect to copies and phonorecords publicly distributed by authority of the copyright owner before the effective date of the Berne Convention Implementation Act of 1988, the omission of the copyright notice described in sections 401 through 403 from copies or phonorecords publicly distributed by authority of the copyright owner does not invalidate the copyright in a work if—

(1) the notice has been omitted from no more than a relatively small number of copies or phonorecords distributed to the public; or

(2) registration for the work has been made before or is made within five years after the publication without notice, and a reasonable effort is made to add notice to all copies or phonorecords that are distributed to the public in the United States after the omission has been discovered; or

(3) the notice has been omitted in violation of an express requirement in writing that, as a condition of the copyright owner's authorization of the public distribution of copies or phonorecords, they bear the prescribed notice.

(b) **Effect of Omission on Innocent Infringers.**—Any person who innocently infringes a copyright, in reliance upon an authorized copy or phonorecord from which the copyright notice has been omitted and which was publicly distributed by authority of the copyright owner before the effective date of the Berne Convention Implementation Act of 1988, incurs no liability for actual or statutory damages under section 504 for any infringing acts committed before receiving actual notice that registration for the work has been made under section 408, if such person proves that he or she was misled by the omission of notice. In a suit for infringement in such a case the court may allow or disallow recovery of any of the infringer's profits attributable to the infringement, and may enjoin the continuation of the infringing undertaking or may require, as a condition for permitting the continuation of the infringing undertaking, that the infringer pay the copyright owner a reasonable license fee in an amount and on terms fixed by the court.

(c) Removal of Notice.—Protection under this title is not affected by the removal, destruction, or obliteration of the notice, without the authorization of the copyright owner, from any publicly distributed copies or phonorecords.

Sec. 406.   Notice of Copyright: Error in Name or Date on Certain Copies and Phonorecords

(a) Error in Name.—With respect to copies and phonorecords publicly distributed by authority of the copyright owner before the effective date of the Berne Convention Implementation Act of 1988, where the person named in the copyright notice on copies or phonorecords publicly distributed by authority of the copyright owner is not the owner of copyright, the validity and ownership of the copyright are not affected. In such a case, however, any person who innocently begins an undertaking that infringes the copyright has a complete defense to any action for such infringement if such person proves that he or she was misled by the notice and began the undertaking in good faith under a purported transfer or license from the person named therein, unless before the undertaking was begun—

    (1) registration for the work had been made in the name of the owner of copyright; or

    (2) a document executed by the person named in the notice and showing the ownership of the copyright had been recorded.

The person named in the notice is liable to account to the copyright owner for all receipts from transfers or licenses purportedly made under the copyright by the person named in the notice.

(b) Error in Date.—When the year date in the notice on copies or phonorecords distributed before the effective date of the Berne Convention Implementation Act of 1988 by authority of the copyright owner is earlier than the year in which publication first occurred, any period computed from the year of first publication under section 302 is to be computed from the year in the notice. Where the year date is more than one year later than the year in which publication first occurred, the work is considered to have been published without any notice and is governed by the provisions of section 405.

(c) Omission of Name or Date.—Where copies or phonorecords publicly distributed before the effective date of the Berne Convention Implementation Act of 1988 by authority of the copyright owner contain no name or no date that could reasonably be considered a part of the notice, the work is considered to have been published without any notice and is governed by the provisions of section 405 as in effect on the day before the effective date of the Berne Convention Implementation Act of 1988.

Sec. 407.   Deposit of Copies or Phonorecords for Library of Congress

(a) Except as provided by subsection (c), and subject to the provisions of subsection (e), the owner of copyright or of the exclusive right of publication in a work published in the United States shall deposit, within three months after the date of such publication—

> (1) two complete copies of the best edition; or

> (2) if the work is a sound recording, two complete phonorecords of the best edition, together with any printed or other visually perceptible material published with such phonorecords.

Neither the deposit requirements of this subsection nor the acquisition provisions of subsection (e) are conditions of copyright protection.

(b) The required copies or phonorecords shall be deposited in the Copyright Office for the use or disposition of the Library of Congress. The Register of Copyrights shall, when requested by the depositor and upon payment of the fee prescribed by section 708, issue a receipt for the deposit.

(c) The Register of Copyrights may by regulation exempt any categories of material from the deposit requirements of this section, or require deposit of only one copy or phonorecord with respect to any categories. Such regulations shall provide either for complete exemption from the deposit requirements of this section, or for alternative forms of deposit aimed at providing a satisfactory archival record of a work without imposing practical or financial hardships on the depositor, where the individual author is the owner of copyright in a pictorial, graphic, or sculptural work and (i) less than five copies of the work have been published, or (ii) the work has been published in a limited edition consisting of numbered copies, the monetary value of which would make the mandatory deposit of two copies of the best edition of the work burdensome, unfair, or unreasonable.

(d) At any time after publication of a work as provided by subsection (a), the Register of Copyrights may make written demand for the required deposit on any of the persons obligated to make the deposit under subsection (a). Unless deposit is made within three months after the demand is received, the person or persons on whom the demand was made are liable—

> (1) to a fine of not more than $250 for each work; and

> (2) to pay into a specially designated fund in the Library of Congress the total retail price of the copies or phonorecords

demanded, or, if no retail price has been fixed, the reasonable cost to the Library of Congress of acquiring them; and

(3) to pay a fine of $2,500, in addition to any fine or liability imposed under clauses (1) and (2), if such person willfully or repeatedly fails or refuses to comply with such a demand.

(e) With respect to transmission programs that have been fixed and transmitted to the public in the United States but have not been published, the Register of Copyrights shall, after consulting with the Librarian of Congress and other interested organizations and officials, establish regulations governing the acquisition, through deposit or otherwise, of copies or phonorecords of such programs for the collections of the Library of Congress.

(1) The Librarian of Congress shall be permitted, under the standards and conditions set forth in such regulations, to make a fixation of a transmission program directly from a transmission to the public, and to reproduce one copy or phonorecord from such fixation for archival purposes.

(2) Such regulations shall also provide standards and procedures by which the Register of Copyrights may make written demand upon the owner of the right of transmission in the United States, for the deposit of a copy or phonorecord of a specific transmission program. Such deposit may, at the option of the owner of the right of transmission in the United States, be accomplished by gift, by loan for purposes of reproduction, or by sale at a price not to exceed the cost of reproducing and supplying the copy or phonorecord. The regulations established under this clause shall provide reasonable periods of not less than three months for compliance with a demand, and shall allow for extensions of such periods and adjustments in the scope of the demand or the methods for fulfilling it, as reasonably warranted by the circumstances. Willful failure or refusal to comply with the conditions prescribed by such regulations shall subject the owner of the right of transmission in the United States to liability for an amount, not to exceed the cost of reproducing and supplying the copy or phonorecord in question, to be paid into a specially designated fund in the Library of Congress.

(3) Nothing in this subsection shall be construed to require the making or retention, for purposes of deposit, of any copy or phonorecord of an unpublished transmission program, the transmission of which occurs before the receipt of a specific written demand as provided by clause (2).

(4) No activity undertaken in compliance with regulations prescribed under clauses (1) or (2) of this subsection shall result in liability if intended solely to assist in the acquisition of copies or phonorecords under this subsection.

Sec. 408.   Copyright Registration in General

(a) **Registration Permissive.**—At any time during the subsistence of the first term of copyright in any published or unpublished work in which the copyright was secured before January 1, 1978, and during the subsistence of any copyright secured on or after that date, the owner of copyright or of any exclusive right in the work may obtain registration of the copyright claim by delivering to the Copyright Office the deposit specified by this section, together with the application and fee specified by sections 409 and 708. Such registration is not a condition of copyright protection.

(b) **Deposit for Copyright Registration.**—Except as provided by subsection (c), the material deposited for registration shall include—

(1) in the case of an unpublished work, one complete copy or phonorecord;

(2) in the case of a published work, two complete copies or phonorecords of the best edition;

(3) in the case of a work first published outside the United States, one complete copy or phonorecord as so published;

(4) in the case of a contribution to a collective work, one complete copy or phonorecord of the best edition of the collective work.

Copies or phonorecords deposited for the Library of Congress under section 407 may be used to satisfy the deposit provisions of this section, if they are accompanied by the prescribed application and fee, and by any additional identifying material that the Register may, by regulation, require. The Register shall also prescribe regulations establishing requirements under which copies or phonorecords acquired for the Library of Congress under subsection (e) of section 407, otherwise than by deposit, may be used to satisfy the deposit provisions of this section.

(c) **Administrative Classification and Optional Deposit.**—

(1) The Register of Copyrights is authorized to specify by regulation the administrative classes into which works are to be placed for purposes of deposit and registration, and the nature of the copies or phonorecords to be deposited in the various classes specified. The regulations may require or permit, for particular classes, the deposit of identifying material instead of copies or phonorecords, the deposit of only one copy or phonorecord where two would normally be required, or a single registration for a group of related works. This administrative classification of works has no significance with respect to the subject matter of copyright or the exclusive rights provided by this title.

(2) Without prejudice to the general authority provided under clause (1), the Register of Copyrights shall establish regulations specifically permitting a single registration for a group of works by the same individual author, all first published as contributions to

periodicals, including newspapers, within a twelve-month period, on the basis of a single deposit, application, and registration fee, under the following conditions—

(A) if the deposit consists of one copy of the entire issue of the periodical, or of the entire section in the case of a newspaper, in which each contribution was first published; and

(B) if the application identifies each work separately, including the periodical containing it and its date of first publication.

(3) As an alternative to separate renewal registrations under subsection (a) of section 304, a single renewal registration may be made for a group of works by the same individual author, all first published as contributions to periodicals, including newspapers, upon the filing of a single application and fee, under all of the following conditions:

(A) the renewal claimant or claimants, and the basis of claim or claims under section 304(a), is the same for each of the works; and

(B) the works were all copyrighted upon their first publication, either through separate copyright notice and registration or by virtue of a general copyright notice in the periodical issue as a whole; and

(C) the renewal application and fee are received not more than twenty-eight or less than twenty-seven years after the thirty-first day of December of the calendar year in which all of the works were first published; and

(D) the renewal application identifies each work separately, including the periodical containing it and its date of first publication.

(d) Corrections and Amplifications.—The Register may also establish, by regulation, formal procedures for the filing of an application for supplementary registration, to correct an error in a copyright registration or to amplify the information given in a registration. Such application shall be accompanied by the fee provided by section 708, and shall clearly identify the registration to be corrected or amplified. The information contained in a supplementary registration augments but does not supersede that contained in the earlier registration.

(e) Published Edition of Previously Registered Work.— Registration for the first published edition of a work previously registered in unpublished form may be made even though the work as published is substantially the same as the unpublished version.

(f) Preregistration of Works Being Prepared for Commercial Distribution.—

(1) Rulemaking.—Not later than 180 days after the date of enactment of this subsection, the Register of Copyrights shall issue regulations to establish procedures for preregistration of a work that is being prepared for commercial distribution and has not been published.

(2) Class of Works.—The regulations established under paragraph (1) shall permit preregistration for any work that is in a class of works that the Register determines has had a history of infringement prior to authorized commercial distribution.

(3) Application for Registration.—Not later than 3 months after the first publication of a work preregistered under this subsection, the applicant shall submit to the Copyright Office—

(A) an application for registration of the work;

(B) a deposit; and

(C) the applicable fee.

(4) Effect of Untimely Application.—An action under this chapter for infringement of a work preregistered under this subsection, in a case in which the infringement commenced no later than 2 months after the first publication of the work, shall be dismissed if the items described in paragraph (3) are not submitted to the Copyright Office in proper form within the earlier of—

(A) 3 months after the first publication of the work; or

(B) 1 month after the copyright owner has learned of the infringement.

Sec. 409.   Application for Copyright Registration

The application for copyright registration shall be made on a form prescribed by the Register of Copyrights and shall include—

(1) the name and address of the copyright claimant;

(2) in the case of a work other than an anonymous or pseudonymous work, the name and nationality or domicile of the author or authors, and, if one or more of the authors is dead, the dates of their deaths;

(3) if the work is anonymous or pseudonymous, the nationality or domicile of the author or authors;

(4) in the case of a work made for hire, a statement to this effect;

(5) if the copyright claimant is not the author, a brief statement of how the claimant obtained ownership of the copyright;

(6) the title of the work, together with any previous or alternative titles under which the work can be identified;

(7) the year in which creation of the work was completed;

(8) if the work has been published, the date and nation of its first publication;

(9) in the case of a compilation or derivative work, an identification of any preexisting work or works that it is based on or incorporates, and a brief, general statement of the additional material covered by the copyright claim being registered; and

(10) any other information regarded by the Register of Copyrights as bearing upon the preparation or identification of the work or the existence, ownership, or duration of the copyright.

If an application is submitted for the renewed and extended term provided for in section 304(a)(3)(A) and an original term registration has not been made, the Register may request information with respect to the existence, ownership, or duration of the copyright for the original term.

Sec. 410.   Registration of Claim and Issuance of Certificate

(a) When, after examination, the Register of Copyrights determines that, in accordance with the provisions of this title, the material deposited constitutes copyrightable subject matter and that the other legal and formal requirements of this title have been met, the Register shall register the claim and issue to the applicant a certificate of registration under the seal of the Copyright Office. The certificate shall contain the information given in the application, together with the number and effective date of the registration.

(b) In any case in which the Register of Copyrights determines that, in accordance with the provisions of this title, the material deposited does not constitute copyrightable subject matter or that the claim is invalid for any other reason, the Register shall refuse registration and shall notify the applicant in writing of the reasons for such refusal.

(c) In any judicial proceedings the certificate of a registration made before or within five years after first publication of the work shall constitute prima facie evidence of the validity of the copyright and of the facts stated in the certificate. The evidentiary weight to be accorded the certificate of a registration made thereafter shall be within the discretion of the court.

(d) The effective date of a copyright registration is the day on which an application, deposit, and fee, which are later determined by the Register of Copyrights or by a court of competent jurisdiction to be acceptable for registration, have all been received in the Copyright Office.

Sec. 411.   Registration and Civil Infringement Actions

(a) Except for an action brought for violation of the rights of the author under section 106A(a), and subject to the provisions of subsection (b), no civil action for infringement of the copyright in any United States work shall be instituted until preregistration or registration of the copyright claim has been made in accordance with this title. In any case, however, where the deposit, application, and fee required for registration have been delivered to the Copyright Office in proper form and registration has been refused, the applicant is entitled to institute a civil action for infringement if notice thereof, with a copy of the complaint, is served on the Register of Copyrights. The Register may, at his or her option, become a party to the action with respect to the issue of registrability of the copyright claim by entering an appearance within sixty days after such service, but the Register's failure to become a party shall not deprive the court of jurisdiction to determine that issue.

(b)(1) A certificate of registration satisfies the requirements of this section and section 412, regardless of whether the certificate contains any inaccurate information, unless—

(A) the inaccurate information was included on the application for copyright registration with knowledge that it was inaccurate; and

(B) the inaccuracy of the information, if known, would have caused the Register of Copyrights to refuse registration.

(2) In any case in which inaccurate information described under paragraph (1) is alleged, the court shall request the Register of Copyrights to advise the court whether the inaccurate information, if known, would have caused the Register of Copyrights to refuse registration.

(3) Nothing in this subsection shall affect any rights, obligations, or requirements of a person related to information contained in a registration certificate, except for the institution of and remedies in infringement actions under this section and section 412.

(c) In the case of a work consisting of sounds, images, or both, the first fixation of which is made simultaneously with its transmission, the copyright owner may, either before or after such fixation takes place, institute an action for infringement under section 501, fully subject to the remedies provided by sections 502 through 505 and section 510, if, in accordance with requirements that the Register of Copyrights shall prescribe by regulation, the copyright owner—

(1) serves notice upon the infringer, not less than 48 hours before such fixation, identifying the work and the specific time and source of its first transmission, and declaring an intention to secure copyright in the work; and

(2) makes registration for the work, if required by subsection (a), within three months after its first transmission.

Sec. 412.   Registration as Prerequisite to Certain Remedies for Infringement

In any action under this title, other than an action brought for a violation of the rights of the author under section 106A(a), an action for infringement of the copyright of a work that has been preregistered under section 408(f) before the commencement of the infringement and that has an effective date of registration not later than the earlier of 3 months after the first publication of the work or 1 month after the copyright owner has learned of the infringement, or an action instituted under section 411(c), no award of statutory damages or of attorney's fees, as provided by sections 504 and 505, shall be made for—

(1) any infringement of copyright in an unpublished work commenced before the effective date of its registration; or

(2) any infringement of copyright commenced after first publication of the work and before the effective date of its registration, unless such registration is made within three months after the first publication of the work.

CHAPTER 5.—COPYRIGHT INFRINGEMENT AND REMEDIES

Sec. 501.   Infringement of Copyright

(a) Anyone who violates any of the exclusive rights of the copyright owner as provided by sections 106 through 122 or of the author as provided in section 106A(a), or who imports copies or phonorecords into the United States in violation of section 602, is an infringer of the copyright or right of the author, as the case may be. For purposes of this chapter (other than section 506), any reference to copyright shall be deemed to include the rights conferred by section 106A(a). As used in this subsection, the term "anyone" includes any State, any instrumentality of a State, and any officer or employee of a State or instrumentality of a State acting in his or her official capacity. Any State, and any such instrumentality, officer, or employee, shall be subject to the provisions of this title in the same manner and to the same extent as any nongovernmental entity.

(b) The legal or beneficial owner of an exclusive right under a copyright is entitled, subject to the requirements of section 411, to institute an action for any infringement of that particular right committed while he or she is the owner of it. The court may require such owner to serve written notice of the action with a copy of the complaint upon any person shown, by the records of the Copyright Office or otherwise, to have or claim an interest in the copyright, and shall require that such notice be served upon any person whose interest is likely to be affected by a decision in the case. The court may require the joinder, and shall permit the intervention, of any person having or claiming an interest in the copyright.

(c) For any secondary transmission by a cable system that embodies a performance or a display of a work which is actionable as an act of infringement under subsection (c) of section 111, a television broadcast station holding a copyright or other license to transmit or perform the same version of that work shall, for purposes of subsection (b) of this section, be treated as a legal or beneficial owner if such secondary transmission occurs within the local service area of that television station.

(d) For any secondary transmission by a cable system that is actionable as an act of infringement pursuant to section 111(c)(3), the following shall also have standing to sue: (i) the primary transmitter whose transmission has been altered by the cable system; and (ii) any broadcast station within whose local service area the secondary transmission occurs.

(e) With respect to any secondary transmission that is made by a satellite carrier of a performance or display of a work embodied in a primary transmission and is actionable as an act of infringement under section 119(a)(5), a network station holding a copyright or other license to transmit or perform the same version of that work shall, for purposes of subsection (b) of this section, be treated as a legal or beneficial owner if such secondary transmission occurs within the local service area of that station.

(f)(1) With respect to any secondary transmission that is made by a satellite carrier of a performance or display of a work embodied in a primary transmission and is actionable as an act of infringement under section 122, a television broadcast station holding a copyright or other license to transmit or perform the same version of that work shall, for purposes of subsection (b) of this section, be treated as a legal or beneficial owner if such secondary transmission occurs within the local market of that station.

(2) A television broadcast station may file a civil action against any satellite carrier that has refused to carry television broadcast signals, as required under section 122(a)(2), to enforce that television broadcast station's rights under section 338(a) of the Communications Act of 1934 [47 U.S.C.A. § 338(a)].

Sec. 502.   Remedies for Infringement: Injunctions

(a) Any court having jurisdiction of a civil action arising under this title may, subject to the provisions of section 1498 of title 28, grant temporary and final injunctions on such terms as it may deem reasonable to prevent or restrain infringement of a copyright.

(b) Any such injunction may be served anywhere in the United States on the person enjoined; it shall be operative throughout the United States and shall be enforceable, by proceedings in contempt or otherwise, by any United States court having jurisdiction of that person. The clerk of the court granting the injunction shall, when requested by any other court in which enforcement of the injunction is sought, transmit promptly to the other court a certified copy of all the papers in the case on file in such clerk's office.

Sec. 503.   Remedies   for   Infringement: Impounding   and Disposition of Infringing Articles

(a)(1) At any time while an action under this title is pending, the court may order the impounding, on such terms as it may deem reasonable—

(A) of all copies or phonorecords claimed to have been made or used in violation of the exclusive right of the copyright owner;

(B) of all plates, molds, matrices, masters, tapes, film negatives, or other articles by means of which such copies or phonorecords may be reproduced; and

(C) of records documenting the manufacture, sale, or receipt of things involved in any such violation, provided that any records seized under this subparagraph shall be taken into the custody of the court.

(2) For impoundments of records ordered under paragraph (1)(C), the court shall enter an appropriate protective order with respect to discovery and use of any records or information that has been impounded. The protective order shall provide for appropriate procedures to ensure that confidential, private, proprietary, or privileged information contained in such records is not improperly disclosed or used.

(3) The relevant provisions of paragraphs (2) through (11) of section 34(d) of the Trademark Act (15 U.S.C. 1116(d)(2) through (11)) shall extend to any impoundment of records ordered under paragraph (1)(C) that is based upon an ex parte application, notwithstanding the provisions of rule 65 of the Federal Rules of Civil Procedure. Any references in paragraphs (2) through (11) of section 34(d) of the Trademark Act to section 32 of such Act shall be read as references to section 501 of this title, and references to use of a counterfeit mark in connection with the sale, offering for sale, or distribution of goods or services shall be read as references to infringement of a copyright.

(b) As part of a final judgment or decree, the court may order the destruction or other reasonable disposition of all copies or phonorecords found to have been made or used in violation of the copyright owner's exclusive rights, and of all plates, molds, matrices, masters, tapes, film negatives, or other articles by means of which such copies or phonorecords may be reproduced.

Sec. 504. Remedies for Infringement: Damages and Profits

(a) In General.—Except as otherwise provided by this title, an infringer of copyright is liable for either—

(1) the copyright owner's actual damages and any additional profits of the infringer, as provided by subsection (b); or

(2) statutory damages, as provided by subsection (c).

(b) Actual Damages and Profits.—The copyright owner is entitled to recover the actual damages suffered by him or her as a result of the infringement, and any profits of the infringer that are attributable to the infringement and are not taken into account in computing the actual damages. In establishing the infringer's profits, the copyright owner is required to present proof only of the infringer's gross revenue, and the infringer is required to prove his or her deductible expenses and the elements of profit attributable to factors other than the copyrighted work.

(c) Statutory Damages.—

(1) Except as provided by clause (2) of this subsection, the copyright owner may elect, at any time before final judgment is rendered, to recover, instead of actual damages and profits, an award of statutory damages for all infringements involved in the action, with respect to any one work, for which any one infringer is liable individually, or for which any two or more infringers are liable jointly and severally, in a sum of not less than $750 or more than $30,000 as the court considers just. For the purposes of this subsection, all the parts of a compilation or derivative work constitute one work.

(2) In a case where the copyright owner sustains the burden of proving, and the court finds, that infringement was committed willfully, the court in its discretion may increase the award of statutory damages to a sum of not more than $150,000. In a case where the infringer sustains the burden of proving, and the court finds, that such infringer was not aware and had no reason to believe that his or her acts constituted an infringement of copyright, the court in its discretion may reduce the award of statutory damages to a sum of not less than $200. The court shall remit statutory damages in any case where an infringer believed and had reasonable grounds for believing that his or her use of the copyrighted work was a fair use under section 107, if the infringer was: (i) an employee or agent of a nonprofit educational institution, library, or archives acting within the scope of his or her employment who, or such institution, library, or archives itself, which infringed by reproducing the work in copies or phonorecords; or (ii) a public broadcasting entity which or a person who, as a regular part of the nonprofit activities of a public broadcasting entity (as defined in section 118(f)) infringed by performing a published nondramatic literary work or

by reproducing a transmission program embodying a performance of such a work.

(3)(A) In a case of infringement, it shall be a rebuttable presumption that the infringement was committed willfully for purposes of determining relief if the violator, or a person acting in concert with the violator, knowingly provided or knowingly caused to be provided materially false contact information to a domain name registrar, domain name registry, or other domain name registration authority in registering, maintaining, or renewing a domain name used in connection with the infringement.

(B) Nothing in this paragraph limits what may be considered willful infringement under this subsection.

(C) For purposes of this paragraph, the term "domain name" has the meaning given that term in section 45 of the Act entitled "An Act to provide for the registration and protection of trademarks used in commerce, to carry out the provisions of certain international conventions, and for other purposes" approved July 5, 1946 (commonly referred to as the "Trademark Act of 1946"; 15 U.S.C. 1127).

(d) Additional Damages in Certain Cases.—In any case in which the court finds that a defendant proprietor of an establishment who claims as a defense that its activities were exempt under section 110(5) did not have reasonable grounds to believe that its use of a copyrighted work was exempt under such section, the plaintiff shall be entitled to, in addition to any award of damages under this section, an additional award of two times the amount of the license fee that the proprietor of the establishment concerned should have paid the plaintiff for such use during the preceding period of up to 3 years.

Sec. 505.   Remedies for Infringement: Costs and Attorney's Fees

In any civil action under this title, the court in its discretion may allow the recovery of full costs by or against any party other than the United States or an officer thereof. Except as otherwise provided by this title, the court may also award a reasonable attorney's fee to the prevailing party as part of the costs.

Sec. 506.   Criminal Offenses

(a) Criminal Infringement.—

(1) In General.—Any person who willfully infringes a copyright shall be punished as provided under section 2319 of title 18, if the infringement was committed—

(A) for purposes of commercial advantage or private financial gain;

(B) by the reproduction or distribution, including by electronic means, during any 180-day period, of 1 or more copies or phonorecords of 1 or more copyrighted works, which have a total retail value of more than $1,000; or

(C) by the distribution of a work being prepared for commercial distribution, by making it available on a computer network accessible to members of the public, if such person knew or should have known that the work was intended for commercial distribution.

(2) Evidence.—For purposes of this subsection, evidence of reproduction or distribution of a copyrighted work, by itself, shall not be sufficient to establish willful infringement of a copyright.

(3) Definition.—In this subsection, the term "work being prepared for commercial distribution" means—

(A) a computer program, a musical work, a motion picture or other audiovisual work, or a sound recording, if, at the time of unauthorized distribution—

(i) the copyright owner has a reasonable expectation of commercial distribution; and

(ii) the copies or phonorecords of the work have not been commercially distributed; or

(B) a motion picture, if, at the time of unauthorized distribution, the motion picture—

(i) has been made available for viewing in a motion picture exhibition facility; and

(ii) has not been made available in copies for sale to the general public in the United States in a format intended to permit viewing outside a motion picture exhibition facility.

(b) Forfeiture, Destruction, and Restitution.—Forfeiture, destruction, and restitution relating to this section shall be subject to section 2323 of title 18, to the extent provided in that section, in addition to any other similar remedies provided by law.

(c) Fraudulent Copyright Notice.—Any person who, with fraudulent intent, places on any article a notice of copyright or words of the same purport that such person knows to be false, or who, with fraudulent intent, publicly distributes or imports for public distribution any article bearing such notice or words that such person knows to be false, shall be fined not more than $2,500.

(d) Fraudulent Removal of Copyright Notice.—Any person who, with fraudulent intent, removes or alters any notice of copyright appearing on a copy of a copyrighted work shall be fined not more than $2,500.

(e) False Representation.—Any person who knowingly makes a false representation of a material fact in the application for copyright registration provided for by section 409, or in any written statement filed in connection with the application, shall be fined not more than $2,500.

(f) Rights of Attribution and Integrity.—Nothing in this section applies to infringement of the rights conferred by section 106A(a).

Sec. 507.   Limitations on Actions

(a) Criminal   Proceedings.—Except   as   expressly   provided otherwise in this title, no criminal proceeding shall be maintained under the provisions of this title unless it is commenced within five years after the cause of action arose.

(b) Civil Actions.—No civil action shall be maintained under the provisions of this title unless it is commenced within three years after the claim accrued.

Sec. 508.   Notification of Filing and Determination of Actions

(a) Within one month after the filing of any action under this title, the clerks of the courts of the United States shall send written notification to the Register of Copyrights setting forth, as far as is shown by the papers filed in the court, the names and addresses of the parties and the title, author, and registration number of each work involved in the action. If any other copyrighted work is later included in the action by amendment, answer, or other pleading, the clerk shall also send a notification concerning it to the Register within one month after the pleading is filed.

(b) Within one month after any final order or judgment is issued in the case, the clerk of the court shall notify the Register of it, sending with the notification a copy of the order or judgment together with the written opinion, if any, of the court.

(c) Upon receiving the notifications specified in this section, the Register shall make them a part of the public records of the Copyright Office.

[Sec. 509.   Repealed]

Sec. 510.   Remedies for Alteration of Programming by Cable Systems

(a) In any action filed pursuant to section 111(c)(3), the following remedies shall be available:

(1) Where an action is brought by a party identified in subsections (b) or (c) of section 501, the remedies provided by sections 502 through 505, and the remedy provided by subsection (b) of this section; and

(2) When an action is brought by a party identified in subsection (d) of section 501, the remedies provided by sections 502 and 505, together with any actual damages suffered by such party as a result of the infringement, and the remedy provided by subsection (b) of this section.

(b) In any action filed pursuant to section 111(c)(3), the court may decree that, for a period not to exceed thirty days, the cable system shall be deprived of the benefit of a statutory license for one or more distant signals carried by such cable system.

Sec. 511. Liability of States, Instrumentalities of States, and State Officials for Infringement of Copyright

(a) In General.—Any State, any instrumentality of a State, and any officer or employee of a State or instrumentality of a State acting in his or her official capacity, shall not be immune, under the Eleventh Amendment of the Constitution of the United States or under any other doctrine of sovereign immunity, from suit in Federal court by any person, including any governmental or nongovernmental entity, for a violation of any of the exclusive rights of a copyright owner provided by sections 106 through 122, for importing copies or phonorecords in violation of section 602, or for any other violation under this title.

(b) Remedies.—In a suit described in subsection (a) for a violation described in that subsection, remedies (including remedies both at law and in equity) are available for the violation to the same extent as such remedies are available for such a violation in a suit against any public or private entity other than a State, instrumentality of a State, or officer or employee of a State acting in his or her official capacity. Such remedies include impounding and disposition of infringing articles under section 503, actual damages and profits and statutory damages under section 504, costs and attorney's fees under section 505, and the remedies provided in section 510.

Sec. 512. Limitations on Liability Relating to Material Online

(a) Transitory Digital Network Communications.—A service provider shall not be liable for monetary relief, or, except as provided in subsection (j), for injunctive or other equitable relief, for infringement of copyright by reason of the provider's transmitting, routing, or providing connections for, material through a system or network controlled or operated by or for the service provider, or by reason of the intermediate and transient storage of that material in the course of such transmitting, routing, or providing connections, if—

(1) the transmission of the material was initiated by or at the direction of a person other than the service provider;

(2) the transmission, routing, provision of connections, or storage is carried out through an automatic technical process without selection of the material by the service provider;

(3) the service provider does not select the recipients of the material except as an automatic response to the request of another person;

(4) no copy of the material made by the service provider in the course of such intermediate or transient storage is maintained on

the system or network in a manner ordinarily accessible to anyone other than anticipated recipients, and no such copy is maintained on the system or network in a manner ordinarily accessible to such anticipated recipients for a longer period than is reasonably necessary for the transmission, routing, or provision of connections; and

(5) the material is transmitted through the system or network without modification of its content.

(b) System Caching.—

(1) Limitation on Liability.—A service provider shall not be liable for monetary relief, or, except as provided in subsection (j), for injunctive or other equitable relief, for infringement of copyright by reason of the intermediate and temporary storage of material on a system or network controlled or operated by or for the service provider in a case in which—

(A) the material is made available online by a person other than the service provider;

(B) the material is transmitted from the person described in subparagraph (A) through the system or network to a person other than the person described in subparagraph (A) at the direction of that other person; and

(C) the storage is carried out through an automatic technical process for the purpose of making the material available to users of the system or network who, after the material is transmitted as described in subparagraph (B), request access to the material from the person described in subparagraph (A), if the conditions set forth in paragraph (2) are met.

(2) Conditions.—The conditions referred to in paragraph (1) are that—

(A) the material described in paragraph (1) is transmitted to the subsequent users described in paragraph (1)(C) without modification to its content from the manner in which the material was transmitted from the person described in paragraph (1)(A);

(B) the service provider described in paragraph (1) complies with rules concerning the refreshing, reloading, or other updating of the material when specified by the person making the material available online in accordance with a generally accepted industry standard data communications protocol for the system or network through which that person makes the material available, except that this subparagraph applies only if those rules are not used by the person described in paragraph

(1)(A) to prevent or unreasonably impair the intermediate storage to which this subsection applies;

(C) the service provider does not interfere with the ability of technology associated with the material to return to the person described in paragraph (1)(A) the information that would have been available to that person if the material had been obtained by the subsequent users described in paragraph (1)(C) directly from that person, except that this subparagraph applies only if that technology—

(i) does not significantly interfere with the performance of the provider's system or network or with the intermediate storage of the material;

(ii) is consistent with generally accepted industry standard communications protocols; and

(iii) does not extract information from the provider's system or network other than the information that would have been available to the person described in paragraph (1)(A) if the subsequent users had gained access to the material directly from that person;

(D) if the person described in paragraph (1)(A) has in effect a condition that a person must meet prior to having access to the material, such as a condition based on payment of a fee or provision of a password or other information, the service provider permits access to the stored material in significant part only to users of its system or network that have met those conditions and only in accordance with those conditions; and

(E) if the person described in paragraph (1)(A) makes that material available online without the authorization of the copyright owner of the material, the service provider responds expeditiously to remove, or disable access to, the material that is claimed to be infringing upon notification of claimed infringement as described in subsection (c)(3), except that this subparagraph applies only if—

(i) the material has previously been removed from the originating site or access to it has been disabled, or a court has ordered that the material be removed from the originating site or that access to the material on the originating site be disabled; and

(ii) the party giving the notification includes in the notification a statement confirming that the material has been removed from the originating site or access to it has been disabled or that a court has ordered that the material be removed from the originating site or that access to the material on the originating site be disabled.

(c) Information Residing on Systems or Networks at Direction of Users.—

(1) In General.—A service provider shall not be liable for monetary relief, or, except as provided in subsection (j), for injunctive or other equitable relief, for infringement of copyright by reason of the storage at the direction of a user of material that resides on a system or network controlled or operated by or for the service provider, if the service provider—

(A)(i) does not have actual knowledge that the material or an activity using the material on the system or network is infringing;

(ii) in the absence of such actual knowledge, is not aware of facts or circumstances from which infringing activity is apparent; or

(iii) upon obtaining such knowledge or awareness, acts expeditiously to remove, or disable access to, the material;

(B) does not receive a financial benefit directly attributable to the infringing activity, in a case in which the service provider has the right and ability to control such activity; and

(C) upon notification of claimed infringement as described in paragraph (3), responds expeditiously to remove, or disable access to, the material that is claimed to be infringing or to be the subject of infringing activity.

(2) Designated Agent.—The limitations on liability established in this subsection apply to a service provider only if the service provider has designated an agent to receive notifications of claimed infringement described in paragraph (3), by making available through its service, including on its website in a location accessible to the public, and by providing to the Copyright Office, substantially the following information:

(A) the name, address, phone number, and electronic mail address of the agent.

(B) other contact information which the Register of Copyrights may deem appropriate.

The Register of Copyrights shall maintain a current directory of agents available to the public for inspection, including through the Internet, and may require payment of a fee by service providers to cover the costs of maintaining the directory.

(3) Elements of Notification.—

(A) To be effective under this subsection, a notification of claimed infringement must be a written communication provided to the designated agent of a service provider that includes substantially the following:

(i) A physical or electronic signature of a person authorized to act on behalf of the owner of an exclusive right that is allegedly infringed.

(ii) Identification of the copyrighted work claimed to have been infringed, or, if multiple copyrighted works at a single online site are covered by a single notification, a representative list of such works at that site.

(iii) Identification of the material that is claimed to be infringing or to be the subject of infringing activity and that is to be removed or access to which is to be disabled, and information reasonably sufficient to permit the service provider to locate the material.

(iv) Information reasonably sufficient to permit the service provider to contact the complaining party, such as an address, telephone number, and, if available, an electronic mail address at which the complaining party may be contacted.

(v) A statement that the complaining party has a good faith belief that use of the material in the manner complained of is not authorized by the copyright owner, its agent, or the law.

(vi) A statement that the information in the notification is accurate, and under penalty of perjury, that the complaining party is authorized to act on behalf of the owner of an exclusive right that is allegedly infringed.

(B)(i) Subject to clause (ii), a notification from a copyright owner or from a person authorized to act on behalf of the copyright owner that fails to comply substantially with the provisions of subparagraph (A) shall not be considered under paragraph (1)(A) in determining whether a service provider has actual knowledge or is aware of facts or circumstances from which infringing activity is apparent.

(ii) In a case in which the notification that is provided to the service provider's designated agent fails to comply substantially with all the provisions of subparagraph (A) but substantially complies with clauses (ii), (iii), and (iv) of subparagraph (A), clause (i) of this subparagraph applies only if the service provider promptly attempts to contact the person making the notification or takes other reasonable steps to assist in the receipt of notification that substantially complies with all the provisions of subparagraph (A).

(d) Information Location Tools.—A service provider shall not be liable for monetary relief, or, except as provided in subsection (j), for injunctive or other equitable relief, for infringement of copyright by reason of the provider referring or linking users to an online location containing infringing material or infringing activity, by using information location tools, including a directory, index, reference, pointer, or hypertext link, if the service provider—

(1)(A) does not have actual knowledge that the material or activity is infringing;

(B) in the absence of such actual knowledge, is not aware of facts or circumstances from which infringing activity is apparent; or

(C) upon obtaining such knowledge or awareness, acts expeditiously to remove, or disable access to, the material;

(2) does not receive a financial benefit directly attributable to the infringing activity, in a case in which the service provider has the right and ability to control such activity; and

(3) upon notification of claimed infringement as described in subsection (c)(3), responds expeditiously to remove, or disable access to, the material that is claimed to be infringing or to be the subject of infringing activity, except that, for purposes of this paragraph, the information described in subsection (c)(3)(A)(iii) shall be identification of the reference or link, to material or activity claimed to be infringing, that is to be removed or access to which is to be disabled, and information reasonably sufficient to permit the service provider to locate that reference or link.

(e) Limitation on Liability of Nonprofit Educational Institutions.—

(1) When a public or other nonprofit institution of higher education is a service provider, and when a faculty member or graduate student who is an employee of such institution is performing a teaching or research function, for the purposes of subsections (a) and (b) such faculty member or graduate student shall be considered to be a person other than the institution, and for the purposes of subsections (c) and (d) such faculty member's or graduate student's knowledge or awareness of his or her infringing activities shall not be attributed to the institution, if—

(A) such faculty member's or graduate student's infringing activities do not involve the provision of online access to instructional materials that are or were required or recommended, within the preceding 3-year period, for a course taught at the institution by such faculty member or graduate student;

(B) the institution has not, within the preceding 3-year period, received more than two notifications described in subsection (c)(3) of claimed infringement by such faculty member or graduate student, and such notifications of claimed infringement were not actionable under subsection (f); and

(C) the institution provides to all users of its system or network informational materials that accurately describe, and promote compliance with, the laws of the United States relating to copyright.

(2) For the purposes of this subsection, the limitations on injunctive relief contained in subsections (j)(2) and (j)(3), but not those in (j)(1), shall apply.

(f) Misrepresentations.—Any person who knowingly materially misrepresents under this section—

(1) that material or activity is infringing, or

(2) that material or activity was removed or disabled by mistake or misidentification,

shall be liable for any damages, including costs and attorneys' fees, incurred by the alleged infringer, by any copyright owner or copyright owner's authorized licensee, or by a service provider, who is injured by such misrepresentation, as the result of the service provider relying upon such misrepresentation in removing or disabling access to the material or activity claimed to be infringing, or in replacing the removed material or ceasing to disable access to it

(g) Replacement of Removed or Disabled Material and Limitation on Other Liability.—

(1) No Liability for Taking Down Generally.—Subject to paragraph (2), a service provider shall not be liable to any person for any claim based on the service provider's good faith disabling of access to, or removal of, material or activity claimed to be infringing or based on facts or circumstances from which infringing activity is apparent, regardless of whether the material or activity is ultimately determined to be infringing.

(2) Exception.—Paragraph (1) shall not apply with respect to material residing at the direction of a subscriber of the service provider on a system or network controlled or operated by or for the service provider that is removed, or to which access is disabled by the service provider, pursuant to a notice provided under subsection (c)(1)(C), unless the service provider—

(A) takes reasonable steps promptly to notify the subscriber that it has removed or disabled access to the material;

(B) upon receipt of a counter notification described in paragraph (3), promptly provides the person who provided the notification under subsection (c)(1)(C) with a copy of the counter notification, and informs that person that it will replace the removed material or cease disabling access to it in 10 business days; and

(C) replaces the removed material and ceases disabling access to it not less than 10, nor more than 14, business days following receipt of the counter notice, unless its designated agent first receives notice from the person who submitted the notification under subsection (c)(1)(C) that such person has filed an action seeking a court order to restrain the subscriber from engaging in infringing activity relating to the material on the service provider's system or network.

(3) Contents of Counter Notification.—To be effective under this subsection, a counter notification must be a written communication provided to the service provider's designated agent that includes substantially the following:

(A) A physical or electronic signature of the subscriber.

(B) Identification of the material that has been removed or to which access has been disabled and the location at which the material appeared before it was removed or access to it was disabled.

(C) A statement under penalty of perjury that the subscriber has a good faith belief that the material was removed or disabled as a result of mistake or misidentification of the material to be removed or disabled.

(D) The subscriber's name, address, and telephone number, and a statement that the subscriber consents to the jurisdiction of Federal District Court for the judicial district in which the address is located, or if the subscriber's address is outside of the United States, for any judicial district in which the service provider may be found, and that the subscriber will accept service of process from the person who provided notification under subsection (c)(1)(C) or an agent of such person.

(4) Limitation on Other Liability.—A service provider's compliance with paragraph (2) shall not subject the service provider to liability for copyright infringement with respect to the material identified in the notice provided under subsection (c)(1)(C).

(h) Subpoena to Identify Infringer.—

(1) Request.—A copyright owner or a person authorized to act on the owner's behalf may request the clerk of any United States district court to issue a subpoena to a service provider for identification of an alleged infringer in accordance with this subsection.

(2) Contents of Request.—The request may be made by filing with the clerk—

(A) a copy of a notification described in subsection (c)(3)(A);

(B) a proposed subpoena; and

(C) a sworn declaration to the effect that the purpose for which the subpoena is sought is to obtain the identity of an alleged infringer and that such information will only be used for the purpose of protecting rights under this title.

(3) Contents of Subpoena.—The subpoena shall authorize and order the service provider receiving the notification and the subpoena to expeditiously disclose to the copyright owner or person authorized by the copyright owner information sufficient to identify the alleged infringer of the material described in the notification to the extent such information is available to the service provider.

(4) Basis for Granting Subpoena.—If the notification filed satisfies the provisions of subsection (c)(3)(A), the proposed subpoena is in proper form, and the accompanying declaration is properly executed, the clerk shall expeditiously issue and sign the proposed subpoena and return it to the requester for delivery to the service provider.

(5) Actions of Service Provider Receiving Subpoena.— Upon receipt of the issued subpoena, either accompanying or subsequent to the receipt of a notification described in subsection (c)(3)(A), the service provider shall expeditiously disclose to the copyright owner or person authorized by the copyright owner the information required by the subpoena, notwithstanding any other provision of law and regardless of whether the service provider responds to the notification.

(6) Rules Applicable to Subpoena.—Unless otherwise provided by this section or by applicable rules of the court, the procedure for issuance and delivery of the subpoena, and the remedies for noncompliance with the subpoena, shall be governed to the greatest extent practicable by those provisions of the Federal Rules of Civil Procedure governing the issuance, service, and enforcement of a subpoena duces tecum.

(i) Conditions for Eligibility.—

(1) Accommodation of Technology.—The limitations on liability established by this section shall apply to a service provider only if the service provider—

> (A) has adopted and reasonably implemented, and informs subscribers and account holders of the service provider's system or network of, a policy that provides for the termination in appropriate circumstances of subscribers and account holders of the service provider's system or network who are repeat infringers; and

> (B) accommodates and does not interfere with standard technical measures.

(2) Definition.—As used in this subsection, the term "standard technical measures" means technical measures that are used by copyright owners to identify or protect copyrighted works and—

(A) have been developed pursuant to a broad consensus of copyright owners and service providers in an open, fair, voluntary, multi-industry standards process;

(B) are available to any person on reasonable and nondiscriminatory terms; and

(C) do not impose substantial costs on service providers or substantial burdens on their systems or networks.

(j) Injunctions.—The following rules shall apply in the case of any application for an injunction under section 502 against a service provider that is not subject to monetary remedies under this section:

(1) Scope of Relief.—

(A) With respect to conduct other than that which qualifies for the limitation on remedies set forth in subsection (a), the court may grant injunctive relief with respect to a service provider only in one or more of the following forms:

(i) An order restraining the service provider from providing access to infringing material or activity residing at a particular online site on the provider's system or network.

(ii) An order restraining the service provider from providing access to a subscriber or account holder of the service provider's system or network who is engaging in infringing activity and is identified in the order, by terminating the accounts of the subscriber or account holder that are specified in the order.

(iii) Such other injunctive relief as the court may consider necessary to prevent or restrain infringement of copyrighted material specified in the order of the court at a particular online location, if such relief is the least burdensome to the service provider among the forms of relief comparably effective for that purpose.

(B) If the service provider qualifies for the limitation on remedies described in subsection (a), the court may only grant injunctive relief in one or both of the following forms:

(i) An order restraining the service provider from providing access to a subscriber or account holder of the service provider's system or network who is using the provider's service to engage in infringing activity and is identified in the order, by terminating the accounts of the subscriber or account holder that are specified in the order.

(ii) An order restraining the service provider from providing access, by taking reasonable steps specified in the order to block access, to a specific, identified, online location outside the United States.

(2) Considerations.—The court, in considering the relevant criteria for injunctive relief under applicable law, shall consider—

(A) whether such an injunction, either alone or in combination with other such injunctions issued against the same service provider under this subsection, would significantly burden either the provider or the operation of the provider's system or network;

(B) the magnitude of the harm likely to be suffered by the copyright owner in the digital network environment if steps are not taken to prevent or restrain the infringement;

(C) whether implementation of such an injunction would be technically feasible and effective, and would not interfere with access to noninfringing material at other online locations; and

(D) whether other less burdensome and comparably effective means of preventing or restraining access to the infringing material are available.

(3) Notice and Ex Parte Orders.—Injunctive relief under this subsection shall be available only after notice to the service provider and an opportunity for the service provider to appear are provided, except for orders ensuring the preservation of evidence or other orders having no material adverse effect on the operation of the service provider's communications network.

(k) Definitions.—

(1) Service Provider.—

(A) As used in subsection (a), the term "service provider" means an entity offering the transmission, routing, or providing of connections for digital online communications, between or among points specified by a user, of material of the user's choosing, without modification to the content of the material as sent or received.

(B) As used in this section, other than subsection (a), the term "service provider" means a provider of online services or network access, or the operator of facilities therefor, and includes an entity described in subparagraph (A).

(2) Monetary Relief.—As used in this section, the term "monetary relief" means damages, costs, attorneys' fees, and any other form of monetary payment.

(*l*) Other Defenses Not Affected.—The failure of a service provider's conduct to qualify for limitation of liability under this section shall not bear adversely upon the consideration of a defense by the service provider that the service provider's conduct is not infringing under this title or any other defense.

(m) Protection of Privacy.—Nothing in this section shall be construed to condition the applicability of subsections (a) through (d) on—

(1) a service provider monitoring its service or affirmatively seeking facts indicating infringing activity, except to the extent consistent with a standard technical measure complying with the provisions of subsection (i); or

(2) a service provider gaining access to, removing, or disabling access to material in cases in which such conduct is prohibited by law.

(n) Construction.—Subsections (a), (b), (c), and (d) describe separate and distinct functions for purposes of applying this section. Whether a service provider qualifies for the limitation on liability in any one of those subsections shall be based solely on the criteria in that subsection, and shall not affect a determination of whether that service provider qualifies for the limitations on liability under any other such subsection.

Sec. 513.   Determination of Reasonable License Fees for Individual Proprietors

In the case of any performing rights society subject to a consent decree which provides for the determination of reasonable license rates or fees to be charged by the performing rights society, notwithstanding the provisions of that consent decree, an individual proprietor who owns or operates fewer than 7 non-publicly traded establishments in which nondramatic musical works are performed publicly and who claims that any license agreement offered by that performing rights society is unreasonable in its license rate or fee as to that individual proprietor, shall be entitled to determination of a reasonable license rate or fee as follows:

(1) The individual proprietor may commence such proceeding for determination of a reasonable license rate or fee by filing an application in the applicable district court under paragraph (2) that a rate disagreement exists and by serving a copy of the application on the performing rights society. Such proceeding shall commence in the applicable district court within 90 days after the service of such copy, except that such 90-day requirement shall be subject to the administrative requirements of the court.

(2) The proceeding under paragraph (1) shall be held, at the individual proprietor's election, in the judicial district of the district court with jurisdiction over the applicable consent decree or in that place of holding court of a district court that is the seat of the Federal circuit (other than the Court of Appeals for the Federal Circuit) in which the proprietor's establishment is located.

(3) Such proceeding shall be held before the judge of the court with jurisdiction over the consent decree governing the performing

rights society. At the discretion of the court, the proceeding shall be held before a special master or magistrate judge appointed by such judge. Should that consent decree provide for the appointment of an advisor or advisors to the court for any purpose, any such advisor shall be the special master so named by the court.

(4) In any such proceeding, the industry rate shall be presumed to have been reasonable at the time it was agreed to or determined by the court. Such presumption shall in no way affect a determination of whether the rate is being correctly applied to the individual proprietor.

(5) Pending the completion of such proceeding, the individual proprietor shall have the right to perform publicly the copyrighted musical compositions in the repertoire of the performing rights society by paying an interim license rate or fee into an interest bearing escrow account with the clerk of the court, subject to retroactive adjustment when a final rate or fee has been determined, in an amount equal to the industry rate, or, in the absence of an industry rate, the amount of the most recent license rate or fee agreed to by the parties.

(6) Any decision rendered in such proceeding by a special master or magistrate judge named under paragraph (3) shall be reviewed by the judge of the court with jurisdiction over the consent decree governing the performing rights society. Such proceeding, including such review, shall be concluded within 6 months after its commencement.

(7) Any such final determination shall be binding only as to the individual proprietor commencing the proceeding, and shall not be applicable to any other proprietor or any other performing rights society, and the performing rights society shall be relieved of any obligation of nondiscrimination among similarly situated music users that may be imposed by the consent decree governing its operations.

(8) An individual proprietor may not bring more than one proceeding provided for in this section for the determination of a reasonable license rate or fee under any license agreement with respect to any one performing rights society.

(9) For purposes of this section, the term "industry rate" means the license fee a performing rights society has agreed to with, or which has been determined by the court for, a significant segment of the music user industry to which the individual proprietor belongs.

CHAPTER 6.—IMPORTATION AND EXPORTATION

Sec.

Sec. 602.   Infringing Importation or Exportation of Copies or Phonorecords

(a) Infringing Importation or Exportation.—

(1) Importation.—Importation into the United States, without the authority of the owner of copyright under this title, of copies or phonorecords of a work that have been acquired outside the United States is an infringement of the exclusive right to distribute copies or phonorecords under section 106, actionable under section 501.

(2) Importation or Exportation of Infringing Items.—Importation into the United States or exportation from the United States, without the authority of the owner of copyright under this title, of copies or phonorecords, the making of which either constituted an infringement of copyright, or which would have constituted an infringement of copyright if this title had been applicable, is an infringement of the exclusive right to distribute copies or phonorecords under section 106, actionable under sections 501 and 506.

(3) Exceptions.—This subsection does not apply to—

(A) importation or exportation of copies or phonorecords under the authority or for the use of the Government of the United States or of any State or political subdivision of a State, but not including copies or phonorecords for use in schools, or copies of any audiovisual work imported for purposes other than archival use;

(B) importation or exportation, for the private use of the importer or exporter and not for distribution, by any person with respect to no more than one copy or phonorecord of any one work at any one time, or by any person arriving from outside the United States or departing from the United States with respect to copies or phonorecords forming part of such person's personal baggage; or

(C) importation by or for an organization operated for scholarly, educational, or religious purposes and not for private gain, with respect to no more than one copy of an audiovisual work solely for its archival purposes, and no more than five copies or phonorecords of any other work for its library lending or archival purposes, unless the importation of such copies or phonorecords is part of an activity consisting of systematic reproduction or distribution, engaged in by such organization in violation of the provisions of section 108(g)(2).

(b) Import Prohibition.—In a case where the making of the copies or phonorecords would have constituted an infringement of copyright if this title had been applicable, their importation is prohibited. In a case where the copies or phonorecords were lawfully made, the United States Customs and Border Protection has no authority to prevent their importation. In either case, the Secretary of the Treasury is authorized to prescribe, by regulation, a procedure under which any person claiming an interest in the copyright in a particular work may, upon payment of a specified fee, be entitled to notification by United States Customs and Border Protection of the importation of articles that appear to be copies or phonorecords of the work.

Sec. 603. Importation Prohibitions: Enforcement and Disposition of Excluded Articles

(a) The Secretary of the Treasury and the United States Postal Service shall separately or jointly make regulations for the enforcement of the provisions of this title prohibiting importation.

(b) These regulations may require, as a condition for the exclusion of articles under section 602—

> (1) that the person seeking exclusion obtain a court order enjoining importation of the articles; or

> (2) that the person seeking exclusion furnish proof, of a specified nature and in accordance with prescribed procedures, that the copyright in which such person claims an interest is valid and that the importation would violate the prohibition in section 602; the person seeking exclusion may also be required to post a surety bond for any injury that may result if the detention or exclusion of the articles proves to be unjustified.

(c) Articles imported in violation of the importation prohibitions of this title are subject to seizure and forfeiture in the same manner as property imported in violation of the customs revenue laws. Forfeited articles shall be destroyed as directed by the Secretary of the Treasury or the court, as the case may be.

CHAPTER 7.—COPYRIGHT OFFICE

Sec. 701.   The Copyright Office: General Responsibilities and Organization

(a) All administrative functions and duties under this title, except as otherwise specified, are the responsibility of the Register of Copyrights as director of the Copyright Office of the Library of Congress. The Register of Copyrights, together with the subordinate officers and employees of the Copyright Office, shall be appointed by the Librarian of Congress, and shall act under the Librarian's general direction and supervision.

(b) In addition to the functions and duties set out elsewhere in this chapter, the Register of Copyrights shall perform the following functions:

(1) Advise Congress on national and international issues relating to copyright, other matters arising under this title, and related matters.

(2) Provide information and assistance to Federal departments and agencies and the Judiciary on national and international issues relating to copyright, other matters arising under this title, and related matters.

(3) Participate in meetings of international intergovernmental organizations and meetings with foreign government officials relating to copyright, other matters arising under this title, and related matters, including as a member of United States delegations as authorized by the appropriate Executive branch authority.

(4) Conduct studies and programs regarding copyright, other matters arising under this title, and related matters, the administration of the Copyright Office, or any function vested in the Copyright Office by law, including educational programs conducted cooperatively with foreign intellectual property offices and international intergovernmental organizations.

(5) Perform such other functions as Congress may direct, or as may be appropriate in furtherance of the functions and duties specifically set forth in this title.

(c) The Register of Copyrights shall adopt a seal to be used on and after January 1, 1978, to authenticate all certified documents issued by the Copyright Office.

(d) The Register of Copyrights shall make an annual report to the Librarian of Congress of the work and accomplishments of the Copyright Office during the previous fiscal year. The annual report of the Register of Copyrights shall be published separately and as a part of the annual report of the Librarian of Congress.

(e) Except as provided by section 706(b) and the regulations issued thereunder, all actions taken by the Register of Copyrights under this title are subject to the provisions of the Administrative Procedure Act of

June 11, 1946, as amended (c. 324, 60 Stat. 237, title 5, United States Code, Chapter 5, Subchapter II and Chapter 7).

(f) The Register of Copyrights shall be compensated at the rate of pay in effect for level III of the Executive Schedule under section 5314 of title 5. The Librarian of Congress shall establish not more than four positions for Associate Registers of Copyrights, in accordance with the recommendations of the Register of Copyrights. The Librarian shall make appointments to such positions after consultation with the Register of Copyrights. Each Associate Register of Copyrights shall be paid at a rate not to exceed the maximum annual rate of basic pay payable for GS-18 of the General Schedule under section 5332 of title 5.

Sec. 702.   Copyright Office Regulations

The Register of Copyrights is authorized to establish regulations not inconsistent with law for the administration of the functions and duties made the responsibility of the Register under this title. All regulations established by the Register under this title are subject to the approval of the Librarian of Congress.

Sec. 703.   Effective Date of Actions in Copyright Office

In any case in which time limits are prescribed under this title for the performance of an action in the Copyright Office, and in which the last day of the prescribed period falls on a Saturday, Sunday, holiday, or other nonbusiness day within the District of Columbia or the Federal Government, the action may be taken on the next succeeding business day, and is effective as of the date when the period expired.

Sec. 704.   Retention and Disposition of Articles Deposited in Copyright Office

(a) Upon their deposit in the Copyright Office under sections 407 and 408, all copies, phonorecords, and identifying material, including those deposited in connection with claims that have been refused registration, are the property of the United States Government.

(b) In the case of published works, all copies, phonorecords, and identifying material deposited are available to the Library of Congress for its collections, or for exchange or transfer to any other library. In the case of unpublished works, the Library is entitled, under regulations that the Register of Copyrights shall prescribe, to select any deposits for its collections or for transfer to the National Archives of the United States or to a Federal records center, as defined in section 2901 of title 44.

(c) The Register of Copyrights is authorized, for specific or general categories of works, to make a facsimile reproduction of all or any part of the material deposited under section 408, and to make such reproduction a part of the Copyright Office records of the registration, before transferring such material to the Library of Congress as provided by subsection (b), or before destroying or otherwise disposing of such material as provided by subsection (d).

(d) Deposits not selected by the Library under subsection (b), or identifying portions or reproductions of them, shall be retained under the control of the Copyright Office, including retention in Government storage facilities, for the longest period considered practicable and desirable by the Register of Copyrights and the Librarian of Congress. After that period it is within the joint discretion of the Register and the Librarian to order their destruction or other disposition; but, in the case of unpublished works, no deposit shall be knowingly or intentionally destroyed or otherwise disposed of during its term of copyright unless a facsimile reproduction of the entire deposit has been made a part of the Copyright Office records as provided by subsection (c).

(e) The depositor of copies, phonorecords, or identifying material under section 408, or the copyright owner of record, may request retention, under the control of the Copyright Office, of one or more of such articles for the full term of copyright in the work. The Register of Copyrights shall prescribe, by regulation, the conditions under which such requests are to be made and granted, and shall fix the fee to be charged under section 708(a) if the request is granted.

Sec. 705.   Copyright   Office   Records: Preparation, Maintenance, Public Inspection, and Searching

(a) The Register of Copyrights shall ensure that records of deposits, registrations, recordations, and other actions taken under this title are maintained, and that indexes of such records are prepared.

(b) Such records and indexes, as well as the articles deposited in connection with completed copyright registrations and retained under the control of the Copyright Office, shall be open to public inspection.

(c) Upon request and payment of the fee specified by section 708, the Copyright Office shall make a search of its public records, indexes, and deposits, and shall furnish a report of the information they disclose with respect to any particular deposits, registrations, or recorded documents.

Sec. 706.   Copies of Copyright Office Records

(a) Copies may be made of any public records or indexes of the Copyright Office; additional certificates of copyright registration and copies of any public records or indexes may be furnished upon request and payment of the fees specified by section 708.

(b) Copies or reproductions of deposited articles retained under the control of the Copyright Office shall be authorized or furnished only under the conditions specified by the Copyright Office regulations.

Sec. 707.   Copyright Office Forms and Publications

(a) Catalog of Copyright Entries.—The Register of Copyrights shall compile and publish at periodic intervals catalogs of all copyright registrations. These catalogs shall be divided into parts in accordance with the various classes of works, and the Register has discretion to determine, on the basis of practicability and usefulness, the form and frequency of publication of each particular part.

(b) Other Publications.—The Register shall furnish, free of charge upon request, application forms for copyright registration and general informational material in connection with the functions of the Copyright Office. The Register also has the authority to publish compilations of information, bibliographies, and other material he or she considers to be of value to the public.

(c) Distribution of Publications.—All publications of the Copyright Office shall be furnished to depository libraries as specified under section 1905 of title 44, and, aside from those furnished free of charge, shall be offered for sale to the public at prices based on the cost of reproduction and distribution.

Sec. 708.   Copyright Office Fees*

(a) *Fees.* Fees shall be paid to the Register of Copyrights—

(1) on filing each application under section 408 for registration of a copyright claim or for a supplementary registration, including the issuance of a certificate of registration if registration is made;

(2) on filing each application for registration of a claim for renewal of a subsisting copyright under section 304(a), including the issuance of a certificate of registration if registration is made;

(3) for the issuance of a receipt for a deposit under section 407;

(4) for the recordation, as provided by section 205, of a transfer of copyright ownership or other document;

(5) for the filing, under section 115(b), of a notice of intention to obtain a compulsory license;

(6) for the recordation, under section 302(c), of a statement revealing the identity of an author of an anonymous or pseudonymous work, or for the recordation, under section 302(d), of a statement relating to the death of an author;

(7) for the issuance, under section 706, of an additional certificate of registration;

(8) for the issuance of any other certification;

(9) for the making and reporting of a search as provided by section 705, and for any related services;

(10) on filing a statement of account based on secondary transmissions of primary transmissions pursuant to section 119 or 122; and

(11) on filing a statement of account based on secondary transmissions of primary transmissions pursuant to section 111.

---

*   For the current fee amounts, see Copyright Office Regulations, 37 C.F.R. § 201.3, at http://copyright.gov/title37/.

The Register is authorized to fix fees for other services, including the cost of preparing copies of Copyright Office records, whether or not such copies are certified, based on the cost of providing the service. Fees established under paragraphs (10) and (11) shall be reasonable and may not exceed one-half of the cost necessary to cover reasonable expenses incurred by the Copyright Office for the collection and administration of the statements of account and any royalty fees deposited with such statements

(b) *Adjustment of Fees.* The Register of Copyrights may, by regulation, adjust the fees for the services specified in subsection (a) in the following manner:

(1) The Register shall conduct a study of the costs incurred by the Copyright Office for the registration of claims, the recordation of documents, and the provision of services. The study shall also consider the timing of any adjustment in fees and the authority to use such fees consistent with the budget.

(2) The Register may, on the basis of the study under paragraph (1), and subject to paragraph (5), adjust fees to not more than that necessary to cover the reasonable costs incurred by the Copyright Office for the services described in paragraph (1), plus a reasonable inflation adjustment to account for any estimated increase in costs.

(3) Any fee established under paragraph (2) shall be rounded off to the nearest dollar, or for a fee less than $12, rounded off to the nearest 50 cents.

(4) Fees established under this subsection shall be fair and equitable and give due consideration to the objectives of the copyright system.

(5) If the Register determines under paragraph (2) that fees should be adjusted, the Register shall prepare a proposed fee schedule and submit the schedule with the accompanying economic analysis to the Congress. The fees proposed by the Register may be instituted after the end of 120 days after the schedule is submitted to the Congress unless, within that 120-day period, a law is enacted stating in substance that the Congress does not approve the schedule.

Sec. 709.   Delay in Delivery Caused by Disruption of Postal or Other Services

In any case in which the Register of Copyrights determines, on the basis of such evidence as the Register may by regulation require, that a deposit, application, fee, or any other material to be delivered to the Copyright Office by a particular date, would have been received in the Copyright Office in due time except for a general disruption or suspension of postal or other transportation or communications services, the actual receipt of such material in the Copyright Office within one month after the date on which the Register determines that the disruption or suspension of such services has terminated, shall be considered timely.

CHAPTER 8.—PROCEEDINGS BY COPYRIGHT ROYALTY JUDGES

Sec.
801. Copyright Royalty Judges; Appointment and Functions.
802. Copyright Royalty Judgeships; Staff.
803. Proceedings of Copyright Royalty Judges.
804. Institution of Proceedings.
805. General Rule for Voluntarily Negotiated Agreements.

Sec. 801. Copyright Royalty Judges; Appointment and Functions

(a) Appointment.—The Librarian of Congress shall appoint 3 full-time Copyright Royalty Judges, and shall appoint 1 of the 3 as the Chief Copyright Royalty Judge. The Librarian shall make appointments to such positions after consultation with the Register of Copyrights.

(b) Functions.—Subject to the provisions of this chapter, the functions of the Copyright Royalty Judges shall be as follows:

(1) To make determinations and adjustments of reasonable terms and rates of royalty payments as provided in sections 112(e), 114, 115, 116, 118, 119, and 1004. The rates applicable under sections 114(f)(1)(B), 115, and 116 shall be calculated to achieve the following objectives:

(A) To maximize the availability of creative works to the public.

(B) To afford the copyright owner a fair return for his or her creative work and the copyright user a fair income under existing economic conditions.

(C) To reflect the relative roles of the copyright owner and the copyright user in the product made available to the public with respect to relative creative contribution, technological contribution, capital investment, cost, risk, and contribution to the opening of new markets for creative expression and media for their communication.

(D) To minimize any disruptive impact on the structure of the industries involved and on generally prevailing industry practices.

(2) To make determinations concerning the adjustment of the copyright royalty rates under section 111 solely in accordance with the following provisions:

(A) The rates established by section 111(d)(1)(B) may be adjusted to reflect—

(i) national monetary inflation or deflation; or

(ii) changes in the average rates charged cable subscribers for the basic service of providing secondary transmissions to maintain the real constant dollar level of the royalty fee per subscriber which existed as of the date of October 19, 1976, except that—

(I) if the average rates charged cable system subscribers for the basic service of providing secondary transmissions are changed so that the average rates exceed national monetary inflation, no change in the rates established by section 111(d)(1)(B) shall be permitted; and

(II) no increase in the royalty fee shall be permitted based on any reduction in the average number of distant signal equivalents per subscriber.

The Copyright Royalty Judges may consider all factors relating to the maintenance of such level of payments, including, as an extenuating factor, whether the industry has been restrained by subscriber rate regulating authorities from increasing the rates for the basic service of providing secondary transmissions.

(B) In the event that the rules and regulations of the Federal Communications Commission are amended at any time after April 15, 1976, to permit the carriage by cable systems of additional television broadcast signals beyond the local service area of the primary transmitters of such signals, the royalty rates established by section 111(d)(1)(B) may be adjusted to ensure that the rates for the additional distant signal equivalents resulting from such carriage are reasonable in the light of the changes effected by the amendment to such rules and regulations. In determining the reasonableness of rates proposed following an amendment of Federal Communications Commission rules and regulations, the Copyright Royalty Judges shall consider, among other factors, the economic impact on copyright owners and users; except that no adjustment in royalty rates shall be made under this subparagraph with respect to any distant signal equivalent or fraction thereof represented by—

(i) carriage of any signal permitted under the rules and regulations of the Federal Communications Commission in effect on April 15, 1976, or the carriage of a signal of the same type (that is, independent, network, or noncommercial educational) substituted for such permitted signal; or

(ii) a television broadcast signal first carried after April 15, 1976, pursuant to an individual waiver of the rules and regulations of the Federal Communications Commission, as such rules and regulations were in effect on April 15, 1976.

(C) In the event of any change in the rules and regulations of the Federal Communications Commission with respect to syndicated and sports program exclusivity after April 15, 1976, the rates established by section 111(d)(1)(B) may be adjusted to assure that such rates are reasonable in light of the changes to such rules and regulations, but any such adjustment shall apply only to the affected television broadcast signals carried on those systems affected by the change.

(D) The gross receipts limitations established by section 111(d)(1)(C) and (D) shall be adjusted to reflect national monetary inflation or deflation or changes in the average rates charged cable system subscribers for the basic service of providing secondary transmissions to maintain the real constant dollar value of the exemption provided by such section, and the royalty rate specified therein shall not be subject to adjustment.

(3)(A) To authorize the distribution, under sections 111, 119, and 1007, of those royalty fees collected under sections 111, 119, and 1005, as the case may be, to the extent that the Copyright Royalty Judges have found that the distribution of such fees is not subject to controversy.

(B) In cases where the Copyright Royalty Judges determine that controversy exists, the Copyright Royalty Judges shall determine the distribution of such fees, including partial distributions, in accordance with section 111, 119, or 1007, as the case may be.

(C) Notwithstanding section 804(b)(8), the Copyright Royalty Judges, at any time after the filing of claims under section 111, 119, or 1007, may, upon motion of one or more of the claimants and after publication in the Federal Register of a request for responses to the motion from interested claimants, make a partial distribution of such fees, if, based upon all responses received during the 30-day period beginning on the date of such publication, the Copyright Royalty Judges conclude that no claimant entitled to receive such fees has stated a reasonable objection to the partial distribution, and all such claimants—

(i) agree to the partial distribution;

(ii) sign an agreement obligating them to return any excess amounts to the extent necessary to comply with the final determination on the distribution of the fees made under subparagraph (B);

(iii) file the agreement with the Copyright Royalty Judges; and

(iv) agree that such funds are available for distribution.

(D) The Copyright Royalty Judges and any other officer or employee acting in good faith in distributing funds under subparagraph (C) shall not be held liable for the payment of any excess fees under subparagraph (C). The Copyright Royalty Judges shall, at the time the final determination is made, calculate any such excess amounts.

(4) To accept or reject royalty claims filed under sections 111, 119, and 1007, on the basis of timeliness or the failure to establish the basis for a claim.

(5) To accept or reject rate adjustment petitions as provided in section 804 and petitions to participate as provided in section 803(b)(1) and (2).

(6) To determine the status of a digital audio recording device or a digital audio interface device under sections 1002 and 1003, as provided in section 1010.

(7)(A) To adopt as a basis for statutory terms and rates or as a basis for the distribution of statutory royalty payments, an agreement concerning such matters reached among some or all of the participants in a proceeding at any time during the proceeding, except that—

(i) the Copyright Royalty Judges shall provide to those that would be bound by the terms, rates, or other determination set by any agreement in a proceeding to determine royalty rates an opportunity to comment on the agreement and shall provide to participants in the proceeding under section 803(b)(2) that would be bound by the terms, rates, or other determination set by the agreement an opportunity to comment on the agreement and object to its adoption as a basis for statutory terms and rates; and

(ii) the Copyright Royalty Judges may decline to adopt the agreement as a basis for statutory terms and rates for participants that are not parties to the agreement, if any participant described in clause (i) objects to the agreement and the Copyright Royalty Judges conclude, based on the record before them if one exists, that the agreement does not provide a reasonable basis for setting statutory terms or rates.

(B) License agreements voluntarily negotiated pursuant to section 112(e)(5), 114(f)(3), 115(c)(3)(E)(i), 116(c), or 118(b)(2) that do not result in statutory terms and rates shall not be subject to clauses (i) and (ii) of subparagraph (A).

(C) Interested parties may negotiate and agree to, and the Copyright Royalty Judges may adopt, an agreement that specifies as terms notice and recordkeeping requirements that apply in lieu of those that would otherwise apply under regulations.

(8) To perform other duties, as assigned by the Register of Copyrights within the Library of Congress, except as provided in section 802(g), at times when Copyright Royalty Judges are not engaged in performing the other duties set forth in this section.

(c) Rulings.—The Copyright Royalty Judges may make any necessary procedural or evidentiary rulings in any proceeding under this chapter and may, before commencing a proceeding under this chapter, make any such rulings that would apply to the proceedings conducted by the Copyright Royalty Judges.

(d) Administrative Support.—The Librarian of Congress shall provide the Copyright Royalty Judges with the necessary administrative services related to proceedings under this chapter.

(e) Location in Library of Congress.—The offices of the Copyright Royalty Judges and staff shall be in the Library of Congress.

(f) Effective Date of Actions.—On and after the date of the enactment of the Copyright Royalty and Distribution Reform Act of 2004, in any case in which time limits are prescribed under this title for performance of an action with or by the Copyright Royalty Judges, and in which the last day of the prescribed period falls on a Saturday, Sunday, holiday, or other nonbusiness day within the District of Columbia or the Federal Government, the action may be taken on the next succeeding business day, and is effective as of the date when the period expired.

Sec. 802.   Copyright Royalty Judgeships; Staff

(a) Qualifications of Copyright Royalty Judges.—

(1) In general.—Each Copyright Royalty Judge shall be an attorney who has at least 7 years of legal experience. The Chief Copyright Royalty Judge shall have at least 5 years of experience in adjudications, arbitrations, or court trials. Of the other 2 Copyright Royalty Judges, 1 shall have significant knowledge of copyright law, and the other shall have significant knowledge of economics. An individual may serve as a Copyright Royalty Judge only if the individual is free of any financial conflict of interest under subsection (h).

(2) Definition.—In this subsection, the term "adjudication" has the meaning given that term in section 551 of title 5, but does not include mediation.

(b) Staff.—The Chief Copyright Royalty Judge shall hire 3 full-time staff members to assist the Copyright Royalty Judges in performing their functions.

(c) Terms.—The individual first appointed as the Chief Copyright Royalty Judge shall be appointed to a term of 6 years, and of the remaining individuals first appointed as Copyright Royalty Judges, 1 shall be appointed to a term of 4 years, and the other shall be appointed to a term of 2 years. Thereafter, the terms of succeeding Copyright Royalty Judges shall each be 6 years. An individual serving as a Copyright Royalty Judge may be reappointed to subsequent terms. The term of a Copyright Royalty Judge shall begin when the term of the predecessor of that Copyright Royalty Judge ends. When the term of office of a Copyright Royalty Judge ends, the individual serving that term may continue to serve until a successor is selected.

(d) Vacancies or incapacity.—

(1) Vacancies.—If a vacancy should occur in the position of Copyright Royalty Judge, the Librarian of Congress shall act expeditiously to fill the vacancy, and may appoint an interim Copyright Royalty Judge to serve until another Copyright Royalty Judge is appointed under this section. An individual appointed to fill the vacancy occurring before the expiration of the term for which the predecessor of that individual was appointed shall be appointed for the remainder of that term.

(2) Incapacity.—In the case in which a Copyright Royalty Judge is temporarily unable to perform his or her duties, the Librarian of Congress may appoint an interim Copyright Royalty Judge to perform such duties during the period of such incapacity.

(e) Compensation.—

(1) Judges.—The Chief Copyright Royalty Judge shall receive compensation at the rate of basic pay payable for level AL-1 for administrative law judges pursuant to section 5372(b) of title 5, and each of the other two Copyright Royalty Judges shall receive compensation at the rate of basic pay payable for level AL-2 for administrative law judges pursuant to such section. The compensation of the Copyright Royalty Judges shall not be subject to any regulations adopted by the Office of Personnel Management pursuant to its authority under section 5376(b)(1) of title 5.

(2) Staff Members.—Of the staff members appointed under subsection (b)—

(A) the rate of pay of 1 staff member shall be not more than the basic rate of pay payable for level 10 of GS-15 of the General Schedule;

(B) the rate of pay of 1 staff member shall be not less than the basic rate of pay payable for GS-13 of the General Schedule and not more than the basic rate of pay payable for level 10 of GS-14 of such Schedule; and

(C) the rate of pay for the third staff member shall be not less than the basic rate of pay payable for GS-8 of the General Schedule and not more than the basic rate of pay payable for level 10 of GS-11 of such Schedule.

(3) Locality pay.—All rates of pay referred to under this subsection shall include locality pay.

(f) Independence of Copyright Royalty Judge.—

(1) In making determinations.—

(A) In general.—

(i) Subject to subparagraph (B) and clause (ii) of this subparagraph, the Copyright Royalty Judges shall have full independence in making determinations concerning adjustments and determinations of copyright royalty rates and terms, the distribution of copyright royalties, the acceptance or rejection of royalty claims, rate adjustment petitions, and petitions to participate, and in issuing other rulings under this title, except that the Copyright Royalty Judges may consult with the Register of Copyrights on any matter other than a question of fact.

(ii) One or more Copyright Royalty Judges may, or by motion to the Copyright Royalty Judges, any participant in a proceeding may, request from the Register of Copyrights an interpretation of any material questions of substantive law that relate to the construction of provisions of this title and arise in the course of the proceeding. Any request for a written interpretation shall be in writing and on the record, and reasonable provision shall be made to permit participants in the proceeding to comment on the material questions of substantive law in a manner that minimizes duplication and delay. Except as provided in subparagraph (B), the Register of Copyrights shall deliver to the Copyright Royalty Judges a written response within 14 days after the receipt of all briefs and comments from the participants. The Copyright Royalty Judges shall apply the legal interpretation embodied in the response of the Register of Copyrights if it is timely delivered, and the response shall be included in the record that accompanies the final determination. The authority under this clause shall not be construed to authorize the Register of Copyrights to provide an interpretation of questions of procedure before the Copyright Royalty Judges, the ultimate adjustments and determinations of copyright royalty rates and terms, the ultimate distribution of copyright royalties, or the acceptance or rejection of royalty claims, rate adjustment petitions, or petitions to participate in a proceeding.

(B) Novel questions.—

(i) In any case in which a novel material question of substantive law concerning an interpretation of those provisions of this title that are the subject of the proceeding is presented, the Copyright Royalty Judges shall request a decision of the Register of Copyrights, in writing, to resolve such novel question. Reasonable provision shall be made for comment on such request by the participants in the proceeding, in such a way as to minimize duplication and delay. The Register of Copyrights shall transmit his or her decision to the Copyright Royalty Judges within 30 days after the Register of Copyrights receives all of the briefs or comments of the participants. Such decision shall be in writing and included by the Copyright Royalty Judges in the record that accompanies their final determination. If such a decision is timely delivered to the Copyright Royalty Judges, the Copyright Royalty Judges shall apply the legal determinations embodied in the decision of the Register of Copyrights in resolving material questions of substantive law.

(ii) In clause (i), a "novel question of law" is a question of law that has not been determined in prior decisions, determinations, and rulings described in section 803(a).

(C) Consultation.—Notwithstanding the provisions of subparagraph (A), the Copyright Royalty Judges shall consult with the Register of Copyrights with respect to any determination or ruling that would require that any act be performed by the Copyright Office, and any such determination or ruling shall not be binding upon the Register of Copyrights.

(D) Review of legal conclusions by the Register of Copyrights.—The Register of Copyrights may review for legal error the resolution by the Copyright Royalty Judges of a material question of substantive law under this title that underlies or is contained in a final determination of the Copyright Royalty Judges. If the Register of Copyrights concludes, after taking into consideration the views of the participants in the proceeding, that any resolution reached by the Copyright Royalty Judges was in material error, the Register of Copyrights shall issue a written decision correcting such legal error, which shall be made part of the record of the proceeding. The Register of Copyrights shall issue such written decision not later than 60 days after the date on which the final determination by the Copyright Royalty Judges is issued. Additionally, the Register of Copyrights shall cause to be published in the Federal Register such written decision, together with a specific identification of the legal conclusion of the Copyright Royalty Judges that is determined to be erroneous. As to conclusions of substantive law involving an interpretation of the statutory provisions of this title, the decision of the Register of Copyrights shall be binding as precedent upon the Copyright Royalty Judges in subsequent proceedings under this chapter. When a decision has been rendered pursuant to this subparagraph, the Register of Copyrights may, on the basis of and in accordance with such decision, intervene as of right in any appeal of a final determination of the Copyright Royalty Judges pursuant to section 803(d) in the United States Court of Appeals for the District of Columbia Circuit. If, prior to intervening in such an appeal, the Register of Copyrights gives notification to, and undertakes to consult with, the Attorney General with respect to such intervention, and the Attorney General fails, within a reasonable period after receiving such notification, to intervene in such appeal, the Register of Copyrights may intervene in such appeal in his or her own name by any attorney designated by the Register of Copyrights for such purpose. Intervention by the Register of Copyrights in his or her own name shall not preclude the Attorney General from intervening on behalf of the United States in such an appeal as may be otherwise provided or required by law.

(E) Effect on judicial review.—Nothing in this section shall be interpreted to alter the standard applied by a court in reviewing legal determinations involving an interpretation or construction of the provisions of this title or to affect the extent to which any construction or interpretation of the provisions of this title shall be accorded deference by a reviewing court.

(2) Performance appraisals.—

(A) In general.—Notwithstanding any other provision of law or any regulation of the Library of Congress, and subject to subparagraph (B), the Copyright Royalty Judges shall not receive performance appraisals.

(B) Relating to sanction or removal.—To the extent that the Librarian of Congress adopts regulations under subsection (h) relating to the sanction or removal of a Copyright Royalty Judge and such regulations require documentation to establish the cause of such sanction or removal, the Copyright Royalty Judge may receive an appraisal related specifically to the cause of the sanction or removal.

(g) Inconsistent duties barred.—No Copyright Royalty Judge may undertake duties that conflict with his or her duties and responsibilities as a Copyright Royalty Judge.

(h) Standards of conduct.—The Librarian of Congress shall adopt regulations regarding the standards of conduct, including financial conflict of interest and restrictions against ex parte communications, which shall govern the Copyright Royalty Judges and the proceedings under this chapter.

(i) Removal or sanction.—The Librarian of Congress may sanction or remove a Copyright Royalty Judge for violation of the standards of conduct adopted under subsection (h), misconduct, neglect of duty, or any disqualifying physical or mental disability. Any such sanction or removal may be made only after notice and opportunity for a hearing, but the Librarian of Congress may suspend the Copyright Royalty Judge during the pendency of such hearing. The Librarian shall appoint an interim Copyright Royalty Judge during the period of any such suspension.

Sec. 803.   Proceedings of Copyright Royalty Judges

(a) Proceedings.—

(1) In general.—The Copyright Royalty Judges shall act in accordance with this title, and to the extent not inconsistent with this title, in accordance with subchapter II of chapter 5 of title 5, in carrying out the purposes set forth in section 801. The Copyright Royalty Judges shall act in accordance with regulations issued by the Copyright Royalty Judges and the Librarian of Congress, and on the basis of a written record, prior determinations and interpretations of the Copyright Royalty Tribunal, Librarian of Congress, the Register of Copyrights, copyright arbitration royalty panels (to the extent those determinations are not inconsistent with a decision of the Librarian of Congress or the Register of Copyrights), and the Copyright Royalty Judges (to the extent those determinations are not inconsistent with a decision of the Register of Copyrights that was timely delivered to the Copyright Royalty Judges pursuant to section 802(f)(1)(A) or (B), or with a decision of the Register of Copyrights pursuant to section 802(f)(1)(D)), under this chapter, and decisions of the court of appeals under this chapter before, on, or after the effective date of the Copyright Royalty and Distribution Reform Act of 2004.

(2) Judges acting as panel and individually.—The Copyright Royalty Judges shall preside over hearings in proceedings under this chapter en banc. The Chief Copyright Royalty Judge may designate a Copyright Royalty Judge to preside individually over such collateral and administrative proceedings, and over such proceedings under paragraphs (1) through (5) of subsection (b), as the Chief Judge considers appropriate.

(3) Determinations.—Final determinations of the Copyright Royalty Judges in proceedings under this chapter shall be made by majority vote. A Copyright Royalty Judge dissenting from the majority on any determination under this chapter may issue his or her dissenting opinion, which shall be included with the determination.

(b) Procedures.—

(1) Initiation.—

(A) Call for petitions to participate.—

(i) The Copyright Royalty Judges shall cause to be published in the Federal Register notice of commencement of proceedings under this chapter, calling for the filing of petitions to participate in a proceeding under this chapter for the purpose of making the relevant determination under section 111, 112, 114, 115, 116, 118, 119, 1004, or 1007, as the case may be—

(I) promptly upon a determination made under section 804(a);

(II) by no later than January 5 of a year specified in paragraph (2) of section 804(b) for the commencement of proceedings;

(III) by no later than January 5 of a year specified in subparagraph (A) or (B) of paragraph (3) of section 804(b) for the commencement of proceedings, or as otherwise provided in subparagraph (A) or (C) of such paragraph for the commencement of proceedings;

(IV) as provided under section 804(b)(8); or

(V) by no later than January 5 of a year specified in any other provision of section 804(b) for the filing of petitions for the commencement of proceedings, if a petition has not been filed by that date, except that the publication of notice requirement shall not apply in the case of proceedings under section 111 that are scheduled to commence in 2005.

(ii) Petitions to participate shall be filed by no later than 30 days after publication of notice of commencement of a proceeding under clause (i), except that the Copyright Royalty Judges may, for substantial good cause shown and if there is no prejudice to the participants that have already filed petitions, accept late petitions to participate at any time up to the date that is 90 days before the date on which participants in the proceeding are to file their written direct statements. Notwithstanding the preceding sentence, petitioners whose petitions are filed more than 30 days after publication of notice of commencement of a proceeding are not eligible to object to a settlement reached during the voluntary negotiation period under paragraph (3), and any objection filed by such a petitioner shall not be taken into account by the Copyright Royalty Judges.

(B) Petitions to participate. Each petition to participate in a proceeding shall describe the petitioner's interest in the subject matter of the proceeding. Parties with similar interests may file a single petition to participate.

(2) Participation in general.—Subject to paragraph (4), a person may participate in a proceeding under this chapter, including through the submission of briefs or other information, only if—

(A) that person has filed a petition to participate in accordance with paragraph (1) (either individually or as a group under paragraph (1)(B));

(B) the Copyright Royalty Judges have not determined that the petition to participate is facially invalid;

(C) the Copyright Royalty Judges have not determined, sua sponte or on the motion of another participant in the proceeding, that the person lacks a significant interest in the proceeding; and

(D) the petition to participate is accompanied by either—

(i) in a proceeding to determine royalty rates, a filing fee of $150; or

(ii) in a proceeding to determine distribution of royalty fees—

(I) a filing fee of $150; or

(II) a statement that the petitioner (individually or as a group) will not seek a distribution of more than $1000, in which case the amount distributed to the petitioner shall not exceed $1000.

(3) Voluntary negotiation period.—

(A) Commencement of proceedings.—

(i) Rate adjustment proceeding.—Promptly after the date for filing of petitions to participate in a proceeding, the Copyright Royalty Judges shall make available to all participants in the proceeding a list of such participants and shall initiate a voluntary negotiation period among the participants.

(ii) Distribution proceeding.—Promptly after the date for filing of petitions to participate in a proceeding to determine the distribution of royalties, the Copyright Royalty Judges shall make available to all participants in the proceeding a list of such participants. The initiation of a voluntary negotiation period among the participants shall be set at a time determined by the Copyright Royalty Judges.

(B) Length of proceedings.—The voluntary negotiation period initiated under subparagraph (A) shall be 3 months.

(C) Determination of subsequent proceedings.—At the close of the voluntary negotiation proceedings, the Copyright Royalty Judges shall, if further proceedings under this chapter are necessary, determine whether and to what extent paragraphs (4) and (5) will apply to the parties.

(4) Small claims procedure in distribution proceedings.—

(A) In general.—If, in a proceeding under this chapter to determine the distribution of royalties, the contested amount of a claim is $10,000 or less, the Copyright Royalty Judges shall decide the controversy on the basis of the filing of the written direct statement by the participant, the response by any opposing participant, and 1 additional response by each such party.

(B) Bad faith inflation of claim.—If the Copyright Royalty Judges determine that a participant asserts in bad faith an amount in controversy in excess of $10,000 for the purpose of avoiding a determination under the procedure set forth in subparagraph (A), the Copyright Royalty Judges shall impose a fine on that participant in an amount not to exceed the difference between the actual amount distributed and the amount asserted by the participant.

(5) Paper proceedings.—The Copyright Royalty Judges in proceedings under this chapter may decide, sua sponte or upon motion of a participant, to determine issues on the basis of the filing of the written direct statement by the participant, the response by any opposing participant, and one additional response by each such participant. Prior to making such decision to proceed on such a paper record only, the Copyright Royalty Judges shall offer to all parties to the proceeding the opportunity to comment on the decision. The procedure under this paragraph—

(A) shall be applied in cases in which there is no genuine issue of material fact, there is no need for evidentiary hearings, and all participants in the proceeding agree in writing to the procedure; and

(B) may be applied under such other circumstances as the Copyright Royalty Judges consider appropriate.

(6) Regulations.—

(A) In general.—The Copyright Royalty Judges may issue regulations to carry out their functions under this title. All regulations issued by the Copyright Royalty Judges are subject to the approval of the Librarian of Congress and are subject to judicial review pursuant to chapter 7 of title 5, except as set forth in subsection (d). Not later than 120 days after Copyright Royalty Judges or interim Copyright Royalty Judges, as the case may be, are first appointed after the enactment of the Copyright Royalty and Distribution Reform Act of 2004, such judges shall issue regulations to govern proceedings under this chapter.

(B) Interim regulations.—Until regulations are adopted under subparagraph (A), the Copyright Royalty Judges shall apply the regulations in effect under this chapter on the day before the effective date of the Copyright Royalty and Distribution Reform Act of 2004, to the extent such regulations are not inconsistent with this chapter, except that functions carried out under such regulations by the Librarian of Congress, the Register of Copyrights, or copyright arbitration royalty panels that, as of such date of enactment, are to be carried out by the Copyright Royalty Judges under this chapter, shall be carried out by the Copyright Royalty Judges under such regulations.

(C) Requirements.—Regulations issued under subparagraph (A) shall include the following:

(i) The written direct statements and written rebuttal statements of all participants in a proceeding under paragraph (2) shall be filed by a date specified by the Copyright Royalty Judges, which, in the case of written direct statements, may be not earlier than 4 months, and not later than 5 months, after the end of the voluntary negotiation period under paragraph (3). Notwithstanding the preceding sentence, the Copyright Royalty Judges may allow a participant in a proceeding to file an amended written direct statement based on new information received during the discovery process, within 15 days after the end of the discovery period specified in clause (iv).

(ii)(I) Following the submission to the Copyright Royalty Judges of written direct statements and written rebuttal statements by the participants in a proceeding under paragraph (2), the Copyright Royalty Judges, after taking into consideration the views of the participants in the proceeding, shall determine a schedule for conducting and completing discovery.

(II) In this chapter, the term "written direct statements" means witness statements, testimony, and exhibits to be presented in the proceedings, and such other information that is necessary to establish terms and rates, or the distribution of royalty payments, as the case may be, as set forth in regulations issued by the Copyright Royalty Judges.

(iii) Hearsay may be admitted in proceedings under this chapter to the extent deemed appropriate by the Copyright Royalty Judges.

(iv) Discovery in connection with written direct statements shall be permitted for a period of 60 days, except for discovery ordered by the Copyright Royalty Judges in connection with the resolution of motions, orders, and disputes pending at the end of such period. The Copyright Royalty Judges may order a discovery schedule in connection with written rebuttal statements.

(v) Any participant under paragraph (2) in a proceeding under this chapter to determine royalty rates may request of an opposing participant nonprivileged documents directly related to the written direct statement or written rebuttal statement of that participant. Any objection to such a request shall be resolved by a motion or request to compel production made to the Copyright Royalty Judges in accordance with regulations adopted by the Copyright Royalty Judges. Each motion or request to compel discovery shall be determined by the Copyright Royalty Judges, or by a Copyright Royalty Judge when permitted under subsection (a)(2). Upon such motion, the Copyright Royalty Judges may order discovery pursuant to regulations established under this paragraph.

(vi)(I) Any participant under paragraph (2) in a proceeding under this chapter to determine royalty rates may, by means of written motion or on the record, request of an opposing participant or witness other relevant information and materials if, absent the discovery sought, the Copyright Royalty Judges' resolution of the proceeding would be substantially impaired. In determining whether discovery will be granted under this clause, the Copyright Royalty Judges may consider—

    (aa) whether the burden or expense of producing the requested information or materials outweighs the likely benefit, taking into account the needs and resources of the participants, the importance of the issues at stake, and the probative value of the requested information or materials in resolving such issues;

    (bb) whether the requested information or materials would be unreasonably cumulative or duplicative, or are obtainable from another source that is more convenient, less burdensome, or less expensive; and (cc) whether the participant seeking discovery has had ample opportunity by discovery in the proceeding or by other means to obtain the information sought.

(II) This clause shall not apply to any proceeding scheduled to commence after December 31, 2010.

(vii) In a proceeding under this chapter to determine royalty rates, the participants entitled to receive royalties shall collectively be permitted to take no more than 10 depositions and secure responses to no more than 25 interrogatories, and the participants obligated to pay royalties shall collectively be permitted to take no more than 10 depositions and secure responses to no more than 25 interrogatories. The Copyright Royalty Judges shall resolve any disputes among similarly aligned participants to allocate the number of depositions or interrogatories permitted under this clause.

(viii) The rules and practices in effect on the day before the effective date of the Copyright Royalty and Distribution Reform Act of 2004, relating to discovery in proceedings under this chapter to determine the distribution of royalty fees, shall continue to apply to such proceedings on and after such effective date.

(ix) In proceedings to determine royalty rates, the Copyright Royalty Judges may issue a subpoena commanding a participant or witness to appear and give testimony, or to produce and permit inspection of documents or tangible things, if the Copyright Royalty Judges' resolution of the proceeding would be substantially impaired by the absence of such testimony or production of documents or tangible things. Such subpoena shall specify with reasonable particularity the materials to be produced or the scope and nature of the required testimony. Nothing in this clause shall preclude the Copyright Royalty Judges from requesting the production by a nonparticipant of information or materials relevant to the resolution by the Copyright Royalty Judges of a material issue of fact.

(x) The Copyright Royalty Judges shall order a settlement conference among the participants in the proceeding to facilitate the presentation of offers of settlement among the participants. The settlement conference shall be held during a 21-day period following the 60-day discovery period specified in clause (iv) and shall take place outside the presence of the Copyright Royalty Judges.

(xi) No evidence, including exhibits, may be submitted in the written direct statement or written rebuttal statement of a participant without a sponsoring witness, except where the Copyright Royalty Judges have taken official notice, or in the case of incorporation by reference of past records, or for good cause shown.

(c) Determination of Copyright Royalty Judges.—

(1) Timing.—The Copyright Royalty Judges shall issue their determination in a proceeding not later than 11 months after the conclusion of the 21-day settlement conference period under subsection (b)(6)(C)(x), but, in the case of a proceeding to determine successors to rates or terms that expire on a specified date, in no event later than 15 days before the expiration of the then current statutory rates and terms.

(2) Rehearings.—

(A) In general.—The Copyright Royalty Judges may, in exceptional cases, upon motion of a participant in a proceeding under subsection (b)(2), order a rehearing, after the determination in the proceeding is issued under paragraph (1), on such matters as the Copyright Royalty Judges determine to be appropriate.

(B) Timing for filing motion.—Any motion for a rehearing under subparagraph (A) may only be filed within 15 days after the date on which the Copyright Royalty Judges deliver to the participants in the proceeding their initial determination.

(C) Participation by opposing party not required.—In any case in which a rehearing is ordered, any opposing party shall not be required to participate in the rehearing, except that nonparticipation may give rise to the limitations with respect to judicial review provided for in subsection (d)(1).

(D) No negative inference.—No negative inference shall be drawn from lack of participation in a rehearing.

(E) Continuity of rates and terms.—

(i) If the decision of the Copyright Royalty Judges on any motion for a rehearing is not rendered before the expiration of the statutory rates and terms that were previously in effect, in the case of a proceeding to determine successors to rates and terms that expire on a specified date, then—

(I) the initial determination of the Copyright Royalty Judges that is the subject of the rehearing motion shall be effective as of the day following the date on which the rates and terms that were previously in effect expire; and

(II) in the case of a proceeding under section 114(f)(1)(C) or 114(f)(2)(C), royalty rates and terms shall, for purposes of section 114(f)(4)(B), be deemed to have been set at those rates and terms contained in the initial determination of the Copyright Royalty Judges that is the subject of the rehearing motion, as of the date of that determination.

(ii) The pendency of a motion for a rehearing under this paragraph shall not relieve persons obligated to make royalty payments who would be affected by the determination on that motion from providing the statements of account and any reports of use, to the extent required, and paying the royalties required under the relevant determination or regulations.

(iii) Notwithstanding clause (ii), whenever royalties described in clause (ii) are paid to a person other than the Copyright Office, the entity designated by the Copyright Royalty Judges to which such royalties are paid by the copyright user (and any successor thereto) shall, within 60 days after the motion for rehearing is resolved or, if the motion is granted, within 60 days after the rehearing is concluded, return any excess amounts previously paid to the extent necessary to comply with the final determination of royalty rates by the Copyright Royalty Judges. Any underpayment of royalties resulting from a rehearing shall be paid within the same period.

(3) **Contents of determination.**—A determination of the Copyright Royalty Judges shall be supported by the written record and shall set forth the findings of fact relied on by the Copyright Royalty Judges. Among other terms adopted in a determination, the Copyright Royalty Judges may specify notice and recordkeeping requirements of users of the copyrights at issue that apply in lieu of those that would otherwise apply under regulations.

(4) **Continuing jurisdiction.**—The Copyright Royalty Judges may, issue an amendment to a written determination to correct any technical or clerical errors in the determination or to modify the terms, but not the rates, of royalty payments in response to unforeseen circumstances that would frustrate the proper implementation of such determination. Such amendment shall be set forth in a written addendum to the determination that shall be distributed to the participants of the proceeding and shall be published in the Federal Register.

(5) Protective order.—The Copyright Royalty Judges may issue such orders as may be appropriate to protect confidential information, including orders excluding confidential information from the record of the determination that is published or made available to the public, except that any terms or rates of royalty payments or distributions may not be excluded.

(6) Publication of determination.—By no later than the end of the 60-day period provided in section 802(f)(1)(D), the Librarian of Congress shall cause the determination, and any corrections thereto, to be published in the Federal Register. The Librarian of Congress shall also publicize the determination and corrections in such other manner as the Librarian considers appropriate, including, but not limited to, publication on the Internet. The Librarian of Congress shall also make the determination, corrections, and the accompanying record available for public inspection and copying.

(7) Late payment.—A determination of the Copyright Royalty Judges may include terms with respect to late payment, but in no way shall such terms prevent the copyright holder from asserting other rights or remedies provided under this title.

(d) Judicial Review.—

(1) Appeal.—Any determination of the Copyright Royalty Judges under subsection (c) may, within 30 days after the publication of the determination in the Federal Register, be appealed, to the United States Court of Appeals for the District of Columbia Circuit, by any aggrieved participant in the proceeding under subsection (b)(2) who fully participated in the proceeding and who would be bound by the determination. Any participant that did not participate in a rehearing may not raise any issue that was the subject of that rehearing at any stage of judicial review of the hearing determination. If no appeal is brought within that 30-day period, the determination of the Copyright Royalty Judges shall be final, and the royalty fee or determination with respect to the distribution of fees, as the case may be, shall take effect as set forth in paragraph (2).

(2) Effect of rates.—

(A) Expiration on specified date.—When this title provides that the royalty rates and terms that were previously in effect are to expire on a specified date, any adjustment or determination by the Copyright Royalty Judges of successor rates and terms for an ensuing statutory license period shall be effective as of the day following the date of expiration of the rates and terms that were previously in effect, even if the determination of the Copyright Royalty Judges is rendered on a later date. A licensee shall be obligated to continue making payments under the rates and terms previously in effect until such time as rates and terms for the successor period are established. Whenever royalties pursuant to this section are paid to a person other than the Copyright Office, the entity designated by the Copyright Royalty Judges to which such royalties are paid by the copyright user (and any successor thereto) shall, within 60 days after the final determination of the Copyright Royalty Judges establishing rates and terms for a successor period or the exhaustion of all rehearings or appeals of such determination, if any, return any excess amounts previously paid to the extent necessary to comply with the final determination of royalty rates. Any underpayment of royalties by a copyright user shall be paid to the entity designated by the Copyright Royalty Judges within the same period.

(B) Other cases.—In cases where rates and terms have not, prior to the inception of an activity, been established for that particular activity under the relevant license, such rates and terms shall be retroactive to the inception of activity under the relevant license covered by such rates and terms. In other cases where rates and terms do not expire on a specified date, successor rates and terms shall take effect on the first day of the second month that begins after the publication of the determination of the Copyright Royalty Judges in the Federal Register, except as otherwise provided in this title, or by the Copyright Royalty Judges, or as agreed by the participants in a proceeding that would be bound by the rates and terms. Except as otherwise provided in this title, the rates and terms, to the extent applicable, shall remain in effect until such successor rates and terms become effective.

(C) Obligation to make payments.—

(i) The pendency of an appeal under this subsection shall not relieve persons obligated to make royalty payments under section 111, 112, 114, 115, 116, 118, 119, or 1003, who would be affected by the determination on appeal, from—

(I) providing the applicable statements of account and report of use; and

(II) paying the royalties required under the relevant determination or regulations.

(ii) Notwithstanding clause (i), whenever royalties described in clause (i) are paid to a person other than the Copyright Office, the entity designated by the Copyright Royalty Judges to which such royalties are paid by the copyright user (and any successor thereto) shall, within 60 days after the final resolution of the appeal, return any excess amounts previously paid (and interest thereon, if ordered pursuant to paragraph (3)) to the extent necessary to comply with the final determination of royalty rates on appeal. Any underpayment of royalties resulting from an appeal (and interest thereon, if ordered pursuant to paragraph (3)) shall be paid within the same period.

(3) Jurisdiction of court.—Section 706 of title 5 shall apply with respect to review by the court of appeals under this subsection. If the court modifies or vacates a determination of the Copyright Royalty Judges, the court may enter its own determination with respect to the amount or distribution of royalty fees and costs, and order the repayment of any excess fees, the payment of any underpaid fees, and the payment of interest pertaining respectively thereto, in accordance with its final judgment. The court may also vacate the determination of the Copyright Royalty Judges and remand the case to the Copyright Royalty Judges for further proceedings in accordance with subsection (a).

(e) Administrative matters.—

(1) Deduction of costs of Library of Congress and Copyright Office from filing fees.—

(A) Deduction from filing fees.—The Librarian of Congress may, to the extent not otherwise provided under this title, deduct from the filing fees collected under subsection (b) for a particular proceeding under this chapter the reasonable costs incurred by the Librarian of Congress, the Copyright Office, and the Copyright Royalty Judges in conducting that proceeding, other than the salaries of the Copyright Royalty Judges and the 3 staff members appointed under section 802(b).

(B) Authorization of appropriations.—There are authorized to be appropriated such sums as may be necessary to pay the costs incurred under this chapter not covered by the filing fees collected under subsection (b). All funds made available pursuant to this subparagraph shall remain available until expended.

(2) Positions required for administration of compulsory licensing.—Section 307 of the Legislative Branch Appropriations Act, 1994, shall not apply to employee positions in the Library of Congress that are required to be filled in order to carry out section 111, 112, 114, 115, 116, 118, or 119 or chapter 10.

Sec. 804.   Institution of Proceedings

(a) Filing of Petition.—With respect to proceedings referred to in paragraphs (1) and (2) of section 801(b) concerning the determination or adjustment of royalty rates as provided in sections 111, 112, 114, 115, 116, 118, 119, and 1004, during the calendar years specified in the schedule set forth in subsection (b), any owner or user of a copyrighted work whose royalty rates are specified by this title, or are established under this chapter before or after the enactment of the Copyright Royalty and Distribution Reform Act of 2004, may file a petition with the Copyright Royalty Judges declaring that the petitioner requests a determination or adjustment of the rate. The Copyright Royalty Judges shall make a determination as to whether the petitioner has such a significant interest in the royalty rate in which a determination or adjustment is requested. If the Copyright Royalty Judges determine that the petitioner has such a significant interest, the Copyright Royalty Judges shall cause notice of this determination, with the reasons for such determination, to be published in the Federal Register, together with the notice of commencement of proceedings under this chapter. With respect to proceedings under paragraph (1) of section 801(b) concerning the determination or adjustment of royalty rates as provided in sections 112 and 114, during the calendar years specified in the schedule set forth in subsection (b), the Copyright Royalty Judges shall cause notice of commencement of proceedings under this chapter to be published in the Federal Register as provided in section 803(b)(1)(A).

(b) **Timing of Proceedings.—**

(1) **Section 111 Proceedings.—**

(A) A petition described in subsection (a) to initiate proceedings under section 801(b)(2) concerning the adjustment of royalty rates under section 111 to which subparagraph (A) or (D) of section 801(b)(2) applies may be filed during the year 2015 and in each subsequent fifth calendar year.

(B) In order to initiate proceedings under section 801(b)(2) concerning the adjustment of royalty rates under section 111 to which subparagraph (B) or (C) of section 801(b)(2) applies, within 12 months after an event described in either of those subsections, any owner or user of a copyrighted work whose royalty rates are specified by section 111, or by a rate established under this chapter before or after the enactment of the Copyright Royalty and Distribution Reform Act of 2004, may file a petition with the Copyright Royalty Judges declaring that the petitioner requests an adjustment of the rate. The Copyright Royalty Judges shall then proceed as set forth in subsection (a) of this section. Any change in royalty rates made under this chapter pursuant to this subparagraph may be reconsidered in the year 2015, and each fifth calendar year thereafter, in accordance with the provisions in section 801(b)(2)(B) or (C), as the case may be. A petition for adjustment of rates established by section 111(d)(1)(B) as a result of a change in the rules and regulations of the Federal Communications Commission shall set forth the change on which the petition is based.

(C) Any adjustment of royalty rates under section 111 shall take effect as of the first accounting period commencing after the publication of the determination of the Copyright

Royalty Judges in the Federal Register, or on such other date as is specified in that determination.

(2) Certain Section 112 Proceedings.—Proceedings under this chapter shall be commenced in the year 2007 to determine reasonable terms and rates of royalty payments for the activities described in section 112(e)(1) relating to the limitation on exclusive rights specified by section 114(d)(1)(C)(iv), to become effective on January 1, 2009. Such proceedings shall be repeated in each subsequent fifth calendar year.

(3) Section 114 and Corresponding 112 Proceedings.—

(A) For Eligible Nonsubscription Services and New Subscription Services.—Proceedings under this chapter shall be commenced as soon as practicable after the date of enactment of the Copyright Royalty and Distribution Reform Act of 2004 to determine reasonable terms and rates of royalty payments under sections 114 and 112 for the activities of eligible nonsubscription transmission services and new subscription services, to be effective for the period beginning on January 1, 2006, and ending on December 31, 2010. Such proceedings shall next be commenced in January 2009 to determine reasonable terms and rates of royalty payments, to become effective on January 1, 2011. Thereafter, such proceedings shall be repeated in each subsequent fifth calendar year.

(B) For Preexisting Subscription and Satellite Digital Audio Radio Services.—Proceedings under this chapter shall be commenced in January 2006 to determine reasonable terms and rates of royalty payments under sections 114 and 112 for the activities of preexisting subscription services, to be effective during the period beginning on January 1, 2008, and ending on December 31, 2012, and preexisting satellite digital audio radio services, to be effective during the period beginning on January 1, 2007, and ending on December 31, 2012. Such proceedings shall next be commenced in 2011 to determine reasonable terms and rates of royalty payments, to become effective on January 1, 2013. Thereafter, such proceedings shall be repeated in each subsequent fifth calendar year.

(C)(i) Notwithstanding any other provision of this chapter, this subparagraph shall govern proceedings commenced pursuant to section 114(f)(1)(C) and 114(f)(2)(C) concerning new types of services.

(ii) Not later than 30 days after a petition to determine rates and terms for a new type of service is filed by any copyright owner of sound recordings, or such new type of service, indicating that such new type of service is or is about to become operational, the Copyright Royalty Judges shall issue a notice for a proceeding to determine rates and terms for such service.

(iii) The proceeding shall follow the schedule set forth in subsections (b), (c), and (d) of section 803, except that—

(I)   the determination shall be issued by not later than 24 months after the publication of the notice under clause (ii); and

(II) the decision shall take effect as provided in subsections (c)(2) and (d)(2) of section 803 and section 114(f)(4)(B)(ii) and (C).

(iv) The rates and terms shall remain in effect for the period set forth in section 114(f)(1)(C) or 114(f)(2)(C), as the case may be.

(4) Section 115 Proceedings.—A petition described in subsection (a) to initiate proceedings under section 801(b)(1) concerning the adjustment or determination of royalty rates as provided in section 115 may be filed in the year 2006 and in each subsequent fifth calendar year, or at such other times as the parties have agreed under section 115(c)(3) (B) and (C).

(5) Section 116 Proceedings.—

(A) A petition described in subsection (a) to initiate proceedings under section 801(b) concerning the determination of royalty rates and terms as provided in section 116 may be filed at any time within 1 year after negotiated licenses authorized by section 116 are terminated or expire and are not replaced by subsequent agreements.

(B) If a negotiated license authorized by section 116 is terminated or expires and is not replaced by another such license agreement which provides permission to use a quantity of musical works not substantially smaller than the quantity of such works performed on coin-operated phonorecord players during the 1-year period ending March 1, 1989, the Copyright Royalty Judges shall, upon petition filed under paragraph (1) within 1 year after such termination or expiration, commence a proceeding to promptly establish an interim royalty rate or rates for the public performance by means of a coin-operated phonorecord player of nondramatic musical works embodied in phonorecords which had been subject to the terminated or expired negotiated license agreement. Such rate or rates shall be the same as the last such rate or rates and shall remain in force until the conclusion of proceedings by the Copyright Royalty Judges, in accordance with section 803, to adjust the royalty rates applicable to such works, or until superseded by a new negotiated license agreement, as provided in section 116(b).

(6) Section 118 Proceedings.—A petition described in subsection (a) to initiate proceedings under section 801(b)(1) concerning the determination of reasonable terms and rates of royalty payments as provided in section 118 may be filed in the year 2006 and in each subsequent fifth calendar year.

(7) Section 1004 Proceedings.—A petition described in subsection (a) to initiate proceedings under section 801(b)(1) concerning the adjustment of reasonable royalty rates under section 1004 may be filed as provided in section 1004(a)(3).

(8) Proceedings Concerning Distribution of Royalty Fees.—With respect to proceedings under section 801(b)(3) concerning the distribution of royalty fees in certain circumstances under section 111, 119, or 1007, the Copyright Royalty Judges shall, upon a determination that a controversy exists concerning such distribution, cause to be published in the Federal Register notice of commencement of proceedings under this chapter.

Sec. 805. General Rule for Voluntarily Negotiated Agreements

Any rates or terms under this title that—

(1) are agreed to by participants to a proceeding under section 803(b)(3),

(2) are adopted by the Copyright Royalty Judges as part of a determination under this chapter, and

(3) are in effect for a period shorter than would otherwise apply under a determination pursuant to this chapter,

shall remain in effect for such period of time as would otherwise apply under such determination, except that the Copyright Royalty Judges shall adjust the rates pursuant to the voluntary negotiations to reflect national monetary inflation during the additional period the rates remain in effect.

CHAPTER 9.—PROTECTION OF SEMICONDUCTOR CHIP PRODUCTS

(Pub.L. 98–620, 98 Stat. 3347 (1984)).

Sec. 901.   Definitions

(a) As used in this chapter—

(1) a "semiconductor chip product" is the final or intermediate form of any product—

(A) having two or more layers of metallic, insulating, or semiconductor material, deposited or otherwise placed on, or etched away or otherwise removed from, a piece of semiconductor material in accordance with a predetermined pattern; and

(B) intended to perform electronic circuitry functions;

(2) a "mask work" is a series of related images, however fixed or encoded—

(A) having or representing the predetermined, three-dimensional pattern of metallic, insulating, or semiconductor material present or removed from the layers of a semiconductor chip product; and

(B) in which series the relation of the images to one another is that each image has the pattern of the surface of one form of the semiconductor chip product;

(3) a mask work is "fixed" in a semiconductor chip product when its embodiment in the product is sufficiently permanent or stable to permit the mask work to be perceived or reproduced from the product for a period of more than transitory duration;

(4) to "distribute" means to sell, or to lease, bail, or otherwise transfer, or to offer to sell, lease, bail, or otherwise transfer;

(5) to "commercially exploit" a mask work is to distribute to the public for commercial purposes a semiconductor chip product embodying the mask work; except that such term includes an offer to sell or transfer a semiconductor chip product only when the offer is in writing and occurs after the mask work is fixed in the semiconductor chip product;

(6) the "owner" of a mask work is the person who created the mask work, the legal representative of that person if that person is deceased or under a legal incapacity, or a party to whom all the rights under this chapter of such person or representative are transferred in accordance with section 903(b); except that, in the case of a work made within the scope of a person's employment, the owner is the employer for whom the person created the mask work or a party to whom all the rights under this chapter of the employer are transferred in accordance with section 903(b);

(7) an "innocent purchaser" is a person who purchases a semiconductor chip product in good faith and without having notice of protection with respect to the semiconductor chip product;

(8) having "notice of protection" means having actual knowledge that, or reasonable grounds to believe that, a mask work is protected under this chapter; and

(9) an "infringing semiconductor chip product" is a semiconductor chip product which is made, imported, or distributed in violation of the exclusive rights of the owner of a mask work under this chapter.

(b) For purposes of this chapter, the distribution or importation of a product incorporating a semiconductor chip product as a part thereof is a distribution or importation of that semiconductor chip product.

Sec. 902.   Subject Matter of Protection

(a)(1) Subject to the provisions of subsection (b), a mask work fixed in a semiconductor chip product, by or under the authority of the owner of the mask work, is eligible for protection under this chapter if—

(A) on the date on which the mask work is registered under section 908, or is first commercially exploited anywhere in the world, whichever occurs first, the owner of the mask work is (i) a national or domiciliary of the United States, (ii) a national, domiciliary, or sovereign authority of a foreign nation that is a party to a treaty affording protection to mask works to which the United States is also a party, or (iii) a stateless person, wherever that person may be domiciled;

(B) the mask work is first commercially exploited in the United States; or

(C) the mask work comes within the scope of a Presidential proclamation issued under paragraph (2).

(2) Whenever the President finds that a foreign nation extends, to mask works of owners who are nationals or domiciliaries of the United States protection (A) on substantially the same basis as that on which the foreign nation extends protection to mask works of its own nationals and domiciliaries and mask works first commercially exploited in that nation, or (B) on substantially the same basis as provided in this chapter, the President may by proclamation extend protection under this chapter to mask works (i) of owners who are, on the date on which the mask works are registered under section 908, or the date on which the mask works are first commercially exploited anywhere in the world, whichever occurs first, nationals, domiciliaries, or sovereign authorities of that nation, or (ii) which are first commercially exploited in that nation. The President may revise, suspend, or revoke any such proclamation or impose any conditions or limitations on protection extended under any such proclamation.

(b) Protection under this chapter shall not be available for a mask work that—

(1) is not original; or

(2) consists of designs that are staple, commonplace, or familiar in the semiconductor industry, or variations of such designs, combined in a way that, considered as a whole, is not original.

(c) In no case does protection under this chapter for a mask work extend to any idea, procedure, process, system, method of operation, concept, principle, or discovery, regardless of the form in which it is described, explained, illustrated, or embodied in such work.

Sec. 903.   Ownership, Transfer, Licensing, and Recordation

(a) The exclusive rights in a mask work subject to protection under this chapter belong to the owner of the mask work.

(b) The owner of the exclusive rights in a mask work may transfer all of those rights, or license all or less than all of those rights, by any written instrument signed by such owner or a duly authorized agent of the owner. Such rights may be transferred or licensed by operation of law, may be bequeathed by will, and may pass as personal property by the applicable laws of intestate succession.

(c)(1) Any document pertaining to a mask work may be recorded in the Copyright Office if the document filed for recordation bears the actual signature of the person who executed it, or if it is accompanied by a sworn or official certification that it is a true copy of the original, signed document. The Register of Copyrights shall, upon receipt of the document and the fee specified pursuant to section 908(d), record the document and return it with a certificate of recordation. The recordation of any transfer or license under this paragraph gives all persons constructive notice of the facts stated in the recorded document concerning the transfer or license.

(2) In any case in which conflicting transfers of the exclusive rights in a mask work are made, the transfer first executed shall be void as against a subsequent transfer which is made for a valuable consideration and without notice of the first transfer, unless the first transfer is recorded in accordance with paragraph (1) within three months after the date on which it is executed, but in no case later than the day before the date of such subsequent transfer.

(d) Mask works prepared by an officer or employee of the United States Government as part of that person's official duties are not protected under this chapter, but the United States Government is not precluded from receiving and holding exclusive rights in mask works transferred to the Government under subsection (b).

Sec. 904.   Duration of Protection

(a) The protection provided for a mask work under this chapter shall commence on the date on which the mask work is registered under section 908, or the date on which the mask work is first commercially exploited anywhere in the world, whichever occurs first.

(b) Subject to subsection (c) and the provisions of this chapter, the protection provided under this chapter to a mask work shall end ten years after the date on which such protection commences under subsection (a).

(c) All terms of protection provided in this section shall run to the end of the calendar year in which they would otherwise expire.

Sec. 905. Exclusive Rights in Mask Works

The owner of a mask work provided protection under this chapter has the exclusive rights to do and to authorize any of the following:

(1) to reproduce the mask work by optical, electronic, or any other means;

(2) to import or distribute a semiconductor chip product in which the mask work is embodied; and

(3) to induce or knowingly to cause another person to do any of the acts described in paragraphs (1) and (2).

Sec. 906. Limitation on Exclusive Rights: Reverse Engineering; First Sale

(a) Notwithstanding the provisions of section 905, it is not an infringement of the exclusive rights of the owner of a mask work for—

(1) a person to reproduce the mask work solely for the purpose of teaching, analyzing, or evaluating the concepts or techniques embodied in the mask work or the circuitry, logic flow, or organization of components used in the mask work; or

(2) a person who performs the analysis or evaluation described in paragraph (1) to incorporate the results of such conduct in an original mask work which is made to be distributed.

(b) Notwithstanding the provisions of section 905(2), the owner of a particular semiconductor chip product made by the owner of the mask work, or by any person authorized by the owner of the mask work, may import, distribute, or otherwise dispose of or use, but not reproduce, that particular semiconductor chip product without the authority of the owner of the mask work.

Sec. 907. Limitation on Exclusive Rights: Innocent Infringement

(a) Notwithstanding any other provision of this chapter, an innocent purchaser of an infringing semiconductor chip product—

(1) shall incur no liability under this chapter with respect to the importation or distribution of units of the infringing semiconductor chip product that occurs before the innocent purchaser has notice of

protection with respect to the mask work embodied in the semiconductor chip product; and

(2) shall be liable only for a reasonable royalty on each unit of the infringing semiconductor chip product that the innocent purchaser imports or distributes after having notice of protection with respect to the mask work embodied in the semiconductor chip product.

(b) The amount of the royalty referred to in subsection (a)(2) shall be determined by the court in a civil action for infringement unless the parties resolve the issue by voluntary negotiation, mediation, or binding arbitration.

(c) The immunity of an innocent purchaser from liability referred to in subsection (a)(1) and the limitation of remedies with respect to an innocent purchaser referred to in subsection (a)(2) shall extend to any person who directly or indirectly purchases an infringing semiconductor chip product from an innocent purchaser.

(d) The provisions of subsections (a), (b), and (c) apply only with respect to those units of an infringing semiconductor chip product that an innocent purchaser purchased before having notice of protection with respect to the mask work embodied in the semiconductor chip product.

Sec. 908.   Registration of Claims of Protection

(a) The owner of a mask work may apply to the Register of Copyrights for registration of a claim of protection in a mask work. Protection of a mask work under this chapter shall terminate if application for registration of a claim of protection in the mask work is not made as provided in this chapter within two years after the date on which the mask work is first commercially exploited anywhere in the world.

(b) The Register of Copyrights shall be responsible for all administrative functions and duties under this chapter. Except for section 708, the provisions of chapter 7 of this title relating to the general responsibilities, organization, regulatory authority, actions, records, and publications of the Copyright Office shall apply to this chapter, except that the Register of Copyrights may make such changes as may be necessary in applying those provisions to this chapter.

(c) The application for registration of a mask work shall be made on a form prescribed by the Register of Copyrights. Such form may require any information regarded by the Register as bearing upon the preparation or identification of the mask work, the existence or duration of protection of the mask work under this chapter, or ownership of the mask work. The application shall be accompanied by the fee set pursuant to subsection (d) and the identifying material specified pursuant to such subsection.

(d) The Register of Copyrights shall by regulation set reasonable fees for the filing of applications to register claims of protection in mask works under this chapter, and for other services relating to the administration of this chapter or the rights under this chapter, taking into consideration the cost of providing those services, the benefits of a public record, and statutory fee schedules under this title. The Register shall also specify the identifying material to be deposited in connection with the claim for registration.

(e) If the Register of Copyrights, after examining an application for registration, determines, in accordance with the provisions of this chapter, that the application relates to a mask work which is entitled to protection under this chapter, then the Register shall register the claim of protection and issue to the applicant a certificate of registration of the claim of protection under the seal of the Copyright Office. The effective date of registration of a claim of protection shall be the date on which an application, deposit of identifying material, and fee, which are determined by the Register of Copyrights or by a court of competent jurisdiction to be acceptable for registration of the claim, have all been received in the Copyright Office.

(f) In any action for infringement under this chapter, the certificate of registration of a mask work shall constitute prima facie evidence (1) of the facts stated in the certificate, and (2) that the applicant issued the certificate has met the requirements of this chapter, and the regulations issued under this chapter, with respect to the registration of claims.

(g) Any applicant for registration under this section who is dissatisfied with the refusal of the Register of Copyrights to issue a certificate of registration under this section may seek judicial review of that refusal by bringing an action for such review in an appropriate United States district court not later than sixty days after the refusal. The provisions of chapter 7 of title 5 shall apply to such judicial review. The failure of the Register of Copyrights to issue a certificate of registration within four months after an application for registration is filed shall be deemed to be a refusal to issue a certificate of registration for purposes of this subsection and section 910(b)(2), except that, upon a showing of good cause, the district court may shorten such four-month period.

Sec. 909.   Mask Work Notice

(a) The owner of a mask work provided protection under this chapter may affix notice to the mask work, and to masks and semiconductor chip products embodying the mask work, in such manner and location as to give reasonable notice of such protection. The Register of Copyrights shall prescribe by regulation, as examples, specific methods of affixation and positions of notice for purposes of this section, but these specifications shall not be considered exhaustive. The affixation of such notice is not a condition of protection under this chapter, but shall constitute prima facie evidence of notice of protection.

(b) the notice referred to in subsection (a) shall consist of—

(1) the words "mask work", the symbol *M*, or the symbol M (the letter M in a circle); and

(2) the name of the owner or owners of the mask work or an abbreviation by which the name is recognized or is generally known.

Sec. 910.   Enforcement of Exclusive Rights

(a) Except as otherwise provided in this chapter, any person who violates any of the exclusive rights of the owner of a mask work under this chapter, by conduct in or affecting commerce, shall be liable as an infringer of such rights. As used in this subsection, the term "any person" includes any State, any instrumentality of a State, and any officer or employee of a State or instrumentality of a State acting in his or her official capacity. Any State, and any such instrumentality, officer, or employee, shall be subject to the provisions of this chapter in the same manner and to the same extent as any nongovernmental entity.

(b)(1) The owner of a mask work protected under this chapter, or the exclusive licensee of all rights under this chapter with respect to the mask work, shall, after a certificate of registration of a claim of protection in that mask work has been issued under section 908, be entitled to institute a civil action for any infringement with respect to the mask work which is committed after the commencement of protection of the mask work under section 904(a).

(2) In any case in which an application for registration of a claim of protection in a mask work and the required deposit of identifying material and fee have been received in the Copyright Office in proper form and registration of the mask work has been refused, the applicant is entitled to institute a civil action for infringement under this chapter with respect to the mask work if notice of the action, together with a copy of the complaint, is served on the Register of Copyrights, in accordance with the Federal Rules of Civil Procedure. The Register may, at his or her option, become a party to the action with respect to the issue of whether the claim of protection is eligible for registration by entering an appearance within sixty days after such service, but the failure of the Register to become a party to the action shall not deprive the court of jurisdiction to determine that issue.

(c)(1) The Secretary of the Treasury and the United States Postal Service shall separately or jointly issue regulations for the enforcement of the rights set forth in section 905 with respect to importation. These regulations may require, as a condition for the exclusion of articles from the United States, that the person seeking exclusion take any one or more of the following actions:

(A) Obtain a court order enjoining, or an order of the International Trade Commission under section 337 of the Tariff Act of 1930 excluding, importation of the articles.

(B) Furnish proof that the mask work involved is protected under this chapter and that the importation of the articles would infringe the rights in the mask work under this chapter.

(C) Post a surety bond for any injury that may result if the detention or exclusion of the articles proves to be unjustified.

(2) Articles imported in violation of the rights set forth in section 905 are subject to seizure and forfeiture in the same manner as property imported in violation of the customs laws. Any such forfeited articles shall be destroyed as directed by the Secretary of the Treasury or the court, as the case may be, except that the articles may be returned to the country of export whenever it is shown to the satisfaction of the Secretary of the Treasury that the importer had no reasonable grounds for believing that his or her acts constituted a violation of the law.

Sec. 911.   Civil Actions

(a) Any court having jurisdiction of a civil action arising under this chapter may grant temporary restraining orders, preliminary injunctions, and permanent injunctions on such terms as the court may deem reasonable to prevent or restrain infringement of the exclusive rights in a mask work under this chapter.

(b) Upon finding an infringer liable, to a person entitled under section 910(b)(1) to institute a civil action, for an infringement of any exclusive right under this chapter, the court shall award such person actual damages suffered by the person as a result of the infringement. The court shall also award such person the infringer's profits that are attributable to the infringement and are not taken into account in computing the award of actual damages. In establishing the infringer's profits, such person is required to present proof only of the infringer's gross revenue, and the infringer is required to prove his or her deductible expenses and the elements of profit attributable to factors other than the mask work.

(c) At any time before final judgment is rendered, a person entitled to institute a civil action for infringement may elect, instead of actual damages and profits as provided by subsection (b), an award of statutory damages for all infringements involved in the action, with respect to any one mask work for which any one infringer is liable individually, or for which any two or more infringers are liable jointly and severally, in an amount not more than $250,000 as the court considers just.

(d) An action for infringement under this chapter shall be barred unless the action is commenced within three years after the claim accrues.

(e)(1) At any time while an action for infringement of the exclusive rights in a mask work under this chapter is pending, the court may order the impounding, on such terms as it may deem reasonable, of all semiconductor chip products, and any drawings, tapes, masks, or other products by means of which such products may be reproduced, that are claimed to have been made, imported, or used in violation of those exclusive rights. Insofar as practicable, applications for orders under this paragraph shall be heard and determined in the same manner as an application for a temporary restraining order or preliminary injunction.

(2) As part of a final judgment or decree, the court may order the destruction or other disposition of any infringing semiconductor chip products, and any masks, tapes, or other articles by means of which such products may be reproduced.

(f) In any civil action arising under this chapter, the court in its discretion may allow the recovery of full costs, including reasonable attorneys' fees, to the prevailing party.

(g)(1) Any State, any instrumentality of a State, and any officer or employee of a State or instrumentality of a State acting in his or her official capacity, shall not be immune, under the Eleventh Amendment of the Constitution of the United States or under any other doctrine of sovereign immunity, from suit in Federal court by any person, including any governmental or nongovernmental entity, for a violation of any of the exclusive rights of the owner of a mask work under this chapter, or for any other violation under this chapter.

(2) In a suit described in paragraph (1) for a violation described in that paragraph, remedies (including remedies both at law and in equity) are available for the violation to the same extent as such remedies are available for such a violation in a suit against any public or private entity other than a State, instrumentality of a State, or officer or employee of a State acting in his or her official capacity. Such remedies include actual damages and profits under subsection (b), statutory damages under subsection (c), impounding and disposition of infringing articles under subsection (e), and costs and attorney's fees under subsection (f).

Sec. 912.   Relation to Other Laws

(a) Nothing in this chapter shall affect any right or remedy held by any person under chapters 1 through 8 or 10 of this title, or under title 35.

(b) Except as provided in section 908(b) of this title, references to "this title" or "title 17" in chapters 1 through 8 or 10 of this title shall be deemed not to apply to this chapter.

(c) The provisions of this chapter shall preempt the laws of any State to the extent those laws provide any rights or remedies with respect to a mask work which are equivalent to those rights or remedies provided by this chapter, except that such preemption shall be effective only with respect to actions filed on or after January 1, 1986.

(d) Notwithstanding subsection (c), nothing in this chapter shall detract from any rights of a mask work owner, whether under Federal law (exclusive of this chapter) or under the common law or the statutes of a State, heretofore or hereafter declared or enacted, with respect to any mask work first commercially exploited before July 1, 1983.

Sec. 913.   Transitional Provisions

(a) No application for registration under section 908 may be filed, and no civil action under section 910 or other enforcement proceeding under this chapter may be instituted, until sixty days after the date of the enactment of this chapter.

(b) No monetary relief under section 911 may be granted with respect to any conduct that occurred before the date of the enactment of this chapter, except as provided in subsection (d).

(c) Subject to subsection (a), the provisions of this chapter apply to all mask works that are first commercially exploited or are registered under this chapter, or both, on or after the date of the enactment of this chapter.

(d)(1) Subject to subsection (a), protection is available under this chapter to any mask work that was first commercially exploited on or after July 1, 1983, and before the date of the enactment of this chapter, if a claim of protection in the mask work is registered in the Copyright Office before July 1, 1985, under section 908.

(2) In the case of any mask work described in paragraph (1) that is provided protection under this chapter, infringing semiconductor chip product units manufactured before the date of the enactment of this chapter may, without liability under sections 910 and 911, be imported into or distributed in the United States, or both, until two years after the date of registration of the mask work under section 908, but only if the importer or distributor, as the case may be, first pays or offers to pay the reasonable royalty referred to in section 907(a)(2) to the mask work owner, on all such units imported or distributed, or both, after the date of the enactment of this chapter.

(3) In the event that a person imports or distributes infringing semiconductor chip product units described in paragraph (2) of this subsection without first paying or offering to pay the reasonable royalty specified in such paragraph, or if the person refuses or fails to make such payment, the mask work owner shall be entitled to the relief provided in sections 910 and 911.

Sec. 914.   International Transitional Provisions

(a) Notwithstanding the conditions set forth in subparagraphs (A) and (C) of section 902(a)(1) with respect to the availability of protection under this chapter to nationals, domiciliaries, and sovereign authorities of a foreign nation, the Secretary of Commerce may, upon the petition of any person, or upon the Secretary's own motion, issue an order extending protection under this chapter to such foreign nationals, domiciliaries, and sovereign authorities if the Secretary finds—

(1) that the foreign nation is making good faith efforts and reasonable progress toward—

(A) entering into a treaty described in section 902(a)(1)(A); or

(B) enacting or implementing legislation that would be in compliance with subparagraphs (A) or (B) of section 902(a)(2); and

(2) that the nationals, domiciliaries, and sovereign authorities of the foreign nation, and persons controlled by them, are not engaged in the misappropriation, or unauthorized distribution or commercial exploitation, of mask works; and

(3) that issuing the order would promote the purposes of this chapter and international comity with respect to the protection of mask works.

(b) While an order under subsection (a) is in effect with respect to a foreign nation, no application for registration of a claim for protection in a mask work under this chapter may be denied solely because the owner of the mask work is a national, domiciliary, or sovereign authority of that foreign nation, or solely because the mask work was first commercially exploited in that foreign nation.

(c) Any order issued by the Secretary of Commerce under subsection (a) shall be effective for such period as the Secretary designates in the order, except that no such order may be effective after the date on which the authority of the Secretary of Commerce terminates under subsection (e). The effective date of any such order shall also be designated in the order. In the case of an order issued upon the petition of a person, such effective date may be no earlier than the date on which the Secretary receives such petition.

(d)(1) Any order issued under this section shall terminate if—

(A) the Secretary of Commerce finds that any of the conditions set forth in paragraphs (1), (2), and (3) of subsection (a) no longer exist; or

(B) mask works of nationals, domiciliaries, and sovereign authorities of that foreign nation or mask works first commercially exploited in that foreign nation become eligible for protection under subparagraph (A) or (C) of section 902(a)(1).

(2) Upon the termination or expiration of an order issued under this section, registrations of claims of protection in mask works made pursuant to that order shall remain valid for the period specified in section 904.

(e) The authority of the Secretary of Commerce under this section shall commence on the date of the enactment of this chapter, and shall terminate on July 1, 1995.

(f)(1) The Secretary of Commerce shall promptly notify the Register of Copyrights and the Committees on the Judiciary of the Senate and the House of Representatives of the issuance or termination of any order under this section, together with a statement of the reasons for such action. The Secretary shall also publish such notification and statement of reasons in the Federal Register.

(2) Two years after the date of the enactment of this chapter, the Secretary of Commerce, in consultation with the Register of Copyrights, shall transmit to the Committees on the Judiciary of the Senate and the House of Representatives a report on the actions taken under this section and on the current status of international recognition of mask work protection. The report shall include such recommendations for modifications of the protection accorded under this chapter to mask works owned by nationals, domiciliaries, or sovereign authorities of foreign nations as the Secretary, in consultation with the Register of Copyrights, considers would promote the purposes of this chapter and international comity with respect to mask work protection. Not later than July 1, 1994, the Secretary of Commerce, in consultation with the Register of Copyrights, shall transmit to the Committees on the Judiciary of the Senate and the House of Representatives a report updating the matters contained in the report transmitted under the preceding sentence.

CHAPTER 10.—DIGITAL AUDIO RECORDING DEVICES AND MEDIA

(Pub.L. 102–563, 106 Stat. 4237 (1992)).

Subchapter A—Definitions

Subchapter B—Copying Controls

Subchapter C—Royalty Payments

Subchapter D—Prohibition on Certain Infringement Actions, Remedies, and Arbitration

Subchapter A—Definitions

Sec. 1001.   Definitions

As used in this chapter, the following terms have the following meanings:

(1) A "digital audio copied recording" is a reproduction in a digital recording format of a digital musical recording, whether that reproduction is made directly from another digital musical recording or indirectly from a transmission.

(2) A "digital audio interface device" is any machine or device that is designed specifically to communicate digital audio information and related interface data to a digital audio recording device through a nonprofessional interface.

(3) A "digital audio recording device" is any machine or device of a type commonly distributed to individuals for use by individuals, whether or not included with or as part of some other machine or device, the digital recording function of which is designed or marketed for the primary purpose of, and that is capable of, making a digital audio copied recording for private use, except for—

(A) professional model products, and

(B) dictation machines, answering machines, and other audio recording equipment that is designed and marketed primarily for the creation of sound recordings resulting from the fixation of nonmusical sounds.

(4)(A) A "digital audio recording medium" is any material object in a form commonly distributed for use by individuals, that is primarily marketed or most commonly used by consumers for the purpose of making digital audio copied recordings by use of a digital audio recording device.

(B) Such term does not include any material object—

(i) that embodies a sound recording at the time it is first distributed by the importer or manufacturer; or

(ii) that is primarily marketed and most commonly used by consumers either for the purpose of making copies of motion pictures or other audiovisual works or for the purpose of making copies of nonmusical literary works, including computer programs or data bases.

(5)(A) A "digital musical recording" is a material object—

(i) in which are fixed, in a digital recording format, only sounds, and material, statements, or instructions incidental to those fixed sounds, if any, and

(ii) from which the sounds and material can be perceived, reproduced, or otherwise communicated, either directly or with the aid of a machine or device.

(B) A "digital musical recording" does not include a material object—

(i) in which the fixed sounds consist entirely of spoken word recordings, or

(ii) in which one or more computer programs are fixed, except that a digital musical recording may contain statements or instructions constituting the fixed sounds and incidental material, and statements or instructions to be used directly or indirectly in order to bring about the perception, reproduction, or communication of the fixed sounds and incidental material.

(C) For purposes of this paragraph—

(i) a "spoken word recording" is a sound recording in which are fixed only a series of spoken words, except that the spoken words may be accompanied by incidental musical or other sounds, and

(ii) the term "incidental" means related to and relatively minor by comparison.

(6) "Distribute" means to sell, lease, or assign a product to consumers in the United States, or to sell, lease, or assign a product in the United States for ultimate transfer to consumers in the United States.

(7) An "interested copyright party" is—

(A) the owner of the exclusive right under section 106(1) of this title to reproduce a sound recording of a musical work that has been embodied in a digital musical recording or analog musical recording lawfully made under this title that has been distributed;

(B) the legal or beneficial owner of, or the person that controls, the right to reproduce in a digital musical recording or analog musical recording a musical work that has been embodied in a digital musical recording or analog musical recording lawfully made under this title that has been distributed;

(C) a featured recording artist who performs on a sound recording that has been distributed; or

(D) any association or other organization—

(i) representing persons specified in subparagraph (A), (B), or (C), or

(ii) engaged in licensing rights in musical works to music users on behalf of writers and publishers.

(8) To "manufacture" means to produce or assemble a product in the United States. A "manufacturer" is a person who manufactures.

(9) A "music publisher" is a person that is authorized to license the reproduction of a particular musical work in a sound recording.

(10) A "professional model product" is an audio recording device that is designed, manufactured, marketed, and intended for use by recording professionals in the ordinary course of a lawful business, in accordance

with such requirements as the Secretary of Commerce shall establish by regulation.

(11) The term "serial copying" means the duplication in a digital format of a copyrighted musical work or sound recording from a digital reproduction of a digital musical recording. The term "digital reproduction of a digital musical recording" does not include a digital musical recording as distributed, by authority of the copyright owner, for ultimate sale to consumers.

(12) The "transfer price" of a digital audio recording device or a digital audio recording medium—

(A) is, subject to subparagraph (B)—

(i) in the case of an imported product, the actual entered value at United States Customs (exclusive of any freight, insurance, and applicable duty), and

(ii) in the case of a domestic product, the manufacturer's transfer price (FOB the manufacturer, and exclusive of any direct sales taxes or excise taxes incurred in connection with the sale); and

(B) shall, in a case in which the transferor and transferee are related entities or within a single entity, not be less than a reasonable arms-length price under the principles of the regulations adopted pursuant to section 482 of the Internal Revenue Code of 1986, or any successor provision to such section.

(13) A "writer" is the composer or lyricist of a particular musical work.

Subchapter B—Copying Controls

Sec. 1002.   Incorporation of Copying Controls

(a) Prohibition on Importation, Manufacture, and Distribution.—No person shall import, manufacture, or distribute any digital audio recording device or digital audio interface device that does not conform to—

(1) the Serial Copy Management System;

(2) a system that has the same functional characteristics as the Serial Copy Management System and requires that copyright and generation status information be accurately sent, received, and acted upon between devices using the system's method of serial copying regulation and devices using the Serial Copy Management System; or

(3) any other system certified by the Secretary of Commerce as prohibiting unauthorized serial copying.

(b) Development of Verification Procedure.—The Secretary of Commerce shall establish a procedure to verify, upon the petition of an interested party, that a system meets the standards set forth in subsection (a)(2).

(c) Prohibition on Circumvention of the System.—No person shall import, manufacture, or distribute any device, or offer or perform any service, the primary purpose or effect of which is to avoid, bypass, remove, deactivate, or otherwise circumvent any program or circuit which implements, in whole or in part, a system described in subsection (a).

(d) Encoding   of   Information   on   Digital   Musical Recordings.—

   (1) Prohibition on encoding inaccurate information.—No person shall encode a digital musical recording of a sound recording with inaccurate information relating to the category code, copyright status, or generation status of the source material for the recording.

   (2) Encoding of copyright status not required.—Nothing in this chapter requires any person engaged in the importation or manufacture of digital musical recordings to encode any such digital musical recording with respect to its copyright status.

(e) Information Accompanying Transmissions in Digital Format.—Any person who transmits or otherwise communicates to the public any sound recording in digital format is not required under this chapter to transmit or otherwise communicate the information relating to the copyright status of the sound recording. Any such person who does transmit or otherwise communicate such copyright status information shall transmit or communicate such information accurately.

Subchapter C—Royalty Payments

Sec. 1003.   Obligation to Make Royalty Payments

(a) Prohibition on Importation and Manufacture.—No person shall import into and distribute, or manufacture and distribute, any digital audio recording device or digital audio recording medium unless such person records the notice specified by this section and subsequently deposits the statements of account and applicable royalty payments for such device or medium specified in section 1004.

(b) Filing of Notice.—The importer or manufacturer of any digital audio recording device or digital audio recording medium, within a product category or utilizing a technology with respect to which such manufacturer or importer has not previously filed a notice under this subsection, shall file with the Register of Copyrights a notice with respect to such device or medium, in such form and content as the Register shall prescribe by regulation.

(c) Filing of Quarterly and Annual Statements of Account.—

   (1) Generally.—Any   importer   or   manufacturer   that distributes any digital audio recording device or digital audio recording medium that it manufactured or imported shall file with the Register of Copyrights, in such form and content as the Register shall prescribe by regulation, such quarterly and annual statements of account with respect to such distribution as the Register shall prescribe by regulation.

(2) Certification, verification, and confidentiality.—Each such statement shall be certified as accurate by an authorized officer or principal of the importer or manufacturer. The Register shall issue regulations to provide for the verification and audit of such statements and to protect the confidentiality of the information contained in such statements. Such regulations shall provide for the disclosure, in confidence, of such statements to interested copyright parties.

(3) Royalty payments.—Each such statement shall be accompanied by the royalty payments specified in section 1004.

Sec. 1004.   Royalty Payments

(a) Digital Audio Recording Devices.—

(1) Amount of payment.—The royalty payment due under section 1003 for each digital audio recording device imported into and distributed in the United States, or manufactured and distributed in the United States, shall be 2 percent of the transfer price. Only the first person to manufacture and distribute or import and distribute such device shall be required to pay the royalty with respect to such device.

(2) Calculation for devices distributed with other devices.—With respect to a digital audio recording device first distributed in combination with one or more devices, either as a physically integrated unit or as separate components, the royalty payment shall be calculated as follows:

(A) If the digital audio recording device and such other devices are part of a physically integrated unit, the royalty payment shall be based on the transfer price of the unit, but shall be reduced by any royalty payment made on any digital audio recording device included within the unit that was not first distributed in combination with the unit.

(B) If the digital audio recording device is not part of a physically integrated unit and substantially similar devices have been distributed separately at any time during the preceding 4 calendar quarters, the royalty payment shall be based on the average transfer price of such devices during those 4 quarters.

(C) If the digital audio recording device is not part of a physically integrated unit and substantially similar devices have not been distributed separately at any time during the preceding 4 calendar quarters, the royalty payment shall be based on a constructed price reflecting the proportional value of such device to the combination as a whole.

(3) Limits on Royalties.—Notwithstanding paragraph (1) or (2), the amount of the royalty payment for each digital audio recording device shall not be less than $1 nor more than the royalty maximum. The royalty maximum shall be $8 per device, except that in the case of a physically integrated unit containing more than 1 digital audio recording device, the royalty maximum for such unit shall be $12. During the 6th year after the effective date of this chapter, and not more than once each year thereafter, any interested copyright party may petition the Copyright Royalty Judges to increase the royalty maximum and, if more than 20 percent of the royalty payments are at the relevant royalty maximum, the Copyright Royalty Judges shall prospectively increase such royalty maximum with the goal of having no more than 10 percent of such payments at the new royalty maximum; however the amount of any such increase as a percentage of the royalty maximum shall in no event exceed the percentage increase in the Consumer Price Index during the period under review.

(b) Digital Audio Recording Media.—The royalty payment due under section 1003 for each digital audio recording medium imported into and distributed in the United States, or manufactured and distributed in the United States, shall be 3 percent of the transfer price. Only the first person to manufacture and distribute or import and distribute such medium shall be required to pay the royalty with respect to such medium.

Sec. 1005. Deposit of Royalty Payments and Deduction of Expenses

The Register of Copyrights shall receive all royalty payments deposited under this chapter and, after deducting the reasonable costs incurred by the Copyright Office under this chapter, shall deposit the balance in the Treasury of the United States as offsetting receipts, in such manner as the Secretary of the Treasury directs. All funds held by the Secretary of the Treasury shall be invested in interest-bearing United States securities for later distribution with interest under section 1007. The Register may, in the Register's discretion, 4 years after the close of any calendar year, close out the royalty payments account for that calendar year, and may treat any funds remaining in such account and any subsequent deposits that would otherwise be attributable to that calendar year as attributable to the succeeding calendar year.

Sec. 1006. Entitlement to Royalty Payments

(a) Interested Copyright Parties.—The royalty payments deposited pursuant to section 1005 shall, in accordance with the procedures specified in section 1007, be distributed to any interested copyright party—

(1) whose musical work or sound recording has been—

(A) embodied in a digital musical recording or an analog musical recording lawfully made under this title that has been distributed, and

(B) distributed in the form of digital musical recordings or analog musical recordings or disseminated to the public in transmissions, during the period to which such payments pertain; and

(2) who has filed a claim under section 1007.

(b) Allocation of Royalty Payments to Groups.—The royalty payments shall be divided into 2 funds as follows:

(1) The sound recordings fund.—66⅔ percent of the royalty payments shall be allocated to the Sound Recordings Fund. 2 ⅝ percent of the royalty payments allocated to the Sound Recordings Fund shall be placed in an escrow account managed by an independent administrator jointly appointed by the interested copyright parties described in section 1001(7)(A) and the American Federation of Musicians (or any successor entity) to be distributed to nonfeatured musicians (whether or not members of the American Federation of Musicians or any successor entity) who have performed on sound recordings distributed in the United States. 1⅜ percent of the royalty payments allocated to the Sound Recordings Fund shall be placed in an escrow account managed by an independent administrator jointly appointed by the interested copyright parties described in section 1001(7)(A) and the American Federation of Television and Radio Artists (or any successor entity) to be distributed to nonfeatured vocalists (whether or not members of the American Federation of Television and Radio Artists or any successor entity) who have performed on sound recordings distributed in the United States. 40 percent of the remaining royalty payments in the Sound Recordings Fund shall be distributed to the interested copyright parties described in section 1001(7)(C), and 60 percent of such remaining royalty payments shall be distributed to the interested copyright parties described in section 1001(7)(A).

(2) The musical works fund.—

(A) 33⅓ percent of the royalty payments shall be allocated to the Musical Works Fund for distribution to interested copyright parties described in section 1001(7)(B).

(B)(i) Music publishers shall be entitled to 50 percent of the royalty payments allocated to the Musical Works Fund.

(ii) Writers shall be entitled to the other 50 percent of the royalty payments allocated to the Musical Works Fund.

(c) Allocation of Royalty Payments Within Groups.—If all interested copyright parties within a group specified in subsection (b) do not agree on a voluntary proposal for the distribution of the royalty payments within each group, the Copyright Royalty Judges shall, pursuant to the procedures specified under section 1007(c), allocate royalty payments under this section based on the extent to which, during the relevant period—

(1) for the Sound Recordings Fund, each sound recording was distributed in the form of digital musical recordings or analog musical recordings; and

(2) for the Musical Works Fund, each musical work was distributed in the form of digital musical recordings or analog musical recordings or disseminated to the public in transmissions.

Sec. 1007. Procedures for Distributing Royalty Payments

(a) Filing of Claims and Negotiations.—

(1) **Filing of Claims.**—During the first two months of each calendar year, every interested copyright party seeking to receive royalty payments to which such party is entitled under section 1006 shall file with the Copyright Royalty Judges a claim for payments collected during the preceding year in such form and manner as the Copyright Royalty Judges shall prescribe by regulation.

(2) **Negotiations.**—Notwithstanding any provision of the antitrust laws, for purposes of this section interested copyright parties within each group specified in section 1006(b) may agree among themselves to the proportionate division of royalty payments, may lump their claims together and file them jointly or as a single claim, or may designate a common agent, including any organization described in section 1001(7)(D), to negotiate or receive payment on their behalf; except that no agreement under this subsection may modify the allocation of royalties specified in section 1006(b).

(b) Distribution of Payments in the Absence of a Dispute.—

After the period established for the filing of claims under subsection (a), in each year, the Copyright Royalty Judges shall determine whether there exists a controversy concerning the distribution of royalty payments under section 1006(c). If the Copyright Royalty Judges determine that no such controversy exists, the Copyright Royalty Judges shall, within 30 days after such determination, authorize the distribution of the royalty payments as set forth in the agreements regarding the distribution of royalty payments entered into pursuant to subsection (a). The Librarian of Congress shall, before such royalty payments are distributed, deduct the reasonable administrative cost incurred under this section.

(c) Resolution of Disputes.—

If the Copyright Royalty Judges find the existence of a controversy, the Copyright Royalty Judges shall, pursuant to chapter 8 of this title, conduct a proceeding to determine the distribution of royalty payments. During the pendency of such a proceeding, the Copyright Royalty Judges shall withhold from distribution an amount sufficient to satisfy all claims with respect to which a controversy exists, but shall, to the extent feasible, authorize the distribution of any amounts that are not in controversy. The Librarian of Congress shall, before such royalty payments are distributed, deduct the reasonable administrative costs incurred under this section.

Subchapter D—Prohibition on Certain Infringement Actions, Remedies, and Arbitration

Sec. 1008.   Prohibition on Certain Infringement Actions

No action may be brought under this title alleging infringement of copyright based on the manufacture, importation, or distribution of a digital audio recording device, a digital audio recording medium, an analog recording device, or an analog recording medium, or based on the noncommercial use by a consumer of such a device or medium for making digital musical recordings or analog musical recordings.

Sec. 1009.   Civil Remedies

(a) Civil Actions.—Any interested copyright party injured by a violation of section 1002 or 1003 may bring a civil action in an appropriate United States district court against any person for such violation.

(b) Other Civil Actions.—Any person injured by a violation of this chapter may bring a civil action in an appropriate United States district court for actual damages incurred as a result of such violation.

(c) Powers of the Court.—In an action brought under subsection (a), the court—

(1) may grant temporary and permanent injunctions on such terms as it deems reasonable to prevent or restrain such violation;

(2) in the case of a violation of section 1002, or in the case of an injury resulting from a failure to make royalty payments required by section 1003, shall award damages under subsection (d);

(3) in its discretion may allow the recovery of costs by or against any party other than the United States or an officer thereof; and

(4) in its discretion may award a reasonable attorney's fee to the prevailing party.

(d) Award of Damages.—

(1) Damages for section 1002 or 1003 violations.—

(A) Actual damages.—

(i) In an action brought under subsection (a), if the court finds that a violation of section 1002 or 1003 has occurred, the court shall award to the complaining party its actual damages if the complaining party elects such damages at any time before final judgment is entered.

(ii) In the case of section 1003, actual damages shall constitute the royalty payments that should have been paid under section 1004 and deposited under section 1005. In such a case, the court, in its discretion, may award an additional amount of not to exceed 50 percent of the actual damages.

(B) Statutory damages for section 1002 violations.—

(i) Device.—A complaining party may recover an award of statutory damages for each violation of section 1002(a) or (c) in the sum of not more than $2,500 per device involved in such violation or per device on which a service prohibited by section 1002(c) has been performed, as the court considers just.

(ii) Digital musical recording.—A complaining party may recover an award of statutory damages for each violation of section 1002(d) in the sum of not more than $25 per digital musical recording involved in such violation, as the court considers just.

(iii) Transmission.—A complaining party may recover an award of damages for each transmission or communication that violates section 1002(e) in the sum of not more than $10,000, as the court considers just.

(2) Repeated violations.—In any case in which the court finds that a person has violated section 1002 or 1003 within 3 years after a final judgment against that person for another such violation was entered, the court may increase the award of damages to not more than double the amounts that would otherwise be awarded under paragraph (1), as the court considers just.

(3) Innocent violations of section 1002.—The court in its discretion may reduce the total award of damages against a person violating section 1002 to a sum of not less than $250 in any case in which the court finds that the violator was not aware and had no reason to believe that its acts constituted a violation of section 1002.

(e) Payment of Damages.—Any award of damages under subsection (d) shall be deposited with the Register pursuant to section 1005 for distribution to interested copyright parties as though such funds were royalty payments made pursuant to section 1003.

(f) Impounding of Articles.—At any time while an action under subsection (a) is pending, the court may order the impounding, on such terms as it deems reasonable, of any digital audio recording device, digital musical recording, or device specified in section 1002(c) that is in the custody or control of the alleged violator and that the court has reasonable cause to believe does not comply with, or was involved in a violation of, section 1002.

(g) Remedial Modification and Destruction of Articles.—In an action brought under subsection (a), the court may, as part of a final judgment or decree finding a violation of section 1002, order the remedial modification or the destruction of any digital audio recording device, digital musical recording, or device specified in section 1002(c) that

(1) does not comply with, or was involved in a violation of, section 1002, and

(2) is in the custody or control of the violator or has been impounded under subsection (f).

Sec. 1010.   Determination of Certain Disputes

(a) Scope of determination.—Before the date of first distribution in the United States of a digital audio recording device or a digital audio interface device, any party manufacturing, importing, or distributing such device, and any interested copyright party may mutually agree to petition the Copyright Royalty Judges to determine whether such device is subject to section 1002, or the basis on which royalty payments for such device are to be made under section 1003.

(b) Initiation of proceedings.—The parties under subsection (a) shall file the petition with the Copyright Royalty Judges requesting the commencement of a proceeding. Within 2 weeks after receiving such a petition, the Chief Copyright Royalty Judge shall cause notice to be published in the Federal Register of the initiation of the proceeding.

(c) Stay of judicial proceedings.—Any civil action brought under section 1009 against a party to a proceeding under this section shall, on application of one of the parties to the proceeding, be stayed until completion of the proceeding.

(d) Proceeding.—The Copyright Royalty Judges shall conduct a proceeding with respect to the matter concerned, in accordance with such procedures as the Copyright Royalty Judges may adopt. The Copyright Royalty Judges shall act on the basis of a fully documented written record. Any party to the proceeding may submit relevant information and proposals to the Copyright Royalty Judges. The parties to the proceeding shall each bear their respective costs of participation.

(e) Judicial review.—Any determination of the Copyright Royalty Judges under subsection (d) may be appealed, by a party to the proceeding, in accordance with section 803(d) of this title. The pendency of an appeal under this subsection shall not stay the determination of the Copyright Royalty Judges. If the court modifies the determination of the Copyright Royalty Judges, the court shall have jurisdiction to enter its own decision in accordance with its final judgment. The court may further vacate the determination of the Copyright Royalty Judges and remand the case for proceedings as provided in this section.

CHAPTER 11.—SOUND RECORDINGS AND MUSIC VIDEOS

Sec. 1101. Unauthorized Fixation and Trafficking in Sound Recordings and Music Videos

(a) Unauthorized Acts.—Anyone who, without the consent of the performer or performers involved—

(1) fixes the sounds or sounds and images of a live musical performance in a copy or phonorecord, or reproduces copies or phonorecords of such a performance from an unauthorized fixation,

(2) transmits or otherwise communicates to the public the sounds or sounds and images of a live musical performance, or

(3) distributes or offers to distribute, sells or offers to sell, rents or offers to rent, or traffics in any copy or phonorecord fixed as described in paragraph (1), regardless of whether the fixations occurred in the United States,

shall be subject to the remedies provided in sections 502 through 505, to the same extent as an infringer of copyright.

(b) Definition.—As used in this section, the term "traffic in" means transport, transfer, or otherwise dispose of, to another, as consideration for anything of value, or make or obtain control of with intent to transport, transfer, or dispose of.

(c) Applicability.—This section shall apply to any act or acts that occur on or after the date of the enactment of the Uruguay Round Agreements Act.

(d) State Law Not Preempted.—Nothing in this section may be construed to annul or limit any rights or remedies under the common law or statutes of any State.

CHAPTER 12.—COPYRIGHT PROTECTION AND MANAGEMENT SYSTEMS

(Pub.L. 105–304, 112 Stat. 2863 (1998)).

Sec. 1201. Circumvention of Copyright Protection Systems

(a) Violations Regarding Circumvention of Technological Measures.—

(1)(A) No person shall circumvent a technological measure that effectively controls access to a work protected under this title. The prohibition contained in the preceding sentence shall take effect at the end of the 2-year period beginning on the date of the enactment of this chapter.

(B) The prohibition contained in subparagraph (A) shall not apply to persons who are users of a copyrighted work which is in a particular class of works, if such persons are, or are likely to be in the succeeding 3-year period, adversely affected by virtue of such prohibition in their ability to make noninfringing uses of that particular class of works under this title, as determined under subparagraph (C).

(C) During the 2-year period described in subparagraph (A), and during each succeeding 3-year period, the Librarian of Congress, upon the recommendation of the Register of Copyrights, who shall consult with the Assistant Secretary for Communications and Information of the Department of Commerce and report and comment on his or her views in making such recommendation, shall make the determination in a rulemaking proceeding for purposes of subparagraph (B) of whether persons who are users of a copyrighted work are, or are likely to be in the succeeding 3-year period, adversely affected by the prohibition under subparagraph (A) in their ability to make noninfringing uses under this title of a particular class of copyrighted works. In conducting such rulemaking, the Librarian shall examine—

(i) the availability for use of copyrighted works;

(ii) the availability for use of works for nonprofit archival, preservation, and educational purposes;

(iii) the impact that the prohibition on the circumvention of technological measures applied to copyrighted works has on criticism, comment, news reporting, teaching, scholarship, or research;

(iv) the effect of circumvention of technological measures on the market for or value of copyrighted works; and

(v) such other factors as the Librarian considers appropriate.

(D) The Librarian shall publish any class of copyrighted works for which the Librarian has determined, pursuant to the rulemaking conducted under subparagraph (C), that noninfringing uses by persons who are users of a copyrighted work are, or are likely to be, adversely affected, and the prohibition contained in subparagraph (A) shall not apply to such users with respect to such class of works for the ensuing 3-year period.

(E) Neither the exception under subparagraph (B) from the applicability of the prohibition contained in subparagraph (A), nor any determination made in a rulemaking conducted under subparagraph (C), may be used as a defense in any action to enforce any provision of this title other than this paragraph.

(2) No person shall manufacture, import, offer to the public, provide, or otherwise traffic in any technology, product, service, device, component, or part thereof, that—

    (A) is primarily designed or produced for the purpose of circumventing a technological measure that effectively controls access to a work protected under this title;

    (B) has only limited commercially significant purpose or use other than to circumvent a technological measure that effectively controls access to a work protected under this title; or

    (C) is marketed by that person or another acting in concert with that person with that person's knowledge for use in circumventing a technological measure that effectively controls access to a work protected under this title.

(3) As used in this subsection—

    (A) to "circumvent a technological measure" means to descramble a scrambled work, to decrypt an encrypted work, or otherwise to avoid, bypass, remove, deactivate, or impair a technological measure, without the authority of the copyright owner; and

    (B) a technological measure "effectively controls access to a work" if the measure, in the ordinary course of its operation, requires the application of information, or a process or a treatment, with the authority of the copyright owner, to gain access to the work.

(b) Additional Violations.—

(1) No person shall manufacture, import, offer to the public, provide, or otherwise traffic in any technology, product, service, device, component, or part thereof, that—

    (A) is primarily designed or produced for the purpose of circumventing protection afforded by a technological measure that effectively protects a right of a copyright owner under this title in a work or a portion thereof;

    (B) has only limited commercially significant purpose or use other than to circumvent protection afforded by a technological measure that effectively protects a right of a copyright owner under this title in a work or a portion thereof; or

    (C) is marketed by that person or another acting in concert with that person with that person's knowledge for use in circumventing protection afforded by a technological measure that effectively protects a right of a copyright owner under this title in a work or a portion thereof.

(2) As used in this subsection—

(A) to "circumvent protection afforded by a technological measure" means avoiding, bypassing, removing, deactivating, or otherwise impairing a technological measure; and

(B) a technological measure "effectively protects a right of a copyright owner under this title" if the measure, in the ordinary course of its operation, prevents, restricts, or otherwise limits the exercise of a right of a copyright owner under this title.

(c) Other Rights, Etc., Not Affected.—

(1) Nothing in this section shall affect rights, remedies, limitations, or defenses to copyright infringement, including fair use, under this title.

(2) Nothing in this section shall enlarge or diminish vicarious or contributory liability for copyright infringement in connection with any technology, product, service, device, component, or part thereof.

(3) Nothing in this section shall require that the design of, or design and selection of parts and components for, a consumer electronics, telecommunications, or computing product provide for a response to any particular technological measure, so long as such part or component, or the product in which such part or component is integrated, does not otherwise fall within the prohibitions of subsection (a)(2) or (b)(1).

(4) Nothing in this section shall enlarge or diminish any rights of free speech or the press for activities using consumer electronics, telecommunications, or computing products.

(d) Exemption for Nonprofit Libraries, Archives, and Educational Institutions.—

(1) A nonprofit library, archives, or educational institution which gains access to a commercially exploited copyrighted work solely in order to make a good faith determination of whether to acquire a copy of that work for the sole purpose of engaging in conduct permitted under this title shall not be in violation of subsection (a)(1)(A). A copy of a work to which access has been gained under this paragraph—

(A) may not be retained longer than necessary to make such good faith determination; and

(B) may not be used for any other purpose.

(2) The exemption made available under paragraph (1) shall only apply with respect to a work when an identical copy of that work is not reasonably available in another form.

(3) A nonprofit library, archives, or educational institution that willfully for the purpose of commercial advantage or financial gain violates paragraph (1)—

(A) shall, for the first offense, be subject to the civil remedies under section 1203; and

(B) shall, for repeated or subsequent offenses, in addition to the civil remedies under section 1203, forfeit the exemption provided under paragraph (1).

(4) This subsection may not be used as a defense to a claim under subsection (a)(2) or (b), nor may this subsection permit a nonprofit library, archives, or educational institution to manufacture, import, offer to the public, provide, or otherwise traffic in any technology, product, service, component, or part thereof, which circumvents a technological measure.

(5) In order for a library or archives to qualify for the exemption under this subsection, the collections of that library or archives shall be—

(A) open to the public; or

(B) available not only to researchers affiliated with the library or archives or with the institution of which it is a part, but also to other persons doing research in a specialized field.

(e) Law Enforcement, Intelligence, and Other Government Activities.—This section does not prohibit any lawfully authorized investigative, protective, information security, or intelligence activity of an officer, agent, or employee of the United States, a State, or a political subdivision of a State, or a person acting pursuant to a contract with the United States, a State, or a political subdivision of a State. For purposes of this subsection, the term "information security" means activities carried out in order to identify and address the vulnerabilities of a government computer, computer system, or computer network.

(f) Reverse Engineering.—

(1) Notwithstanding the provisions of subsection (a)(1)(A), a person who has lawfully obtained the right to use a copy of a computer program may circumvent a technological measure that effectively controls access to a particular portion of that program for the sole purpose of identifying and analyzing those elements of the program that are necessary to achieve interoperability of an independently created computer program with other programs, and that have not previously been readily available to the person engaging in the circumvention, to the extent any such acts of identification and analysis do not constitute infringement under this title.

(2) Notwithstanding the provisions of subsections (a)(2) and (b), a person may develop and employ technological means to circumvent a technological measure, or to circumvent protection afforded by a technological measure, in order to enable the identification and analysis under paragraph (1), or for the purpose of enabling

interoperability of an independently created computer program with other programs, if such means are necessary to achieve such interoperability, to the extent that doing so does not constitute infringement under this title.

(3) The information acquired through the acts permitted under paragraph (1), and the means permitted under paragraph (2), may be made available to others if the person referred to in paragraph (1) or (2), as the case may be, provides such information or means solely for the purpose of enabling interoperability of an independently created computer program with other programs, and to the extent that doing so does not constitute infringement under this title or violate applicable law other than this section.

(4) For purposes of this subsection, the term "interoperability" means the ability of computer programs to exchange information, and of such programs mutually to use the information which has been exchanged.

(g) Encryption Research.—

(1) Definitions.—For purposes of this subsection—

(A) the term "encryption research" means activities necessary to identify and analyze flaws and vulnerabilities of encryption technologies applied to copyrighted works, if these activities are conducted to advance the state of knowledge in the field of encryption technology or to assist in the development of encryption products; and

(B) the term "encryption technology" means the scrambling and descrambling of information using mathematical formulas or algorithms.

(2) Permissible Acts of Encryption Research.—Notwithstanding the provisions of subsection (a)(1)(A), it is not a violation of that subsection for a person to circumvent a technological measure as applied to a copy, phonorecord, performance, or display of a published work in the course of an act of good faith encryption research if—

(A) the person lawfully obtained the encrypted copy, phonorecord, performance, or display of the published work;

(B) such act is necessary to conduct such encryption research;

(C) the person made a good faith effort to obtain authorization before the circumvention; and

(D) such act does not constitute infringement under this title or a violation of applicable law other than this section, including section 1030 of title 18 and those provisions of title 18 amended by the Computer Fraud and Abuse Act of 1986.

(3) Factors in Determining Exemption.—In determining whether a person factors to be considered shall include—

(A) whether the information derived from the encryption research was disseminated, and if so, whether it was disseminated in a manner reasonably calculated to advance the state of knowledge or development of encryption technology, versus whether it was disseminated in a manner that facilitates infringement under this title or a violation of applicable law other than this section including a violation of privacy or breach of security;

(B) whether the person is engaged in a legitimate course of study, is employed, or is appropriately trained or experienced, in the field of encryption technology; and

(C) whether the person provides the copyright owner of the work to which the technological measure is applied with notice of the findings and documentation of the research, and the time when such notice is provided.

(4) Use of Technological Means for Research Activities.— Notwithstanding the provisions of subsection (a)(2), it is not a violation of that subsection for a person to—

(A) develop and employ technological means to circumvent a technological measure for the sole purpose of that person performing the acts of good faith encryption research described in paragraph (2); and

(B) provide the technological means to another person with whom he or she is working collaboratively for the purpose of conducting the acts of good faith encryption research described in paragraph (2) or for the purpose of having that other person verify his or her acts of good faith encryption research described in paragraph (2).

(5) Report to Congress.—Not later than 1 year after the date of the enactment of this chapter, the Register of Copyrights and the Assistant Secretary for Communications and Information of the Department of Commerce shall jointly report to the Congress on the effect this subsection has had on—

(A) encryption research and the development of encryption technology;

(B) the adequacy and effectiveness of technological measures designed to protect copyrighted works; and

(C) protection of copyright owners against the unauthorized access to their encrypted copyrighted works.

The report shall include legislative recommendations, if any.

(h) Exceptions Regarding Minors.—In applying subsection (a) to a component or part, the court may consider the necessity for its intended and actual incorporation in a technology, product, service, or device, which—

(1) does not itself violate the provisions of this title; and

(2) has the sole purpose to prevent the access of minors to material on the Internet.

(i) Protection of Personally Identifying Information.—

(1) Circumvention Permitted.—Notwithstanding the provisions of subsection (a)(1)(A), it is not a violation of that subsection for a person to circumvent a technological measure that effectively controls access to a work protected under this title, if—

(A) the technological measure, or the work it protects, contains the capability of collecting or disseminating personally identifying information reflecting the online activities of a natural person who seeks to gain access to the work protected;

(B) in the normal course of its operation, the technological measure, or the work it protects, collects or disseminates personally identifying information about the person who seeks to gain access to the work protected, without providing conspicuous notice of such collection or dissemination to such person, and without providing such person with the capability to prevent or restrict such collection or dissemination;

(C) the act of circumvention has the sole effect of identifying and disabling the capability described in subparagraph (A), and has no other effect on the ability of any person to gain access to any work; and

(D) the act of circumvention is carried out solely for the purpose of preventing the collection or dissemination of personally identifying information about a natural person who seeks to gain access to the work protected, and is not in violation of any other law.

(2) Inapplicability to Certain Technological Measures.—This subsection does not apply to a technological measure, or a work it protects, that does not collect or disseminate personally identifying information and that is disclosed to a user as not having or using such capability.

(j) Security Testing.—

(1) Definition.—For purposes of this subsection, the term "security testing" means accessing a computer network, solely for the purpose of good faith testing, investigating, or correcting, a security flaw or vulnerability, with the authorization of the owner or operator of such computer, computer system, or computer network.

(2) Permissible Acts of Security Testing.—Notwithstanding the provisions of subsection (a)(1)(A), it is not a violation of that subsection for a person to engage in an act of security testing, if such act does not constitute infringement under this title or a violation of applicable law other than this section, including section 1030 of title 18 and those provisions of title 18 amended by the Computer Fraud and Abuse Act of 1986.

(3) Factors in Determining Exemption.—In determining whether a person qualifies for the exemption under paragraph (2), the factors to be considered shall include—

(A) whether the information derived from the security testing was used solely to promote the security of the owner or operator of such computer, computer system or computer network, or shared directly with the developer of such computer, computer system, or computer network; and

(B) whether the information derived from the security testing was used or maintained in a manner that does not facilitate infringement under this title or a violation of applicable law other than this section, including a violation of privacy or breach of security.

(4) Use of Technological Means for Security Testing.—Notwithstanding the provisions of subsection (a)(2), it is not a violation of that subsection for a person to develop, produce, distribute or employ technological means for the sole purpose of performing the acts of security testing described in subsection (2), provided such technological means does not otherwise violate section (a)(2).

(k) Certain Analog Devices and Certain Technological Measures.—

(1) Certain Analog Devices.—

(A) Effective 18 months after the date of the enactment of this chapter, no person shall manufacture, import, offer to the public, provide or otherwise traffic in any—

(i) VHS format analog video cassette recorder unless such recorder conforms to the automatic gain control copy control technology;

(ii) 8mm format analog video cassette camcorder unless such camcorder conforms to the automatic gain control technology;

(iii) Beta format analog video cassette recorder, unless such recorder conforms to the automatic gain control copy control technology, except that this requirement shall not apply until there are 1,000 Beta format analog video cassette recorders sold in the United States in any one calendar year after the date of the enactment of this chapter;

(iv) 8mm format analog video cassette recorder that is not an analog video cassette camcorder, unless such recorder conforms to the automatic gain control copy control technology, except that this requirement shall not apply until there are 20,000 such recorders sold in the United States in any one calendar year after the date of the enactment of this chapter; or

(v) analog video cassette recorder that records using an NTSC format video input and that is not otherwise covered under clauses (i) through (iv), unless such device conforms to the automatic gain control copy control technology.

(B) Effective on the date of the enactment of this chapter, no person shall manufacture, import, offer to the public, provide or otherwise traffic in—

(i) any VHS format analog video cassette recorder or any 8mm format analog video cassette recorder if the design of the model of such recorder has been modified after such date of enactment so that a model of recorder that previously conformed to the automatic gain control copy control technology no longer conforms to such technology; or

(ii) any VHS format analog video cassette recorder, or any 8mm format analog video cassette recorder that is not an 8mm analog video cassette camcorder, if the design of the model of such recorder has been modified after such date of enactment so that a model of recorder that previously conformed to the four-line colorstripe copy control technology no longer conforms to such technology.

Manufacturers that have not previously manufactured or sold a VHS format analog video cassette recorder, or an 8mm format analog cassette recorder, shall be required to conform to the four-line colorstripe copy control technology in the initial model of any such recorder manufactured after the date of the enactment of this chapter, and thereafter to continue conforming to the four-line colorstripe copy control technology. For purposes of this subparagraph, an analog video cassette recorder "conforms to" the four-line colorstripe copy control technology if it records a signal that, when played back by the playback function of that recorder in the normal viewing mode, exhibits, on a reference display device, a display containing distracting visible lines through portions of the viewable picture.

(2) Certain Encoding Restrictions.—No person shall apply the automatic gain control copy control technology or colorstripe copy control technology to prevent or limit consumer copying except such copying—

(A) of a single transmission, or specified group of transmissions, of live events or of audiovisual works for which a member of the public has exercised choice in selecting the transmissions, including the content of the transmissions or the time of receipt of such transmissions, or both, and as to which such member is charged a separate fee for each such transmission or specified group of transmissions;

(B) from a copy of a transmission of a live event or an audiovisual work if such transmission is provided by a channel or service where payment is made by a member of the public for such channel or service in the form of a subscription fee that entitles the member of the public to receive all of the programming contained in such channel or service;

(C) from a physical medium containing one or more prerecorded audiovisual works; or

(D) from a copy of a transmission described in subparagraph (A) or from a copy made from a physical medium described in subparagraph (C).

In the event that a transmission meets both the conditions set forth in subparagraph (A) and those set forth in subparagraph (B), the transmission shall be treated as a transmission described in subparagraph (A).

(3) Inapplicability.—This subsection shall not—

(A) require any analog video cassette camcorder to conform to the automatic gain control copy control technology with respect to any video signal received through a camera lens;

(B) apply to the manufacture, importation, offer for sale, provision of, or other trafficking in, any professional analog video cassette recorder; or

(C) apply to the offer for sale or provision of, or other trafficking in, any previously owned analog video cassette recorder, if such recorder was legally manufactured and sold when new and not subsequently modified in violation of paragraph (1)(B).

(4) Definitions.—For purposes of this subsection:

(A) An "analog video cassette recorder" means a device that records, or a device that includes a function that records, on electromagnetic tape in an analog format the electronic impulses produced by the video and audio portions of a television program, motion picture, or other form of audiovisual work.

(B) An "analog video cassette camcorder" means an analog video cassette recorder that contains a recording function that operates through a camera lens and through a video input that may be connected with a television or other video playback device.

(C) An analog video cassette recorder "conforms" to the automatic gain control copy control technology if it—

(i) detects one or more of the elements of such technology and does not record the motion picture or transmission protected by such technology; or

(ii) records a signal that, when played back, exhibits a meaningfully distorted or degraded display.

(D) The term "professional analog video cassette recorder" means an analog video cassette recorder that is designed, manufactured, marketed, and intended for use by a person who regularly employs such a device for a lawful business or industrial use, including making, performing, displaying, distributing, or transmitting copies of motion pictures on a commercial scale.

(E) The terms "VHS format", "8mm format", "Beta format", "automatic gain control copy control technology", "colorstripe copy control technology", "four-line version of the colorstripe copy control technology", and "NTSC" have the meanings that are commonly understood in the consumer electronics and motion picture industries as of the date of the enactment of this chapter.

(5) Violations.—Any violation of paragraph (1) of this subsection shall be treated as a violation of subsection (b)(1) of this section. Any violation of paragraph (2) of this subsection shall be deemed an "act of circumvention" for the purposes of section 1203(c)(3)(A) of this chapter.

Sec. 1202.   Integrity of Copyright Management Information

(a) False Copyright Management Information.—No person shall knowingly and with the intent to induce, enable, facilitate, or conceal infringement—

(1) provide copyright management information that is false, or

(2) distribute or import for distribution copyright management information that is false.

(b) Removal or Alteration of Copyright Management Information.—No person shall, without the authority of the copyright owner or the law—

(1) intentionally remove or alter any copyright management information,

(2) distribute or import for distribution copyright management information knowing that the copyright management information has been removed or altered without authority of the copyright owner or the law, or

(3) distribute, import for distribution, or publicly perform works, copies of works, or phonorecords, knowing that copyright management information has been removed or altered without authority of the copyright owner or the law,

knowing, or, with respect to civil remedies under section 1203, having reasonable grounds to know, that it will induce, enable, facilitate, or conceal an infringement of any right under this title.

(c) Definition.—As used in this section, the term "copyright management information" means any of the following information conveyed in connection with copies or phonorecords of a work or performances or displays of a work, including in digital form, except that such term does not include any personally identifying information about a user of a work or of a copy, phonorecord, performance, or display of a work:

(1) The title and other information identifying the work, including the information set forth on a notice of copyright.

(2) The name of, and other identifying information about, the author of a work.

(3) The name of, and other identifying information about, the copyright owner of the work, including the information set forth in a notice of copyright.

(4) With the exception of public performances of works by radio and television broadcast stations, the name of, and other identifying information about, a performer whose performance is fixed in a work other than an audiovisual work.

(5) With the exception of public performances of works by radio and television broadcast stations, in the case of an audiovisual work, the name of, and other identifying information about, a writer, performer, or director who is credited in the audiovisual work.

(6) Terms and conditions for use of the work.

(7) Identifying numbers or symbols referring to such information or links to such information.

(8) Such other information as the Register of Copyrights may prescribe by regulation, except that the Register of Copyrights may not require the provision of any information concerning the user of a copyrighted work.

(d) Law Enforcement, Intelligence, and Other Government Activities.—This section does not prohibit any lawfully authorized investigative, protective, information security, or intelligence activity of an officer, agent, or employee of the United States, a State, or a political subdivision of a State, or a person acting pursuant to a contract with the United States, a State, or a political subdivision of a State. For purposes of this subsection, the term "information security" means activities carried out in order to identify and address the vulnerabilities of a government computer, computer system, or computer network.

(e) Limitations on Liability.—

(1) Analog Transmissions.—In the case of an analog transmission, a person who is making transmissions in its capacity as a broadcast station, or as a cable system, or someone who provides programming to such station or system, shall not be liable for a violation of subsection (b) if—

(A) avoiding the activity that constitutes such violation is not technically feasible or would create an undue financial hardship on such person; and

(B) such person did not intend, by engaging in such activity, to induce, enable, facilitate, or conceal infringement of a right under this title.

(2) Digital Transmissions.—

(A) If a digital transmission standard for the placement of copyright management information for a category of works is set in a voluntary, consensus standard-setting process involving a representative cross-section of broadcast stations or cable systems and copyright owners of a category of works that are intended for public performance by such stations or systems, a person identified in paragraph (1) shall not be liable for a violation of subsection (b) with respect to the particular copyright management information addressed by such standard if—

(i) the placement of such information by someone other than such person is not in accordance with such standard; and

(ii) the activity that constitutes such violation is not intended to induce, enable, facilitate, or conceal infringement of a right under this title.

(B) Until a digital transmission standard has been set pursuant to subparagraph (A) with respect to the placement of copyright management information for a category of works, a person identified in paragraph (1) shall not be liable for a violation of subsection (b) with respect to such copyright management information, if the activity that constitutes such violation is not intended to induce, enable, facilitate, or conceal infringement of a right under this title, and if—

> (i) the transmission of such information by such person would result in a perceptible visual or aural degradation of the digital signal; or

> (ii) the transmission of such information by such person would conflict with—

>> (I) an applicable government regulation relating to transmission of information in a digital signal;

>> (II) an applicable industry-wide standard relating to the transmission of information in a digital signal that was adopted by a voluntary consensus standards body prior to the effective date of this chapter; or

>> (III) an applicable industry-wide standard relating to the transmission of information in a digital signal that was adopted in a voluntary, consensus standards-setting process open to participation by a representative cross-section of broadcast stations or cable systems and copyright owners of a category of works that are intended for public performance by such stations or systems.

(3) Definitions.—As used in this subsection—

> (A) the term "broadcast station" has the meaning given that term in section 3 of the Communications Act of 1934 (47 U.S.C. 153); and

> (B) the term "cable system" has the meaning given that term in section 602 of the Communications Act of 1934 (47 U.S.C. 522).

Sec. 1203.   Civil Remedies

(a) Civil Actions.—Any person injured by a violation of section 1201 or 1202 may bring a civil action in an appropriate United States district court for such violation.

(b) Powers of the Court.—In an action brought under subsection (a), the court—

> (1) may grant temporary and permanent injunctions on such terms as it deems reasonable to prevent or restrain a violation, but in no event shall impose a prior restraint on free speech or the press protected under the 1st amendment to the Constitution;

> (2) at any time while an action is pending, may order the impounding, on such terms as it deems reasonable, of any device or product that is in the custody or control of the alleged violator and that the court has reasonable cause to believe was involved in a violation;

(3) may award damages under subsection (c);

(4) in its discretion may allow the recovery of costs by or against any party other than the United States or an officer thereof;

(5) in its discretion may award reasonable attorney's fees to the prevailing party; and

(6) may, as part of a final judgment or decree finding a violation, order the remedial modification or the destruction of any device or product involved in the violation that is in the custody or control of the violator or has been impounded under paragraph (2).

(c) Award of Damages.—

(1) In General.—Except as otherwise provided in this title, a person committing a violation of section 1201 or 1202 is liable for either—

(A) the actual damages and any additional profits of the violator, as provided in paragraph (2), or

(B) statutory damages, as provided in paragraph (3).

(2) Actual Damages.—The court shall award to the complaining party the actual damages suffered by the party as a result of the violation, and any profits of the violator that are attributable to the violation and are not taken into account in computing the actual damages, if the complaining party elects such damages at any time before final judgment is entered.

(3) Statutory Damages.—

(A) At any time before final judgment is entered, a complaining party may elect to recover an award of statutory damages for each violation of section 1201 in the sum of not less than $200 or more than $2,500 per act of circumvention, device, product, component, offer, or performance of service, as the court considers just.

(B) At any time before final judgment is entered, a complaining party may elect to recover an award of statutory damages for each violation of section 1202 in the sum of not less than $2,500 or more than $25,000.

(4) Repeated Violations.—In any case in which the injured party sustains the burden of proving, and the court finds, that a person has violated section 1201 or 1202 within 3 years after a final judgment was entered against the person for another such violation, the court may increase the award of damages up to triple the amount that would otherwise be awarded, as the court considers just.

(5) Innocent Violations.—

(A) In General.—The court in its discretion may reduce or remit the total award of damages in any case in which the violator sustains the burden of proving, and the court finds, that the violator was not aware and had no reason to believe that its acts constituted a violation.

(B) Nonprofit Library, Archives, Educational Institutions, or Public Broadcasting Entities.—

(i) Definition.—In this subparagraph, the term "public broadcasting entity" has the meaning given such term under section 118(f).

(ii) In general.—In the case of a nonprofit library, archives, educational institution, or public broadcasting entity, the court shall remit damages in any case in which the library, archives, educational institution, or public broadcasting entity sustains the burden of proving, and the court finds, that the library, archives, educational institution, or public broadcasting entity was not aware and had no reason to believe that its acts constituted a violation.

Sec. 1204. Criminal Offenses and Penalties

(a) In General.—Any person who violates section 1201 or 1202 willfully and for purposes of commercial advantage or private financial gain—

(1) shall be fined not more than $500,000 or imprisoned for not more than 5 years, or both, for the first offense; and

(2) shall be fined not more than $1,000,000 or imprisoned for not more than 10 years, or both, for any subsequent offense.

(b) Limitation for Nonprofit Library, Archives, Educational Institution, or Public Broadcasting Entity.—Subsection (a) shall not apply to a nonprofit library, archives, educational institution, or public broadcasting entity (as defined under section 118(f)).

(c) Statute of Limitations.—No criminal proceeding shall be brought under this section unless such proceeding is commenced within 5 years after the cause of action arose.

Sec. 1205. Savings Clause

Nothing in this chapter abrogates, diminishes, or weakens the provisions of, nor provides any defense or element of mitigation in a criminal prosecution or civil action under, any Federal or State law that prevents the violation of the privacy of an individual in connection with the individual's use of the Internet.

CHAPTER 13.—PROTECTION OF ORIGINAL DESIGNS

(Pub.L. 105–304, 112 Stat. 2905 (1998)).

Sec. 1301. Designs Protected

(a) Designs Protected.—

(1) In General.—The designer or other owner of an original design of a useful article which makes the article attractive or distinctive in appearance to the purchasing or using public may secure the protection provided by this chapter upon complying with and subject to this chapter.

(2) Vessel features.—The design of a vessel hull, deck, or combination of a hull and deck, including a plug or mold, is subject to protection under this chapter, notwithstanding section 1302(4).

(3) Exceptions.—Department of Defense rights in a registered design under this chapter, including the right to build to such registered design, shall be determined solely by operation of section 2320 of title 10 or by the instrument under which the design was developed for the United States Government.

(b) Definitions.—For the purpose of this chapter, the following terms have the following meanings:

(1) A design is "original" if it is the result of the designer's creative endeavor that provides a distinguishable variation over prior work pertaining to similar articles which is more than merely trivial and has not been copied from another source.

(2) A "useful article" is a vessel hull or deck, including a plug or mold, which in normal use has an intrinsic utilitarian function that is not merely to portray the appearance of the article or to convey information. An article which normally is part of a useful article shall be deemed to be a useful article.

(3) A "vessel" is a craft—

(A) that is designed and capable of independently steering a course on or through water through its own means of propulsion; and

(B) that is designed and capable of carrying and transporting one or more passengers.

(4) A "hull" is the exterior frame or body of a vessel, exclusive of the deck, superstructure, masts, sails, yards, rigging, hardware, fixtures, and other attachments.

(5) A "plug" means a device or model used to make a mold for the purpose of exact duplication, regardless of whether the device or model has an intrinsic utilitarian function that is not only to portray the appearance of the product or to convey information.

(6) A "mold" means a matrix or form in which a substance for material is used, regardless of whether the matrix or form has an intrinsic utilitarian function that is not only to portray the appearance of the product or to convey information.

(7) A "deck" is the horizontal surface of a vessel that covers the hull, including exterior cabin and cockpit surfaces, and exclusive of masts, sails, yards, rigging, hardware, fixtures, and other attachments.

Sec. 1302.   Designs not Subject to Protection

Protection under this chapter shall not be available for a design that is—

(1) not original;

(2) staple or commonplace, such as a standard geometric figure, a familiar symbol, an emblem, or a motif, or another shape, pattern, or configuration which has become standard, common, prevalent, or ordinary;

(3) different from a design excluded by paragraph (2) only in insignificant details or in elements which are variants commonly used in the relevant trades;

(4) dictated solely by a utilitarian function of the article that embodies it; or

(5) embodied in a useful article that was made public by the designer or owner in the United States or a foreign country more than 2 years before the date of the application for registration under this chapter.

Sec. 1303.   Revisions, Adaptations, and Rearrangements

Protection for a design under this chapter shall be available notwithstanding the employment in the design of subject matter excluded from protection under section 1302 if the design is a substantial revision, adaptation, or rearrangement of such subject matter. Such protection shall be independent of any subsisting protection in subject matter employed in the design, and shall not be construed as securing any right to subject matter excluded from protection under this chapter or as extending any subsisting protection under this chapter.

Sec. 1304.   Commencement of Protection

The protection provided for a design under this chapter shall commence upon the earlier of the date of publication of the registration under section 1313(a) or the date the design is first made public as defined by section 1310(b).

Sec. 1305.   Term of Protection

(a) In General.—Subject to subsection (b), the protection provided under this chapter for a design shall continue for a term of 10 years beginning on the date of the commencement of protection under section 1304.

(b) Expiration.—All terms of protection provided in this section shall run to the end of the calendar year in which they would otherwise expire.

(c) Termination of Rights.—Upon expiration or termination of protection in a particular design under this chapter, all rights under this chapter in the design shall terminate, regardless of the number of different articles in which the design may have been used during the term of its protection.

Sec. 1306.   Design Notice

(a) Contents of Design Notice.—

(1) Whenever any design for which protection is sought under this chapter is made public under section 1310(b), the owner of the design shall, subject to the provisions of section 1307, mark it or have it marked legibly with a design notice consisting of—

(A) the words "Protected Design", the abbreviation "Prot'd Des.", or the letter "D" with a circle, or the symbol " *D* ";

(B) the year of the date on which protection for the design commenced; and

(C) the name of the owner, an abbreviation by which the name can be recognized, or a generally accepted alternative designation of the owner.

Any distinctive identification of the owner may be used for purposes of subparagraph (C) if it has been recorded by the Administrator before the design marked with such identification is registered.

(2) After registration, the registration number may be used instead of the elements specified in subparagraphs (B) and (C) of paragraph (1).

(b) Location of Notice.—The design notice shall be so located and applied as to give reasonable notice of design protection while the useful article embodying the design is passing through its normal channels of commerce.

(c) Subsequent Removal of Notice.—When the owner of a design has complied with the provisions of this section, protection under this chapter shall not be affected by the removal, destruction, or obliteration by others of the design notice on an article.

Sec. 1307.   Effect of Omission of Notice

(a) Actions with Notice.—Except as provided in subsection (b), the omission of the notice prescribed in section 1306 shall not cause loss of the protection under this chapter or prevent recovery for infringement under this chapter against any person who, after receiving written notice of the design protection, begins an undertaking leading to infringement under this chapter.

(b) Actions Without Notice.—The omission of the notice prescribed in section 1306 shall prevent any recovery under section 1323 against a person who began an undertaking leading to infringement under this chapter before receiving written notice of the design protection. No injunction shall be issued under this chapter with respect to such undertaking unless the owner of the design reimburses that person for any reasonable expenditure or contractual obligation in connection with such undertaking that was incurred before receiving written notice of the design protection, as the court in its discretion directs. The burden of providing written notice of design protection shall be on the owner of the design.

Sec. 1308.   Exclusive Rights

The owner of a design protected under this chapter has the exclusive right to—

(1) make, have made, or import, for sale or for use in trade, any useful article embodying that design; and

(2) sell or distribute for sale or for use in trade any useful article embodying that design.

Sec. 1309.   Infringement

(a) **Acts of Infringement.**—Except as provided in subsection (b), it shall be infringement of the exclusive rights in a design protected under this chapter for any person, without the consent of the owner of the design, within the United States and during the term of such protection, to—

(1) make, have made, or import, for sale or for use in trade, any infringing article as defined in subsection (e); or

(2) sell or distribute for sale or for use in trade any such infringing article.

(b) **Acts of Sellers and Distributors.**—A seller or distributor of an infringing article who did not make or import the article shall be deemed to have infringed on a design protected under this chapter only if that person—

(1) induced or acted in collusion with a manufacturer to make, or an importer to import such article, except that merely purchasing or giving an order to purchase such article in the ordinary course of business shall not of itself constitute such inducement or collusion; or

(2) refused or failed, upon the request of the owner of the design, to make a prompt and full disclosure of that person's source of such article, and that person orders or reorders such article after receiving notice by registered or certified mail of the protection subsisting in the design.

(c) **Acts Without Knowledge.**—It shall not be infringement under this section to make, have made, import, sell, or distribute, any article embodying a design which was created without knowledge that a design was protected under this chapter and was copied from such protected design.

(d) **Acts in Ordinary Course of Business.**—A person who incorporates into that person's product of manufacture an infringing article acquired from others in the ordinary course of business, or who, without knowledge of the protected design embodied in an infringing article, makes or processes the infringing article for the account of another person in the ordinary course of business, shall not be deemed to have infringed the rights in that design under this chapter except under a condition contained in paragraph (1) or (2) of subsection (b). Accepting an order or reorder from the source of the infringing article shall be deemed ordering or reordering within the meaning of subsection (b)(2).

(e) **Infringing Article Defined.**—As used in this section, an "infringing article" is any article the design of which has been copied from a design protected under this chapter, without the consent of the owner of the protected design. An infringing article is not an illustration or picture of a protected design in an advertisement, book, periodical, newspaper, photograph, broadcast, motion picture, or similar medium. A design shall not be deemed to have been copied from a protected design if it is original and not substantially similar in appearance to a protected design.

(f) Establishing Originality.—The party to any action or proceeding under this chapter who alleges rights under this chapter in a design shall have the burden of establishing the design's originality whenever the opposing party introduces an earlier work which is identical to such design, or so similar as to make prima facie showing that such design was copied from such work.

(g) Reproduction for Teaching or Analysis.—It is not an infringement of the exclusive rights of a design owner for a person to reproduce the design in a useful article or in any other form solely for the purpose of teaching, analyzing, or evaluating the appearance, concepts, or techniques embodied in the design, or the function of the useful article embodying the design.

Sec. 1310.   Application for Registration

(a) Time Limit for Application for Registration.—Protection under this chapter shall be lost if application for registration of the design is not made within 2 years after the date on which the design is first made public.

(b) When Design is Made Public.—A design is made public when an existing useful article embodying the design is anywhere publicly exhibited, publicly distributed, or offered for sale or sold to the public by the owner of the design or with the owner's consent.

(c) Application by Owner of Design.—Application for registration may be made by the owner of the design.

(d) Contents of Application.—The application for registration shall be made to the Administrator and shall state—

(1) the name and address of the designer or designers of the design;

(2) the name and address of the owner if different from the designer;

(3) the specific name of the useful article embodying the design;

(4) the date, if any, that the design was first made public, if such date was earlier than the date of the application;

(5) affirmation that the design has been fixed in a useful article; and

(6) such other information as may be required by the Administrator.

The application for registration may include a description setting forth the salient features of the design, but the absence of such a description shall not prevent registration under this chapter.

(e) Sworn Statement.—The application for registration shall be accompanied by a statement under oath by the applicant or the applicant's duly authorized agent or representative, setting forth, to the best of the applicant's knowledge and belief—

(1) that the design is original and was created by the designer or designers named in the application;

(2) that the design has not previously been registered on behalf of the applicant or the applicant's predecessor in title; and

(3) that the applicant is the person entitled to protection and to registration under this chapter.

If the design has been made public with the design notice prescribed in section 1306, the statement shall also describe the exact form and position of the design notice

(f) Effect of Errors.—

(1) Error in any statement or assertion as to the utility of the useful article named in the application under this section, the design of which is sought to be registered, shall not affect the protection secured under this chapter.

(2) Errors in omitting a joint designer or in naming an alleged joint designer shall not affect the validity of the registration, or the actual ownership or the protection of the design, unless it is shown that the error occurred with deceptive intent.

(g) Design Made in Scope of Employment.—In a case in which the design was made within the regular scope of the designer's employment and individual authorship of the design is difficult or impossible to ascribe and the application so states, the name and address of the employer for whom the design was made may be stated instead of that of the individual designer.

(h) Pictorial Representation of Design.—The application for registration shall be accompanied by two copies of a drawing or other pictorial representation of the useful article embodying the design, having one or more views, adequate to show the design, in a form and style suitable for reproduction, which shall be deemed a part of the application.

(i) Design in More Than One Useful Article.—If the distinguishing elements of a design are in substantially the same form in different useful articles, the design shall be protected as to all such useful articles when protected as to one of them, but not more than one registration shall be required for the design.

(j) Application for More Than One Design.—More than one design may be included in the same application under such conditions as may be prescribed by the Administrator. For each design included in an application the fee prescribed for a single design shall be paid.

Sec. 1311.   Benefit of Earlier Filing Date in Foreign Country

An application for registration of a design filed in the United States by any person who has, or whose legal representative or predecessor or successor in title has, previously filed an application for registration of the same design in a foreign country which extends to designs of owners who are citizens of the United States, or to applications filed under this chapter, similar protection to that provided under this chapter shall have that same effect as if filed in the United States on the date on which the application was first filed in such foreign country, if the application in the United States is filed within 6 months after the earliest date on which any such foreign application was filed.

Sec. 1312.   Oaths and Acknowledgments

(a) In General.—Oaths and acknowledgments required by this chapter—

(1) may be made—

(A) before any person in the United States authorized by law to administer oaths; or

(B) when made in a foreign country, before any diplomatic or consular officer of the United States authorized to administer oaths, or before any official authorized to administer oaths in the foreign country concerned, whose authority shall be proved by a certificate of a diplomatic or consular officer of the United States; and

(2) shall be valid if they comply with the laws of the State or country where made.

(b) Written Declaration in Lieu of Oath.—

(1) The Administrator may by rule prescribe that any document which is to be filed under this chapter in the Office of the Administrator and which is required by any law, rule, or other regulation to be under oath, may be subscribed to by a written declaration in such form as the Administrator may prescribe, and such declaration shall be in lieu of the oath otherwise required.

(2) Whenever a written declaration under paragraph (1) is used, the document containing the declaration shall state that willful false statements are punishable by fine or imprisonment, or both, pursuant to section 1001 of title 18, and may jeopardize the validity of the application or document or a registration resulting therefrom.

Sec. 1313.   Examination of Application and Issue or Refusal of Registration

(a) Determination of Registrability of Design; Registration.—
Upon the filing of an application for registration in proper form under section 1310, and upon payment of the fee prescribed under section 1316, the Administrator shall determine whether or not the application relates

to a design which on its face appears to be subject to protection under this chapter, and, if so, the Register shall register the design. Registration under this subsection shall be announced by publication. The date of registration shall be the date of publication.

(b) Refusal to Register; Reconsideration.—If, in the judgment of the Administrator, the application for registration relates to a design which on its face is not subject to protection under this chapter, the Administrator shall send to the applicant a notice of refusal to register and the grounds for the refusal. Within 3 months after the date on which the notice of refusal is sent, the applicant may, by written request, seek reconsideration of the application. After consideration of such a request, the Administrator shall either register the design or send to the applicant a notice of final refusal to register.

(c) Application to Cancel Registration.—Any person who believes he or she is or will be damaged by a registration under this chapter may, upon payment of the prescribed fee, apply to the Administrator at any time to cancel the registration on the ground that the design is not subject to protection under this chapter, stating the reasons for the request. Upon receipt of an application for cancellation, the Administrator shall send to the owner of the design, as shown in the records of the Office of the Administrator, a notice of the application, and the owner shall have a period of 3 months after the date on which such notice is mailed in which to present arguments to the Administrator for support of the validity of the registration. The Administrator shall also have the authority to establish, by regulation, conditions under which the opposing parties may appear and be heard in support of their arguments. If, after the periods provided for the presentation of arguments have expired, the Administrator determines that the applicant for cancellation has established that the design is not subject to protection under this chapter, the Administrator shall order the registration stricken from the record. Cancellation under this subsection shall be announced by publication, and notice of the Administrator's final determination with respect to any application for cancellation shall be sent to the applicant and to the owner of record. Costs of the cancellation procedure under this subsection shall be borne by the nonprevailing party or parties, and the Administrator shall have the authority to assess and collect such costs.

Sec. 1314.   Certification of Registration

Certificates of registration shall be issued in the name of the United States under the seal of the Office of the Administrator and shall be recorded in the official records of the Office. The certificate shall state the name of the useful article, the date of filing of the application, the date of registration, and the date the design was made public, if earlier than the date of filing of the application, and shall contain a reproduction of the drawing or other pictorial representation of the design. If a description of the salient features of the design appears in the application, the description shall also appear in the certificate. A certificate of registration shall be admitted in any court as prima facie evidence of the facts stated in the certificate.

Sec. 1315.   Publication of Announcements and Indexes

(a) Publications of the Administrator.—The Administrator shall publish lists and indexes of registered designs and cancellations of designs and may also publish the drawings or other pictorial representations of registered designs for sale or other distribution.

(b) File of Representatives of Registered Designs.—The Administrator shall establish and maintain a file of the drawings or other pictorial representations of registered designs. The file shall be available for use by the public under such conditions as the Administrator may prescribe.

Sec. 1316.   Fees

The Administrator shall by regulation set reasonable fees for the filing of applications to register designs under this chapter and for other services relating to the administration of this chapter, taking into consideration the cost of providing these services and the benefit of a public record.

Sec. 1317.   Regulations

The Administrator may establish regulations for the administration of this chapter.

Sec. 1318.   Copies of Records

Upon payment of the prescribed fee, any person may obtain a certified copy of any official record of the Office of the Administrator that relates to this chapter. That copy shall be admissible in evidence with the same effect as the original.

Sec. 1319.   Correction of Errors in Certificates

The Administrator may, by a certificate of correction under seal, correct any error in a registration incurred through the fault of the Office, or, upon payment of the required fee, any error of a clerical or typographical nature occurring in good faith but not through the fault of the Office. Such registration, together with the certificate, shall thereafter have the same effect as if it had been originally issued in such corrected form.

Sec. 1320.   Ownership and Transfer

(a) Property Right in Design.—The property right in a design subject to protection under this chapter shall vest in the designer, the legal representatives of a deceased designer or of one under legal incapacity, the employer for whom the designer created the design in the case of a design made within the regular scope of the designer's employment, or a person to whom the rights of the designer or of such employer have been transferred. The person in whom the property right is vested shall be considered the owner of the design.

(b) Transfer of Property Right.—The property right in a registered design, or a design for which an application for registration has been or may be filed, may be assigned, granted, conveyed, or mortgaged by an instrument in writing, signed by the owner, or may be bequeathed by will.

(c) Oath or Acknowledgment of Transfer.—An oath or acknowledgment under section 1312 shall be prima facie evidence of the execution of an assignment, grant, conveyance, or mortgage under subsection (b).

(d) Recordation of Transfer.—An assignment, grant, conveyance, or mortgage under subsection (b) shall be void as against any subsequent purchaser or mortgagee for a valuable consideration, unless it is recorded in the Office of the Administrator within 3 months after its date of execution or before the date of such subsequent purchase or mortgage.

Sec. 1321.   Remedy for Infringement

(a) In General.—The owner of a design is entitled, after issuance of a certificate of registration of the design under this chapter, to institute an action for any infringement of the design.

(b) Review of Refusal to Register.—

(1) Subject to paragraph (2), the owner of a design may seek judicial review of a final refusal of the Administrator to register the design under this chapter by bringing a civil action, and may in the same action, if the court adjudges the design subject to protection under this chapter, enforce the rights in that design under this chapter.

(2) The owner of a design may seek judicial review under this section if—

(A) the owner has previously duly filed and prosecuted to final refusal an application in proper form for registration of the design;

(B) the owner causes a copy of the complaint in the action to be delivered to the Administrator within 10 days after the commencement of the action; and

(C) the defendant has committed acts in respect to the design which would constitute infringement with respect to a design protected under this chapter.

(c) Administrator as Party to Action.—The Administrator may, at the Administrator's option, become a party to the action with respect to the issue of registrability of the design claim by entering an appearance within 60 days after being served with the complaint, but the failure of the Administrator to become a party shall not deprive the court of jurisdiction to determine that issue.

(d) Use of Arbitration to Resolve Dispute.—The parties to an infringement dispute under this chapter, within such time as may be specified by the Administrator by regulation, may determine the dispute, or any aspect of the dispute, by arbitration. Arbitration shall be governed by title 9. The parties shall give notice of any arbitration award to the Administrator, and such award shall, as between the parties to the arbitration, be dispositive of the issues to which it relates. The arbitration award shall be unenforceable until such notice is given. Nothing in this subsection shall preclude the Administrator from determining whether a design is subject to registration in a cancellation proceeding under section 1313(c).

Sec. 1322.   Injunctions

(a) In General.—A court having jurisdiction over actions under this chapter may grant injunctions in accordance with the principles of equity to prevent infringement of a design under this chapter, including, in its discretion, prompt relief by temporary restraining orders and preliminary injunctions.

(b) Damages for Injunctive Relief Wrongfully Obtained.—A seller or distributor who suffers damage by reason of injunctive relief wrongfully obtained under this section has a cause of action against the applicant for such injunctive relief and may recover such relief as may be appropriate, including damages for lost profits, cost of materials, loss of good will, and punitive damages in instances where the injunctive relief was sought in bad faith, and, unless the court finds extenuating circumstances, reasonable attorney's fees.

Sec. 1323.   Recovery for Infringement

(a) Damages.—Upon a finding for the claimant in an action for infringement under this chapter, the court shall award the claimant damages adequate to compensate for the infringement. In addition, the court may increase the damages to such amount, not exceeding $50,000 or $1 per copy, whichever is greater, as the court determines to be just. The damages awarded shall constitute compensation and not a penalty. The court may receive expert testimony as an aid to the determination of damages.

(b) Infringer's Profits.—As an alternative to the remedies provided in subsection (a), the court may award the claimant the infringer's profits resulting from the sale of the copies if the court finds that the infringer's sales are reasonably related to the use of the claimant's design. In such a case, the claimant shall be required to prove only the amount of the infringer's sales and the infringer shall be required to prove its expenses against such sales.

(c) Statute of Limitations.—No recovery under subsection (a) or (b) shall be had for any infringement committed more than 3 years before the date on which the complaint is filed.

(d) Attorney's Fees.—In an action for infringement under this chapter, the court may award reasonable attorney's fees to the prevailing party.

(e) Disposition of Infringing and Other Articles.—The court may order that all infringing articles, and any plates, molds, patterns, models, or other means specifically adapted for making the articles, be delivered up for destruction or other disposition as the court may direct.

Sec. 1324.   Power of Court Over Registration

In any action involving the protection of a design under this chapter, the court, when appropriate, may order registration of a design under this chapter or the cancellation of such a registration. Any such order shall be certified by the court to the Administrator, who shall make an appropriate entry upon the record.

Sec. 1325.   Liability for Action on Registration Fraudulently Obtained

Any person who brings an action for infringement knowing that registration of the design was obtained by a false or fraudulent representation materially affecting the rights under this chapter, shall be liable in the sum of $10,000, or such part of that amount as the court may determine. That am amount shall be to compensate the defendant and shall be charged against the plaintiff and paid to the defendant, in addition to such costs and attorney's fees of the defendant as may be assessed by the court.

Sec. 1326.   Penalty for False Marking

(a) In General.—Whoever, for the purpose of deceiving the public, marks upon, applies to, or uses in advertising in connection with an article made, used, distributed, or sold, a design which is not protected under this chapter, a design notice specified in section 1306, or any other words or symbols importing that the design is protected under this chapter, knowing that the design is not so protected, shall pay a civil fine of not more than $500 for each such offense.

(b) Suit by Private Persons.—Any person may sue for the penalty established by subsection (a), in which event one-half of the penalty shall be awarded to the person suing and the remainder shall be awarded to the United States.

Sec. 1327.   Penalty for False Representation

Whoever knowingly makes a false representation materially affecting the rights obtainable under this chapter for the purpose of obtaining registration of a design under this chapter shall pay a penalty of not less than $500 and not more than $1,000, and any rights or privileges that individual may have in the design under this chapter shall be forfeited.

Sec. 1328. Enforcement by Treasury and Postal Service

(a) Regulations.—The Secretary of the Treasury and the United States Postal Service shall separately or jointly issue regulations for the enforcement of the rights set forth in section 1308 with respect to importation. Such regulations may require, as a condition for the exclusion of articles from the United States, that the person seeking exclusion take any one or more of the following actions:

(1) Obtain a court order enjoining, or an order of the International Trade Commission under section 337 of the Tariff Act of 1930 excluding, importation of the articles.

(2) Furnish proof that the design involved is protected under this chapter and that the importation of the articles would infringe the rights in the design under this chapter.

(3) Post a surety bond for any injury that may result if the detention or exclusion of the articles proves to be unjustified.

(b) Seizure and Forfeiture.—Articles imported in violation of the rights set forth in section 1308 are subject to seizure and forfeiture in the same manner as property imported in violation of the customs laws. Any such forfeited articles shall be destroyed as directed by the Secretary of the Treasury or the court, as the case may be, except that the articles may be returned to the country of export whenever it is shown to the satisfaction of the Secretary of the Treasury that the importer had no reasonable grounds for believing that his or her acts constituted a violation of the law.

Sec. 1329. Relation to Design Patent Law

The issuance of a design patent under title 35, United States Code, for an original design for an article of manufacture shall terminate any protection of the original design under this chapter.

Sec. 1330. Common Law and Other Rights Unaffected

Nothing in this chapter shall annul or limit—

(1) common law or other rights or remedies, if any, available to or held by any person with respect to a design which has not been registered under this chapter; or

(2) any right under the trademark laws or any right protected against unfair competition.

Sec. 1331. Administrator; Office of the Administrator

In this chapter, the "Administrator" is the Register of Copyrights, and the "Office of the Administrator" and the "Office" refer to the Copyright Office of the Library of Congress.

Sec. 1332.   No Retroactive Effect

Protection under this chapter shall not be available for any design that has been made public under section 1310(b) before the effective date of this chapter.

APPENDIX B

THE 1909 COPYRIGHT ACT (EXCERPTS)

CHAPTER 1—REGISTRATION OF COPYRIGHTS

§ 1. Exclusive Rights as to Copyrighted Works.—Any person entitled thereto, upon complying with the provisions of this title, shall have the exclusive right:

(a) To print, reprint, publish, copy, and vend the copyrighted work;

(b) To translate the copyrighted work into other languages or dialects, or make any other version thereof, if it be a literary work; to dramatize it if it be a nondramatic work; to convert it into a novel or other nondramatic work if it be a drama; to arrange or adapt it if it be a musical work; to complete, execute, and finish it if it be a model or design for a work of art;

(c) To deliver, authorize the delivery of, read, or present the copyrighted work in public for profit if it be a lecture, sermon, address or similar production, or other nondramatic literary work; to make or procure the making of any transcription or record thereof by or from which, in whole or in part, it may in any manner or by any method be exhibited, delivered, presented, produced, or reproduced; and to play or perform it in public for profit, and to exhibit, represent, produce, or reproduce it in any manner or by any method whatsoever. The damages for the infringement by broadcast of any work referred to in this subsection shall not exceed the sum of $100 where the infringing broadcaster shows that he was not aware that he was infringing and that such infringement could not have been reasonably foreseen; and

(d) To perform or represent the copyrighted work publicly if it be a drama or, if it be a dramatic work and not reproduced in copies for sale, to vend any manuscript or any record whatsoever thereof; to make or to procure the making of any transcription or record thereof by or from which, in whole or in part, it may in any manner or by any method be exhibited, performed, represented, produced, or reproduced; and to exhibit, perform, represent, produce, or reproduce it in any manner or by any method whatsoever; and

(e) To perform the copyrighted work publicly for profit if it be a musical composition; and for the purpose of public performance for profit, and for the purposes set forth in subsection (a) hereof, to make any arrangement or setting of it or of the melody of it in any system of notation or any form of record in which the thought of an author may be recorded and from which it may be read or reproduced: *Provided,* That the provisions of this title, so far as they secure copyright controlling the parts of instruments serving to reproduce mechanically the musical work, shall include only compositions published and copyrighted after July 1, 1909, and shall not include the works of a foreign author or composer unless the foreign state or nation of which such author or composer is a citizen or subject grants, either by treaty, convention, agreement, or law, to citizens of the United States similar rights. And as a condition of extending the copyrighted control to such mechanical reproductions, that whenever the owner of a musical copyright has used or permitted or knowingly acquiesced in the use of the copyrighted work upon the parts of instruments serving to reproduce mechanically the musical work, any other person may make similar use of the copyrighted work upon the payment to the copyright proprietor of a royalty of 2 cents on each such part manufactured, to be paid by the manufacturer thereof; and the copyright proprietor may require, and if so the manufacturer shall furnish, a report under oath on the 20th day of each month on the number of parts of instruments manufactured during the previous month serving to reproduce mechanically said musical work, and royalties shall be due on the parts manufactured during any month upon the 20th of the next succeeding month. The payment of the royalty provided for by this section shall free the articles or devices for which such royalty has been paid from further contribution to the copyright except in case of public performance for profit. It shall be the duty of the copyright owner, if he uses the musical composition himself for the manufacture of parts of instruments serving to reproduce mechanically the musical work, or licenses others to do so, to file notice thereof, accompanied by a recording fee, in the copyright office, and any failure to file such notice shall be a complete defense to any suit, action, or proceeding for any infringement of such copyright.

In case of failure of such manufacturer to pay to the copyright proprietor within thirty days after demand in writing the full sum of royalties due at said rate at the date of such demand, the court may award taxable costs to the plaintiff and a reasonable counsel fee, and the court may, in its discretion, enter judgment therein for any sum in addition over the amount found to be due as royalty in accordance with the terms of this title, not exceeding three times such amount.

The reproduction or rendition of a musical composition by or upon coin-operated machines shall not be deemed a public performance for profit unless a fee is charged for admission to the place where such reproduction or rendition occurs.

(f) To reproduce and distribute to the public by sale or other transfer of ownership, or by rental, lease, or lending, reproductions of the copyrighted work if it be a sound recording: *Provided,* That the exclusive right of the owner of a copyright in a sound recording to reproduce it is limited to the right to duplicate the sound recording in a tangible form that directly or indirectly recaptures the actual sounds fixed in the recording: *Provided further,* That this right does not extend to the making or duplication of another sound recording that is an independent fixation of other sounds, even though such sounds imitate or simulate those in the copyrighted sound recording; or to reproductions made by transmitting organizations exclusively for their own use.

§ 2. Rights of Author or Proprietor of Unpublished Work.— Nothing in this title shall be construed to annul or limit the right of the author or proprietor of an unpublished work, at common law or in equity, to prevent the copying, publication, or use of such unpublished work without his consent, and to obtain damages therefor.

§ 3. Protection of Component Parts of Work Copyrighted; Composite Works or Periodicals.— The copyright provided by this title shall protect all the copyrightable component parts of the work copyrighted, and all matter therein in which copyright is already subsisting, but without extending the duration or scope of such copyright. The copyright upon composite works or periodicals shall give to the proprietor thereof all the rights in respect thereto which he would have if each part were individually copyrighted under this title.

§ 4. All Writings of Author Included.—The works for which copyright may be secured under this title shall include all the writings of an author.

§ 5. Classification of Works for Registration.—The application for registration shall specify to which of the following classes the work in which copyright is claimed belongs:

(a) Books, including composite and cyclopedic works, directories, gazetteers, and other compilations.

(b) Periodicals, including newspapers.

(c) Lectures, sermons, addresses (prepared for oral delivery).

(d) Dramatic or dramatico-musical compositions.

(e) Musical compositions.

(f) Maps.

(g) Works of art; models or designs for works of art.

(h) Reproductions of a work of art.

(i) Drawings or plastic works of a scientific or technical character.

(j) Photographs.

(k) Prints and pictorial illustrations including prints or labels used for articles of merchandise.

(l) Motion-picture photoplays.

(m) Motion pictures other than photoplays.

(n) Sound recordings.

The above specifications shall not be held to limit the subject matter of copyright as defined in section 4 of this title, nor shall any error in classification invalidate or impair the copyright protection secured under this title.

* * * *

§ 7. Copyright on Compilations of Works in Public Domain or of Copyrighted Works; Subsisting Copyrights Not Affected.—Compilations or abridgements, adaptations, arrangements, dramatizations, translations, or other versions of works in the public domain or of copyrighted works when produced with the consent of the proprietor of the copyright in such works, or works republished with new matter, shall be regarded as new works subject to copyright under the provisions of this title; but the publication of any such new works shall not affect the force or validity of any subsisting copyright upon the matter employed or any part thereof, or be construed to imply an exclusive right to such use of the original works, or to secure or extend copyright in such original works.

* * * *

§ 9. Authors or Proprietors, Entitled; Aliens.—The author or proprietor of any work made the subject of copyright by this title, or his executors, administrators, or assigns, shall have copyright for such work under the conditions and for the terms specified in this title: *Provided, however,* That the copyright secured by this title shall extend to the work of an author or proprietor who is a citizen or subject of a foreign state or nation only under the conditions described in subsections (a), (b), or (c) below:

(a) When an alien author or proprietor shall be domiciled within the United States at the time of the first publication of his work; or

(b) When the foreign state or nation of which such author or proprietor is a citizen or subject grants, either by treaty, convention, agreement, or law, to citizens of the United States the benefit of copyright on substantially the same basis as to its own citizens, or copyright protection, substantially equal to the protection secured to such foreign author under this title or by treaty; or when such foreign state or nation is a party to an international agreement which provides for reciprocity in the granting of copyright, by the terms of which agreement the United States may, at its pleasure, become a party thereto.

The existence of the reciprocal conditions aforesaid shall be determined by the President of the United States, by proclamation made from time to time, as the purposes of this title may require: *Provided,* That whenever the President shall find that the authors, copyright owners, or proprietors of works first produced or published abroad and subject to copyright or to renewal of copyright under the laws of the United States, including works subject to ad interim copyright, are or may have been temporarily unable to comply with the conditions and formalities prescribed with respect to such works by the copyright laws of the United States, because of the disruption or suspension of facilities essential for such compliance, he may by proclamation grant such extension of time as he may deem appropriate for the fulfillment of such conditions or formalities by authors, copyright owners, or proprietors who are citizens of the United States or who are nationals of countries which accord substantially equal treatment in this respect to authors, copyright owners, or proprietors who are citizens of the United States: *Provided further,* That no liability shall attach under this title for lawful uses made or acts done prior to the effective date of such proclamation in connection with such works, or in respect to the continuance for one year subsequent to such date of any business undertaking or enterprise lawfully undertaken prior to such date involving expenditure or contractual obligation in connection with the exploitation, production, reproduction, circulation, or performance of any such work.

The President may at any time terminate any proclamation authorized herein or any part thereof or suspend or extend its operation for such period or periods of time as in his judgment the interests of the United States may require.

(c) When the Universal Copyright Convention, signed at Geneva on September 6, 1952, shall be in force between the United States of America and the foreign state or nation of which such author is a citizen or subject, or in which the work was first published. Any work to which copyright is extended pursuant to this subsection shall be exempt from the following provisions of this title: (1) The requirement in section 1(e) that a foreign state or nation must grant to United States citizens mechanical reproduction rights similar to those specified therein; (2) the obligatory deposit requirements of the first sentence of section 13; (3) the provisions of sections 14, 16, 17, and 18; (4) the import prohibitions of section 107, to the extent that they are related to the manufacturing requirements of section 16; and (5) the requirements of sections 19 and 20: *Provided, however,* That such exemptions shall apply only if from the time of first publication all the copies of the work published with the authority of the author or other copyright proprietor shall bear the symbol © accompanied by the name of the copyright proprietor and the year of first publication placed in such manner and location as to give reasonable notice of claim of copyright.

Upon the coming into force of the Universal Copyright Convention in a foreign state or nation as hereinbefore provided, every book or periodical of a citizen or subject thereof in which ad interim copyright was subsisting on the effective date of said coming into force shall have copyright for twenty-eight years from the date of first publication abroad without the necessity of complying with the further formalities specified in section 23 of this title.

The provisions of this subsection shall not be extended to works of an author who is a citizen of, or domiciled in the United States of America regardless of place of first publication, or to works first published in the United States.

§ 10.   Publication of Work With Notice.—Any person entitled thereto by this title may secure copyright for his work by publication thereof with the notice of copyright required by this title; and such notice shall be affixed to each copy thereof published or offered for sale in the United States by authority of the copyright proprietor, except in the case of books seeking ad interim protection under section 22 of this title.

§ 11.   Registration of Claim and Issuance of Certificate.— Such person may obtain registration of his claim to copyright by complying with the provisions of this title, including the deposit of copies, and upon such compliance the Register of Copyrights shall issue to him the certificates provided for in section 209 of this title.

§ 12.   Works Not Reproduced for Sale.—Copyright may also be had of the works of an author, of which copies are not reproduced for sale, by the deposit, with claim of copyright, of one complete copy of such work if it be a lecture or similar production or a dramatic, musical, or dramatico-musical composition; of a title and description, with one print taken from each scene or act, if the work be a motion-picture photoplay;

of a photographic print if the work be a photograph; of a title and description, with not less than two prints taken from different sections of a complete motion picture, if the work be a motion picture other than a photoplay; or of a photograph or other identifying reproduction thereof, if it be a work of art or a plastic work or drawing. But the privilege of registration of copyright secured hereunder shall not exempt the copyright proprietor from the deposit of copies, under sections 13 and 14 of this title, where the work is later reproduced in copies for sale.

§ 13.   Deposit of Copies After Publication; Action or Proceeding for Infringement.—After copyright has been secured by publication of the work with the notice of copyright as provided in section 10 of this title, there shall be promptly deposited in the Copyright Office or in the mail addressed to the Register of Copyrights, Washington, District of Columbia, two complete copies of the best edition thereof then published, or if the work is by an author who is a citizen or subject of a foreign state or nation and has been published in a foreign country, one complete copy of the best edition then published in such foreign country, which copies or copy, if the work be a book or periodical, shall have been produced in accordance with the manufacturing provisions specified in section 16 of this title; or if such work be a contribution to a periodical, for which contribution special registration is requested, one copy of the issue or issues containing such contribution; or if the work belongs to a class specified in subsections (g), (h), (i) or (k) of section 5 of this title, and if the Register of Copyrights determines that it is impracticable to deposit copies because of their size, weight, fragility, or monetary value he may permit the deposit of photographs or other identifying reproductions in lieu of copies of the work as published under such rules and regulations as he may prescribe with the approval of the Librarian of Congress; or if the work is not reproduced in copies for sale there shall be deposited the copy, print, photograph, or other identifying reproduction provided by section 12 of this title, such copies or copy, print, photograph, or other reproduction to be accompanied in each case by a claim of copyright. No action or proceeding shall be maintained for infringement of copyright in any work until the provisions of this title with respect to the deposit of copies and registration of such work shall have been complied with.

§ 14.   Same; Failure to Deposit; Demand; Penalty.—Should the copies called for by section 13 of this title not be promptly deposited as provided in this title, the Register of Copyrights may at any time after the publication of the work, upon actual notice, require the proprietor of the copyright to deposit them, and after the said demand shall have been made, in default of the deposit of copies of the work within three months from any part of the United States, except an outlying territorial possession of the United States, or within six months from any outlying territorial possession of the United States, or from any foreign country, the proprietor of the copyright shall be liable to a fine of $100 and to pay to the Library of Congress twice the amount of the retail price of the best edition of the work, and the copyright shall become void.

* * * *

§ 19.   Notice; Form.—The notice of copyright required by section 10 of this title shall consist either of the word "Copyright", the abbreviation "Copr.", or the symbol ©, accompanied by the name of the copyright proprietor, and if the work be a printed literary, musical, or dramatic work, the notice shall include also the year in which the copyright was secured by publication. In the case, however, of copies of works specified in subsections (f) to (k), inclusive, of section 5 of this title, the notice may consist of the letter C enclosed within a circle, thus ©, accompanied by the initials, monogram, mark, or symbol of the copyright proprietor: *Provided,* That on some accessible portion of such copies or of the margin, back, permanent base, or pedestal, or of the substance on which such copies shall be mounted, his name shall appear. But in the case of works in which copyright was subsisting on July 1, 1909, the notice of copyright may be either in one of the forms prescribed herein or may consist of the following words: "Entered according to Act of Congress, in the year ___, by A.B., and in the office of the Librarian of Congress, at Washington, D.C.," or, at his option the word "Copyright", together with the year the copyright was entered and the name of the party by whom it was taken out; thus, "Copyright, 19__, by A.B."

In the case of reproductions of works specified in subsection (n) of section 5 of this title, the notice shall consist of the symbol P (the letter P in a circle), the year of first publication of the sound recording, and the name of the owner of copyright in the sound recording, or an abbreviation by which the name can be recognized, or a generally known alternative designation of the owner: *Provided,* That if the producer of the sound recording is named on the labels or containers of the reproduction, and if no other name appears in conjunction with the notice, his name shall be considered a part of the notice.

§ 20.   Same; Place of Application of; One Notice in Each Volume or Number of Newspaper or Periodical.—The notice of copyright shall be applied, in the case of a book or other printed publication, upon its title page or the page immediately following, or if a periodical either upon the title page or upon the first page of text of each separate number or under the title heading, or if a musical work either upon its title page or the first page of music, or if a sound recording on the surface of reproductions thereof or on the label or container in such manner and location as to give reasonable notice of the claim of copyright. One notice of copyright in each volume or in each number of a newspaper or periodical published shall suffice.

§ 21.   Same; Effect of Accidental Omission From Copy or Copies.—Where the copyright proprietor has sought to comply with the provisions of this title with respect to notice, the omission by accident or mistake of the prescribed notice from a particular copy or copies shall not invalidate the copyright or prevent recovery for infringement against any person who, after actual notice of the copyright, begins an undertaking to infringe it, but shall prevent the recovery of damages against an innocent infringer who has been misled by the omission of the notice; and in a suit for infringement no permanent injunction shall be had unless the copyright proprietor shall reimburse to the innocent infringer his reasonable outlay innocently incurred if the court, in its discretion, shall so direct.

* * * *

§ 24. Duration, Renewal and Extension.—The copyright secured by this title shall endure for twenty-eight years from the date of first publication, whether the copyrighted work bears the author's true name or is published anonymously or under an assumed name: *Provided,* That in the case of any posthumous work or of any periodical, cyclopedic, or other composite work upon which the copyright was originally secured by the proprietor thereof, or of any work copyrighted by a corporate body (otherwise than as assignee or licensee of the individual author) or by an employer for whom such work is made for hire, the proprietor of such copyright shall be entitled to a renewal and extension of the copyright in such work for the further term of twenty-eight years when application for such renewal and extension shall have been made to the copyright office and duly registered therein within one year prior to the expiration of the original term of copyright: *And provided further,* That in the case of any other copyrighted work, including a contribution by an individual author to a periodical or to a cyclopedic or other composite work, the author of such work, if still living, or the widow, widower, or children of the author, if the author be not living, or if such author, widow, widower or children be not living, then the author's executors, or in the absence of a will, his next of kin shall be entitled to a renewal and extension of the copyright in such work for a further term of twenty-eight years when application for such renewal and extension shall have been made to the copyright office and duly registered therein within one year prior to the expiration of the original term of copyright: *And provided further,* That in default of the registration of such application for renewal and extension, the copyright in any work shall determine at the expiration of twenty-eight years from first publication.

* * * *

§ 26. Terms Defined.—In the interpretation and construction of this title "the date of publication" shall in the case of a work of which copies are reproduced for sale or distribution be held to be the earliest date when copies of the first authorized edition were placed on sale, sold, or publicly distributed by the proprietor of the copyright or under his authority, and the word "author" shall include an employer in the case of works made for hire.

For the purposes of this section and sections 10, 11, 13, 14, 21, 101, 106, 109, 209, 215, but not for any other purpose, a reproduction of a work described in subsection 5(n) shall be considered to be a copy thereof. "Sound recordings" are works that result from the fixation of a series of musical, spoken, or other sounds, but not including the sounds accompanying a motion picture. "Reproductions of sound recordings" are material objects in which sounds other than those accompanying a motion picture are fixed by any method now known or later developed, and from which the sounds can be perceived, reproduced, or otherwise communicated, either directly or with the aid of a machine or device, and include the "parts of instruments serving to reproduce mechanically the musical work", "mechanical reproductions", and "interchangeable parts, such as discs or tapes for use in mechanical music-producing machines" referred to in sections 1(e) and 101(e) of this title.

§ 27.   Copyright Distinct From Property in Object Copyrighted; Effect of Sale of Object, and of Assignment of Copyright.—The copyright is distinct from the property in the material object copyrighted, and the sale or conveyance, by gift or otherwise, of the material object shall not of itself constitute a transfer of the copyright, nor shall the assignment of the copyright constitute a transfer of the title to the material object; but nothing in this title shall be deemed to forbid, prevent, or restrict the transfer of any copy of a copyrighted work the possession of which has been lawfully obtained.

§ 28.   Assignments and Bequests.—Copyright secured under this title or previous copyright laws of the United States may be assigned, granted, or mortgaged by an instrument in writing signed by the proprietor of the copyright, or may be bequeathed by will.

* * * *

§ 30.   Same; Record.—Every assignment of copyright shall be recorded in the copyright office within three calendar months after its execution in the United States or within six calendar months after its execution without the limits of the United States, in default of which it shall be void as against any subsequent purchaser or mortgagee for a valuable consideration, without notice, whose assignment has been duly recorded.

§ 31.   Same; Certificate of Record.—The Register of Copyrights shall, upon payment of the prescribed fee, record such assignment, and shall return it to the sender with a certificate of record attached under seal of the copyright office, and upon the payment of the fee prescribed by this title he shall furnish to any person requesting the same a certified copy thereof under the said seal.

§ 32.   Same; Use of Name of Assignee in Notice.—When an assignment of the copyright in a specified book or other work has been recorded the assignee may substitute his name for that of the assignor in the statutory notice of copyright prescribed by this title.

CHAPTER 2—INFRINGEMENT PROCEEDINGS

§ 101.   Infringement.—If any person shall infringe the copyright in any work protected under the copyright laws of the United States such person shall be liable:

(a) Injunction.—To an injunction restraining such infringement;

(b) Damages and Profits; Amount; Other Remedies.—To pay to the copyright proprietor such damages as the copyright proprietor may have suffered due to the infringement, as well as all the profits which the infringer shall have made from such infringement, and in proving profits the plaintiff shall be required to prove sales only, and the defendant shall be required to prove every element of cost which he claims, or in lieu of actual damages and profits, such damages as to the court shall appear to be just, and in assessing such damages the court may, in its discretion, allow the amounts as hereinafter stated, but in case of a newspaper reproduction of a copyrighted photograph, such damages shall not exceed the sum of $200 nor be less than the sum of $50, and in the case of the infringement of an undramatized or nondramatic work by means of motion pictures, where the infringer shall show that he was not aware that he was infringing, and that such infringement could not have been reasonably foreseen, such damages shall not exceed the sum of $100; and in the case of an infringement of a copyrighted dramatic or dramatico-musical work by a maker of motion pictures and his agencies for distribution thereof to exhibitors, where such infringer shows that he was not aware that he was infringing a copyrighted work, and that such infringements could not reasonably have been foreseen, the entire sum of such damages recoverable by the copyright proprietor from such infringing maker and his agencies for the distribution to exhibitors of such infringing motion picture shall not exceed the sum of $5,000 nor be less than $250, and such damages shall in no other case exceed the sum of $5,000 nor be less than $250, and shall not be regarded as a penalty. But the foregoing exceptions shall not deprive the copyright proprietor of any other remedy given him under this law, nor shall the limitation as to the amount of recovery apply to infringements occurring after the actual notice to a defendant, either by service of process in a suit or other written notice served upon him. . . .

* * * *

§ 104.   Willful Infringement for Profit.—(a) Except as provided in subsection (b), any person who willfully and for profit shall infringe any copyright secured by this title, or who shall knowingly and willfully aid or abet such infringement, shall be deemed guilty of a misdemeanor, and upon conviction thereof shall be punished by imprisonment for not exceeding one year or by a fine of not less than $100 nor more than $1,000, or both, in the discretion of the court: *Provided, however,* That nothing in this title shall be so construed as to prevent the performance of religious or secular works such as oratorios, cantatas, masses, or octavo choruses by public schools, church choirs, or vocal societies, rented, borrowed, or obtained from some public library, public school, church choir, school choir, or vocal society, provided the performance is given for charitable or educational purposes and not for profit.

(b) Any person who willfully and for profit shall infringe any copyright provided by section 1(f) of this title, or who should knowingly and willfully aid or abet such infringement, shall be fined not more than $25,000 or imprisoned not more than one year, or both, for the first offense and shall be fined not more than $50,000 or imprisoned not more than two years, or both for any subsequent offense.

* * * *

APPENDIX C

REGULATIONS OF THE U.S. COPYRIGHT OFFICE

The current text of the regulations of the U.S. Copyright Office, codified at Chapter II of Title 37 of the Code of Federal Regulations, is available online at http://www.copyright.gov/title37/. The current text of the regulations of the Copyright Royalty Board, including the rates and terms for statutory licenses, codified at Chapter III of Title 37 of the Code of Federal Regulations, is available online at http://www.loc.gov/crb/laws/title37/.

BERNE CONVENTION FOR THE PROTECTION OF LITERARY AND ARTISTIC WORKS (EXCERPTS)

(Paris Text 1971)

The countries of the Union, being equally animated by the desire to protect, in as effective and uniform a manner as possible, the rights of authors in their literary and artistic works,

Recognising the importance of the work of the Revision Conference held at Stockholm in 1967,

Having resolved to revise the Act adopted by the Stockholm Conference, while maintaining without change Article 1 to 20 and 22 to 26 of that Act.

Consequently, the undersigned Plenipotentiaries, having presented their full powers, recognised as in good and due form, have agreed as follows:

Article 1

The countries to which this Convention applies constitute a Union for the protection of the rights of authors in their literary and artistic works.

Article 2

(1) The expression "literary and artistic works" shall include every production in the literary, scientific and artistic domain, whatever may be the mode or form of its expression, such as books, pamphlets and other writings; lectures, addresses, sermons and other works of the same nature; dramatic or dramatico-musical works; choreographic works and entertainments in dumb show; musical compositions with or without words; cinematographic works to which are assimilated works expressed by a process analogous to cinematography; works of drawing, painting, architecture, sculpture, engraving and lithography; photographic works to which are assimilated works expressed by a process analogous to photography; works of applied art; illustrations, maps, plans, sketches and three-dimensional works relative to geography, topography, architecture or science.

(2) It shall, however, be a matter for legislation in the countries of the Union to prescribe that works in general or any specified categories

of works shall not be protected unless they have been fixed in some material form.

(3) Translations, adaptations, arrangements of music and other alterations of a literary or artistic work shall be protected as original works without prejudice to the copyright in the original work.

(4) It shall be a matter for legislation in the countries of the Union to determine the protection to be granted to official texts of a legislative, administrative and legal nature, and to official translations of such texts.

(5) Collections of literary or artistic works such as encyclopaedias and anthologies which, by reason of the selection and arrangement of their contents, constitute intellectual creations shall be protected as such, without prejudice to the copyright in each of the works forming part of such collections.

(6) The works mentioned in this Article shall enjoy protection in all countries of the Union. This protection shall operate for the benefit of the author and his successors in title.

(7) Subject to the provisions of Article 7(4) of this Convention, it shall be a matter for legislation in the countries of the Union to determine the extent of the application of their laws to works of applied art and industrial designs and models, as well as the conditions under which such works, designs and models shall be protected. Works protected in the country of origin solely as designs and models shall be entitled in another country of the Union only to such special protection as is granted in that country to designs and models; however, if no such special protection is granted in that country, such works shall be protected as artistic works.

(8) The protection of this Convention shall not apply to news of the day or to miscellaneous facts having the character of mere items of press information.

Article 2bis

(1) It shall be a matter for legislation in the countries of the Union to exclude, wholly or in part, from the protection provided by the preceding Article political speeches and speeches delivered in the course of legal proceedings.

(2) It shall also be a matter for legislation in the countries of the Union to determine the conditions under which lectures, addresses and other works of the same nature which are delivered in public may be reproduced by the press, broadcast, communicated to the public by wire and made the subject of public communication as envisaged in Article 11bis (1) of this Convention, when such use is justified by the informatory purpose.

(3) Nevertheless, the author shall enjoy the exclusive right of making a collection of his works mentioned in the preceding paragraphs.

Article 3

(1) The protection of this Convention shall apply to:

(a) authors who are nationals of one of the countries of the Union, for their works, whether published or not;

(b) authors who are not nationals of one of the countries of the Union, for their works first published in one of those countries, or simultaneously in a country outside the Union and in a country of the Union.

(2) Authors who are not nationals of one of the countries of the Union but who have their habitual residence in one of them shall, for the purposes of this Convention, be assimilated to nationals of that country.

(3) The expression "published works" means works published with the consent of their authors, whatever may be the means of manufacture of the copies, provided that the availability of such copies has been such as to satisfy the reasonable requirements of the public, having regard to the nature of the work. The performance of a dramatic, dramatico-musical, cinematographic or musical work, the public recitation of a literary work, the communication by wire or the broadcasting of literary or artistic works, the exhibition of a work of art and the construction of a work of architecture shall not constitute publication.

(4) A work shall be considered as having been published simultaneously in several countries if it has been published in two or more countries within thirty days of its first publication.

Article 4

The protection of this Convention shall apply, even if the conditions of Article 3 are not fulfilled, to:

(a) authors of cinematographic works the maker of which has his headquarters or habitual residence in one of the countries of the Union;

(b) authors of works of architecture erected in a country of the Union or of other artistic works incorporated in a building or other structure located in a country of the Union.

Article 5

(1) Authors shall enjoy, in respect of works for which they are protected under this Convention, in countries of the Union other than the country of origin, the rights which their respective laws do now or may hereafter grant to their nationals, as well as the rights specially granted by this Convention.

(2) The enjoyment and the exercise of these rights shall not be subject to any formality; such enjoyment and such exercise shall be independent of the existence of protection in the country of origin of the work. Consequently, apart from the provisions of this Convention, the extent of protection, as well as the means of redress afforded to the

author to protect his rights, shall be governed exclusively by the laws of the country where protection is claimed.

(3) Protection in the country of origin is governed by domestic law. However, when the author is not a national of the country of origin of the work for which he is protected under this Convention, he shall enjoy in that country the same rights as national authors.

(4) The country of origin shall be considered to be:

(a) in the case of works first published in a country of the Union, that country; in the case of works published simultaneously in several countries of the Union which grant different terms of protection, the country whose legislation grants the shortest term of protection;

(b) in the case of works published simultaneously in a country outside the Union and in a country of the Union, the latter country;

(c) in the case of unpublished works or of works first published in a country outside the Union, without simultaneous publication in a country of the Union, the country of the Union of which the author is a national, provided that:

> (i) when these are cinematographic works the maker of which has his headquarters or his habitual residence in a country of the Union, the country of origin shall be that country, and

> (ii) when these are works of architecture erected in a country of the Union or other artistic works incorporated in a building or other structure located in a country of the Union, the country of origin shall be that country.

Article 6

(1) Where any country outside the Union fails to protect in an adequate manner the works of authors who are nationals of one of the countries of the Union, the latter country may restrict the protection given to the works of authors who are, at the date of the first publication thereof, nationals of the other country and are not habitually resident in one of the countries of the Union. If the country of first publication avails itself of this right, the other countries of the Union shall not be required to grant to works thus subjected to special treatment a wider protection than that granted to them in the country of first publication.

(2) No restrictions introduced by virtue of the preceding paragraph shall affect the rights which an author may have acquired in respect of a work published in a country of the Union before such restrictions were put into force.

(3) The countries of the Union which restrict the grant of copyright in accordance with this Article shall give notice thereof to the Director General of the World Intellectual Property Organisation (hereinafter designated as "the Director General") by a written declaration specifying the countries in regard to which protection is restricted, and the restrictions to which rights of authors who are nationals of those

countries are subjected. The Director General shall immediately communicate this declaration to all the countries of the Union.

Article 6bis

(1) Independently of the author's economic rights, and even after the transfer of the said rights, the author shall have the right to claim authorship of the work and to object to any distortion, mutilation or other modification of, or other derogatory action in relation to, the said work, which would be prejudicial to his honour or reputation.

(2) The rights granted to the author in accordance with the preceding paragraph shall, after his death, be maintained, at least until the expiry of the economic rights, and shall be exercisable by the persons or institutions authorized by the legislation of the country where protection is claimed. However, those countries whose legislation, at the moment of their ratification of or accession to this Act, does not provide for the protection after the death of the author of all the rights set out in the preceding paragraph may provide that some of these rights may, after his death, cease to be maintained.

(3) The means of redress for safeguarding the rights granted by this Article shall be governed by the legislation of the country where protection is claimed.

Article 7

(1) The term of protection granted by this Convention shall be the life of the author and fifty years after his death.

(2) However, in the case of cinematographic works, the countries of the Union may provide that the term of protection shall expire fifty years after the work has been made available to the public with the consent of the author, or, failing such an event within fifty years from the making of such a work, fifty years after the making.

(3) In the case of anonymous or pseudonymous works, the terms of protection granted by this Convention shall expire fifty years after the work has been lawfully made available to the public. However, when the pseudonym adopted by the author leaves no doubt as to his identity, the term of protection shall be that provided in paragraph (1). If the author of an anonymous or pseudonymous work discloses his identity during the above-mentioned period, the term of protection applicable shall be that provided in paragraph (1). The countries of the Union shall not be required to protect anonymous or pseudonymous works in respect of which it is reasonable to presume that their author has been dead for fifty years.

(4) It shall be a matter for legislation in the countries of the Union to determine the term of protection of photographic works and that of works of applied art in so far as they are protected as artistic works; however, this term shall last at least until the end of a period of twenty-five years from the making of such a work.

(5) The term of protection subsequent to the death of the author and the terms provided by paragraphs (2), (3) and (4) shall run from the date of death or of the event referred to in those paragraphs, but such terms shall always be deemed to begin on the first of January of the year following the death or such event.

(6) The countries of the Union may grant a term of protection in excess of those provided by the preceding paragraphs.

(7) Those countries of the Union bound by the Rome Act of this Convention which grant, in their national legislation in force at the time of signature of the present Act, shorter terms of protection than those provided for in the preceding paragraphs shall have the right to maintain such terms when ratifying or acceding to the present Act.

(8) In any case, the term shall be governed by the legislation of the country where protection is claimed; however, unless the legislation of that country otherwise provides, the term shall not exceed the term fixed in the country of origin of the work.

Article 7bis

The provisions of the preceding Article shall also apply in the case of a work of joint authorship, provided that the terms measured from the death of the author shall be calculated from the death of the last surviving author.

Article 8

Authors of literary and artistic works protected by this Convention shall enjoy the exclusive right of making and of authorising the translation of their works throughout the term of protection of their rights in the original works.

Article 9

(1) Authors of literary and artistic works protected by this Convention shall have the exclusive right of authorising the reproduction of these works, in any manner or form.

(2) It shall be a matter for legislation in the countries of the Union to permit the reproduction of such works in certain special cases, provided that such reproduction does not conflict with a normal exploitation of the work and does not unreasonably prejudice the legitimate interests of the author.

(3) Any sound or visual recording shall be considered as a reproduction for the purposes of this Convention.

Article 10

(1) It shall be permissible to make quotations from a work which has already been lawfully made available to the public, provided that their making is compatible with fair practice, and their extent does not exceed that justified by the purpose, including quotations from newspaper articles and periodicals in the form of press summaries.

(2) It shall be a matter for legislation in the countries of the Union, and for special agreements existing or to be concluded between them, to permit the utilisation, to the extent justified by the purpose, of literary or artistic works by way of illustration in publications, broadcasts or sound or visual recordings for teaching, provided such utilisation is compatible with fair practice.

(3) Where use is made of works in accordance with the preceding paragraphs of this Article, mention shall be made of the source, and of the name of the author if it appears thereon.

Article 10bis

(1) It shall be a matter for legislation in the countries of the Union to permit the reproduction by the press, the broadcasting or the communication to the public by wire of articles published in newspapers or periodicals on current economic, political or religious topics, and of broadcast works of the same character, in cases in which the reproduction, broadcasting or such communication thereof is not expressly reserved. Nevertheless, the source must always be clearly indicated; the legal consequences of a breach of this obligation shall be determined by the legislation of the country where protection is claimed.

(2) It shall also be a matter for legislation in the countries of the Union to determine the conditions under which, for the purpose of reporting current events by means of photography, cinematography, broadcasting or communication to the public by wire, literary or artistic works seen or heard in the course of the event may, to the extent justified by the informatory purpose, be reproduced and made available to the public.

Article 11

(1) Authors of dramatic, dramatico-musical and musical works shall enjoy the exclusive right of authorising:

(i) the public performance of their works, including such public performance by any means or process;

(ii) any communication to the public of the performance of their works.

(2) Authors of dramatic or dramatico-musical works shall enjoy, during the full term of their rights in the original works, the same rights with respect to translations thereof.

Article 11bis

(1) Authors of literary and artistic works shall enjoy the exclusive right of authorising:

(i) the broadcasting of their works or the communication thereof to the public by any other means of wireless diffusion of signs, sounds or images;

(ii) any communication to the public by wire or by rebroadcasting of the broadcast of the work, when this communication is made by an organisation other than the original one;

(iii) the public communication by loudspeaker or any other analogous instrument transmitting, by signs, sounds or images, the broadcast of the work.

(2) It shall be a matter for legislation in the countries of the Union to determine the conditions under which the rights mentioned in the preceding paragraph may be exercised, but these conditions shall apply only in the countries where they have been prescribed. They shall not in any circumstances be prejudicial to the moral rights of the author, nor to his right to obtain equitable remuneration which, in the absence of agreement, shall be fixed by competent authority.

(3) In the absence of any contrary stipulation, permission granted in accordance with paragraph (1) of this Article shall not imply permission to record, by means of instruments recording sounds or images, the work broadcast. It shall, however, be a matter for legislation in the countries of the Union to determine the regulations for ephemeral recordings made by a broadcasting organisation by means of its own facilities and used for its own broadcasts. The preservation of these recordings in official archives may, on the ground of their exceptional documentary character, be authorised by such legislation.

Article 11ter

(1) Authors of literary works shall enjoy the exclusive right of authorising:

(i) the public recitation of their words, including such public recitation by any means or process;

(ii) any communication to the public of the recitation of their works.

(2) Authors of literary works shall enjoy, during the full term of their rights in the original works, the same rights with respect to translations thereof.

Article 12

Authors of literary or artistic works shall enjoy the exclusive right of authorising adaptations, arrangements and other alterations of their works.

Article 13

(1) Each country of the Union may impose for itself reservations and conditions on the exclusive right granted to the author of a musical work and to the author of any words, the recording of which together with the musical work has already been authorised by the latter, to authorise the sound recording of that musical work, together with such words, if any; but all such reservations and conditions shall apply only in the countries which have imposed them and shall not, in any circumstances, be

prejudicial to the rights of these authors to obtain equitable remuneration which, in the absence of agreement, shall be fixed by competent authority.

(2) Recordings of musical works made in a country of the Union in accordance with Article 13(3) of the Conventions signed at Rome on 2 June 1928, and at Brussels on 26 June 1948, may be reproduced in that country without the permission of the author of the musical work until a date two years after that country becomes bound by this Act.

(3) Recordings made in accordance with paragraphs (1) and (2) of this Article and imported without permission from the parties concerned into a country where they are treated as infringing recordings shall be liable to seizure.

Article 14

(1) Authors of literary or artistic works shall have the exclusive right of authorising:

(i) the cinematographic adaptation and reproduction of these works, and the distribution of the works thus adapted or reproduced;

(ii) the public performance and communication to the public by wire of the works thus adapted or reproduced.

(2) The adaptation into any other artistic form of a cinematographic production derived from literary or artistic works shall, without prejudice to the authorisation of the author of the cinematographic production, remain subject to the authorisation of the authors of the original works.

(3) The provisions of Article 13(1) shall not apply.

Article 14bis

(1) Without prejudice to the copyright in any work which may have been adapted or reproduced, a cinematographic work shall be protected as an original work. The owner of copyright in a cinematographic work shall enjoy the same rights as the author of an original work, including the rights referred to in the preceding Article.

(2)(a) Ownership of copyright in a cinematographic work shall be a matter for legislation in a country where protection is claimed.

(b) However, in the countries of the Union which, by legislation, include among the owners of copyright in a cinematographic work authors who have brought contributions to the making of the work, such authors, if they have undertaken to bring such contributions, may not, in the absence of any contrary or special stipulation, object to the reproduction, distribution, public performance, communication to the public by wire, broadcasting or any other communication to the public, or to the subtitling or dubbing of texts, of the work.

(c) The question whether or not the form of the undertaking referred to above should, for the application of the preceding subparagraph (b), be in a written agreement or a written act of the same effect shall be a matter for the legislation of the country where the maker of the cinematographic work has his headquarters or habitual residence. However, it shall be a matter for the legislation of the country of the Union where protection is claimed to provide that the said undertaking shall be in a written agreement or a written act of the same effect. The countries whose legislation so provides shall notify the Director General by means of a written declaration, which will be immediately communicated by him to all the other countries of the Union.

(d) By "contrary or special stipulation" is meant any restrictive condition which is relevant to the aforesaid undertaking.

(3) Unless the national legislation provides to the contrary, the provisions of paragraph (2)(b) above shall not be applicable to authors of scenarios, dialogues and musical works created for the making of the cinematographic work, or to the principal director thereof. However, those countries of the Union whose legislation does not contain rules providing for the application of the said paragraph (2)(b) to such director shall notify the Director General by means of a written declaration, which will be immediately communicated by him to all the other countries of the Union.

Article 14[ter]

(1) The author, or after his death the persons or institutions authorised by national legislation, shall, with respect to original works of art and original manuscripts of writers and composers, enjoy the inalienable right to an interest in any sale of the work subsequent to the first transfer by the author of the work.

(2) The protection provided by the preceding paragraph may be claimed in a country of the Union only if legislation in the country to which the author belongs so permits, and to the extent permitted by the country where this protection is claimed.

(3) The procedure for collection and the amounts shall be matters for determination by national legislation.

Article 15

(1) In order that the author of a literary or artistic work protected by this Convention shall, in the absence of proof to the contrary, be regarded as such, and consequently be entitled to institute infringement proceedings in the countries of the Union, it shall be sufficient for his name to appear on the work in the usual manner. This paragraph shall be applicable even if this name is a pseudonym, where the pseudonym adopted by the author leaves no doubt as to his identity.

(2) The person or body corporate whose name appears on a cinematographic work in the usual manner shall, in the absence of proof to the contrary, be presumed to be the maker of the said work.

(3) In the case of anonymous and pseudonymous works, other than those referred to in paragraph (1) above, the publisher whose name appears on the work shall, in the absence of proof to the contrary, be deemed to represent the author, and in this capacity he shall be entitled to protect and enforce the author's rights. The provisions of this paragraph shall cease to apply when the author reveals his identity and establishes his claim to authorship of the work.

(4)(a) In the case of unpublished works where the identity of the author is unknown, but where there is every ground to presume that he is a national of a country of the Union, it shall be a matter for legislation in that country to designate the competent authority which shall represent the author and shall be entitled to protect and enforce his rights in the countries of the Union.

(b) Countries of the Union which makes such designation under the terms of this provision shall notify the Director General by means of a written declaration giving full information concerning the authority thus designated. The Director General shall at once communicate this declaration to all other countries of the Union.

Article 16

(1) Infringing copies of a work shall be liable to seizure in any country of the Union where the work enjoys legal protection.

(2) The provisions of the preceding paragraph shall also apply to reproductions coming from a country where the work is not protected, or has ceased to be protected.

(3) The seizure shall take place in accordance with the legislation of each country.

Article 17

The provisions of this Convention cannot in any way affect the right of the Government of each country of the Union to permit, to control, or to prohibit, by legislation or regulation, the circulation, presentation, or exhibition of any work or production in regard to which the competent authority may find it necessary to exercise that right.

Article 18

(1) This Convention shall apply to all works which, at the moment of its coming into force, have not yet fallen into the public domain in the country of origin through the expiry of the term of protection.

(2) If, however, through the expiry of the term of protection which was previously granted, a work has fallen into the public domain of the country where protection is claimed, that work shall not be protected anew.

(3) The application of this principle shall be subject to any provisions contained in special conventions to that effect existing or to be concluded between countries of the Union. In the absence of such provisions, the

respective countries shall determine, each in so far as it is concerned, the conditions of application of this principle.

(4) The preceding provisions shall also apply in the case of new accessions to the Union and to cases in which protection is extended by the application of Article 7 or by the abandonment of reservations.

Article 19

The provisions of this Convention shall not preclude the making of a claim to the benefit of any greater protection which may be granted by legislation in a country of the Union.

Article 20

The Governments of the countries of the Union reserve the right to enter into special agreements among themselves, in so far as such agreements grant to authors more extensive rights than those granted by the Convention, or contain other provisions not contrary to this Convention. The provisions of existing agreements which satisfy these conditions shall remain applicable.

* * * *

Article 27

(1) This Convention shall be submitted to revision with a view to the introduction of amendments designed to improve the system of the Union.

(2) For this purpose, conferences shall be held successively in one of the countries of the Union among the delegates of the said countries.

(3) . . . any revision of this Act, including the Appendix, shall require the unanimity of the votes cast.

* * * *

Article 30

(1) . . . ratification or accession shall automatically entail acceptance of all the provisions and admission to all the advantages of this Convention.

* * * *

Article 33

(1) Any dispute between two or more countries of the Union concerning the interpretation or application of this Convention, not settled by negotiation, may, by any one of the countries concerned, be brought before the International Court of Justice by application in conformity with the Statute of the Court, unless the countries concerned agree on some other method of settlement. The country bringing the dispute before the Court shall inform the International Bureau; the International Bureau shall bring the matter to the attention of the other countries of the Union.

(2) Each country may, at the time it signs this Act or deposits its instrument of ratification or accession, declare that it does not consider itself bound by the provisions of paragraph (1). With regard to any dispute between such country and any other country of the Union, the provisions of paragraph (1) shall not apply.

(3) Any country having made a declaration in accordance with the provisions of paragraph (2) may, at any time, withdraw its declaration by notification addressed to the Director General.

* * * *

Article 36

(1) Any country party to this Convention undertakes to adopt, in accordance with its constitution, the measures necessary to ensure the application of this Convention.

(2) It is understood that, at the time a country becomes bound by this Convention, it will be in a position under its domestic law to give effect to the provisions of this Convention.

* * * *

Article 37

(1)

(a) This Act shall be signed in a single copy in the French and English languages and, subject to paragraph (2), shall be deposited with the Director General.

(b) Official texts shall be established by the Director General, after consultation with the interested Governments, in the Arabic, German, Italian, Portuguese and Spanish languages, and such other languages as the Assembly may designate.

(c) In case of differences of opinion on the interpretation of the various texts, the French text shall prevail.

* * * *

APPENDIX E

UNIVERSAL COPYRIGHT CONVENTION, AS REVISED AT PARIS, 1971 (EXCERPTS)

The Contracting States,

Moved by the desire to ensure in all countries copyright protection of literary, scientific and artistic works,

Convinced that a system of copyright protection appropriate to all nations of the world and expressed in a universal convention, additional to, and without impairing international systems already in force, will ensure respect for the rights of the individual and encourage the development of literature, the sciences and the arts,

Persuaded that such a universal copyright system will facilitate a wider dissemination of works of the human mind and increase international understanding,

Have resolved to revise the Universal Copyright Convention as signed at Geneva on 6 September 1952 (hereinafter called "the 1952 Convention"), and consequently,

Have agreed as follows:

Article I

Each Contracting State undertakes to provide for the adequate and effective protection of the rights of authors and other copyright proprietors in literary, scientific and artistic works, including writings, musical, dramatic and cinematographic works, and paintings, engravings and sculpture.

Article II

1.   Published works of nationals of any Contracting State and works first published in that State shall enjoy in each other Contracting State the same protection as that other State accords to works of its nationals first published in its own territory, as well as the protection specially granted by this Convention.

2.   Unpublished works of nationals of each Contracting State shall enjoy in each other Contracting State the same protection as that other State accords to unpublished works of its own nationals, as well as the protection specially granted by this Convention.

3.   For the purpose of this Convention any Contracting State may, by domestic legislation, assimilate to its own nationals any person domiciled in that State.

Article III

1. Any Contracting State which, under its domestic law, requires as a condition of copyright, compliance with formalities such as deposit, registration, notice, notarial certificates, payment of fees or manufacture or publication in that Contracting State, shall regard these requirements as satisfied with respect to all works protected in accordance with this Convention and first published outside its territory and the author of which is not one of its nationals, if from the time of the first publication all the copies of the work published with the authority of the author or other copyright proprietor bear the symbol © accompanied by the name of the copyright proprietor and the year of first publication placed in such manner and location as to give reasonable notice of claim of copyright.

2. The provisions of paragraph 1 shall not preclude any Contracting State from requiring formalities or other conditions for the acquisition and enjoyment of copyright in respect of works first published in its territory or works of its nationals wherever published.

3. The provisions of paragraph 1 shall not preclude any Contracting State from providing that a person seeking judicial relief must, in bringing the action, comply with procedural requirements, such as that the complainant must appear through domestic counsel or that the complainant must deposit with the court or an administrative office, or both, a copy of the work involved in the litigation; provided that failure to comply with such requirements shall not affect the validity of the copyright, nor shall any such requirement be imposed upon a national of another Contracting State if such requirement is not imposed on nationals of the State in which protection is claimed.

4. In each Contracting State there shall be legal means of protecting without formalities the unpublished works of nationals of other Contracting States.

5. If a Contracting State grants protection for more than one term of copyright and the first term is for a period longer than one of the minimum periods prescribed in Article IV, such State shall not be required to comply with the provisions of paragraph 1 of this Article in respect of the second or any subsequent term of copyright.

Article IV

1. The duration of protection of a work shall be governed, in accordance with the provisions of Article II and this Article, by the law of the Contracting State in which protection is claimed.

2. (a) The term of protection for works protected under this Convention shall not be less than the life of the author and twenty-five years after his death. However, any Contracting State which, on the effective date of this Convention in that State, has limited this term for certain classes of works to a period computed from the first publication of the work, shall be entitled to maintain these exceptions and to extend

them to other classes of works. For all these classes the term of protection shall not be less than twenty-five years from the date of first publication.

(b) Any Contracting State which, upon the effective date of this Convention in that State, does not compute the term of protection upon the basis of the life of the author, shall be entitled to compute the term of protection from the date of the first publication of the work or from its registration prior to publication, as the case may be, provided the term of protection shall not be less than twenty-five years from the date of first publication or from its registration prior to publication, as the case may be.

(c) If the legislation of a Contracting State grants two or more successive terms of protection, the duration of the first term shall not be less than one of the minimum periods specified in sub-paragraphs (a) and (b).

3.   The provisions of paragraph 2 shall not apply to photographic works or to works of applied art; provided, however, that the term of protection in those Contracting States which protect photographic works, or works of applied art in so far as they are protected as artistic works, shall not be less than ten years for each of said classes of works.

4.   (a) No Contracting State shall be obliged to grant protection to a work for a period longer than that fixed for the class of works to which the work in question belongs, in the case of unpublished works by the law of the Contracting State of which the author is a national, and in the case of published works by the law of the Contracting State in which the work has been first published.

(b) For the purposes of the application of sub-paragraph (a), if the law of any Contracting State grants two or more successive terms of protection, the period of protection of that State shall be considered to be the aggregate of those terms. However, if a specified work is not protected by such State during the second or any subsequent term for any reason, the other Contracting States shall not be obliged to protect it during the second or any subsequent term.

5.   For the purposes of the application of paragraph 4, the work of a national of a Contracting State, first published in a non-Contracting State, shall be treated as though first published in the Contracting State of which the author is a national.

6.   For the purposes of the application of paragraph 4, in case of simultaneous publication in two or more Contracting States, the work shall be treated as though first published in the State which affords the shortest term; any work published in two or more Contracting States within thirty days of its first publication shall be considered as having been published simultaneously in said Contracting States.

*Article IV*bis

1.   The rights referred to in Article I shall include the basic rights ensuring the author's economic interests, including the exclusive right to authorize reproduction by any means, public performance and broadcasting. The provisions of this Article shall extend to works protected under this Convention either in their original form or in any form recognizably derived from the original.

2.   However, any Contracting State may, by its domestic legislation, make exceptions that do not conflict with the spirit and provisions of this Convention, to the rights mentioned in paragraph 1 of this Article. Any State whose legislation so provides, shall nevertheless accord a reasonable degree of effective protection to each of the rights to which exception has been made.

Article V

1.   The rights referred to in Article I shall include the exclusive right of the author to make, publish and authorize the making and publication of translations of works protected under this Convention.

2.   However, any Contracting State may, by its domestic legislation, restrict the right of translation of writings, but only subject to the following provisions:

(a) If, after the expiration of a period of seven years from the date of the first publication of a writing, a translation of such writing has not been published in a language in general use in the Contracting State, by the owner of the right of translation or with his authorization, any national of such Contracting State may obtain a non-exclusive licence from the competent authority thereof to translate the work into that language and publish the work so translated.

(b) Such national shall in accordance with the procedure of the State concerned, establish either that he has requested, and been denied, authorization by the proprietor of the right to make and publish the translation, or that, after due diligence on his part, he was unable to find the owner of the right. A licence may also be granted on the same conditions if all previous editions of a translation in a language in general use in the Contracting State are out of print.

(c) If the owner of the right of translation cannot be found, then the applicant for a licence shall send copies of his application to the publisher whose name appears on the work and, if the nationality of the owner of the right of translation is known, to the diplomatic or consular representative of the State of which such owner is a national, or to the organization which may have been designated by the government of that State. The licence shall not be granted before the expiration of a period of two months from the date of the dispatch of the copies of the application.

(d) Due provision shall be made by domestic legislation to ensure to the owner of the right of translation a compensation which is just and conforms to international standards, to ensure payment and transmittal of such compensation, and to ensure a correct translation of the work.

(e) The original title and the name of the author of the work shall be printed on all copies of the published translation. The licence shall be valid only for publication of the translation in the territory of the Contracting State where it has been applied for. Copies so published may be imported and sold in another Contracting State if a language in general use in such other State is the same language as that into which the work has been so translated, and if the domestic law in such other State makes provision for such licences and does not prohibit such importation and sale. Where the foregoing conditions do not exist, the importation and sale of such copies in a Contracting State shall be governed by its domestic law and its agreements. The licence shall not be transferred by the licencee.

(f) The licence shall not be granted when the author has withdrawn from circulation all copies of the work.

* * * *

Article VI

"Publication", as used in this Convention, means the reproduction in tangible form and the general distribution to the public of copies of a work from which it can be read or otherwise visually perceived.

Article VII

This Convention shall not apply to works or rights in works which, at the effective date of this Convention in a Contracting State where protection is claimed, are permanently in the public domain in the said Contracting State.

* * * *

Article X

1. Each Contracting State undertakes to adopt, in accordance with its Constitution, such measures as are necessary to ensure the application of this Convention.

2. It is understood that at the date this Convention comes into force in respect of any State, that State must be in a position under its domestic law to give effect to the terms of this Convention.

* * * *

Article XVII

1. This Convention shall not in any way affect the provisions of the Berne Convention for the Protection of Literary and Artistic Works or membership in the Union created by that Convention.

2.   In application of the foregoing paragraph, a declaration has been annexed to the present Article. This declaration is an integral part of this Convention for the States bound by the Berne Convention on 1 January 1951, or which have or may become bound to it at a later date. The signature of this Convention by such States shall also constitute signature of the said declaration, and ratification, acceptance or accession by such States shall include the declaration, as well as this Convention.

Article XVIII

This Convention shall not abrogate multilateral or bilateral copyright conventions or arrangements that are or may be in effect exclusively between two or more American Republics. In the event of any difference either between the provisions of such existing conventions or arrangements and the provisions of this Convention, or between the provisions of this Convention and those of any new convention or arrangement which may be formulated between two or more American Republics after this Convention comes into force, the convention or arrangement most recently formulated shall prevail between the parties thereto. Rights in works acquired in any Contracting State under existing conventions or arrangements before the date this Convention comes into force in such State shall not be affected.

Article XIX

This Convention shall not abrogate multilateral or bilateral conventions or arrangements in effect between two or more Contracting States. In the event of any difference between the provisions of such existing conventions or arrangements and the provisions of this Convention, the provisions of this Convention shall prevail. Rights in works acquired in any Contracting State under existing conventions or arrangements before the date on which this Convention comes into force in such State shall not be affected. Nothing in this Article shall affect the provisions of Articles XVII and XVIII.

Article XX

Reservations to this Convention shall not be permitted.

Appendix Declaration Relating to Article XVII

The States which are members of the International Union for the Protection of Literary and Artistic Works (hereinafter called "the Berne Union") and which are signatories to this Convention,

Desiring to reinforce their mutual relations on the basis of the said Union and to avoid any conflict which might result from the co-existence of the Berne Convention and the Universal Copyright Convention,

Recognizing the temporary need of some States to adjust their level of copyright protection in accordance with their stage of cultural, social and economic development,

Have, by common agreement, accepted the terms of the following declaration:

(a) Except as provided by paragraph (b), works which, according to the Berne Convention, have as their country of origin a country which has withdrawn from the Berne Union after 1 January 1951, shall not be protected by the Universal Copyright Convention in the countries of the Berne Union;

(b) Where a Contracting State is regarded as a developing country in conformity with the established practice of the General Assembly of the United Nations, and has deposited with the Director-General of the United Nations Educational, Scientific and Cultural Organization, at the time of its withdrawal from the Berne Union, a notification to the effect that it regards itself as a developing country, the provisions of paragraph (a) shall not be applicable as long as such State may avail itself of the exceptions provided for by this Convention in accordance with Article V^{bis};

(c) The Universal Copyright Convention shall not be applicable to the relationships among countries of the Berne Union in so far as it relates to the protection of works having as their country of origin, within the meaning of the Berne Convention, a country of the Berne Union.

APPENDIX F

AGREEMENT ON TRADE-RELATED ASPECTS OF INTELLECTUAL PROPERTY RIGHTS (EXCERPTS)

MTN/FA II-A1C

Members,

Desiring to reduce distortions and impediments to international trade, and taking into account the need to promote effective and adequate protection of intellectual property rights, and to ensure that measures and procedures to enforce intellectual property rights do not themselves become barriers to legitimate trade;

Recognizing, to this end, the need for new rules and disciplines concerning:

(a) the applicability of the basic principles of the GATT 1994 and of relevant international intellectual property agreements or conventions;

(b) the provision of adequate standards and principles concerning the availability, scope and use of trade-related intellectual property rights;

(c) the provision of effective and appropriate means for the enforcement of trade-related intellectual property rights, taking into account differences in national legal systems;

(d) the provision of effective and expeditious procedures for the multilateral prevention and settlement of disputes between governments; and

(e) transitional arrangements aiming at the fullest participation in the results of the negotiations;

Recognizing the need for a multilateral framework of principles, rules and disciplines dealing with international trade in counterfeit goods;

Recognizing that intellectual property rights are private rights;

Recognizing the underlying public policy objectives of national systems for the protection of intellectual property, including development and technological objectives;

Recognizing also the special needs of the least-developed country Members in respect of maximum flexibility in the domestic implementation of laws and regulations in order to enable them to create a sound and viable technological base;

Emphasizing the importance of reducing tensions by reaching strengthened commitments to resolve disputes on trade-related intellectual property issues through multilateral procedures;

Desiring to establish a mutually supportive relationship between the WTO and the World Intellectual Property Organization (WIPO) as well as other relevant international organizations;

Hereby agree as follows:

PART I—GENERAL PROVISIONS AND BASIC PRINCIPLES

Article 1

Nature and Scope of Obligations

1.   Members shall give effect to the provisions of this Agreement. Members may, but shall not be obliged to, implement in their domestic law more extensive protection than is required by this Agreement, provided that such protection does not contravene the provisions of this Agreement. Members shall be free to determine the appropriate method of implementing the provisions of this Agreement within their own legal system and practice.

2.   For the purposes of this Agreement, the term "intellectual property" refers to all categories of intellectual property that are the subject of Sections 1 to 7 of Part II.

3.   Members shall accord the treatment provided for in this Agreement to the nationals of other Members.[1] In respect for the relevant intellectual property right, the nationals of other Members shall be understood as those natural or legal persons that would meet the criteria for eligibility for protection provided for in the Paris Convention (1967), the Berne Convention (1971), the Rome Convention and the Treaty on Intellectual Property in Respect of Integrated Circuits, were all Members of the WTO members of those conventions.[2] Any Member availing itself of the possibilities provided in paragraph 3 of Article 5 or paragraph 2 of Article 6 of the Rome Convention shall make a notification as foreseen in

---

[1]   When "nationals" are referred to in this Agreement, they shall be deemed, in the case of a separate customs territory Member of the WTO, to mean persons, natural or legal, who are domiciled or who have a real and effective industrial or commercial establishment in that customs territory.

[2]   In this Agreement, "Paris Convention" refers to the Paris Convention for the Protection of Industrial Property; "Paris Convention (1967)" refers to the Stockholm Act of this Convention of 14 July 1967. "Berne Convention" refers to the Berne Convention for the Protection of Literary and Artistic Works; "Berne Convention (1971)" refers to the Paris Act of this Convention of 24 July 1971. "Rome Convention" refers to the International Convention for the Protection of Performers, Producers of Phonograms and Broadcasting Organizations, adopted at Rome on 26 October 1961. "Treaty on Intellectual Property in Respect of Integrated Circuits" (IPIC Treaty) refers to the Treaty on Intellectual Property in Respect of Integrated Circuits, adopted at Washington on 26 May 1989.

those provisions to the Council for Trade-Related Aspects of Intellectual Property Rights.

Article 2

Intellectual Property Conventions

* * * *

2.   Nothing in Parts I to IV of this Agreement shall derogate from existing obligations that Members may have to each other under the Paris Convention, the Berne Convention, the Rome Convention and the Treaty on Intellectual Property in Respect of Integrated Circuits.

Article 3

National Treatment

1.   Each Member shall accord to the nationals of other Members treatment no less favourable than that it accords to its own nationals with regard to the protection[3] of intellectual property, subject to the exceptions already provided in, respectively, the Paris Convention (1967), the Berne Convention (1971), the Rome Convention and the Treaty on Intellectual Property in Respect of Integrated Circuits. In respect of performers, producers of phonograms and broadcasting organizations, this obligation only applies in respect of the rights provided under this Agreement. Any Member availing itself of the possibilities provided in Article 6 of the Berne Convention and paragraph 1(b) of Article 16 of the Rome Convention shall make a notification as foreseen in those provisions to the Council for Trade-Related Aspects of Intellectual Property Rights.

2.   Members may avail themselves of the exceptions permitted under paragraph 1 above in relation to judicial and administrative procedures, including the designation of an address for service or the appointment of an agent within the jurisdiction of a Member, only where such exceptions are necessary to secure compliance with laws and regulations which are not inconsistent with the provisions of this Agreement and where such practices are not applied in a manner which would constitute a disguised restriction on trade.

Article 4

Most-Favoured-Nation Treatment

With regard to the protection of intellectual property, any advantage, favour, privilege or immunity granted by a Member to the nationals of any other country shall be accorded immediately and unconditionally to the nationals of all other Members. Exempted from this obligation are any advantage, favour, privilege or immunity accorded by a Member:

---

[3]   For the purposes of Articles 3 and 4 of this Agreement, "protection" shall include matters affecting the availability, acquisition, scope, maintenance and enforcement of intellectual property rights as well as those matters affecting the use of intellectual property rights specifically addressed in this Agreement.

(a) deriving from international agreements on judicial assistance and law enforcement of a general nature and not particularly confined to the protection of intellectual property;

(b) granted in accordance with the provisions of the Berne Convention (1971) or the Rome Convention authorizing that the treatment accorded be a function not of national treatment but of the treatment accorded in another country;

(c) in respect of the rights of performers, producers of phonograms and broadcasting organizations not provided under this Agreement;

(d) deriving from international agreements related to the protection of intellectual property which entered into force prior to the entry into force of the Agreement Establishing the WTO, provided that such agreements are notified to the Council for Trade-Related Aspects of Intellectual Property Rights and do not constitute an arbitrary or unjustifiable discrimination against nationals of other Members.

Article 5

Multilateral Agreements on Acquisition or Maintenance of Protection

The obligations under Articles 3 and 4 above do not apply to procedures provided in multilateral agreements concluded under the auspices of the World Intellectual Property Organization relating to the acquisition or maintenance of intellectual property rights.

Article 6

Exhaustion

For the purposes of dispute settlement under this Agreement, subject to the provisions of Articles 3 and 4 above nothing in this Agreement shall be used to address the issue of the exhaustion of intellectual property rights.

Article 7

Objectives

The protection and enforcement of intellectual property rights should contribute to the promotion of technological innovation and to the transfer and dissemination of technology, to the mutual advantage of producers and users of technological knowledge and in a manner conducive to social and economic welfare, and to a balance of rights and obligations.

Article 8

Principles

1.   Members may, in formulating or amending their national laws and regulations, adopt measures necessary to protect public health and nutrition, and to promote the public interest in sectors of vital importance to their socio-economic and technological development,

provided that such measures are consistent with the provisions of this Agreement.

2.   Appropriate measures, provided that they are consistent with the provisions of this Agreement, may be used to prevent the abuse of intellectual property rights by right holders or the resort to practices which unreasonably restrain trade or adversely affect the international transfer of technology.

PART II—STANDARDS CONCERNING THE AVAILABILITY, SCOPE AND USE OF INTELLECTUAL PROPERTY RIGHTS

Section 1:

Copyright and Related Rights

Article 9

Relation to Berne Convention

1.   Members shall comply with Articles 1–21 and the Appendix of the Berne Convention (1971). However, Members shall not have rights or obligations under this Agreement in respect of the rights conferred under Article 6*bis* of that Convention or of the rights derived therefrom.

2.   Copyright protection shall extend to expressions and not to ideas, procedures, methods of operation or mathematical concepts as such.

Article 10

Computer Programs and Compilations of Data

1.   Computer programs, whether in source or object code, shall be protected as literary works under the Berne Convention (1971).

2.   Compilations of data or other material, whether in machine readable or other form, which by reason of the selection or arrangement of their contents constitute intellectual creations shall be protected as such. Such protection, which shall not extend to the data or material itself, shall be without prejudice to any copyright subsisting in the data or material itself.

Article 11

Rental Rights

In respect of at least computer programs and cinematographic works, a Member shall provide authors and their successors in title the right to authorize or to prohibit the commercial rental to the public of originals or copies of their copyright works. A Member shall be excepted from this obligation in respect of cinematographic works unless such rental has led to widespread copying of such works which is materially impairing the exclusive right of reproduction conferred in that Member on authors and their successors in title. In respect of computer programs, this obligation does not apply to rentals where the program itself is not the essential object of the rental.

Article 12

Term of Protection

Whenever the term of protection of a work, other than a photographic work or a work of applied art, is calculated on a basis other than the life of a natural person, such term shall be no less than fifty years from the end of the calendar year of authorized publication, or, failing such authorized publication within fifty years from the making of the work, fifty years from the end of the calendar year of making.

Article 13

Limitations and Exceptions

Members shall confine limitations or exceptions to exclusive rights to certain special cases which do not conflict with a normal exploitation of the work and do not unreasonably prejudice the legitimate interests of the right holder.

Article 14

Protection of Performers, Producers of Phonograms (Sound Recordings) and Broadcasting Organizations

1.   In respect of a fixation of their performance on a phonogram, performers shall have the possibility of preventing the following acts when undertaken without their authorization: the fixation of their unfixed performance and the reproduction of such fixation. Performers shall also have the possibility of preventing the following acts when undertaken without their authorization: the broadcasting by wireless means and the communication to the public of their live performance.

2.   Producers of phonograms shall enjoy the right to authorize or prohibit the direct or indirect reproduction of their phonograms.

3.   Broadcasting organizations shall have the right to prohibit the following acts when undertaken without their authorization: the fixation, the reproduction of fixations, and the rebroadcasting by wireless means of broadcasts, as well as the communication to the public of television broadcasts of the same. Where Members do not grant such rights to broadcasting organizations, they shall provide owners of copyright in the subject matter of broadcasts with the possibility of preventing the above acts, subject to the provisions of the Berne Convention (1971).

4.   The provisions of Article 11 in respect of computer programs shall apply *mutatis mutandis* to producers of phonograms and any other right holders in phonograms as determined in domestic law. If, on the date of the Ministerial Meeting concluding the Uruguay Round of Multilateral Trade Negotiations, a Member has in force a system of equitable remuneration of right holders in respect of the rental of phonograms, it may maintain such system provided that the commercial rental of phonograms is not giving rise to the material impairment of the exclusive rights of reproduction of right holders.

5.   The term of the protection available under this Agreement to performers and producers of phonograms shall last at least until the end of a period of fifty years computed from the end of the calendar year in which the fixation was made or the performance took place. The term of protection granted pursuant to paragraph 3 above shall last for at least twenty years from the end of the calendar year in which the broadcast took place.

6.   Any Member may, in relation to the rights conferred under paragraphs 1–3 above, provide for conditions, limitations, exceptions and reservations to the extent permitted by the Rome Convention. However, the provisions of Article 18 of the Berne Convention (1971) shall also apply, *mutatis mutandis,* to the rights of performers and producers of phonograms in phonograms.

PART III—ENFORCEMENT OF INTELLECTUAL PROPERTY RIGHTS

Section 1:

General Obligations

Article 41

1.   Members shall ensure that enforcement procedures as specified in this Part are available under their law so as to permit effective action against any act of infringement of intellectual property rights covered by this Agreement, including expeditious remedies to prevent infringements and remedies which constitute a deterrent to further infringements. These procedures shall be applied in such a manner as to avoid the creation of barriers to legitimate trade and to provide for safeguards against their abuse.

2.   Procedures concerning the enforcement of intellectual property rights shall be fair and equitable. They shall not be unnecessarily complicated or costly, or entail unreasonable time-limits or unwarranted delays.

3.   Decisions on the merits of a case shall preferably be in writing and reasoned. They shall be made available at least to the parties to the proceeding without undue delay. Decisions on the merits of a case shall be based only on evidence in respect of which parties were offered the opportunity to be heard.

4.   Parties to a proceeding shall have an opportunity for review by a judicial authority of final administrative decisions and, subject to jurisdictional provisions in a Member's law concerning the importance of a case, of at least the legal aspects of initial judicial decisions on the merits of a case. However, there shall be no obligation to provide an opportunity for review of acquittals in criminal cases.

5.   It is understood that this Part does not create any obligation to put in place a judicial system for the enforcement of intellectual property rights distinct from that for the enforcement of law in general, nor does

it affect the capacity of Members to enforce their law in general. Nothing in this Part creates any obligation with respect to the distribution of resources as between enforcement of intellectual property rights and the enforcement of law in general.

Section 2:

Civil and Administrative Procedures and Remedies

. . .

Article 44

Injunctions

1.   The judicial authorities shall have the authority to order a party to desist from an infringement, inter alia to prevent the entry into the channels of commerce in their jurisdiction of imported goods that involve the infringement of an intellectual property right, immediately after customs clearance of such goods. Members are not obliged to accord such authority in respect of protected subject matter acquired or ordered by a person prior to knowing or having reasonable grounds to know that dealing in such subject matter would entail the infringement of an intellectual property right.

2.   Notwithstanding the other provisions of this Part and provided that the provisions of Part II specifically addressing use by governments, or by third parties authorized by a government, without the authorization of the right holder are complied with, Members may limit the remedies available against such use to payment of remuneration in accordance with subparagraph (h) of Article 31. In other cases, the remedies under this Part shall apply or, where these remedies are inconsistent with a Member's law, declaratory judgments and adequate compensation shall be available.

Article 45

Damages

1.   The judicial authorities shall have the authority to order the infringer to pay the right holder damages adequate to compensate for the injury the right holder has suffered because of an infringement of that person's intellectual property right by an infringer who knowingly, or with reasonable grounds to know, engaged in infringing activity.

2.   The judicial authorities shall also have the authority to order the infringer to pay the right holder expenses, which may include appropriate attorney's fees. In appropriate cases, Members may authorize the judicial authorities to order recovery of profits and/or payment of pre-established damages even where the infringer did not knowingly, or with reasonable grounds to know, engage in infringing activity.

APPENDIX G

WORLD INTELLECTUAL PROPERTY ORGANIZATION COPYRIGHT TREATY (EXCERPTS)

(Geneva 1996)

CRNR/DC/94

Preamble

The Contracting Parties,

Desiring to develop and maintain the protection of the rights of authors in their literary and artistic works in a manner as effective and uniform as possible,

Recognizing the need to introduce new international rules and clarify the interpretation of certain existing rules in order to provide adequate solutions to the questions raised by new economic, social, cultural and technological developments,

Recognizing the profound impact of the development and convergence of information and communication technologies on the creation and use of literary and artistic works,

Emphasizing the outstanding significance of copyright protection as an incentive for literary and artistic creation,

Recognizing the need to maintain a balance between the rights of authors and the larger public interest, particularly education, research and access to information, as reflected in the Berne Convention,

Have agreed as follows:

Article 1

Relation to the Berne Convention

(1) This Treaty is a special agreement within the meaning of Article 20 of the Berne Convention for the Protection of Literary and Artistic Works, as regards Contracting Parties that are countries of the Union established by that Convention. This Treaty shall not have any connection with treaties other than the Berne Convention, nor shall it prejudice any rights and obligations under any other treaties.

(2) Nothing in this Treaty shall derogate from existing obligations that Contracting Parties have to each other under the Berne Convention for the Protection of Literary and Artistic Works.

(3) Hereinafter, "Berne Convention" shall refer to the Paris Act of July 24, 1971 of the Berne Convention for the Protection of Literary and Artistic Works.

(4) Contracting Parties shall comply with Articles 1 to 21 and the Appendix of the Berne Convention.[1]

Article 2

Scope of Copyright Protection

Copyright protection extends to expressions and not to ideas, procedures, methods of operation or mathematical concepts as such.

Article 3

Application of Articles 2 to 6 of the Berne Convention

Contracting Parties shall apply *mutatis mutandis* the provisions of Articles 2 to 6 of the Berne Convention in respect of the protection provided for in this Treaty.[2]

Article 4

Computer Programs

Computer programs are protected as literary works within the meaning of Article 2 of the Berne Convention. Such protection applies to computer programs, whatever may be the mode or form of their expression.[3]

Article 5

Compilations of Data (Databases)

Compilations of data or other material, in any form, which by reason of the selection or arrangement of their contents constitute intellectual creations, are protected as such. This protection does not extend to the

---

[1]   **Agreed statement concerning Article 1(4):** The reproduction right, as set out in Article 9 of the Berne Convention, and the exceptions permitted thereunder, fully apply in the digital environment, in particular to the use of works in digital form. It is understood that the storage of a protected work in digital form in an electronic medium constitutes a reproduction within the meaning of Article 9 of the Berne Convention.

[2]   **Agreed statement concerning Article 3:** It is understood that in applying Article 3 of this Treaty, the expression "country of the Union" in Articles 2 to 6 of the Berne Convention will be read as if it were a reference to a Contracting Party to this Treaty, in the application of those Berne Articles in respect of protection provided for in this Treaty. It is also understood that the expression "country outside the Union" in those Articles in the Berne Convention will, in the same circumstances, be read as if it were a reference to a country that is not a Contracting Party to this Treaty, and that "this Convention" in Articles 2(8), 2*bis*(2), 3, 4 and 5 of the Berne Convention will be read as if it were a reference to the Berne Convention and this Treaty. Finally, it is understood that a reference in Articles 3 to 6 of the Berne Convention to a "national of one of the countries of the Union" will, when these Articles are applied to this Treaty, mean, in regard to an intergovernmental organization that is a Contracting Party to this Treaty, a national of one of the countries that is member of that organization.

[3]   **Agreed statement concerning Article 4:** The scope of protection for computer programs under Article 4 of this Treaty, read with Article 2, is consistent with Article 2 of the Berne Convention and on a par with the relevant provisions of the TRIPS Agreement.

data or the material itself and is without prejudice to any copyright subsisting in the data or material contained in the compilation.[4]

Article 6

Right of Distribution

(1) Authors of literary and artistic works shall enjoy the exclusive right of authorizing the making available to the public of the original and copies of their works through sale or other transfer of ownership.

(2) Nothing in this Treaty shall affect the freedom of Contracting Parties to determine the conditions, if any, under which the exhaustion of the right in paragraph (1) applies after the first sale or other transfer of ownership of the original or a copy of the work with the authorization of the author.[5]

Article 7

Right of Rental

(1) Authors of

(i) computer programs;

(ii) cinematographic works; and

(iii) works embodied in phonograms, as determined in the national law of Contracting Parties, shall enjoy the exclusive right of authorizing commercial rental to the public of the originals or copies of their works.

(2) Paragraph (1) shall not apply

(i) in the case of computer programs, where the program itself is not the essential object of the rental; and

(ii) in the case of cinematographic works, unless such commercial rental has led to widespread copying of such works materially impairing the exclusive right of reproduction.

(3) Notwithstanding the provisions of paragraph (1), a Contracting Party that, on April 15, 1994, had and continues to have in force a system of equitable remuneration of authors for the rental of copies of their works embodied in phonograms may maintain that system provided that the commercial rental of works embodied in phonograms is not giving

---

[4] **Agreed statement concerning Article 5:** The scope of protection for compilations of data (databases) under Article 5 of this Treaty, read with Article 2, is consistent with Article 2 of the Berne Convention and on a par with the relevant provisions of the TRIPS Agreement.

[5] **Agreed statement concerning Articles 6 and 7:** As used in these Articles, the expressions "copies" and "original and copies," being subject to the right of distribution and the right of rental under the said Articles, refer exclusively to fixed copies that can be put into circulation as tangible objects.

rise to the material impairment of the exclusive right of reproduction of authors.[6, 7]

Article 8

Right of Communication to the Public

Without prejudice to the provisions of Articles 11(1)(ii), 11bis(1)(i) and (ii), 11ter(1)(ii), 14(1)(ii) and 14bis(1) of the Berne Convention, authors of literary and artistic works shall enjoy the exclusive right of authorizing any communication to the public of their works, by wire or wireless means, including the making available to the public of their works in such a way that members of the public may access these works from a place and at a time individually chosen by them.[8]

Article 9

Duration of the Protection of Photographic Works

In respect of photographic works, the Contracting Parties shall not apply the provisions of Article 7(4) of the Berne Convention.

Article 10

Limitations and Exceptions

(1) Contracting Parties may, in their national legislation, provide for limitations of or exceptions to the rights granted to authors of literary and artistic works under this Treaty in certain special cases that do not conflict with a normal exploitation of the work and do not unreasonably prejudice the legitimate interests of the author.

(2) Contracting Parties shall, when applying the Berne Convention, confine any limitations of or exceptions to rights provided for therein to certain special cases that do not conflict with a normal exploitation of the work and do not unreasonably prejudice the legitimate interests of the author.[9]

---

[6] **Agreed statement concerning Articles 6 and 7:** As used in these Articles, the expressions "copies" and "original and copies," being subject to the right of distribution and the right of rental under the said Articles, refer exclusively to fixed copies that can be put into circulation as tangible objects.

[7] **Agreed statement concerning Article 7:** It is understood that the obligation under Article 7(1) does not require a Contracting Party to provide an exclusive right of commercial rental to authors who, under that Contracting Party's law, are not granted rights in respect of phonograms. It is understood that this obligation is consistent with Article 14(4) of the TRIPS Agreement.

[8] **Agreed statement concerning Article 8:** It is understood that the mere provision of physical facilities for enabling or making a communication does not in itself amount to communication within the meaning of this Treaty or the Berne Convention. It is further understood that nothing in Article 8 precludes a Contracting Party from applying Article 11bis(2).

[9] **Agreed statement concerning Article 10:** It is understood that the provisions of Article 10 permit Contracting Parties to carry forward and appropriately extend into the digital environment limitations and exceptions in their national laws which have been considered acceptable under the Berne Convention. Similarly, these provisions should be understood to permit Contracting Parties to devise new exceptions and limitations that are appropriate in the digital network environment.

Article 11

Obligations concerning Technological Measures

Contracting Parties shall provide adequate legal protection and effective legal remedies against the circumvention of effective technological measures that are used by authors in connection with the exercise of their rights under this Treaty or the Berne Convention and that restrict acts, in respect of their works, which are not authorized by the authors concerned or permitted by law.

Article 12

Obligations concerning Rights Management Information

(1) Contracting Parties shall provide adequate and effective legal remedies against any person knowingly performing any of the following acts knowing, or with respect to civil remedies having reasonable grounds to know, that it will induce, enable, facilitate or conceal an infringement of any right covered by this Treaty or the Berne Convention:

(i) to remove or alter any electronic rights management information without authority;

(ii) to distribute, import for distribution, broadcast or communicate to the public, without authority, works or copies of works knowing that electronic rights management information has been removed or altered without authority.

(2) As used in this Article, "rights management information" means information which identifies the work, the author of the work, the owner of any right in the work, or information about the terms and conditions of use of the work, and any numbers or codes that represent such information, when any of these items of information is attached to a copy of a work or appears in connection with the communication of a work to the public.[10]

Article 13

Application in Time

Contracting Parties shall apply the provisions of Article 18 of the Berne Convention to all protection provided for in this Treaty.

It is also understood that Article 10(2) neither reduces nor extends the scope of applicability of the limitations and exceptions permitted by the Berne Convention.

[10] **Agreed statement concerning Article 12:** It is understood that the reference to "infringement of any right covered by this Treaty or the Berne Convention" includes both exclusive rights and rights of remuneration.

It is further understood that Contracting Parties will not rely on this Article to devise or implement rights management systems that would have the effect of imposing formalities which are not permitted under the Berne Convention or this Treaty, prohibiting the free movement of goods or impeding the enjoyment of rights under this Treaty.

Article 14

Provisions on Enforcement of Rights

(1) Contracting Parties undertake to adopt, in accordance with their legal systems, the measures necessary to ensure the application of this Treaty.

(2) Contracting Parties shall ensure that enforcement procedures are available under their law so as to permit effective action against any act of infringement of rights covered by this Treaty, including expeditious remedies to prevent infringements and remedies which constitute a deterrent to further infringements.

* * * *

Article 22

No Reservations to the Treaty

No reservation to this Treaty shall be admitted.

* * * *

APPENDIX H

WORLD INTELLECTUAL PROPERTY ORGANIZATION PERFORMANCES AND PHONOGRAMS TREATY (EXCERPTS)

(Geneva 1996)

CRNR/DC/95

Preamble

The Contracting Parties,

Desiring to develop and maintain the protection of the rights of performers and producers of phonograms in a manner as effective and uniform as possible,

Recognizing the need to introduce new international rules in order to provide adequate solutions to the questions raised by economic, social, cultural and technological developments,

Recognizing the profound impact of the development and convergence of information and communication technologies on the production and use of performances and phonograms,

Recognizing the need to maintain a balance between the rights of performers and producers of phonograms and the larger public interest, particularly education, research and access to information,

Have agreed as follows:

CHAPTER I—GENERAL PROVISIONS

Article 1

Relation to Other Conventions

(1) Nothing in this Treaty shall derogate from existing obligations that Contracting Parties have to each other under the International Convention for the Protection of Performers, Producers of Phonograms and Broadcasting Organizations done in Rome, October 26, 1961 (hereinafter the "Rome Convention").

(2) Protection granted under this Treaty shall leave intact and shall in no way affect the protection of copyright in literary and artistic works.

Consequently, no provision of this Treaty may be interpreted as prejudicing such protection.[1]

(3) This Treaty shall not have any connection with, nor shall it prejudice any rights and obligations under, any other treaties.

Article 2

Definitions

For the purposes of this Treaty:

(a) "performers" are actors, singers, musicians, dancers, and other persons who act, sing, deliver, declaim, play in, interpret, or otherwise perform literary or artistic works or expressions of folklore;

(b) "phonogram" means the fixation of the sounds of a performance or of other sounds, or of a representation of sounds, other than in the form of a fixation incorporated in a cinematographic or other audiovisual work;[2]

(c) "fixation" means the embodiment of sounds, or of the representations thereof, from which they can be perceived, reproduced or communicated through a device;

(d) "producer of a phonogram" means the person, or the legal entity, who or which takes the initiative and has the responsibility for the first fixation of the sounds of a performance or other sounds, or the representations of sounds;

(e) "publication" of a fixed performance or a phonogram means the offering of copies of the fixed performance or the phonogram to the public, with the consent of the rightholder, and provided that copies are offered to the public in reasonable quantity;[3]

(f) "broadcasting" means the transmission by wireless means for public reception of sounds or of images and sounds or of the representations thereof; such transmission by satellite is also "broadcasting"; transmission of encrypted signals is "broadcasting" where the means for decrypting are provided to the public by the broadcasting organization or with its consent;

---

[1] **Agreed statement concerning Article 1(2):** It is understood that Article 1(2) clarifies the relationship between rights in phonograms under this Treaty and copyright in works embodied in the phonograms. In cases where authorization is needed from both the author of a work embodied in the phonogram and a performer or producer owning rights in the phonogram, the need for the authorization of the author does not cease to exist because the authorization of the performer or producer is also required, and vice versa.

It is further understood that nothing in Article 1(2) precludes a Contracting Party from providing exclusive rights to a performer or producer of phonograms beyond those required to be provided under this Treaty.

[2] **Agreed statement concerning Article 2(b):** It is understood that the definition of phonogram provided in Article 2(b) does not suggest that rights in the phonogram are in any way affected through their incorporation into a cinematographic or other audiovisual work.

[3] **Agreed statement concerning Articles 2(e), 8, 9, 12 and 13:** As used in these Articles, the expressions "copies" and "original and copies," being subject to the right of distribution and the right of rental under the said Articles, refer exclusively to fixed copies that can be put into circulation as tangible objects.

(g) "communication to the public" of a performance or a phonogram means the transmission to the public by any medium, otherwise than by broadcasting, of sounds of a performance or the sounds or the representations of sounds fixed in a phonogram. For the purposes of Article 15, "communication to the public" includes making the sounds or representations of sounds fixed in a phonogram audible to the public.

Article 3

Beneficiaries of Protection under this Treaty

(1) Contracting Parties shall accord the protection provided under this Treaty to the performers and producers of phonograms who are nationals of other Contracting Parties.

(2) The nationals of other Contracting Parties shall be understood to be those performers or producers of phonograms who would meet the criteria for eligibility for protection provided under the Rome Convention, were all the Contracting Parties to this Treaty Contracting States of that Convention. In respect of these criteria of eligibility, Contracting Parties shall apply the relevant definitions in Article 2 of this Treaty.[4]

(3) Any Contracting Party availing itself of the possibilities provided in Article 5(3) of the Rome Convention or, for the purposes of Article 5 of the same Convention, Article 17 thereof shall make a notification as foreseen in those provisions to the Director General of the World Intellectual Property Organization (WIPO).[5]

Article 4

National Treatment

(1) Each Contracting Party shall accord to nationals of other Contracting Parties, as defined in Article 3(2), the treatment it accords to its own nationals with regard to the exclusive rights specifically granted in this Treaty, and to the right to equitable remuneration provided for in Article 15 of this Treaty.

(2) The obligation provided for in paragraph (1) does not apply to the extent that another Contracting Party makes use of the reservations permitted by Article 15(3) of this Treaty.

CHAPTER II—RIGHTS OF PERFORMERS

Article 5

Moral Rights of Performers

(1) Independently of a performer's economic rights, and even after the transfer of those rights, the performer shall, as regards his live aural

---

[4] **Agreed statement concerning Article 3(2):** For the application of Article 3(2), it is understood that fixation means the finalization of the master tape ("bande-mère").

[5] **Agreed statement concerning Article 3:** It is understood that the reference in Articles 5(a) and 16(a)(iv) of the Rome Convention to "national of another Contracting State" will, when applied to this Treaty, mean, in regard to an intergovernmental organization that is a Contracting Party to this Treaty, a national of one of the countries that is a member of that organization.

performances or performances fixed in phonograms, have the right to claim to be identified as the performer of his performances, except where omission is dictated by the manner of the use of the performance, and to object to any distortion, mutilation or other modification of his performances that would be prejudicial to his reputation.

(2) The rights granted to a performer in accordance with paragraph (1) shall, after his death, be maintained, at least until the expiry of the economic rights, and shall be exercisable by the persons or institutions authorized by the legislation of the Contracting Party where protection is claimed. However, those Contracting Parties whose legislation, at the moment of their ratification of or accession to this Treaty, does not provide for protection after the death of the performer of all rights set out in the preceding paragraph may provide that some of these rights will, after his death, cease to be maintained.

(3) The means of redress for safeguarding the rights granted under this Article shall be governed by the legislation of the Contracting Party where protection is claimed.

Article 6

Economic Rights of Performers in their Unfixed Performances

Performers shall enjoy the exclusive right of authorizing, as regards their performances:

(i) the broadcasting and communication to the public of their unfixed performances except where the performance is already a broadcast performance; and

(ii) the fixation of their unfixed performances.

Article 7

Right of Reproduction

Performers shall enjoy the exclusive right of authorizing the direct or indirect reproduction of their performances fixed in phonograms, in any manner or form.[6]

Article 8

Right of Distribution

(1) Performers shall enjoy the exclusive right of authorizing the making available to the public of the original and copies of their performances fixed in phonograms through sale or other transfer of ownership.

---

[6] **Agreed statement concerning Articles 7, 11 and 16:** The reproduction right, as set out in Articles 7 and 11, and the exceptions permitted thereunder through Article 16, fully apply in the digital environment, in particular to the use of performances and phonograms in digital form. It is understood that the storage of a protected performance or phonogram in digital form in an electronic medium constitutes a reproduction within the meaning of these Articles.

(2) Nothing in this Treaty shall affect the freedom of Contracting Parties to determine the conditions, if any, under which the exhaustion of the right in paragraph (1) applies after the first sale or other transfer of ownership of the original or a copy of the fixed performance with the authorization of the performer.[7]

Article 9

Right of Rental

(1) Performers shall enjoy the exclusive right of authorizing the commercial rental to the public of the original and copies of their performances fixed in phonograms as determined in the national law of Contracting Parties, even after distribution of them by, or pursuant to, authorization by the performer.

(2) Notwithstanding the provisions of paragraph (1), a Contracting Party that, on April 15, 1994, had and continues to have in force a system of equitable remuneration of performers for the rental of copies of their performances fixed in phonograms, may maintain that system provided that the commercial rental of phonograms is not giving rise to the material impairment of the exclusive right of reproduction of performers.[8]

Article 10

Right of Making Available of Fixed Performances

Performers shall enjoy the exclusive right of authorizing the making available to the public of their performances fixed in phonograms, by wire or wireless means, in such a way that members of the public may access them from a place and at a time individually chosen by them.

CHAPTER III—RIGHTS OF PRODUCERS OF PHONOGRAMS

Article 11

Right of Reproduction

Producers of phonograms shall enjoy the exclusive right of authorizing the direct or indirect reproduction of their phonograms, in any manner or form.[9]

---

[7] **Agreed statement concerning Articles 2(e), 8, 9, 12 and 13:** As used in these Articles, the expressions "copies" and "original and copies," being subject to the right of distribution and the right of rental under the said Articles, refer exclusively to fixed copies that can be put into circulation as tangible objects.

[8] **Agreed statement concerning Articles 2(e), 8, 9, 12 and 13:** As used in these Articles, the expressions "copies" and "original and copies," being subject to the right of distribution and the right of rental under the said Articles, refer exclusively to fixed copies that can be put into circulation as tangible objects.

[9] **Agreed statement concerning Articles 7, 11 and 16:** The reproduction right, as set out in Articles 7 and 11, and the exceptions permitted thereunder through Article 16, fully apply in the digital environment, in particular to the use of performances and phonograms in digital form. It is understood that the storage of a protected performance or phonogram in digital form in an electronic medium constitutes a reproduction within the meaning of these Articles.

Article 12

Right of Distribution

(1) Producers of phonograms shall enjoy the exclusive right of authorizing the making available to the public of the original and copies of their phonograms through sale or other transfer of ownership.

(2) Nothing in this Treaty shall affect the freedom of Contracting Parties to determine the conditions, if any, under which the exhaustion of the right in paragraph (1) applies after the first sale or other transfer of ownership of the original or a copy of the phonogram with the authorization of the producer of the phonogram.[10]

Article 13

Right of Rental

(1) Producers of phonograms shall enjoy the exclusive right of authorizing the commercial rental to the public of the original and copies of their phonograms, even after distribution of them by or pursuant to authorization by the producer.

(2) Notwithstanding the provisions of paragraph (1), a Contracting Party that, on April 15, 1994, had and continues to have in force a system of equitable remuneration of producers of phonograms for the rental of copies of their phonograms, may maintain that system provided that the commercial rental of phonograms is not giving rise to the material impairment of the exclusive rights of reproduction of producers of phonograms.[11]

Article 14

Right of Making Available of Phonograms

Producers of phonograms shall enjoy the exclusive right of authorizing the making available to the public of their phonograms, by wire or wireless means, in such a way that members of the public may access them from a place and at a time individually chosen by them.

CHAPTER IV—COMMON PROVISIONS

Article 15

Right to Remuneration for Broadcasting and Communication to the Public

(1) Performers and producers of phonograms shall enjoy the right to a single equitable remuneration for the direct or indirect use of

---

[10] **Agreed statement concerning Articles 2(e), 8, 9, 12 and 13:** As used in these Articles, the expressions "copies" and "original and copies," being subject to the right of distribution and the right of rental under the said Articles, refer exclusively to fixed copies that can be put into circulation as tangible objects.

[11] **Agreed statement concerning Articles 2(e), 8, 9, 12 and 13:** As used in these Articles, the expressions "copies" and "original and copies," being subject to the right of distribution and the right of rental under the said Articles, refer exclusively to fixed copies that can be put into circulation as tangible objects.

phonograms published for commercial purposes for broadcasting or for any communication to the public.

(2) Contracting Parties may establish in their national legislation that the single equitable remuneration shall be claimed from the user by the performer or by the producer of a phonogram or by both. Contracting Parties may enact national legislation that, in the absence of an agreement between the performer and the producer of a phonogram, sets the terms according to which performers and producers of phonograms shall share the single equitable remuneration.

(3) Any Contracting Party may in a notification deposited with the Director General of WIPO, declare that it will apply the provisions of paragraph (1) only in respect of certain uses, or that it will limit their application in some other way, or that it will not apply these provisions at all.

(4) For the purposes of this Article, phonograms made available to the public by wire or wireless means in such a way that members of the public may access them from a place and at a time individually chosen by them shall be considered as if they had been published for commercial purposes.[12, 13]

Article 16

Limitations and Exceptions

(1) Contracting Parties may, in their national legislation, provide for the same kinds of limitations or exceptions with regard to the protection of performers and producers of phonograms as they provide for, in their national legislation, in connection with the protection of copyright in literary and artistic works.

(2) Contracting Parties shall confine any limitations of or exceptions to rights provided for in this Treaty to certain special cases which do not conflict with a normal exploitation of the performance or phonogram and

---

[12] **Agreed statement concerning Article 15:** It is understood that Article 15 does not represent a complete resolution of the level of rights of broadcasting and communication to the public that should be enjoyed by performers and phonogram producers in the digital age. Delegations were unable to achieve consensus on differing proposals for aspects of exclusivity to be provided in certain circumstances or for rights to be provided without the possibility of reservations, and have therefore left the issue to future resolution.

[13] **Agreed statement concerning Article 15:** It is understood that Article 15 does not prevent the granting of the right conferred by this Article to performers of folklore and producers of phonograms recording folklore where such phonograms have not been published for commercial gain.

do not unreasonably prejudice the legitimate interests of the performer or of the producer of the phonogram.[14] [15]

Article 17

Term of Protection

(1) The term of protection to be granted to performers under this Treaty shall last, at least, until the end of a period of 50 years computed from the end of the year in which the performance was fixed in a phonogram.

(2) The term of protection to be granted to producers of phonograms under this Treaty shall last, at least, until the end of a period of 50 years computed from the end of the year in which the phonogram was published, or failing such publication within 50 years from fixation of the phonogram, 50 years from the end of the year in which the fixation was made.

Article 18

Obligations concerning Technological Measures

Contracting Parties shall provide adequate legal protection and effective legal remedies against the circumvention of effective technological measures that are used by performers or producers of phonograms in connection with the exercise of their rights under this Treaty and that restrict acts, in respect of their performances or phonograms, which are not authorized by the performers or the producers of phonograms concerned or permitted by law.

Article 19

Obligations concerning Rights Management Information

(1) Contracting Parties shall provide adequate and effective legal remedies against any person knowingly performing any of the following acts knowing, or with respect to civil remedies having reasonable grounds to know, that it will induce, enable, facilitate or conceal an infringement of any right covered by this Treaty:

---

[14] **Agreed statement concerning Articles 7, 11 and 16:** The reproduction right, as set out in Articles 7 and 11, and the exceptions permitted thereunder through Article 16, fully apply in the digital environment, in particular to the use of performances and phonograms in digital form. It is understood that the storage of a protected performance or phonogram in digital form in an electronic medium constitutes a reproduction within the meaning of these Articles.

[15] **Agreed statement concerning Article 16:** The agreed statement concerning Article 10 (on Limitations and Exceptions) of the WIPO Copyright Treaty is applicable *mutatis mutandis* also to Article 16 (on Limitations and Exceptions) of the WIPO Performances and Phonograms Treaty. [The text of the agreed statement concerning Article 10 of the WCT reads as follows:

It is understood that the provisions of Article 10 permit Contracting Parties to carry forward and appropriately extend into the digital environment limitations and exceptions in their national laws which have been considered acceptable under the Berne Convention. Similarly, these provisions should be understood to permit Contracting Parties to devise new exceptions and limitations that are appropriate in the digital network environment.

It is also understood that Article 10(2) neither reduces nor extends the scope of applicability of the limitations and exceptions permitted by the Berne Convention.]

(i) to remove or alter any electronic rights management information without authority;

(ii) to distribute, import for distribution, broadcast, communicate or make available to the public, without authority, performances, copies of fixed performances or phonograms knowing that electronic rights management information has been removed or altered without authority.

(2) As used in this Article, "rights management information" means information which identifies the performer, the performance of the performer, the producer of the phonogram, the phonogram, the owner of any right in the performance or phonogram, or information about the terms and conditions of use of the performance or phonogram, and any numbers or codes that represent such information, when any of these items of information is attached to a copy of a fixed performance or a phonogram or appears in connection with the communication or making available of a fixed performance or a phonogram to the public.[16]

Article 20

Formalities

The enjoyment and exercise of the rights provided for in this Treaty shall not be subject to any formality.

Article 21

Reservations

Subject to the provisions of Article 15(3), no reservations to this Treaty shall be permitted.

Article 22

Application in Time

(1) Contracting Parties shall apply the provisions of Article 18 of the Berne Convention, *mutatis mutandis*, to the rights of performers and producers of phonograms provided for in this Treaty.

(2) Notwithstanding paragraph (1), a Contracting Party may limit the application of Article 5 of this Treaty to performances which occurred after the entry into force of this Treaty for that Party.

---

[16] **Agreed statement concerning Article 19:** The agreed statement concerning Article 12 (on Obligations concerning Rights Management Information) of the WIPO Copyright Treaty is applicable *mutatis mutandis* also to Article 19 (on Obligations concerning Rights Management Information) of the WIPO Performances and Phonograms Treaty.

[The agreed statement concerning Article 12 of the WIPO Copyright Treaty reads as follows:

It is understood that the reference to "infringement of any right covered by this Treaty or the Berne Convention" includes both exclusive rights and rights of remuneration.

It is further understood that Contracting Parties will not rely on this Article to devise or implement rights management systems that would have the effect of imposing formalities which are not permitted under the Berne Convention or this Treaty, prohibiting the free movement of goods or impeding the enjoyment of rights under this Treaty.]

Article 23

Provisions on Enforcement of Rights

(1) Contracting Parties undertake to adopt, in accordance with their legal systems, the measures necessary to ensure the application of this Treaty.

(2) Contracting Parties shall ensure that enforcement procedures are available under their law so as to permit effective action against any act of infringement of rights covered by this Treaty, including expeditious remedies to prevent infringements and remedies which constitute a deterrent to further infringements.

* * * *